WORDS OF WAR

A volume in the series
Cornell Studies in Security Affairs
Edited by Austin Carson, Alexander B. Downes, Kelly M. Greenhill,
and Caitlin Talmadge
Founding editors: Robert J. Art, Robert Jervis, and Stephen M. Walt

A list of titles in this series is available at cornellpress.cornell.edu.

WORDS OF WAR

Negotiation as a Tool of Conflict

Eric Min

CORNELL UNIVERSITY PRESS   ITHACA AND LONDON

First published 2025 by Cornell University Press

Library of Congress Cataloging-in-Publication Data

Names: Min, Eric (Eric Aram), 1988– author.
Title: Words of war : negotiation as a tool of conflict / Eric Min.
Description: Ithaca : Cornell University Press, 2025. | Series: Cornell studies in
    security affairs | Includes bibliographical references and index.
Identifiers: LCCN 2024021686 (print) | LCCN 2024021687 (ebook) |
    ISBN 9781501779220 (hardcover) | ISBN 9781501779244 (epub) |
    ISBN 9781501779237 (pdf)
Subjects: LCSH: Diplomatic negotiations in international disputes. |
    Mediation, International.
Classification: LCC JZ6045 .M56 2025 (print) | LCC JZ6045 (ebook) |
    DDC 327.2—dc23/eng/20240824
LC record available at https://lccn.loc.gov/2024021686
LC ebook record available at https://lccn.loc.gov/2024021687

To Christina. Forever.

Contents

Figures

Tables

Acknowledgments

At its core, negotiation involves conversations. Many people over the years have been generous enough to have conversations with me, all of which have helped bring this book to fruition.

I was enormously fortunate to have been mentored by Jim Fearon and Ken Schultz at Stanford University. Many days were spent bouncing back and forth between their two offices, absorbing their thoughts. Both individuals were instrumental in pushing my ideas forward, providing perceptive feedback, asking sharp questions that clarified my thinking, and highlighting the importance of knowing your own data. I do my best to emulate their patience and to be even a modest fraction of the scholars that they are. As the core of this book began to emerge, I was pleased to receive additional advice and support from Mike Tomz, Justin Grimmer, and Jonathan Bendor. My entire journey at Stanford was also made much richer by my friends and colleagues: Jonathan Chu, Marc Grinberg, Azusa Katagiri, Melissa Lee, Lizhi Liu, Rebecca Perlman, and John Young. During my final year at Stanford, I was grateful to have the support of the Center for International Security and Cooperation (CISAC), where I received additional encouragement from Jooeun Kim, Rochelle Terman, Harold Trinkunas, and Amy Zegart.

This book would be a mere shadow of itself without the generous assistance of several individuals who participated in a workshop for an early manuscript: Hein Goemans, Dani Reiter, Alex Weisiger, and Amy Yuen. They all went beyond my expectations in providing enormously valuable feedback that fundamentally changed the structure of the book and helped several seemingly disparate pieces fall into place. I owe a great deal to these scholars, both for their contributions in the workshop and for the inspiration their research provided me over the years.

I am deeply privileged to have a wonderful community at UCLA, filled with numerous people who have offered both emotional and intellectual support. Worth particular mention are Graeme Blair, Michael Chwe, Leslie Johns, Debbie Larson, Barry O'Neill, Maggie Peters, Art Stein, Dan Thompson, and Rob Trager. Their advice regarding my book as well as academia in general was vital to facilitating my transition to life as a professor. I also thank Ohnha Ro for her excellent research assistance, which made the quantitative analysis in chapter 6 possible.

I presented assorted parts and versions of material in this book at conferences and workshops over the years. I thank numerous attendees at several meetings of the American Political Science Association, International Studies Association, Midwest Political Science Association, and Peace Science Society for their engagement. I am also deeply indebted to audiences at Stanford (both in the Department of Political Science and at CISAC), the Christopher H. Browne Center for International Politics at the University of Pennsylvania, Korea University, the Massachusetts Institute of Technology (MIT), the University of Chicago, and the University of Wisconsin–Madison.

Many individuals read parts of my manuscript, provided material and comments, and shared guidance along the way. I wish to thank Rosella Cappella Zielinski, Austin Carson, Jason Davis, Taylor Fravel, Ryan Grauer, Michael Joseph, Tyler Jost, Josh Kertzer, Erik Lin-Greenberg, Anne Sartori, Rob Schub, Paul Staniland, and Hohyun Yoon.

Portions of chapter 2 were previously published in Eric Min, "Talking While Fighting: Understanding the Role of Wartime Negotiations," *International Organization* 74, no. 3 (2020): 610–32, and "Interstate War Battle Dataset (1823–2003)," *Journal of Peace Research* 58, no. 2 (2021): 294–303. Portions of chapter 6 were previously published in Eric Min, "Painful Words: The Effect of Battlefield Activity on Conflict Negotiation Behavior," *Journal of Conflict Resolution* 66, no. 4–5 (2022): 595–622.

It has been a fantastic experience to work with Jackie Teoh at Cornell University Press. I thank her, as well as two anonymous reviewers, for their thoroughly constructive feedback and confidence in my work.

The path leading to this book would never have taken form without several additional mentors who shaped the person I am today. Chris Riffer (who in my mind will always be "Mr. Riffer") was the coach of the debate and forensics teams at Blue Valley High School in Stilwell, Kansas. It was through his direction and truly excellent teaching that I discovered my voice and my desire to collect, explore, analyze, question, and communicate information about the world. He was responsible for my decision to major in political science in college. Bruce Bueno de Mesquita and David Stasavage, who instructed me in seminars and my senior thesis as an undergraduate student at New York University, saw potential in me. Their support was essential to opening the doors into the world of academia.

My parents, Young and Natalie Min, arrived in the United States with two suitcases each in 1985 so that my father could earn a master's degree at the Ohio State University. Their original plan was to return to South Korea after he graduated, with potential plans to pursue a doctoral degree. When I was born right as my father was graduating, my parents decided to remain in a foreign country and work tirelessly so that their only child could have better opportunities in the States. It is only as I have grown older that I have better understood the gravity of the sacrifices they made for me. I am endlessly grateful to them and hope that my actions help them feel that their difficult choices were ultimately worthwhile.

Finally, I close by acknowledging and thanking my wife, Christina. I met Christina within two months of arriving in Los Angeles. It is impossible to over-state how lucky I was for that to somehow happen. On every dimension I can fathom, I have been transformed for the better because of her boundless energy, humor, encouragement, and love. I cherish every moment I get to share—often laughing—with her. I could not be more eager for all the conversations we will have for years to come.

A Note about the Online Appendix

The appendix that accompanies this book is online at https://doi.org/10.7910/DVN/KVRXCI. It includes descriptive statistics of all data used in the book, comprehensive results for all quantitative analyses presented in the book, and robustness checks or supplementary materials that are mentioned in the notes. It also features the data, code, and codebook necessary to replicate all statistical findings reported in both the book and the appendix.

INTRODUCTION
Time to Talk

On August 6, 1905, representatives from Russia and Japan arrived in Portsmouth, New Hampshire. For Russian delegation leader Sergei Witte and his team, the occasion in this unfamiliar city was a bitter one. For head Japanese delegate Baron Komura and his diplomats, it was a slightly more auspicious affair. The two empires had spent the last eighteen months fighting a war over their competing ambitions in East Asia, and hostilities had slowly but surely laid bare Japan's military superiority. Tsar Nicholas II had persistently held out hope for victory despite a relentless sequence of battlefield losses. But sixteen days of fighting between February 22 and March 9, 1905, in the Manchurian city of Mukden marked a moment of reckoning. In what would be one of the biggest land battles to be fought prior to World War I, Russia and Japan suffered a collective total of over 150,000 casualties. Japan, however, emerged from that battle with full control of southern Manchuria, one of the key disputed territories between both expanding empires, and as the dust settled at Mukden, the reality of Japan's advantage became harder for the Russian government to ignore. One final naval disaster in the battle of Tsushima in late May sounded the death knell for Russia's cause. By June, Tsar Nicholas II quietly decided to pursue talks with the Japanese,[1] accepting a mediation offer from President Theodore Roosevelt of the United States, who had gotten diplomatically involved in March once a Japanese envoy requested his assistance. It was through Roosevelt's efforts that the two delegations came to sit around a long mahogany table half a world away to discuss peace.

Over twelve sessions spanning August 9 to August 30, the opposing diplomats debated the terms of a potential settlement. Disagreements arose about whether Japan would demand an indemnity from Russia, but many of the other outstanding issues were resolved in short order. Japan would eventually drop its indemnity clause but claim southern Manchuria, the Korean peninsula, and the southern half of Sakhalin (Russia's largest island, dozens of miles away from the coast of northern Japan).[2] The resulting Treaty of Portsmouth was signed on September 5, 1905, ending the war.

The conflict transformed both sides' futures. Russian humiliation would feed the flames of the First Russian Revolution, Japan's military would gain increasing prominence in its government, and Western powers would no longer underestimate the Japanese Empire. Of particular note, however, is when diplomatic interactions started and how long they took. Diplomacy during the war was delayed in starting but moved quickly once it began. The first and only round of negotiations took place 95 percent of the way into the entire conflict. Talks, which came to pass over the remaining 5 percent, promptly reached a settlement.

Diplomatic interactions looked radically different during the Falklands War several decades later. On April 2, 1982, Argentinian troops invaded and occupied the Falkland Islands, which were three hundred miles east of Argentina and had been the subject of a long-standing dispute involving the United Kingdom. A mere three days in, US secretary of state Alexander Haig sprang into action as a mediator between the two sides. Through much of April, Argentina and the United Kingdom exchanged proposals with little room for compromise.[3] The death of one thousand Argentinian soldiers due to the sinking of the ship ARA *General Belgrano* on May 3 brought both sides back to talks, this time led by United Nations secretary-general Javier Pérez de Cuéllar. Discussions once again faltered as Argentina rejected the United Kingdom's terms, which essentially described the prewar status quo. By late May, the languishing discussions became irrelevant. British reinforcements had traversed the Atlantic while the talks were happening and swiftly overwhelmed the Argentinian occupying troops. On June 14, General Mario Menéndez, commander of the Argentinian garrison at the capital town of Stanley, surrendered to Major General Jeremy Moore.[4] The two sides discussed, drafted, and signed a document of surrender the following day, bringing the conflict to a close.

Over the course of the war, two rounds of talks came and went before the third codified British victory. The first attempt began almost immediately once violence erupted—only 5 percent of the way into the war that would come to pass. The second took place at approximately the halfway point. These two efforts together spanned over 50 percent of the conflict's entire duration. The third negotiation, lasting only one day, consolidated the United Kingdom's victory over Argentina.

The Russo-Japanese War and the Falklands War exemplify two very different stories regarding the timing, frequency, and consequences of negotiations that occur during armed conflict. Their contrasts are indicative of the wide range of variation we see in wartime diplomacy across time and space. As this book demonstrates, talks occurred almost immediately in some conflicts, later on in others, and not at all in some. Several negotiations took almost the entire duration of a given war, others a handful of days. And only some talks resulted in peace, whereas others only prolonged, or even exacerbated, the conflict. What explains the differences in the timing, frequency, and consequences of wartime negotiations? When and why do belligerents decide to start negotiating again? What conditions help dictate whether or not these talks result in peace? What effects, if any, can negotiations have on war beyond codifying its potential settlement? To what extent does this line of thought help to promote or revise our understanding of diplomacy—either during conflict or more generally?

This book addresses these questions by developing and substantiating a theory of wartime negotiations. My theory explains what conditions promote the occurrence of negotiations, as well as what impact they have on the subsequent trajectory of the war. I show that negotiations are a far more strategic, complex, and potentially cynical activity than most scholars and practitioners have generally recognized. A central aspect of my argument is that talking while fighting can serve more than one purpose and that we can understand when each purpose is more likely to be prioritized over the other. This claim, as innocuous as it may seem, leads us to recognize what some might consider a "dark side" of diplomacy. Ultimately, negotiations not only are used to help settle conflicts but can also be harnessed to help delay, fight, and potentially win them. Diplomacy does not intrinsically promote peace. Depending on the circumstances, it may promote a belligerent's war aims and be worse than staging no talks at all. If negotiations can indeed worsen conflict, it is crucial to understand the conditions under which negotiations are more likely to do so and how to minimize the risks of diplomacy being exploited to perpetuate violence.

What We Know about Negotiations in War

Up to this point, very few sources of data allowed us to see this variation in a more systematic manner. New negotiation data for ninety-two interstate wars between 1823 and 2003 offer one of our first chances to see this variation across two centuries of violent international conflict. This variation is captured in figure 0.1.

Figure 0.1 shows how dramatically wars vary in the relative timing of their negotiations. We must first note that a fair number of conflicts proceed without a

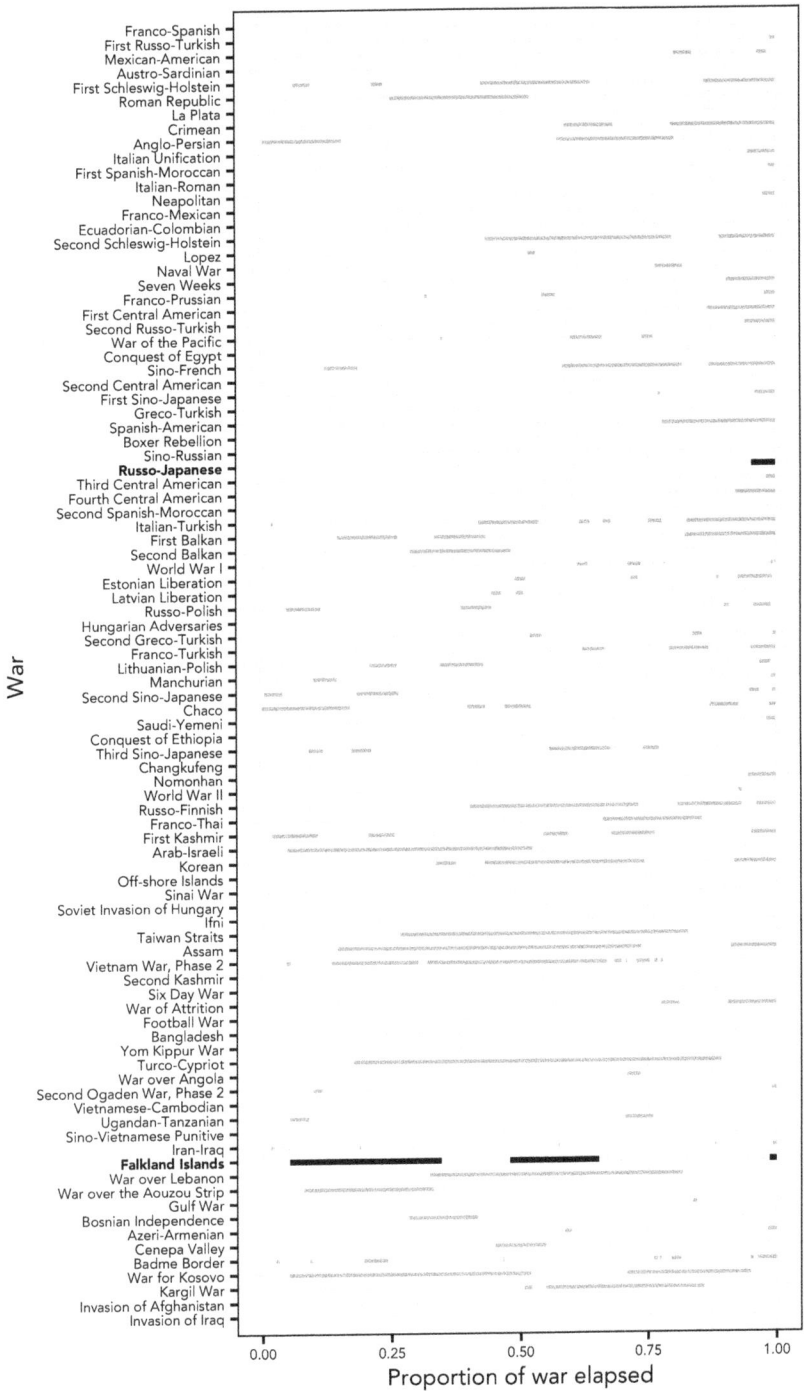

FIGURE 0.1. The relative timing of negotiations across ninety-two interstate wars.

single round of talks between belligerents. The invasions of Afghanistan and Iraq at the turn of the twenty-first century are contemporary examples; the La Plata War between Argentina and an alliance led by Brazil, which began in July 1851 and ended with a Brazilian military victory in February 1852, is a case from the more distant past. For wars that do feature negotiations, some talks occurred almost immediately once hostilities erupted, as was the case in the Falklands War; others started shortly before the conflict came to an end, as in the Russo-Japanese War; and many others began somewhere in the middle. The 1999 Kargil War between India and Pakistan is an instance of this last scenario: the first talks began on June 12, thirty-five days after the war began and thirty-five days before it ended.

Figure 0.1 also demonstrates how many talks failed to produce peace and instead ended up marking what would become the early stages of the war. If all negotiations quickly led to settlement, the plots would feature one short bar on the right-hand side of each conflict. The negotiation data indicate that 49 out of 189 total negotiation efforts across these wars, or about 25 percent, directly resulted in the termination of hostilities. Figure 0.1 also highlights a remarkable degree of variation in how much time warring states chose to communicate with each other while fighting. In a majority of conflicts, belligerents do not afford much time to sit at the bargaining table. Yet in a sizable number of cases, official state representatives spend between 20 percent and 80 percent of the war's overall duration talking to one another.

The reality of wartime negotiation thus appears contradictory. States frequently hesitate to negotiate, but when they do negotiate, talks are intermittent and regularly evince apathy or antipathy toward peace. For all the intricate differences we see across these conflicts, contemporary scholarship presents few explanations for why or how diplomatic interactions take place during war. But before I advance a new theory to tackle these questions, it is worth addressing what answers have already been offered.

Rational Reasons for War

Since the 1990s, scholars of international relations have broadly scrutinized war using a "rational choice" framework, which conceives of war as a form of bargaining.[5] We imagine that two or more actors are in a zero-sum dispute over how to divide a valuable good, such as territory or policy, between themselves. The actors either could split the resource peacefully by striking a mutually acceptable bargain or may attempt to use force to wrest a larger share. Each side's preferences regarding whether to take a pacific or bellicose approach are shaped by beliefs about the distribution of power between them, as well as the potential costs they would be willing to withstand from fighting. These two concepts are commonly referred to as capabilities and resolve. All of these judgments are made under a shroud of uncertainty, where the other side's true capabilities, resolve, and intentions are not fully known.[6]

In an agenda-setting article, James Fearon produces a game-theoretical model reflecting this logic and demonstrates that wars can be understood as a rational process where belligerents use violence to determine their minimally acceptable bargaining offers, which in turn reveals where a mutually acceptable zone of potential agreements—in political science parlance, a bargaining range—may exist. Using this framework, Fearon underscores two mechanisms that could trigger war: incomplete (or asymmetric) information and commitment problems.[7] In an incomplete information dynamic, actors may have incentives to overstate their capabilities and resolve—that is, to bluff. By doing so, one party hopes to convince the other that a war over the disputed good would be unwise, which in turn would produce a more generous diplomatic bargain.[8] The escalatory moves each side makes to demonstrate the credibility of its words can eventually push both sides over the precipice and into an unintended armed conflict.

With respect to commitment problems, an actor that is already or will become powerful cannot reassure anyone that it will not use its power to change the status quo; it would be fully rational for the actor to take advantage of its own growing strength. Other actors may worry that, if left unchecked, the ascending actor will push the bargaining range dramatically in its own favor and be more likely to realize its revisionist goals. These fears could lead concerned parties to launch a war with the goal of precluding such a disadvantageous shift in the first place.[9]

These two mechanisms highlight why actors may engage in war even though there is likely a peaceful and less painful deal that could have been made in the abstract. For whatever way in which actors divide a good, they would both prefer to make the split without fighting, as violence inevitably creates human, economic, and psychological suffering that negates at least some of the gains made. The fact that wars occur despite this fact is commonly called the inefficiency puzzle.[10] War, in this view, is a mechanism through which actors impose and absorb real costs in order—or, rather, because they failed—to demonstrate the validity of their own words.

Three Assumptions in Current Knowledge

The rationalist perspective on war has usefully illuminated the role of information in motivating conflict. Yet while works following this tradition seem intuitive and internally consistent, they harbor three interrelated assumptions regarding wartime diplomacy that are worth identifying and questioning. These involve the timing, cost, and purpose of negotiations.

TIMING

Early rationalist models of war were focused on explaining war initiation and did not directly address the question of what happens once wars erupt, either on the battlefield or at the bargaining table. The outcome of the entire war is viewed as a coin flip weighted by each side's military power. Such models are often called costly lottery models. Most quantitative studies of war adopt a similar methodology in which entire conflicts are taken as the unit of analysis; only fixed or initial characteristics at the outset of hostilities can shape the overall war, which itself is usually understood in terms of the victor or the duration of conflict. These methods preclude the study of how events that occur during the war itself, including negotiations, can reshape the war's trajectory once hostilities have already commenced.[11]

Subsequent bargaining models acknowledged that a comprehensive theory of war should explain not only its initiation but also its duration and termination.[12] These game-theoretic works explore intrawar dynamics and, importantly, acknowledge that diplomacy plays a part in ending many conflicts. Many models of this variety share a roughly similar structure. War is depicted as an alternating process between the exchange of a take-it-or-leave-it bargaining offer and a potentially war-ending battle if the offer is rejected.[13] Bargaining offers made near the outset of conflict may be more extreme. These inordinate proposals could reflect a genuine demand made in the midst of uncertainty, or they may even be intended to strategically manipulate the information environment and signal apparent strength. As the war progresses, each battle fought reveals new and less manipulable information about each side's relative capabilities, and costs incurred from these clashes further test the parties' resolve. Fighting is learning. Through the conduct of war, whatever proposals were initially made at the bargaining table based on less information are pushed aside. Belligerents are forced to update their beliefs about future expectations and thus revise their bargaining positions to be more closely aligned with the harsh truth revealed from hostilities.[14] Wars end either when belligerents reach a common set of expectations such that one side accepts the other's revised offer or when one side is totally defeated through a fatal battle. Critically, this generation of bargaining models explicitly clarified that wars need not end in complete victory or defeat, nor do they even require the belief that either total outcome is possible. War is an attempt by at least one side to improve on the status quo, and not necessarily to vanquish an opponent.[15]

Scholars disagree on the exact mechanism through which actors translate what they learn from fighting into behavior that could settle the conflict. These divergences lead to contrasting implications about the frequency and timing of negotiations. In most cases, models portray talks as a convergence process where belligerents slowly make more generous offers in order to screen out weak actors and to identify genuinely strong actors that are willing to fight longer to obtain more. These models imply that negotiations occur constantly throughout the entirety of a war.[16] A smaller but notable contingent of research instead argues that belligerents' bargaining process is better reflected as a war of attrition, where actors obstinately refuse to change their bargaining positions through most of the conflict before relenting and swiftly reaching an agreement.[17] These works suggest that negotiation does not occur for much of the conflict. Regardless of the specific mechanism, both representations of diplomacy assume that verbal bargaining is essentially instantaneous, allowing belligerents to exchange countless offers while fighting.[18]

More contemporary studies, predominantly focused on civil war, have challenged both views by suggesting that negotiations are a distinct stage of a broader conflict resolution process that is motivated by numerous political and strategic factors.[19] These works follow in the tradition of I. William Zartman's work on ripeness theory.[20] In brief, ripeness theory identifies two conditions that prompt belligerents to seek a negotiated settlement. First, the parties must feel as if they are trapped in a costly deadlock with no victory in sight; second, the belligerents must perceive a way to break out of the deadlock through the possibility of a negotiated and mutually acceptable settlement. When these two conditions are met, warring parties may thus be "ripe" for negotiations. Ripeness theory has for many years been the leading framework to understand the onset of negotiations during hostilities and will be discussed in greater detail in the next chapter.

COSTS

Many formal models of war suggest that the act of negotiating during hostilities, separate from the substantive concessions made, is costless. The idea that negotiations occur in between every round of fighting attests to this notion. Such an assumption is a natural consequence of the costly signaling tradition, which treats most diplomatic communication as "cheap talk." An extensive literature argues that verbal communication is not particularly costly and is thus not credible on its own, because it is hard to verify and easy to take back.[21] If diplomacy that occurs in the midst of crises can be cheap, then diplomacy during war seems even cheaper and less meaningful to understanding active conflict, especially when extraordinarily costly violence is communicating far more credible information.

Oriana Skylar Mastro's work challenges this view.[22] According to her costly conversations thesis (CCT), belligerents generally adopt a "closed" diplomatic posture when they fear the opponent may infer that an interest in diplomacy reveals vulnerability. Mastro refers to this as the "adverse inference of weakness." CCT proposes that belligerents are likelier to adopt open diplomatic postures when they believe they have demonstrated enough strength to overcome any adverse inference and when their opponent has relatively low strategic capacity to exploit any signs of weakness. Impressively researched studies of several wars support these claims.

PURPOSE

Across many formal models, the bargaining positions taken or any concessions made by a belligerent are a mechanical reflection of the battlefield. The more one actor dominates in recent clashes, the more that bargaining positions drift in that actor's favor. The longer one actor continues suffering costs without relenting, the more that bargaining offers will be more generous to that actor. When parties do choose to negotiate, it is because their bargaining positions have become sufficiently similar and their desire to end the conflict supersedes their interest in further bloodshed. Negotiations are a formal manner through which belligerents codify the outcomes of hostilities.

This last element overlaps with conventional notions of negotiation, which assume participants are willing to discuss items in good faith with the sole purpose of reaching an agreement, even if they may ultimately fail. In the bestselling book *Getting to Yes*, the cofounders of the Harvard Negotiation Project, Roger Fisher and William Ury, define negotiations as "back and forth communication designed to reach an agreement."[23] An article reporting on a laboratory experiment by the psychologist Peter Carnevale and the sociologist Edward Lawler describes negotiation as "a form of symbolic communication that involves two or more people attempting to reach agreement on issues where there are perceived differences of interest."[24] Indeed, experimental studies of negotiations often adopt designs that reward participants for reaching a mutually acceptable agreement.[25] In the policymaking realm, former secretary of state Dean Acheson also observes that "negotiation, in the classic diplomatic sense, assumes parties [are] more anxious to agree than to disagree; parties who are, therefore, willing to make concessions in determining what shall be agreed upon."[26]

The Puzzling Reality of Negotiations

The general thrust of conflict research therefore portrays wartime diplomacy as an ever-present, costless, mechanical, and earnest endeavor. Yet this logically consistent and intuitive depiction faces a problem: the empirical record does not support it. As figure 0.1 shows, patterns of negotiations during conflict are highly sporadic, vary widely by conflict, and do not always respond to outcomes in fighting.

Histories of war suggest that leaders frequently feel reticent to talk while fighting and consider the decision to engage in diplomacy a serious one. During the Crimean War of 1853–56, Tsar Nicholas I of Russia refused to negotiate with the Allies (Great Britain, France, and the Ottoman Empire) despite a series of battlefield victories by the Allies in mid and late 1854. It was only once Nicholas I died and was replaced by Alexander II that the belligerents met in Vienna in March 1855. But after several days of talks, all parties realized that nobody was prepared to make significant concessions.[27]

The Vienna talks during the Crimean War also illustrate that the onset of negotiations is not equivalent to the settlement of conflict. According to the negotiation data that I describe later in this book, approximately three-quarters of all periods of negotiation during the last two centuries of interstate war are not associated with the cessation of hostilities. About half of all interstate wars in the same period feature more than one round of negotiation. Each of these statistics suggests that belligerents fluctuate in their willingness to talk, sometimes pulling back from diplomacy after making the initial choice to participate. Current theories of conflict are not well equipped to explain these shifts.[28]

Many negotiations do not simply fail to reach an agreement but seem to reveal complete antipathy toward any form of compromise. Several months into the Second Sino-Japanese War of 1931–33, diplomats at the League of Nations hurriedly attempted to spearhead mediation efforts to stem the explosion of violence. The most notable efforts were formulated by the US and British ministers to China, Nelson T. Johnson and Sir Miles Lampson. The two arrived in Shanghai (the next target of Japan's expansion into China) on behalf of the league on February 12, 1932, with hopes of establishing a neutral zone. The visit went nowhere. By February 18, Japanese military representatives issued the mayor of Shanghai terms of an ultimatum with a deadline of February 20 that, in Lampson's words, were "in so arrogant a tone and dictatorial a form that it was hardly possible to expect their acceptance by the Chinese."[29] The mayor rejected the ultimatum, and Japanese forces that had arrived on February 18 renewed their assault. As such, the idea that belligerents constantly drift toward agreement and that negotiations signify a nearly irreversible shift toward peace is not justified.

One potential interpretation of this multifaceted negotiation behavior is that diplomacy is little more than "noise." Patterns of negotiation could perhaps be motivated by extraneous factors that are disconnected from the conflict itself. If so, then negotiations reveal very little about war, the observed variation is not worth further scrutiny, and conflict scholars have rightly treated diplomacy in the manner I have described thus far. But another interpretation is that we have severely undervalued the highly strategic nature of wartime negotiations and what they reveal about conflict. A lack of detailed data about conflict diplomacy and a paucity of theoretical tools to understand it may have created a vicious cycle that precludes a serious investigation of the topic.

The Argument

How can we understand when, why, and how diplomatic talks are used during war? I offer a straightforward overarching argument: negotiating in the midst of conflict involves costs and benefits, and belligerents continuously weigh these competing forces in order to choose whether to negotiate and how to negotiate. The simplicity of this thesis is somewhat deceptive, as the scholarly literature has not fully appreciated or synthesized the numerous upsides and downsides associated with diplomacy during war.

To develop this argument, I distinguish between two forms of negotiation, which I call *sincere* and *insincere*. Sincere negotiations refer to good-faith attempts by belligerents to reach a mutually acceptable agreement. Sincerity does not guarantee successful compromise but underscores the participants' genuine preference to reach an agreement rather than not. As I will discuss in the next chapter, both our common and scholarly understandings of negotiations overwhelmingly adopt this view. One certainly cannot deny that negotiations are necessary to end conflicts short of complete military victory or defeat. But to assume that this is diplomacy's only function embodies an unsophisticated view of what negotiation can accomplish and reveal during conflicts. My theory therefore emphasizes the insincere mode of negotiation, which refers to interactions where at least one party seeks to use talks for some purpose unrelated or antithetical to agreement. In the wartime context, this means that a belligerent exploits the time spent talking in order to realize some other objective that serves to promote policy aims that aid its war effort. Two significant goals motivate insincere negotiations: deflecting political blame for participating in armed conflict and buying time to regroup and remobilize one's military forces to fight more effectively in the near future.

I am certainly not the first to suggest that negotiations can be orchestrated in bad faith. Numerous scholars and practitioners have identified this phenomenon using terms such as "side effects,"[30] "devious objectives,"[31] "posturing,"[32] "duplicitous negotiations,"[33] "avoidance bargaining,"[34] "phony bargaining,"[35] "striving for no,"[36] "false negotiations,"[37] "false readiness,"[38] "insincere bargaining,"[39] and "insincere negotiations."[40] These works, however, merely note the existence and possibility of bad-faith diplomatic bargaining without providing an explanation for when it should be more prone to occurring. My argument provides one of the first systematic explanations of the conditions in which negotiations would more likely be sincere or insincere.

I establish a theory of wartime negotiations that contends that belligerents' decisions to negotiate and whether to negotiate sincerely or insincerely are dictated by two primary factors. The first is what I call latent external pressure. This reflects the amount of influence that third parties can activate in order to compel belligerents to engage in diplomacy. The descriptive term "latent" captures the notion that the overall degree and quality of pressure that outside parties can place on belligerents in any particular conflict are partially moderated by the broader existence of institutions, norms, and structures that facilitate such behavior. The second factor, already widely accepted in extant research, is information obtained from the battlefield. The interactions of these two factors account for the relative costs and benefits of negotiating during war.

In the absence of any external pressures to negotiate, belligerents perceive enormously high costs to negotiating with the enemy. Looking too eager to talk can be interpreted as a sign of weakness, which may encourage the enemy to fight harder because it thinks victory is at hand or discourage one's own people from fighting because they believe defeat is imminent.[41] The simple act of negotiation, regardless of what positions belligerents espouse when talking, can therefore worsen a belligerent's prospects in a war if talks do not produce a diplomatic settlement. Consequently, when latent external pressures are low, we should expect negotiations to happen infrequently, and most would-be attempts to negotiate insincerely should be deterred. The likelihood of talks will increase as the results of fighting trend heavily in one side's favor, and any talks that do occur have a high probability of being sincere attempts to cease hostilities and minimize one's costs by avoiding needless bloodshed.

The talks in Portsmouth during the Russo-Japanese War are a paradigmatic example of sincere negotiations, which took place in an environment with relatively low latent external pressures for peace and a battlefield solidly trending in one side's favor. Tsar Nicholas II very reluctantly acceded to negotiations because Russia's weakness had been made apparent and few other alternatives remained. Both sides came to the table of their own accord and were therefore able to quickly settle their affairs.

Incentives to engage in diplomacy change considerably when latent external pressures to negotiate are high. Constant attempts by third parties to initiate talks, as well as the pervasiveness of norms or institutions aimed at peace, lower the costs to negotiation. Being willing to talk is interpreted more as a submission to the international community, and belligerents do not have to initiate negotiation efforts on their own. These cost-reducing effects exist regardless of whether third parties wield sufficient leverage to actually alter the prospects of a lasting settlement.[42] On the one hand, this may enable some wars to end more quickly because warring parties can start talking more expeditiously (or at all) without worrying about as many negative repercussions of doing so. On the other hand, this permissive environment also enables belligerents to negotiate more freely regardless of the state of the battlefield. Actors thus have greater liberty to try negotiating insincerely in hopes of improving their ability to prosecute the war effort when talks fall apart by design. While diplomatic communications are relatively common in this high-pressure environment, the battlefield plays an important role in dictating whether talks are sincere or insincere. When the battlefield provides limited or indeterminate information, negotiations that come to pass are probably insincere in nature, exploited to further at least one side's cause. As fighting tilts heavily in one side's favor, negotiations are more likely to be sincere and to bring the war to a diplomatic conclusion.

The two fruitless negotiations that punctuated the Falklands War exemplify insincere negotiations. Both were products of enormous international pressure that was immediately activated once hostilities erupted, occurring before fighting had taken place in earnest. Mediated diplomatic communication moved forward even though neither side had any real desire to reach a settlement. But negotiations were not only unsuccessful in reaching peace. The United Kingdom used the period of diplomatic bargaining to deploy its forces to Argentina, and both sides exploited the apparent diplomatic deadlock to animate their domestic audiences in favor of more conflict. The only sincere talks of the war lasted one day and wrote down the terms of Argentina's military surrender.

The Russo-Japanese War and the Falklands War are two archetypal cases that illustrate my theory in stark terms. But as I will establish in the chapters to come, my argument effectively explains the causes and consequences of wartime diplomacy over two centuries of global conflict. The seemingly arbitrary nature of negotiations in conflict is, I show, not arbitrary at all.

Contributions

The core evidence for my theory relies on new quantitative data of battles and negotiations over two centuries of interstate conflict. These data are based on a wide-scale review of several hundred primary documents, reference materials, and periodicals. By combining these two resources, I am able to track the ebbs and flows of wartime fighting and talking at the daily level. My data afford the opportunity to study wars at a level of breadth and granularity that is unmatched by current studies of war. Figure 0.1, as simple as it looks, reveals variation that cannot be readily explained using extant theories of conflict. This suggests that there is a great deal about negotiations that the fields of international relations, diplomacy, and conflict resolution do not fully appreciate, much less understand.

My battle and negotiation data not only enable a systematic assessment of my theory but may also help to reinvigorate the quantitative study of war. Inspired by Fearon's seminal article, a surge of research around the turn of the twenty-first century used game-theoretic models to further flesh out the notion of war as a bargaining process, but the endeavor has since become a more dormant enterprise. This is likely not a coincidence. Very few resources have been created to directly validate, challenge, or refine the premises or conclusions of these bargaining models—many of which contradict each other—on a larger scale.[43] Debates regarding whether wars are resolved through a convergence or attrition process are one prominent instance where conclusions differ based on the structure, payoffs, and presumptions of the model. My new data represent a sizable step in this direction and may help motivate others to gather more quantitative measures of intrawar activity. Doing so would help further crack open what Scott Gartner memorably called the "black box of war,"[44] breaking the cycle where a lack of data on wartime negotiations precludes an exploration or appreciation of wartime negotiations, which in turn inhibits the collection of data on them.

On the academic front, this endeavor challenges the penchant of international relations scholarship to shortchange the importance of diplomacy during war. It is natural to think of wartime negotiations as being the converse to armed violence; belligerents shed blood on the battlefield and resolve their differences at the bargaining table. But even though all diplomatic settlements require negotiation, not all negotiations lead to diplomatic settlements. The fact that these "unsuccessful" negotiations can have political implications, be harnessed to moderate conflict, alleviate third-party pressures, and reshape battlefield outcomes poses a nontrivial challenge to extant scholarship that does not seriously contemplate intrawar diplomacy or that solely views it as a manner to grant concessions. As such, my theory indicates that the rationalist tradition of dismissing diplomacy as mere "cheap talk," especially during war, is overly reductive and deleterious to our understanding of international conflict. Negotiations during war are not an alternative to war but an essential tool to navigate it.

In pointing out how the bargaining model of war harbors an oversimplified conception of negotiations, I do not mean to suggest that the bargaining model's broader conception of war is fundamentally wrong. My argument adopts a rational approach where actors weigh the balance of costs and benefits when determining their optimal course of action moving forward; concerns about information, capabilities, resolve, and intentions all matter greatly in these calculations. Instead, I emphasize the fact that the occurrence of negotiations—regardless of the specific proposals exchanged during them—can produce new consequences that influence each side's leverage and thus its prospects in the violent bargaining process of war.

While scholars in the realm of international relations have deeply scrutinized the strategic underpinnings of war without as much emphasis on negotiations that could occur at those times, scholars focused on negotiation studies and diplomatic studies have taken the matter of negotiations more seriously. But they frequently do not consider them in a wartime context. My theory thus represents a useful coalescence of insights from, and contributes to, related research tracks on war, conflict resolution, diplomacy, and negotiations.

This book also offers significant insights on conflict resolution when it comes to policymaking. Since most wars involve and end through diplomacy, understanding the incentives that belligerents have with respect to negotiations is vital for producing thoughtful policies that promote peace rather than undermine it. For instance, my theoretical framework and empirical findings advance thinking on the seminal policy debate about the merits of outside intervention in wars. Reflecting on the United Nations' uneven impact in the Bosnian War of 1992–95, Edward Luttwak memorably argued that international actors should stay out of conflicts and "give war a chance," as the only manner to truly end hostilities is to allow belligerents to fight to mutual exhaustion or complete defeat.[45] Such a proposal insinuates that the international institutions we have built since World War II to maintain peace and stability are actually undermining their professed goals. This book indicates that constant efforts to spur diplomacy, even if well meaning, could ultimately be counterproductive. Yet it also identifies moments when diplomacy facilitates peace. By systematically pinpointing the specific conditions of when those moments may (or may not) occur, this book thus furthers our understanding of when and which conflict resolution policies might be effective.

Additionally, my theory highlights the potentially unscrupulous side of diplomacy. US policymakers often treat negotiation as a good-faith activity and do not see the cynical ends that negotiation can facilitate.[46] In a memoir, Dean Acheson lamented many policymakers' naive view of the relationship between negotiation and conflict: "I have heard people who should know better, including a head of government, say happily, 'As long as we keep them talking, they're not fighting.' Nothing could be more untrue: they are fighting. . . . To our minds international conferences and negotiations are so completely means for ending conflict that we are blind to the fact that they may be and, in the hands of experts, are equally adapted to continuing it."[47]

Strong normative beliefs conceive of diplomacy as an inherently genuine process,[48] which perhaps explains why policymakers around the world do not fully appreciate the power of duplicitous negotiations as a weapon of war. This book calls for a serious revision of this unsophisticated view of diplomacy.

The Book to Come

Chapter 1 lays out my full theoretical framework regarding wartime negotiations. To that end, I first define key concepts of the book with reference to current literatures on war, negotiations, and their intersection. The remainder of the chapter develops the central components of my theory and explains the conditions in which we are most likely to see negotiations that may productively resolve hostilities, or when negotiations may be more easily exploited for instrumental ends. I place particular emphasis on insincere negotiations, as their existence and effects introduce the implications that stand in starkest contrast with existing research on conflict and its resolution.

This discussion leads to a series of testable implications that I assess in subsequent chapters. Since my theory features many moving parts, no single test can fully substantiate it in its entirety. I rely instead on several forms of empirical inquiry to assess different aspects of my argument at various levels of analysis, and I have selected case studies to show the validity of the argument across a wide span of time and space.

Chapter 2 discusses the empirical cornerstone of this book: data on battles and negotiations in almost all interstate wars over the last two centuries. I describe the raw materials, definitions, and procedures used to convert hundreds of qualitative historical sources into two quantitative datasets on wartime negotiations and battles across ninety-two conflicts. I demonstrate the utility and plausibility of these two datasets by illustrating patterns of wartime negotiations and battlefield trends within wars. Even these purely descriptive statistics reveal insights about war that would be infeasible with extant resources.

Chapter 3 is the first to directly assess my theory of wartime negotiations. I address the impact that latent external pressures and battlefield outcomes have on the initiation of negotiations, as well as their relationship with the termination of hostilities. While my battle data allow me to create straightforward measures of battlefield outcomes, it was necessary to develop a method to measure latent external pressures on belligerents to negotiate. To that end, I leverage the dramatic change in the international environment before and after 1945. This decision is based on the idea, backed by substantial scholarship, that the post–World War II era witnessed an immense growth of institutions, actors, and norms that promote peace and stability. I argue that these innovations have led to a substantial and systemic decrease in the costs of negotiating, as it becomes easier for third parties to activate pressure on belligerents to talk to one another. I establish that the 1945 line is indeed associated with a dramatic upward shift in the rate of wartime negotiations.

Furthermore, I show that wars before 1945—that is, wars with relatively low latent external pressures—indeed have less frequent negotiations, but that talks become more frequent and promptly terminate wars when the battlefield firmly moves in one side's favor. Meanwhile, in wars after 1945, negotiations occur quite frequently and bear little relationship with the state of the battlefield. Many talks come and go without any steps toward peace. A battlefield where one side has a solid advantage, however, does help to predict whether negotiations that do occur will lead to settlement. A number of supplementary analyses provide more context for why the pre-1945 and post-1945 diplomatic environments look so different, as well as what factors may account for the actual deployment of diplomatic pressure by third parties. I further substantiate my argument regarding latent external pressures by leveraging whether wars involved any major power belligerents, who I expect to be more immune to external diplomatic pressures. In support of my expectations, I find that wars involving only minor powers feature higher rates of reluctant negotiation because the belligerents are more dependent on external material and political support.

Any quantitative study of conflict will inevitably sand away details and nuances of individual events in exchange for evidence of broader trends.[49] As such, the second part of chapter 3 features a qualitative comparison of two conflicts that feature the same main belligerents: the Greco-Turkish War of 1897 and the Turkish invasion of Cyprus in 1974. The case studies show the importance of latent external pressures in influencing negotiation behavior. The 1897 war featured relatively few external sources of diplomatic pressure; the only round of talks that took place codified the Ottoman Empire's victory. In contrast, the 1974 conflict was woven into a broader fabric of international politics. A two-week diplomatic effort spearheaded by the United Kingdom and the United States produced no peace and instead allowed the belligerents to mobilize their political and military assets so that they could fight more effectively once talks ended.

Whereas chapter 3 analyzes how battlefield activity can influence negotiation behavior, chapter 4 explores how negotiations can reshape the battlefield. This tests my claim that insincere negotiations not only fail to end hostilities but can be exploited to help reshape the subsequent trajectory of conflict. I return to my quantitative data to substantiate two implications of my theory. First, I confirm that periods of negotiation are associated with lower levels of active hostilities on the battlefield. These moments of relative quiet on the battlefield are natural for belligerents who want to sincerely stop fighting, but they are also necessary for belligerents that merely want to abuse negotiations to improve their political and military position. Second, I demonstrate that negotiations that do not result in peace are followed by battlefield trends that systematically favor war targets and that are more consistent with prewar expectations. This result is particularly noteworthy and underscores the importance of viewing negotiations as a very real extension of war.

The chapter then uses a qualitative approach to walk through the relationship between fighting and bargaining and to show the deep military and political impacts of negotiation in two distinct wars: the War of the Roman Republic in 1849 and the Cenepa Valley War of 1995. The former is a valuable example of how insincere negotiations can occur in the absence of explicit external pressures. The latter, a South American conflict, is the most recent war for which there is adequately accessible documentation of public and private diplomatic activity.

Chapter 5 offers an in-depth qualitative study of the Arab-Israeli War of 1948–49, a historical clash in the Middle East that is also one of the first cases to erupt in an environment of high latent external pressures after 1945. This conflict illustrates how the dynamics that I examine separately in chapters 3 and 4 can coalesce into a more complex and strategic story. I show that constant mediation efforts by the United Nations, while motivated by optimistic intentions, enabled both Israel and the Arab states to exploit phases of negotiation to rearm themselves and to frame their opponent as the wayward party that was unwilling to consider peace. I argue that Israel's victory and survival in early 1949 is largely the product of how the Ben-Gurion government exploited insincere negotiations to give Israel valuable time to buttress its unprepared military forces.

Up to this point, much of my empirical evidence treats entire periods of negotiation as being sincere or insincere. Chapter 6 explores whether my theory can also explain variation in negotiation behavior within individual rounds of talks. I do so by analyzing the Korean War of 1950–53. The war is notable in that it is still technically active today and in that it also involves major powers on either side. I conduct a hybrid analysis that includes both a qualitative review of the conflict and a highly granular quantitative analysis of battlefield activity and negotiation behavior. Using a combination of text-as-data and machine learning methods, I convert thousands of pages of declassified archival documents that track battlefield movement, casualties, and negotiation behavior to daily-level quantitative measures. These data allow me to directly test how small changes on the battlefield influence a belligerent's proclivity to be more sincere or insincere within longer bouts of negotiation, all while keeping the level of latent external pressures constant. They reveal patterns that are consistent with my theory of wartime negotiations. When the battlefront provided new information through troop movement or losses, both delegations engaged in more substantive and seemingly sincere discussions that were related to settling the conflict. Conversely, when little was learned from fighting, the delegation's negotiation behavior became more overtly hostile, obstinate, and insincere.

The conclusion wraps up the book with directions for future lines of inquiry and policy recommendations regarding the conduct of wartime diplomacy. I emphasize the complicated balancing act that my theory and findings uncover regarding the role that the international community can play in steering the course of conflicts. In some cases, external actors may succeed in their professed goal of preventing wars from causing more suffering. But in other instances, similar diplomatic endeavors not only may fail to strike a peace but may even undermine that objective. When wars cannot end through military means, diplomacy becomes an olive branch in one hand and a sword in the other. This book provides the structure to understand when and why each hand is extended.

A THEORY OF WARTIME NEGOTIATIONS

On July 14, 2015, Secretary of State John Kerry announced at a press conference the formation of the Joint Comprehensive Plan of Action, or JCPOA—a sweeping agreement devised by the permanent five members of the United Nations Security Council, Germany, and Iran to limit Iran's nuclear ambitions in exchange for significant sanctions relief. Many policy experts and politicians hailed the JCPOA as a critical tool to prevent yet another war in the Middle East.[1] Characterizing the gravity of this accomplishment within the context of his personal life, Kerry ended his statements by talking about his service in the Vietnam War. He remarked, "I learned in war the price that is paid when diplomacy fails. . . . I know that war is the failure of diplomacy and the failure of leaders to make alternative decisions."[2]

Kerry is by no means the first or only person to claim that wars begin when diplomacy fails. In his iconic (and inescapable) volume *On War*, Carl von Clausewitz famously states that "war is merely the continuation of policy by other means"—those other means being necessary when diplomacy falls short.[3] The notion is so deeply ingrained in our collective psyche that a version of it is uttered by Captain Kathryn Janeway on an episode of the television show *Star Trek: Voyager*: "When diplomacy fails, there's only one alternative: violence."[4]

The introduction to this book described a puzzling inconsistency within current treatments of conflict: crisis diplomacy is viewed as a highly calculated and manipulable form of communication, but diplomacy is sapped of strategic value once bloodshed begins. The high levels of variation we see in the timing and success rates of negotiation suggest that far more remains to be learned about diplomacy and its relationship with conflict. Against that backdrop, this chapter establishes a theory of wartime negotiations that helps to explain when negotiations are likely to occur, as well as what consequences they have for the future trajectory of conflict.

I begin with a discussion of how to define negotiations. I then explain the importance of a concept in the study of negotiations known as the reversion outcome—more commonly called the best alternative to a negotiated agreement (BATNA). The reversion outcome refers to the best result a negotiator can hope to realize if negotiations do not reach a mutually acceptable agreement. The notion of a reversion outcome is not unfamiliar in the field of international relations, but as I will suggest, it does not play an explicit part in many existing theories of conflict.

With those ideas established, I enumerate the specific costs and benefits that shape belligerents' calculations regarding wartime diplomacy. Importantly, I argue that the primary costs and benefits of negotiating during war are related to the concept of the reversion outcome. A critical cost to starting negotiations is that they can signal weakness to the enemy and one's own constituency. This, in turn, worsens the range of outcomes a belligerent can obtain when negotiations fail, since abortive talks are likely to be followed by an emboldened enemy or political punishment.

My examination of the benefits to talking while fighting introduces two separate modes of negotiation, which I call *sincere* and *insincere*. Negotiations that are conducted sincerely embody the traditional understanding of negotiation, which implies a good-faith effort at reaching agreement by all sides. Actors talk because they would like to avoid the reversion outcome associated with the continuation of war. Negotiations that are pursued for insincere ends, on the other hand, reflect a form of bargaining where at least one actor engages in talks for reasons unrelated to and perhaps antithetical to agreement. Importantly, diplomacy that is used insincerely can be exploited to improve one's ability to prosecute a war after talks fail. Insincere negotiations help to augment a party's reversion outcome, and they can reshape conflicts in ways that current theories would not necessarily anticipate.

Two key factors help to explain the specific balance of costs and benefits that belligerents perceive when considering when and how to negotiate during war: the level of latent diplomatic pressure that can be activated and placed on belligerents by third parties, and the degree of information culled from fighting. Different configurations of each of these two dimensions help to explain not only how frequently belligerents would come to the table during war but also whether these talks would lead to the settlement or exacerbation of conflict. The chapter ends with an enumeration of the core testable implications that arise from my theory.

Defining Negotiations

Intuitively, negotiation is a process through which divergent positions are discussed in hopes of producing a common agreement. This book adopts a more formal definition adapted from Fred Iklé's book on international diplomacy, *How Nations Negotiate*. Negotiation is a process of direct or mediated communication between official representatives of the active disputants, where explicit proposals are put forward with the ostensible aim of reaching a mutually acceptable agreement.[5] This description shares similarities with most definitions of the word and is not limited to a wartime context.

There are several constituent and purposeful parts of this definition worth discussing individually. First, negotiations can be direct or mediated. They can proceed between two parties in isolation, or they can involve a third party that facilitates discussion by either being in the same room as all the disputants or traveling back and forth between them. Negotiation with active but nonbinding participation by a third party is mediation.

Second, official and accredited representatives conduct negotiations.[6] Everyday citizens from different countries speak with each other all the time, but we obviously do not consider their communication to be diplomacy. Perhaps more conspicuously, celebrities receive attention for meeting with government officials; consider Dennis Rodman's basketball-related interactions with Kim Jong-un in North Korea or Angelina Jolie serving as goodwill ambassador for the United Nations High Commissioner for Refugees. The burgeoning prominence of celebrities in international affairs is certainly a worthwhile topic to explore.[7] Nonetheless, many aspects of international relations—and, in particular, conflict resolution—remain the domain of state leaders, officials, diplomats, and other individuals vested with direct authority to speak on behalf of a government or organization.

Third, negotiations involve explicit and verbal or written proposals. Actors must discuss substantive ideas regarding how to deal with a disagreement. This does not imply that actors must agree on these proposals, but it does mean that incidental small talk between representatives in the halls or corners of the United Nations, for example, is too casual to be considered negotiation. Acts of tacit bargaining where parties seek to influence one another through nonverbal behavior, such as troop movements or other physical maneuvers,[8] are important phenomena in international affairs, and they are clearly acts of communication designed to influence behavior, but they do not satisfy my definition of negotiation.

Fourth, the word *ostensible*, which seems innocuous, in fact represents a significant corrective to many seminal definitions of negotiation, which often presuppose that negotiations occur with genuine "interests in reaching agreement," as Ariel Rubinstein puts it.[9] As I explain later in this chapter and in others, negotiations often take place even when belligerents have no desire to realize any agreement with their opponent. The notion that wartime diplomacy is often used to moderate and reshape the trajectory of war, and that the strategy to this behavior can be systematically explained, is a central insight of this book.

It is necessary to delineate negotiations against two adjacent terms: bargaining and diplomacy. The term *bargaining* refers to the general process of deciding how to divide gains from some form of joint action.[10] An article by Rubinstein conceives of bargaining as a noncooperative and zero-sum process where two parties attempt to reach an agreement about how to divide a "pie."[11] Many issues in international relations that can escalate to conflict involve bargaining. This form of interaction can ensue through negotiations but, as the next section clarifies, also transpires through war. As such, negotiations are a form of bargaining.

According to Sir Ernest Mason Satow's classic *Guide to Diplomatic Practice*, diplomacy can be succinctly defined as "the conduct of business between States by peaceful means."[12] Diplomacy is the manner in which states often bargain with one another, and negotiations are a tool through which diplomacy takes place. The *Oxford English Dictionary* goes as far as to define diplomacy as "the management of international relations by negotiation."[13]

That said, two clarifications are worth mentioning. First, the idea that diplomacy occurs via peaceful means does not imply that it is completely removed from violence.[14] Giving verbal ultimatums, performing military exercises, and mobilizing one's military forces are all forms of diplomacy that do not involve direct violence but obviously seek to coerce an opponent by threatening it. By analyzing negotiations during war, this book focuses on the extreme version of this concept, where diplomatic activity takes place alongside active violence (rather than under the threat of violence) and the result of failed diplomacy is the continuation of violence. Second, diplomacy need not require states as actors. Satow's definition is informed by his experience as a foreign officer for the British government in the nineteenth and early twentieth centuries, when the Westphalian notion of the nation-state was robust and nonstate actors were not prominent in international affairs. Today it may be more accurate to say that diplomacy involves the conduct of business between political entities, including negotiations, by peaceful means.[15] Discussions between governments and rebel groups within a state or between governments and terrorist organizations abroad should therefore also count as examples of diplomacy, and my findings on interstate conflicts yield implications regarding these other arenas.

While the above discussion outlines how negotiation, bargaining, and diplomacy are not completely identical, unless otherwise indicated, I will use the terms *negotiation, diplomacy,* and *diplomatic bargaining* interchangeably throughout the text to refer to the central concept of negotiation.

The Reversion Outcome

Negotiations involve the ostensible goal of reaching a mutually acceptable agreement. How do actors determine what potential deals are worth taking or rejecting? When actors make decisions regarding whether to negotiate, what they would seek during negotiations, and how they would utilize negotiations, they must consider what alternatives to talking exist. Scholars and practitioners alike emphasize the significance of a party's best alternative to a negotiated agreement, or BATNA. A term popularized by Fisher and Ury in their book *Getting to Yes*, a BATNA refers to the next-most-favorable alternative that an actor has should negotiations fail to result in agreement.[16] In political science and formal modeling literature, this concept is often called the reversion outcome. I treat these two terms as equivalent throughout the remainder of this book. The reversion outcome is important because it defines each side's bargaining leverage. Actors with a more favorable reversion outcome are freer to walk away from talks or eschew them completely, while those with a less favorable one are more pressed to make a deal because their fallback option is undesirable.

An actor contemplating negotiations in a wartime setting cannot precisely know what will happen if negotiations collapse and fighting continues. In such cases, actors must estimate the benefits, costs, and likelihoods of all possible outcomes or actions should talks fail and then calculate the expected value of the reversion outcome.[17] If a belligerent believes, accurately or not, that defeat with massive casualties is likely, the reversion outcome is highly negative. If a belligerent instead predicts victory but is uncertain about the magnitude of lives and resources that will be lost in the process, the reversion outcome's value is more complicated to appraise. These estimates will change and perhaps sharpen over the course of conflict as each side learns more information that helps it revise its assessment of the war's likely trajectory.

The concept of the reversion outcome is distinct from the concept of a minimally acceptable offer. In standard models of war, actors consider what share of a disputed good they believe they would win from fighting, and they subtract the expected costs of conflict from that share. This quantity is known as a minimally acceptable offer, or the value of war.[18] Wars are fought in order to truthfully unveil each side's minimally acceptable offer. Any diplomatic deal that would give each actor at least this minimum value would be preferable to fighting; any diplomatic deal that is at least as good as both sides' minimally acceptable offer constitutes the viable bargaining range. The BATNA or reversion outcome represents the scenario an actor faces if a negotiation generates an impasse. As an actor's BATNA becomes progressively worse, the minimally acceptable offer it would be willing to accept through negotiations can also fall.

While BATNAs may influence minimally acceptable offers, the two are not identical or permanent.[19] As a brief illustration, suppose an artist hopes to sell a painting for no less than $500, which accounts for the costs of raw supplies and the artist's time. Based on similar past transactions and their own assessment of the painting's quality, the artist initially believes they can easily find a client who will pay $1,000. A client who offers $750 at this point will be turned away. Even though $750 exceeds the minimally acceptable offer of $500, the artist's perceived BATNA—quickly finding a different client who will pay more—has a higher value of $1,000. Suppose, however, that the artist's original intuition is eventually proven wrong, and they struggle to find another interested buyer. The BATNA may then involve putting the painting away and making no money. The artist in this case would accept any bid worth at least $500. Indeed, the new reversion outcome's value of $0 may lead the artist to revise their minimally acceptable offer dramatically below $500, simply to defray some costs instead of no costs at all.

Although many canonical bargaining models of war explicitly capture the notion of a minimally acceptable offer and the bargaining range that exists between two sides, their treatment of the reversion outcome is far more implicit. In some models, negotiations take place only to codify the outcomes of war as determined by the results of fighting.[20] In others that portray war as an alternating process between fighting and negotiating, the diplomacy phase is depicted as a moment of suspended animation. The war freezes in its current configuration while the belligerents exchange, consider, and respond to bargaining offers in an instantaneous fashion. If an offer is rejected, the war proceeds with another battle, where each side's likelihood of victory is based on the characteristics of the belligerents and battlefield immediately before the previous round of talks began.[21] Across both cases, the reversion outcome when negotiations fail is the continuation of hostilities based on little other than the state of affairs that existed prior to negotiations.

Negotiation scholarship suggests that reversion outcomes are far more complex, accounting for situations and changing circumstances that may exist outside the narrow confines of the direct bargaining interaction in question. BATNAs are not necessarily alternatives that exist independent of the other side.[22] As an example, suppose members of a union are considering whether to go on strike in order to demand safer working conditions. Their minimally acceptable offer may involve a series of safety reforms and the installation of newer equipment in their facilities. If the company refused to honor these demands, it may seem as if the union members' reversion outcome would be continuing to work in an unsafe environment while preparing for another collective effort. But more factors exist beyond the scope of the specific negotiation. If union members choose to go on strike but fail to obtain their demands, they may end up being replaced with individuals willing to cross the picket line and could ultimately be fired. The workers' reversion outcome is therefore not necessarily the continuation of their hazardous jobs; it could be the potential end of their jobs. This may cause hesitation about what terms to demand or whether to strike at all. But if local media outlets were already reporting on this dispute, the workers may believe that the strike will attract enough public attention to cast a harsh spotlight on the company, which might reduce the likelihood that anyone would be fired. The reversion outcome in this situation would be an expected value calculated using the estimated prospects that media scrutiny will or will not protect the striking workers' jobs. Regardless of the specific calculation, union members would have greater leverage and more incentives to strike if the media became involved compared to a scenario where they did not. Whether these or any other reversion outcomes are more likely depends on factors internal and external to the specific bargain over workplace conditions. What binds all of these disparate possibilities together is that engaging in negotiations can influence an actor's bargaining leverage if talks fail to reach an agreement.

I contend that wars are equally, if not more, subject to a similar logic. The theory I develop proposes the following: *The basic act of negotiating during war can directly alter a belligerent's reversion outcome and thus its bargaining leverage.* The political and military environment following failed talks may be fundamentally different from the conditions that existed prior to any diplomatic interactions, for good or for ill, and these changes may redirect the trajectory of conflict compared to a scenario where negotiations did not take place. This prospect helps to explain when, why, and how belligerents would choose to talk while fighting. My theory suggests that the costs and benefits of negotiation are all related to how the act of negotiating either worsens or improves belligerents' prospects should talks fail. In some cases, words can be used to fight.

To understand this strategic argument and its implications in full, we must first enumerate and explore the competing costs and benefits entailed by negotiating during war and how they relate to an actor's reversion outcome.

Avoiding Negotiations

I begin by addressing why belligerents often choose not to communicate with their opponent during active hostilities. As my data show, approximately 83 percent of war-days involve no negotiations between actors in interstate wars. This observation is especially puzzling and incongruous with many current conceptions of negotiations in war.

One natural reason negotiations do not occur is that they may not be worth the trouble. In wars primarily driven by credible commitment problems, belligerents would sense very little utility to negotiating an agreement that stands little chance of being upheld over time. The complete surrender or neutralization of the enemy may seem to be the only real and self-enforcing solution.[23] The War of the Triple Alliance of 1864–70—also known as the López or Paraguayan War—provides a useful illustration. Paraguay's access to the Atlantic Ocean, which was vital for its security and economic well-being, ran through Argentina and Uruguay. When Argentina and Brazil began to directly intervene in Uruguayan affairs, President Francisco Solano López feared that his nation would be choked off from the sea. He subsequently launched attacks against Argentina and Brazil to reverse their claims on Uruguay. The attempt failed and instead led the two regional powers plus occupied Uruguay to escalate hostilities against a seemingly irrational opponent. The resulting war was fought to the bitter end, concluding only in 1870 when Solano López was killed in battle. Due to extreme concerns about the opponent's intentions and willingness to uphold any diplomatic settlement, the war raged for six years, wiped out approximately 70 percent of the prewar Paraguayan population, and featured no negotiations.[24]

While commitment problems may explain diplomatic silence in the Paraguayan War, this explanation does not account for the infrequency of talks during conflicts primarily motivated by incomplete information, nor does it address why wars borne of commitment problems—such as the United States' experiences in Korea and Vietnam—may still feature negotiations at different points during hostilities. A more compelling answer emerges when we consider the potential costs of talking with the enemy. Despite many models of war treating negotiation as a costless activity, numerous scholars and practitioners have argued that a major obstacle to initiating negotiations during conflict is the fear that any interest in dialogue will be construed as a sign of weakness or flagging resolve.[25] Practitioners in government and business also commonly suggest that actors refrain from starting a conversation, especially when information asymmetries exist.[26]

Some examples illustrate this point concretely. On February 12, 1964, Fidel Castro of Cuba relayed a back-channel message to President Lyndon Johnson through the ABC News correspondent Lisa Howard. The communication expressed hope that the two countries could "eventually sit down in an atmosphere of good will and of mutual respect and negotiate our differences." Yet tellingly, Castro's message ended by stressing that Johnson "should not interpret my conciliatory attitude, my desire for discussions as a sign of weakness."[27] An entry from the President's Daily Brief—the premier intelligence document of the United States government—also demonstrates the reality of this concern. Discussing tensions between King Hussein of Jordan and militant Palestinian fedayeen who had created a quasi-state within his country, a brief in early 1970 concluded that "[Hussein] has been accused of weakness because he preferred negotiating to fighting."[28]

This mindset is also reflected in popular culture. In an episode of the television show *The Office*, aptly titled "The Negotiation," regional manager Michael Scott clumsily applies bargaining tactics he learned from Wikipedia in a mock negotiation to obtain a pay raise. Several seconds of uncomfortable silence pass before he announces that he is "declining to speak first."[29] In the 2013 film *The Wolf of Wall Street*, the stockbroker Jordan Belfort echoes a similar sentiment when teaching other brokers how to make sales, saying that "whoever speaks first loses."[30]

Returning to the realm of international relations, Thomas Schelling describes the predicament raised by the choice to talk, as "one side or both may fear that even a show of willingness to negotiate will be interpreted as excessive eagerness."[31] Work by Oriana Skylar Mastro refers to this concern as "adverse inference of weakness."[32] Several contributions in economics make a similar point but from the opposite direction, finding that refusal to negotiate can be harnessed as a mechanism to signal one's continuing resolve.[33] Since wars almost universally involve some form of incomplete information, indicating interest in diplomacy may suggest that a party is starting to falter, losing patience, or preparing to sue for peace. Any sign of vulnerability may motivate the opponent to fight harder and adopt an even more hard-line approach.[34] Communicating with an opponent that has been politically villainized can trigger misgivings about appeasing an aggressor or validating their behavior, empowering the opponent to work more assiduously toward its own interests.[35]

History abounds with mentions of this concern during crises and wars.[36] During a meeting on June 5, 1961 (the day after the storied Vienna summit between President John F. Kennedy and Chairman Nikita Khrushchev), Kennedy and British prime minister Harold Macmillan discussed how the quadripartite allies would handle the escalating crisis against the Soviets in Berlin. Both leaders agreed that any act by "the West to offer negotiations might now seem to be a sign of weakness" to the Soviets, emboldening them and endangering the allies' ability to protect West Berlin.[37] In February 1965, ambassador to Vietnam (and former chairman of the Joint Chiefs of Staff) Maxwell Taylor warned against any diplomatic overtures, arguing that "haste to get to the conference table may spark upsurge in [Viet Cong] efforts designed to achieve the maximum negotiating advantage, since Hanoi and Peking may interpret our eagerness as a sign of weakness."[38] In discussions with the Norwegian ambassador to Peking during the Vietnam War, the North Vietnamese ambassador similarly justified refusal to diplomatically engage with the United States by asserting that "when North Vietnam showed an interest in negotiations, Americans had taken such interest as a sign of weakness and with results of stronger escalation."[39]

The Second Russo-Turkish War of 1877–78 affords a fuller example of how deeply belligerents worry about looking weak from seeking negotiations. In early 1877, a conference of powers including the Russian Empire submitted terms to create autonomous Bulgarian provinces using Ottoman territory. The Ottoman Empire, which was then in slow and steady decline, refused these terms, and the conference dissolved by January 20. The war officially began on April 24, 1877, when the Russian Empire broke diplomatic relations with the Turkish government and began an attack against the Ottoman Empire—an endeavor that had not succeeded during the Crimean War two decades before. The ultimate outcome of this new war was not obvious at its outset. Russia had higher numbers in terms of personnel, but its soldiers were poorly equipped and served under relatively incapable commanders. The Ottomans wielded more modern weapons supplied by the Americans, British, and Germans and established strong defenses, but they were not well organized.[40] The war dramatically broke in the Russians' favor on December 9, when, after a monthslong siege, Russian forces seized the critical town of Plevna. This was a devastating outcome for the Ottomans. Not only was Plevna the last stronghold to prevent an unfettered march toward the capital city of Constantinople, but the surrender itself resulted in the capture of forty-three thousand Turks.[41]

On December 12, the Ottomans made their first meaningful attempt to negotiate an end to the conflict. The Porte distributed a diplomatic circular to numerous states that attempted to strike a tone of magnanimity and strength: "What object can there be in prolonging the contest ruinous to both countries? The moment has arrived for the belligerent powers to accept peace without affecting their dignity. Europe might now usefully interpose her good offices, since the Porte is ready to come to terms."[42] The language in this circular attested to how acutely the Ottomans worried about looking weak from requesting negotiations on one hand while confronting the reality of requiring negotiations on the other. The statement "The moment has arrived for the belligerent powers to accept peace" evinced the Ottomans' desire to sound as if they did not need peace but were willing to consider it. The phrase "without affecting their dignity" also spoke to a desire for any potential peace talks not to be interpreted as part of a humiliating loss.

The Porte's deep concern with perceptions of weakness was further highlighted on December 17. In response to the general reactions to their circular from five days earlier, the Ottomans distributed a follow-up notice stating the following: "Erroneous interpretations having been given to the circular dispatch, by which the Porte expresses a desire for peace and requests the mediation of the Powers, it is explained, that Turkey does not approach the Powers as a vanquished State, since she still has two lines of defense which the government believes it would be able to hold. It is pointed out that by its circular dispatch the Porte desires to intimate its willingness to take into consideration the proposals made by the conference."[43] But even this clarification overstated the Turks' position. After the fall of Plevna, Russian troops were making steady progress toward Constantinople. The notion that the war would be resolved by simply accepting the results of the Constantinople Conference in late 1876 and early 1877 was no longer tenable. Indeed, Russian forces arrived in Constantinople by January 30, forcing the Turks to sue for peace. The preliminary agreement signed on January 31 and the subsequent Treaty of San Stefano on March 3 were stacked with onerous concessions. The Ottoman Empire agreed to recognize Romania, Montenegro, and Serbia—territories that had been under Ottoman control—as independent states, and Bulgaria would be considered an autonomous principality. The Turks would pay an indemnity valued at 1,410,000,000 rubles, of which 1,000,000,000 would be paid via the transfer of territory to Russia.

Beyond the international sphere, starting negotiations can also produce domestic political costs. Both troops and citizens that learn of diplomatic overtures may lose motivation to commit themselves to the war effort when they believe the government is contemplating settlement.[44] Audience cost theory implies that if a leader publicly promises that a war they initiated will result in victory, any move that appears to pull back from that promise could attract sizable political punishment.[45] Potential concessions that would be made in negotiations may also upset key constituencies and political coalitions that a leader requires to maintain power, preventing leaders from taking steps toward peace and even pushing them to continue fighting when their true interests hew toward settlement.[46] Notably, leaders of belligerent parties often rally support for war by framing the adversary as evil and uncompromising, which can ultimately impede their ability to later open talks with the enemy.[47]

Both world wars provide useful illustrations of these liabilities. During World War I, the German government was extremely hesitant to make a peace overture with the Allies for fear of signaling weakness and demoralizing troops on the ground. The offer that Germany did make in 1916 was phrased to sound confident, but it was promptly rejected by the Allies and was still interpreted as an indication of Germany's disadvantaged position.[48] In World War II, Prime Minister Winston Churchill had multiple reasons to refuse negotiations with Hitler. One of these was his deep concern that talks with the Axis powers would pose a "slippery slope" and a situation from which Britain would "be unable to turn back," obliterating domestic morale and creating an unrecoverable political climate if talks did not conclude the war.[49]

These examples all illustrate an actor's belief that expressing interest in negotiations would potentially embolden the enemy and perhaps even deflate the war effort at home. These changes, in turn, would simultaneously undermine the likelihood of negotiations producing an acceptable peace agreement and worsen the actor's ability to succeed on the battlefield when diplomacy fails— even before any verbal exchange of offers takes place. In language we have used thus far, sitting down at a bargaining table could directly undercut a belligerent's reversion outcome. Should talks occur but then fail, a belligerent may find itself subjected to even more aggression from an enemy that senses potential victory, or it may become accosted by painful political repercussions at home. Either situation would be worse than what a belligerent might anticipate experiencing by talking without fighting.

Negotiating Anyway

Fears of signaling weakness are thus a powerful reason why warring parties may avoid negotiating with one another. But as my data indicate, about 17 percent of war-days do involve negotiations, and we know that a solid majority of wars end through negotiated settlements. We can logically deduce that diplomacy can sometimes confer benefits that outweigh the aforementioned costs.

I argue that there are two distinct sets of benefits associated with negotiating. Each set of benefits is defined by how it relates to an actor's reversion outcome— namely, whether talks are designed to forestall the continuation of war or to reshape the future trajectory of fighting by potentially improving an actor's political or military situation when talks fail. These objectives are each tied to different modes of negotiating, which I call sincere and insincere, respectively. Belligerents can dynamically choose which mode of negotiation to prioritize over the course of the war in response to circumstances surrounding the conflict. The decision is neither binary nor permanent, so the discussion that follows should be interpreted as an exploration of ideal types that help establish the foundations for my theory.

Sincere Negotiation: Avoiding More Fighting

In the traditional treatment of negotiation, actors come to the table with earnest hopes of resolving the issue in good faith—that is, under the presumption that all parties will communicate and act with genuine desire to reach and fulfill an agreement. I refer to this mode of negotiating as being *sincere*. It bears emphasizing that sincerity is a characterization of intentions rather than outcomes. While all negotiations that settle a conflict are conducted sincerely, agreement is not a requirement for talks to be sincere. Fruitless talks are still sincere if agreement was the goal, free of ulterior motives.

An instructive case of a "failed" sincere negotiation comes from the Russo-Polish War of 1919–20. The conflict was sparked by the Russian Soviet Republic's desire to seize the newly independent state of Poland in hopes of spreading revolution westward, as well as by Poland's hope of expanding eastward to restore its much larger pre-1772 borders. In July 1919, about five months into the war, representatives from each state met in Soviet-held territory to discuss a potential peace. The meeting produced some limited concessions that would have pushed the Soviet-Polish border further east and thus would have favored Poland, but no final agreement was struck. Both delegates nevertheless expressed a clear desire to meet again the following month, and to do so in secret (using the guise of Red Cross prisoner exchanges), indicating that neither wanted to exploit talks for any other purpose than to find compromise.[50]

It also merits noting that sincerity is a characteristic of a negotiation effort and not a descriptor of the actual negotiators. Actors can and do shift between different modes of negotiation depending on the circumstances.[51] Another round of negotiations in the Russo-Polish War helps illustrate this point. Thirteen months after a sincere attempt to find peace, diplomats from the belligerent states met in the Belorussian capital of Minsk. The negotiation round was not only fruitless but intentionally designed to get nowhere. Polish forces had initiated a major offensive against Warsaw the day before scheduled proceedings in Minsk began. Wanting to see how this battle would pan out, both sides backtracked and demanded more onerous preconditions that they anticipated would be rejected.[52] Discussions fell apart within a week.

Intuitively, belligerents seek to negotiate sincerely when they sense that the prospects of continued war are undesirable. A party struggling on the battlefield may consider the trajectory of hostilities to be so poor that the reversion outcome of additional fighting feels worse than accepting a harsh set of negotiated provisions. A party enjoying relative success on the battlefield may eventually believe that the additional costs of fighting are no longer worthwhile in relation to what has already been gained and what the opponent is willing to concede. When both sides feel that a negotiated settlement is preferable to each party's reversion outcome, the benefits of ending the war can outweigh the perceived costs of starting negotiations at all. It is at this point that belligerents engage in the process of ascertaining and codifying what the specific terms of a negotiated settlement might be. The Russo-Polish War ended with the signing of a peace protocol in

October 1920 after Polish forces decisively won in Warsaw and made a steady eastward push toward the Russian Soviet Republic. The Soviet government saw no option but to sue for peace, while the Polish government had little appetite to keep fighting. For both sides, the reversion outcome of the war continuing on its present trajectory was less appealing than an imperfect compromise that established the new states of Ukraine and Belarus in between Poland and Soviet Russia.[53]

Insincere Negotiation: Reshaping Future Fighting

Negotiations can negatively affect a belligerent's reversion outcome by signaling weakness. Yet negotiations can also affect an actor's BATNA in a positive manner, potentially improving the prospects of war outcomes in the next period of hostilities. Stated more dramatically, talking can become an extension of combat.[54]

Most negotiation literature assumes that the only possible objective and effect of negotiations is to make a deal, but some exceptions prove this rule. Classic but often-overlooked treatments of interstate diplomacy by Fred Iklé and Paul Pillar use the term "side-effects" to describe any consequences of talks that are unrelated to reaching an agreement.[55] The two authors' discussions of side effects are somewhat cursory and unsystematic, but their core insight is highly salient. Side effects offer a fundamental modification to our view of negotiation, as they suggest that talks themselves can actively alter the trajectory of conflict. If diplomacy can be harnessed to change the state of affairs between two disputants, then negotiations that apparently "fail" may actually be successful for at least one party by changing its relative ability to prevail against the opponent in the overall bargain. Negotiations used primarily to extract side effects are what I call *insincere*. Talks are not defined as being insincere simply because they failed to forge an agreement but because the disputants attempted to use them to pursue ulterior motives. The inclusion of the word *ostensible* in my definition of negotiation is an important acknowledgment of this insincere mode of diplomacy, where actors may pretend to seek an agreement while actually exploiting talks for other ends.

A commonality across many side effects is that they accomplish extraneous objectives by using negotiations to stall for time, creating space to pursue unrelated ends. The literal process of negotiation—discussing, exchanging, revising, and contemplating proposals—takes time. The atemporal nature of negotiations in bargaining models, as well as the imposed separation of fighting and talking, forestalls the opportunity to think about what time can buy.[56]

Policymakers and trained negotiators have recognized that disadvantaged actors may use talks to drag their feet in hopes of improving their relative position in the future.[57] Numerous examples in and out of international affairs demonstrate how insincere negotiations are exploited to reap benefits for at least one actor. In the fittingly titled book *Stalling for Time*, the former FBI negotiator Gary Noesner recounts multiple hostage negotiations where "time purchased through delays" was essential to grinding down the hostage taker's resolve, gathering information, and allowing law enforcement to develop and execute a complex operation that would maximize the number of lives saved.[58]

Arms reductions negotiations during the 1970s and 1980s also featured insincerity. As détente took hold during the Cold War, several NATO countries sought to reduce their military budgets and scale down their conventional forces. The United States opposed these cuts for fear of having to commit more resources to defend Western Europe. To forestall these proposals, the United States suggested that it and the NATO countries directly negotiate a conventional force reduction agreement with the Warsaw Pact. This resulted in the establishment of the Conference on Security and Cooperation in Europe, or CSCE, in 1972.[59] Both the United States and the Soviet Union encouraged these talks with the intention of making them languish. Many years later, negotiations (and the Soviet Union, for that matter) fell apart, and the NATO states largely maintained their military spending throughout that entire period.[60]

Dilatory negotiation is so common that domestic regulations sometimes expressly prohibit it. Labor law in the United States is dictated by the National Labor Relations Act, which describes permissible conduct in collective bargaining. Its rules indicate that actors must "bargain in good faith," which disallows failing to meet at reasonable times and intervals, engaging in piecemeal bargaining, refusing to provide relevant information, creating impasses using irrelevant topics, and not signing completed agreements.[61] Far fewer tools exist to preclude such obstructive behavior at the international level.

Despite the possibilities and consequences of using talks as a stall tactic, insincere negotiations have not been fully incorporated into our understanding of conflict even as, ironically, the acrimonious and turbulent environment wrought by war arguably presents stronger incentives for parties to consider exploiting diplomacy for side effects. Deftly utilized negotiations, even in interstate conflicts, can be a way to accomplish policy objectives in a more economical manner than violence alone. This is wholly consistent with military doctrine. The use of diplomacy to promote war objectives without as many costs embodies the principle of war known as the economy of force—the employment of force in the most effective manner possible.[62]

Stalling in wartime negotiations can produce myriad side effects.[63] As it is not practical to enumerate every plausible one, I will instead focus on two that are distinctly relevant and consequential in armed conflict.

DEFLECTING PRESSURE AND BLAME

We commonly think of wars as violent interactions between two (sets of) actors, but all wars take place in view of countless third parties. Many of these outside actors wield resources and political capital that could potentially be directed toward a conflict that touches on their own interests or violates principles they deem important.[64] Unsurprisingly, parties at war may harbor concerns about how these third-party actors view their behavior.

Negotiations offer an avenue for belligerents to redirect international scorn and pressure away from themselves and to attract support for their own cause. David C. McGaffey, an academic and storied US diplomat, described these incentives in no uncertain terms: "Negotiations are not always intended to reach a conclusion. They are sometimes intended as a deflection in the face of political pressures. . . . [T]here have been historical cases where Presidents pressed to do something have begun negotiating. I think there have been cases where it has been made clear to the negotiators that they are not to reach a conclusion."[65]

In his book *Between Peace and War*, Richard Ned Lebow proposes a similar idea called the "justification of hostility crisis." Leaders that are already bent on fighting an adversary can use cynical tactics to legitimize the use of force. By making diplomatic offers that are not patently outrageous but designed to be rejected by an adversary, an actor can attempt to cast the other side as the recalcitrant and aggressive party. These theatrics may allow the actor to justify using military force and help bolster support for its cause.[66] Lebow discusses this process in the context of crisis diplomacy that precedes a potential war, but the same story readily applies to diplomacy that occurs during active conflict. Belligerents may be targets of political condemnation for using violence instead of diplomacy, and support for costly wars may falter over time. By convincing both domestic and international audiences that they have tried to reach a settlement but ultimately failed, actors with no real interest in negotiated arrangements can deflect pressures to seek peace. This maneuvering can temporarily resuscitate support for war against a seemingly intransigent enemy, as it seems to bolster the case that all other avenues short of extended hostilities have been exhausted.

The 1948–49 Arab-Israeli War, which chapter 5 explores in detail, offers an example of this behavior. In late October 1948, five months after the conflict began, the Israeli delegation at the United Nations helped to craft Security Council Resolution 62, which called on all states to revert to lines of control that had held two weeks prior and also urged belligerents to arrange a negotiated peace. The resolution was soon adopted on November 16. As much as Resolution 62 seemed against the interests of Israel, which was gaining ground in the conflict, the Israeli delegation intentionally participated in this process in order to look like the magnanimous party offering an olive branch. Israel correctly anticipated that the Arab states would reject the resolution and thus become a new lightning rod for international criticism while Israel continued plowing forward in the Negev Desert without as many objections.[67]

Both sides sought to redirect political pressures in peace talks four decades later. In 1991, riding the momentum of victory in the Persian Gulf War, President George H. W. Bush announced a diplomatic initiative to "put an end to the Arab-Israeli conflict."[68] Secretary of State James Baker spent several months conducting numerous aggressive rounds of shuttle diplomacy to convince the relevant states to participate. The resulting Madrid Conference in October, cochaired by the United States and the Soviet Union, included representatives from Israel, Egypt, Lebanon, Syria, Jordan, and Palestine. This gathering gained widespread attention for being the first-ever direct talks to include all actors that had been embroiled in the conflict. Many lamented the unproductiveness of the talks as they ended in early November, but Israel and the Arab states were satisfied with this result. The two sets of belligerents had attended talks not because they sought or expected peace but because they needed to feign interest in peace to placate the United States.[69]

Analogous developments have played out in the Syrian civil war, which began in 2011. When UN-mediated peace talks in Geneva collapsed around early February 2016, some Syrian rebel commanders expressed enthusiasm and hoped that additional outside states would realize the Assad regime was unreasonable and thus provide rebels with "something new, God willing" that would permit them to fight more effectively against the state.[70]

Belligerents repeatedly demonstrate that an insincere mode of negotiation can help navigate political crosswinds while avoiding settlement. When this strategy proves successful, a belligerent's reversion outcome improves because demands to seek peace are diminished and support for war is revitalized. Both empower an actor to fight more freely compared to a situation in which it did not negotiate.

RESHAPING THE BATTLEFIELD

Although the fortunes of fighting are revealing, they are not inevitable or unidirectional. A party experiencing losses on the battlefield is not necessarily fated to continue losing, or vice versa. An actor who believes that its future costs of fighting will fall and its future battlefield performance will improve may seek to continue fighting and to push through the short-term costs in hopes of turning hostilities in its favor in the longer term.[71]

For some, the idea that a beleaguered belligerent's ability to prosecute a war could improve later in the conflict may sound peculiar. Bargaining models of war view fighting as a costly activity that drains belligerents' finite resources and is dictated by the distribution of power that stood prior to fighting.[72] Yet in reality, having a set of resources or capabilities is not equivalent to being able to effectively or immediately use them. Choices regarding the employment of force and the elements of strategy also play important mediating roles in a belligerent's success on the battlefield.[73] Mobilization, which refers not only to the general production of war materiel or the recruitment of troops (though those are certainly important) but also to the ability of a belligerent to adapt its capabilities to fit the specific needs of the present conflict, does not happen overnight. Belligerents may thus believe they can obtain more positive outcomes in the future once they have a chance to translate more of their latent capabilities—whether those are troops, weapons, vehicles, or the like—into mobilized and functional capabilities on an active battlefield.[74] Military strategists readily point out that a sufficient number of standing forces may be effective at defense once conflict erupts but that more time is typically necessary to prepare the materiel, logistics, and strategies for offensive countermeasures.[75] Literature on the element of surprise is also predicated on the idea that a belligerent can enjoy a temporary strategic and logistical advantage that is not captured by straightforward measures of military might.[76]

Mobilization and planning, in short, both require time.[77] Prussian field marshal August von Gneisenau, a contemporary of Clausewitz and an influential figure in his own right, makes the point succinctly: "Strategy is the art of utilising time and space. I am more economic of the first than of the second. I can always regain space; time lost, never."[78] Different tactics can be used to reclaim or effectively create time. In the realm of military tactics, delaying or retrograde operations are designed to buy time and temporarily hamper an opponent's forces in order to allow the party performing the operation to reorganize its forces, wait for reinforcements, and sap the enemy's resources.[79] Stalling for time through diplomacy can accomplish a similar goal during war.[80] By engaging in insincere negotiations, an embattled party can create an opportunity to rearm and regroup its military forces in hopes of creating a strategic advantage that helps reverse some of its losses once discussions fold.[81]

The Syrian civil war is relevant again here. After Geneva peace talks failed in early February 2016, the United Nations spearheaded a ceasefire that began later that month. Over the following weeks, the anti-Assad coalition accused the government of bargaining in bad faith and using past diplomatic endeavors to stall for time in order to prepare an assault on Aleppo—the country's most populous and economically active city.[82] By December 2016, the Assad government decisively took control of this highly valuable strategic objective.

Another useful example is the Assam War of 1962 between India and China. On October 20, Chinese forces launched offensives across the McMahon Line—a boundary between India and China that had been determined in 1914 but disputed ever since. Within three days, Chinese troops had overrun a series of Indian outposts and largely achieved their limited aims. Mao Zedong's regime proposed an agreement to end the affair before it would draw more international attention, which was then focused on the Cuban Missile Crisis. Jawaharlal Nehru's government in India spent weeks asking for technical clarifications regarding the proposal before accusing China of "cold-blood[ed] . . . massive aggression" and renewing hostilities with remobilized troops in mid-November.[83] Within several days, this burst of activity led the Chinese to offer a more favorable ceasefire that granted India two-thirds of the disputed territory.

For negotiations to potentially facilitate mobilization, they must not only forestall agreement but also temporarily slacken the intensity of hostilities and create breathing room for at least one actor to exploit. As the next section explains, the incentives and reasons for belligerents to reduce hostilities during negotiations are a function of the strategic environment in which negotiations occur.

The Logic of (Not) Negotiating

Up to this point, I have characterized the costs and benefits of negotiating during war. A central danger to negotiating is that an actor may signal weakness and worsen its own reversion outcome, which in turn undermines its bargaining leverage if talks do not produce peace. Conversely, negotiation can afford some valuable benefits, which vary depending on whether an actor adopts a sincere or insincere mode to negotiating. Actors who negotiate sincerely engage in good-faith efforts to reach an agreement, in hopes of avoiding the reversion outcome of continuing a painful war; actors who negotiate insincerely engage in bad-faith attempts to abuse diplomacy by stalling for time, which enables them to improve their reversion outcome by deflecting political pressure and remobilizing their forces to fight more effectively once talks falter. With these concepts now in place, we can address the crucial question: What influences the balance of these costs and benefits of negotiating sincerely, insincerely, or at all during war?

I propose that two central dimensions affect this calculus: the existence of latent external pressures to negotiate and information obtained from the realities of the battlefield. Both have been mentioned in my discussion thus far, but we will now address each explicitly in the context of how they moderate the costs and benefits of conflict diplomacy. Notably, the two key side effects of insincere negotiations that I mentioned—diverting political pressures and remobilizing for further conflict—roughly parallel these two factors.

Latent External Pressures

Belligerents do not exist in a vacuum. Various third parties with some vested interest in peace can encourage warring parties to settle their differences via diplomacy. I use the term *latent external pressure* to refer to the extent to which third parties can readily activate diplomatic pressure on belligerents. Latent external pressures are reflected by the presence of institutions and power structures that exist beyond the specific circumstances that unfold over the course of a particular conflict. These include the existence of international organizations that promote peace, laws and norms that condemn aggression, peace lobbies or ecosystems that supply mediators, and relationships that belligerents have with powerful states that could influence their behavior. Many of these institutions and structures, such as the creation of the United Nations, the advent of nuclear weapons and their potentially pacifying effect on violence, and the strengthening of conflict-averse norms and institutions, are associated with the post-1945 international order.[84] The existence of such structural and institutional conditions define a baseline for the amount and quality of explicit third-party diplomatic pressure—such as mediation efforts or other discrete attempts to initiate dialogue between the belligerents—that can be deployed and placed on the belligerents during a given war.

To be clear, battlefield developments and discrete third-party efforts to advocate diplomacy are almost assuredly related to one another. The United Nations, for instance, may try to wield its influence more forcefully when violence is highly destabilizing and likely to cause negative externalities for specific member states. Literature on conflict mediation also debates the merits of intervening during different stages and circumstances of war.[85] But even if specific events during a conflict influence the degree to which external actors may push actors to negotiate, institutions and power relations supply the infrastructure for such endeavors to occur more readily. Latent external pressures for peace also provide a more useful source of empirical leverage, as they are more exogenous to the conflict itself.

Once actuated, third-party diplomatic pressures have been shown to be effective at obliging belligerents to communicate with one another.[86] Yet getting belligerents to sit at the same table is separate from convincing them to reach a meaningful compromise. External pressures to negotiate, if sufficiently strong, can create perceived costs to avoiding diplomacy and compel actors to engage in talks even when they have no interest in reaching an agreement. Fred Iklé describes these incentives in his classic work on international negotiation:

> Governments are reluctant to refuse negotiation, no matter how unlikely or undesirable an agreement. They fear that such refusal would impair the good will of groups important to them—their own parliament, the public in allied countries, or other governments, for example. These audiences may judge quite superficially in praising those willing to negotiate and censuring those who refuse. Outside groups may have only a vague notion as to what negotiating means and how it relates to the merits of the issue. Governments that negotiate in order to win public approval value the act of negotiating as the Pharisee values prayer. It is not the thoughts behind the prayer that matter, or the purposes pursued, or the deeds before and after—what counts is that the ceremony be performed with the proper gestures.[87]

International organizations can wield a heavy hand in creating diplomatic pressures. During the war over the Aouzou Strip between Libya and Chad in 1986 and 1987, the Organization of African Unity and multiple heads of African states initiated relentless peace missions to bring the two states together for talks. The negotiations that did occur in March 1987 were superficial and dissolved on their first day.[88]

Even major powers are not completely immune to these forces. Throughout the Falklands War of 1982, at least three individuals—US secretary of state Alexander Haig, Peruvian president Fernando Belaúnde Terry, and United Nations secretary-general Javier Pérez de Cuéllar—independently attempted to push Argentinian president Leopoldo Galtieri and British prime minister Margaret Thatcher to accept mediation. Both belligerents eventually caved after one month of constant pressure but proceeded to engage in perfunctory and unproductive talks. The war instead ended when British reinforcements arrived in the Falklands and reclaimed the islands from Argentinian forces. Recounting this conflict more than a decade later, Thatcher would write that she felt "under an almost intolerable pressure to negotiate for the sake of negotiation."[89] It is notable that British opinion strongly supported reclaiming the islands by force.[90] Thatcher's decision to entertain diplomacy represented at least a partial capitulation to third parties and the ideals they espoused.

The Syrian civil war affords a more contemporary illustration of the international community's constant attempts at promoting diplomacy. Between 2012 and 2017, the United Nations organized multiple talks in Geneva, none of which made meaningful progress. Some meetings even failed to get representatives of the Assad government and Syrian rebels in the same room. The majority of these negotiations were backed by United Nations Security Council Resolution 2254 (passed on December 18, 2015), which called for a ceasefire and laid out a plan for formal negotiations that would lead to open elections within eighteen months. As the aforementioned failures of 2016 suggest, this timeline did not come to pass. Starting in early 2017, another diplomatic track opened in Astana, Kazakhstan, under the auspices of Iran, Russia, and Turkey but with the general support of the United Nations. An agreement reached in January 2018 aimed to create a 150-member committee facilitated by the United Nations and populated by representatives from all sides that would draft a constitution. On October 30, 2019, the resulting Syrian Constitutional Committee convened for the first time. Five rounds of talks between October 2019 and February 2021 failed to even settle procedural matters, leading United Nations special envoy and Norwegian diplomat Geir Pederson to suspend talks indefinitely.[91]

Latent external pressures and their activation during conflict introduce a fundamental complication to the calculus of negotiation. When belligerents are left to their own devices, efforts to negotiate require a unilateral attempt to contact the enemy, which incurs potentially high costs from signaling weakness. Any benefits to be gained from negotiating sincerely (making peace) or insincerely (stalling for time) are counterbalanced by the risks associated with appearing hesitant to keep fighting. These concerns decrease the number of scenarios in which belligerents would consider talking while fighting. In contrast, relenting to third-party diplomatic efforts does not signal weakness in the same way as independently seeking negotiations. External actors' active presence and participation may help belligerents reframe their decision to engage in diplomacy by converting it from an expression of weakness to a conscientious recognition of the international community's will.[92] By introducing an outside force that presses actors into talking, warring parties perceive fewer downsides to their reversion outcome if diplomacy fails, making them more willing to negotiate in a wider array of conditions where they experience less pain or foresee fewer benefits. In sum, strong external pressures for diplomacy obfuscate the relationship between negotiating and potentially signaling weakness.

This logic facilitates both sincere and insincere negotiations. Belligerents that earnestly seek to cease hostilities can initiate the peace process more quickly and potentially obtain less unfavorable terms in a settlement without suffering as many negative repercussions associated with looking fragile. Quantitative, experimental, and historical works alike have shown that international institutions and third parties offer political cover that allows actors to make broadly unpopular concessions or policy choices while blunting some political fallout.[93] That said, externally imposed negotiations can interrupt the revelation of information necessary to resolve the original causes of war, undermining prospects for fruit-ful negotiations or a lasting peace even if this is the belligerents' earnest goal.[94]

At the same time, actors without interest in peace can negotiate for side effects without worrying about perceptions of weakness. The Iklé quotation above sug-gests that belligerents may decide that the performance of diplomacy, however empty, is worthwhile specifically because it helps relieve and redirect political pressures for peace. By going through the motions of talking, actors can gain a reprieve from external actors insisting on a diplomatic settlement.[95] Belligerents who believe that buying time will give them an opportunity to fully mobilize their military may also have greater freedom to pursue this strategy.

In sum, if all else is held equal, *higher amounts of latent external pressures for peace increase the likelihood of both sincere and insincere negotiations.* Regardless of an actor's intentions in a specific round of talks, the ability to act on those intentions increases when outside forces help to diminish one of the crucial costs and liabilities of engaging in diplomacy with the enemy.

Information from the Battlefield

The existence of latent external pressures for peace explains the frequency of negotiations. It does not, however, address the question of whether these negotia-tions would be sincere or insincere. For that, we turn to the battlefield.

If wars are a consequence of incomplete information, then war represents a painful yet truthful way to learn each side's actual strength, resolve, and intentions—all of which would help reveal the potential bounds of a bargaining range.[96] By commonly observing an objective reflection of each side's perfor-mance on the battlefield, belligerents obtain new information that may lead them to reduce their uncertainty, update their beliefs, and revise their bargaining posi-tions. In some canonical models, fighting is depicted as a struggle to possess a series of forts. The term *fort* here is used broadly to represent strategically valu-able military resources that can be exchanged and can shape actors' ability to fight.[97] Forts include not only literal military fortifications but also hills critical for communication, ports used for resupply, ships in the sea, units of benefi-cial territory, capital cities where governments sit, and more. Each belligerent is assumed to possess a certain share of forts prior to war, and wartime battles are discrete clashes that result in the potential exchange of a single fort. Observing how forts are given and taken, and also what costs are suffered along the way, will eventually promote convergence on shared expectations about the future course of hostilities. This allows belligerents to develop a firmer understanding of both the opponents' and their own reversion outcomes, as well as how each may evolve if war continues. When both sides are able to identify potential arrangements that are preferable to their reversion outcomes and are at least worth their value to war, they have found a viable bargaining range from which they may develop a mutually acceptable agreement. Active hostilities are therefore crucial to dictating how, in the historian Geoffrey Blainey's words, "rival expectations, initially so far apart, are so close to one another that terms of peace can be agreed upon."[98]

Scholars have noted that outcomes from the battlefield are most effective in shaping common beliefs and ending wars when one side dominates the other over a continuous sequence of battles.[99] While this conclusion is reached using a wide array of methods and evidence, the fort analogy proves particularly useful here. If Actors A and B each win two forts in the first four battles, uncertainty regarding each side's prospects in war remains high. A wider set of actors can sustain a wider set of beliefs about their chances of success should they continue to fight. In contrast, if Actor A seizes four of Actor B's forts in the first four battles, both sides should believe that Actor A is far more likely to succeed in future fighting than Actor B, regardless of what claims each side may have verbally made before or during the opening stages of war. As Actor A's odds of success become more commonly understood, any bargaining range and negotiated settlement that settles the war will heavily favor Actor A.

We can extrapolate this idea to diplomacy that precedes conflict termination. Witnessing a distinct battlefield trend has three intertwining effects on negotiation strategy. First, concerns about looking weak from negotiating will fade. The disadvantaged party is no longer worried about the risk of adverse inference via diplomacy because its weakness has already been made apparent. Simultaneously, the advantaged party will feel more confident that its victories sweep away perceptions of weakness.

Second, the appeal of negotiating sincerely will rise. A persistently poor battlefield performance will push an actor to realize that its reversion outcome is not only poor but likely to worsen if war continues. The prospects of weakening bargaining leverage will lead the actor to make larger diplomatic concessions in hopes of minimizing its prospective losses. It is through these evolving offers that belligerents may find a settlement that both sides find preferable to the continuation of war.[100] This is consistent with the empirical finding that wars have more durable peace settlements when they end on the back of a distinct battlefield trend.[101]

Third, the value of negotiating insincerely will fall. Although belligerents may sometimes be correct in assessing that their fortunes can improve through insincere negotiations, this belief can also be a manifestation of incomplete information. It is easier to believe that political and military mobilization will turn a war in one's favor when this belief has not been disproven through fighting.[102] Once the battlefield reveals a consistent stream of information that also creates real costs, the potential side effects to be extracted from stalling for time will dwindle and be unable to compensate for the increasingly dire reversion outcome that would arise if talks do not end the war. Truly weak belligerents will have little left to remobilize, and both domestic and international tolerance for further violence may disintegrate when an irreversible trajectory seems self-evident.

In sum, if all else is held equal, *higher amounts of information from fighting increase the likelihood that negotiations are sincere, and lower amounts of information from fighting increase the likelihood that negotiations are insincere.*

It bears emphasizing that my argument is consistent with existing schools of thought regarding the role of information in war. My innovation is to highlight the possibility of insincere negotiations and how their propensity is also related to what is learned from the battlefield.

Combining Pressure and Information

By combining the two broad predictions I have presented in this section, we can produce a coherent set of expectations about the frequency and mode of negotiations that take place during war. Figure 1.1 presents two stylized diagrams that illustrate how latent external pressures and battlefield information affect wartime negotiation strategies. As I have previously stated, the choice of negotiation mode is not binary in practice and is simplified here for the sake of outlining broad expectations. Belligerents that genuinely seek peace may still consider which side effects they can accrue if talks fail, and belligerents that primarily want to extract side effects may be willing to stop fighting if they receive a sufficiently appealing offer. We can nonetheless presume that actors predictably prioritize one of these modes of negotiation over the other, depending on the circumstances.

First, the left-hand diagram of figure 1.1 depicts an environment where few mechanisms exist to pressure actors into negotiating. Belligerents would pursue

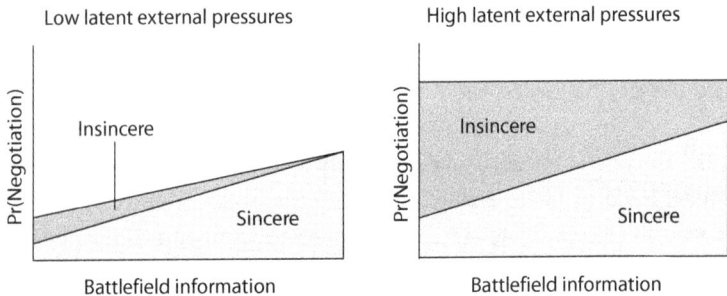

FIGURE 1.1. Predicted negotiation behavior, conditional on environment.

diplomacy only when they sense that the risks of adverse influence are less onerous than the risks from continued conflict. This condition is least likely to be met when hostilities have produced very little information; actors have insufficient incentive to revise their beliefs and avoid further bloodshed. Some parties may believe that they can extract sufficiently large side effects from insincere negotiations to attempt talks, but the costs associated with this choice are too high for most actors to be considered worthwhile. As the battlefield supplies more compelling information about the future trajectory of conflict, the disadvantaged actor would seek to stop fighting and to stem additional costs, and the advantaged actor would want to discuss and codify a settlement from an obvious position of strength. These incentives would push both parties to seek sincere negotiations. This is reflected in the right-hand side of the figure. Since at least one belligerent wants to cease hostilities and may even be incapable of fighting further, negotiations should be associated with a substantial decrease in contemporaneous battlefield activity.[103] The final stages of the 1904–5 Russo-Japanese War, described in the introduction, embody this situation. Peace talks at Portsmouth during August 1905 were associated with a de facto ceasefire.[104] Overall, an environment featuring lower latent external pressures for peace will lead to relatively few negotiations, but talks that do occur are also more likely to be genuine attempts to reach agreement because they are a response to the realities of fighting.

Next, the right-hand side of figure 1.1 illustrates an environment where a great deal of latent external pressure can be activated and directed toward the belligerents. The costs of negotiation are considerably diminished, and fewer benefits are necessary to contemplate negotiating during war. Belligerents have greater liberty—or, in more extreme cases, the obligation—to talk to one another, independent of their underlying interest in peace. Negotiations will thus occur far more frequently across all states of the battlefield. This higher propensity of negotiations reveals a double-edged sword. Some wars may see sincere negotiations that resolve war more quickly than would be the case in the absence of outside parties encouraging settlement. Yet at the same time, these same pressures can unleash insincere negotiations aimed at reshaping belligerents' reversion outcomes and supporting their war efforts.

Whether talks are used sincerely or insincerely is dictated by information from the battlefield, which influences each side's assessment of its reversion outcome and how it can be shaped. In low-information environments where little to nothing has been gleaned through hostilities, diplomacy will commonly be exploited for side effects. The paucity of information about the belligerents' true characteristics—which is further exacerbated by the inorganic motivation for negotiating—allows for many of the informational asymmetries that contributed to the start of war to persist. This point is critical. Belligerents that have not yet learned enough common information about their relative capabilities, resolve, or intentions can sustain misinformed beliefs regarding the value of negotiating, incentivizing one or both sides to enter talks under the impression that stalling for time and producing side effects through diplomacy can recast the reversion outcome in their favor. For all these reasons, talks may be associated with lower levels of battlefield activity, but the motivations to slacken the pace of fighting are cynical and not self-enforcing. Belligerents may temporarily dampen hostilities because this affords them an opportunity to promote their war aims through other means. The appeal of negotiating insincerely should be especially pointed for belligerents that have wider gaps between their latent material capabilities and the actual military force they could rearm, regroup, and remobilize if given some time to do so, but the ability to divert political blame by looking interested in peace and highlighting the opponent's intransigence offers another reason to talk without any desire to strike a lasting agreement.

Importantly, this argument indicates that deception and duplicity are not prerequisite conditions for talks to be used insincerely.[105] If scant information has been culled from fighting, both sides can be fully aware that negotiations could be exploited, but they may simply disagree on the extent to which any side effects will provide one actor an advantage over the other. According to Thucydides's account of the First Peloponnesian War, Sparta chose to enter a one-year truce and diplomatic interactions with Athens because it believed that a temporary peace would deflate Athens's willingness to fight again. For its part, Athens agreed to a truce in order to quietly reinforce its defenses.[106] Similarly, during the lull in hostilities over the first round of Korean War armistice talks, both the United Nations Command and Communist forces harbored the belief that the war would turn in their favor. Each side prepared for further fighting and made statements designed to curry favor with international audiences.[107]

The negotiation calculus becomes more difficult when the battlefield produces moderately clear information in an environment with high latent pressures for peace. This situation is reflected by the center of the right diagram in figure 1.1, where the composition of sincere and insincere talks is more comparable. The belligerent with a relative advantage on the battlefield faces a precarious decision regarding whether to bend to any third-party diplomatic pressures and enter negotiations. On the one hand, the advantaged party could refuse to talk, suffering external costs of avoiding diplomacy and any additional costs from future fighting. On the other hand, the advantaged party could choose to talk, which poses a gamble between two outcomes. In the first, the enemy negotiates sincerely, peace is struck, and no additional costs of war are suffered. In the second, the enemy engages in insincere negotiations and alters the reversion outcome before resuming hostilities. Compared to the scenario where no talks occur, the side effects generated in this case may decrease the advantaged party's likelihood of overall victory, increase the costs it will suffer in future fighting, or both. If the probability of a negotiated settlement, the costs of future fighting, or the costs of eschewing diplomacy are sufficiently high, they will outweigh the possible consequences that side effects may have for the future trajectory of conflict.

This calculus helps to explain why belligerents with even a modest upper hand on the battlefield may choose to engage in negotiations even when they are aware that their opponent may use diplomacy for side effects. First, intermediate levels of information may lead some advantaged actors to believe that the probability of the enemy genuinely seeking peace is sufficiently high to try reaching a settlement. Second, the potential side effects that the enemy could accrue from insincere diplomacy could be deemed low and therefore not a serious threat to ultimate success. Third, as my theory implies, sufficiently stiff latent external pressures may make the costs of rejecting negotiations outright too high, compelling advantaged belligerents to come to the table even if they do not intend to act sincerely. Indeed, side effects are a tool not only of the weak; advantaged parties could also try using talks to augment the war effort in their favor, independent of the opponent's true intentions. Fourth, an advantaged party may have largely accomplished its policy objectives and would gamble on the possibility that the opponent wants to negotiate sincerely and end the war.

As battlefield information becomes increasingly lopsided (reflected by moving rightward on the right-hand diagram in figure 1.1), decisions to negotiate become more straightforward. Any potential side effects that could be accrued from insincere talks are not sufficient to counteract the reality of the battlefield—both because the fortunes of fighting are too strongly imbalanced to easily reverse and because the gap between latent and actual military capabilities, which stalling for time can help close, naturally diminishes as hostilities proceed over time. As such, disadvantaged belligerents that may have otherwise considered adopting an insincere approach are screened out, leaving behind actors who desire sincere negotiations to resolve the conflict. The advantaged party thus gains more confidence that any enemy who is willing to talk must possess a genuine desire to reach peace and cease the creation of any additional costs of conflict.

In sum, an environment featuring high latent external pressures for peace will lead to relatively frequent negotiations, but many more of these talks will be insincere, motivated by the goal of diverting the war's current trajectory rather than ending it entirely. Talks will be more likely to be sincere, however, when the battlefield offers conspicuous information regarding one side's advantage.

Implications

The discussion above produces a number of testable implications. The first three, which address the frequency of negotiations and their propensity to resolve conflicts, are reflected by figure 1.1.

> **Hypothesis 1:** In an environment with low latent external pressures, negotiations will be less frequent but also more predictive of overall conflict termination.
>
> **Hypothesis 2:** In an environment with high latent external pressures, negotiations will be more frequent but also less predictive of overall conflict termination.
>
> **Hypothesis 3:** Negotiations that do take place are more likely to terminate conflict when battlefield information exhibits clear information in one side's favor.

The next two hypotheses speak to the ramifications that negotiations have for the battlefield itself. Based on my theory, negotiations should be linked together with decreased intensity of fighting on the battlefield. Belligerents seeking to negotiate sincerely would tone down their violence out of necessity or a desire to indicate interest in peace. Meanwhile, actors with insincere motivations would also dampen hostilities, though perhaps to a slightly lesser extent, because doing so would allow them to better accrue at least two important side effects: deflecting political pressures for peace and buying time to remobilize their military forces.

> **Hypothesis 4:** Periods of negotiation are associated with lower levels of active hostilities on the battlefield.

If the only impact of negotiations failing to end war were that fighting would resume along the same trajectory as before negotiations began, then existing models of conflict that treat diplomacy as a costless, perpetual, and instantaneous activity might be making reasonable simplifying assumptions. I argue that this is not the case. The act of negotiating itself can potentially improve a belligerent's reversion outcome, which would boost its leverage in the next stage of bargaining. If my theory is valid, then negotiations that do not end wars are more likely to be insincere, and insincere negotiations should reshape the battlefield so that it differs from the state of fighting prior to talks.

> **Hypothesis 5:** Negotiations that do not lead to settlement are likely to be followed by battlefield trends that are distinct from those that existed prior to the start of talks.

Caveats

Several matters are worth clarification at this point. Critically, I do not claim that every attempt to negotiate insincerely is successful in reaping the desired side effects. In the 1974 Turco-Cypriot War, explored in chapter 3, the Greeks dragged their feet during ceasefire negotiations pushed by the United Nations, United States, and United Kingdom in late July and early August. Greece hoped to use this diplomatic interlude to amass international sympathy, frame the Turkish initiators as military occupiers, and prepare for further hostilities. Their diplomatic stall tactics failed to stop Turkey's advance two weeks later.[108] Insincere negotiations are a strategic gamble to disrupt the current trend and turn it in one's favor, and gambles can be in vain. Even so, my argument does suggest that these attempts should work often enough to produce some measurable overall effect. Evidence in favor of this prediction poses a major challenge to the common scholarly assumption that negotiations bear no consequences of their own besides arranging agreements. Negotiations are not a mere reflection of the battlefield but a tool that can be used to help reshape it.

My theory and implications assume rational actors that objectively process information and make decisions based on specific cost-benefit calculations. But a body of work underscores the psychological biases and flawed rationality that permeate real-world decision-making.[109] Actors that fight and negotiate in wars are humans, and humans unconsciously tend to rely on mental shortcuts and heuristics that are based more on intuition than on the reasoning process involved in theories of rational choice.[110] Humans also possess different dispositional traits that affect their underlying preferences for using force, as well as how these individuals behave in policy deliberations with others.[111] Moreover, actors' decisions are also influenced by their emotions.[112] Decisions made in the shadow of strong emotions are more likely to result in biased views about an actor's own likelihood of victory, which further exacerbates the actor's penchant for dismissing information that calls their prior beliefs into doubt. The desire to restore one's honor or to seek revenge can lead to similar tendencies to discuss inauspicious information and to fight for retribution, which may lead to greater unwillingness to negotiate with an enemy.[113] Such emotional motivations may be partially responsible for explaining the protracted nature of World War I.[114]

Psychological factors are undoubtedly relevant to understanding war and some of its worst excesses, and my theory does not suggest otherwise. Rational and psychological considerations can coexist in explaining conflict. If I find systematic evidence that negotiation patterns can be largely captured by analyzing patterns of fighting and external diplomatic pressures as reflected in figure 1.1, then a fundamentally rational logic does motivate at least a considerable degree of negotiation activity, and additional behavioral considerations can exist on top of this foundation. Such a result would push back against an attempt to study wars using a purely behavioral perspective and support a more open approach. Subsequent studies could then characterize the specific conditions in which psychological and emotional dimensions pull wartime behavior away from what is predicted by rationalist theories such as the one I advance.

Comparisons with Ripeness Theory

One of the most prominent research agendas regarding negotiations during war stems from I. William Zartman's work on ripeness theory. Ripeness theory represents the leading framework on conflict-based diplomacy and is more commonly discussed in studies of civil war mediation.[115] The introduction provided a brief summary of ripeness theory, but its outsized importance in both scholarly and policymaking circles compels us to return to Zartman's argument and understand its relationship with mine.

Ripeness theory suggests two necessary but not sufficient conditions for belligerents to seek a negotiated settlement. First, the parties must feel as if they are stuck in a costly deadlock that cannot be pushed to a complete victory. This is called a mutually hurting stalemate, and it presses actors to reassess the viability of fighting through severe losses for little anticipated gain. Second, the belligerents must perceive a "way out" of their deadlock, referring to the general perception that a negotiated mutually acceptable settlement may exist. It is when both conditions hold that warring parties may be more "ripe" for negotiations. The opening of armistice talks during the Korean War (discussed in chapter 6) is often presented as a textbook example of this dynamic. It was only after lines of control stabilized after several offensives and counteroffensives at the thirty-eighth parallel that both sides realized complete victory was impossible, stepped away from their original demands, and agreed to negotiate in July 1951.[116]

The notion of a hurting stalemate may reflect a relatively low-information environment where belligerents are caught in a stagnant environment and neither side is able to produce a distinct battlefield trend in its favor. The second requirement of ripeness theory, "a way out," is highly subjective—a point Zartman readily makes. The fact that perceptions of a way out are so malleable is meant to be a feature, rather than a shortcoming, of the theory. The intentional flexibility of this concept is designed to elevate the importance of third parties and their role in shaping the perceptions of the belligerents and pushing them to sit at the negotiating table.[117] As such, while my theory does not directly capture a way out, the notion of a way out as constructed in ripeness theory presumes an environment that could constantly press belligerents to reconsider their views and return to the negotiating table. Ripeness theory therefore implies that negotiations are most likely to occur when battlefield information is low and latent external pressures are high. This is represented by the left side of the left-hand diagram in figure 1.1.

Ripeness theory has been disputed on theoretical grounds,[118] and quantitative empirical support for its predictions has been mixed at best.[119] Beyond those direct responses to Zartman's argument, my theory offers at least three related advancements over ripeness theory's understanding of wartime diplomacy. First, I outline additional sets of conditions in which belligerents may be more willing to negotiate: when latent external pressures are low but battlefield information is high, and when both latent external pressure and battlefield information are high. Ripeness theory best addresses when third parties should attempt to promote diplomacy in more protracted and stagnant conflicts, but in doing so, it places less emphasis on the fact that belligerents would also organically seek negotiations when fighting consistently and heavily tilts in favor of one actor.

Second, I systematically flesh out the idea of insincere negotiations. The precondition of a way out tacitly suggests that negotiations begin when both sides believe that a viable settlement is at hand. My framework expressly argues that negotiations can occur even when belligerents do not see eye to eye about a potential bargain. Zartman transiently acknowledges this point, remarking that "it is difficult at the outset to determine whether negotiations are indeed serious or sincere" and that some negotiations "may be a tactical interlude, a breather for rest and rearmament, a sop to external pressure, without any intent of opening a sincere search for a joint outcome."[120] These are acute concerns that subvert the professed goal of helping belligerents negotiate peace.

Third, and as a natural consequence of the previous point, ripeness theory does not address the question of which negotiations are more or less likely to be sincere. Zartman appears to recognize this issue.[121] His subsequent refinement of ripeness theory establishes an additional condition that is necessary but not sufficient for negotiations to occur and also to succeed: a "mutually enticing opportunity" that not only pushes belligerents to talk but also pulls them toward an actual settlement.[122] The purposely vague and subjective character of this concept further emphasizes the role that third parties have in crafting ideas and thrusting them on the actors directly at war, making ripeness theory relevant in situations where belligerents experience lower costs of negotiation and therefore have a lower likelihood of diplomacy leading to settlement. The fact that ripeness theory presupposes third-party intervention precludes the question of whether external pressure for diplomacy could enable insincere behavior.[123] My theory addresses when such disingenuous forms of diplomacy are more likely to pass and how they may affect the conflict itself.

Assessing a Theory of Wartime Negotiations

My theoretical framework, which calls attention to the existence of insincere negotiations and enables us to understand when and why they occur, substantially revises what we know of what diplomacy can accomplish during war. Interestingly, extant studies of wartime negotiation acknowledge the possibility that diplomacy can be exploited, but the idea is more broached as a passing thought than highlighted as a central puzzle. As previously mentioned, Zartman only briefly raises the possibility that negotiations can be exploited, but he then says no more on the matter. Mastro's explication of CCT also mentions that "wartime diplomacy can have *negative* externalities."[124] Her discussion touches on the concept of side effects, but the core theory does not explain when and why belligerents may have greater incentives to engage in a cynical mode of negotiation. My theory advances a systematic manner to understand when negotiations are more likely to occur, when these negotiations are more likely to be sincere, and what impacts—pacifying or otherwise—these negotiations have on the future trajectory of a conflict.

In the chapters to come, I evaluate my theory using a series of statistical and qualitative analyses, each of which features its own strengths and weaknesses. While no single piece of evidence can validate every aspect of my theory, the separate studies I present work together to support it as a whole.

A principal empirical contribution of this book is to analyze patterns of fighting and negotiating across two centuries of interstate wars. Doing so not only tests whether my theory can broadly explain a wide range of conflicts across space and time, but also provides novel and valuable sets of tools for future research on conflict. With that in mind, we now turn to reviewing the data constructed for this purpose.

QUANTIFYING TWO CENTURIES OF WAR

The previous chapter laid out a theory to understand the role of negotiation during war. The implications that follow from it portray wartime diplomacy as a highly strategic activity that is shaped by additional factors beyond the status of the battlefield.

Many of my hypotheses speak to activities—such as the initiation of negotiations, the level of hostilities on the battlefield, and changes in fighting following failed talks—that occur and fluctuate within individual conflicts. Very few extant resources, however, allow for the systematic analysis of these dynamics across a multitude of wars. Indeed, one noteworthy reason why studies of conflict have undervalued diplomacy is that the shortage of data regarding battlefield and diplomatic activity has led to overly simplified assumptions about them.

A more faithful test of my theory requires information on the ebbs and flows of activity within conflicts. To that end, this chapter describes data I have gathered to analyze the relationship between fighting and negotiating across more than ninety interstate wars that span 1823 (the Franco-Spanish War) to 2003 (the invasion of Iraq).[1] I consequently produce two novel sets of data that capture bouts of negotiation and battles across these conflicts at the daily level. These resources, particularly when combined, afford an unprecedented and systematic view of intrawar dynamics across a wide array of individual conflicts. Beyond helping to assess my theory of wartime negotiation, they represent a significant step forward in the broader study of war.

I will first describe the definitions and processes used to develop data on wartime negotiations before discussing the matter of battles. In both sections,

I provide numerous illustrations of how the criteria are applied to create individual data points that are manipulated to create my final datasets. I also display and discuss general trends in the data. These descriptive statistics not only are inherently interesting but also provide suggestive evidence in favor of my theoretical argument. The next two chapters use these data to assess my theory more rigorously.

Negotiation Data

While some efforts have been made to capture diplomatic behavior during civil wars from the last several decades, no such resource exists to track negotiation activity over two hundred years of interstate war.[2] I therefore collect this information using over 350 unique sources. These resources include but are not limited to diplomatic documents, reputable periodicals reporting contemporaneously on the conflict, books on individual wars, and peer-reviewed historical texts.[3]

These data are a significant step forward, but we must also be cognizant of at least two potential shortcomings. First, there is no guarantee that these sources capture all relevant negotiations. While some may believe that older wars are harder to track, the opposite is more true. Historians have invested enormous effort to find, document, and write about diplomatic activity uncovered through archival materials. Modern-day conflicts, on the other hand, may feature some diplomatic interactions that took place behind closed doors and still remain classified. The last secret negotiation in my dataset involves the "XYZ meetings," which were extraordinarily sensitive discussions that took place in 1965 between former US ambassador Edmund Gullion and North Vietnamese representative Mai Van Bo.[4] It is entirely possible that my data collection effort misses other secret negotiations that have transpired during more contemporary wars. The only practical solution for this issue is to stay apprised of additional revelations and document declassifications. That said, as I will show, the data I collect include more negotiations in modern-day conflicts. This does not completely allay concerns about coverage bias, but it does suggest that my data are not systematically biased against contemporary negotiations.

Second, information on more modern-day negotiations relies more on periodicals. Approximately 6 percent of sources used to document negotiations in pre-1945 conflicts are periodicals; the number rises to 35 percent for wars since 1945. Two mitigating factors help alleviate concerns of bias. For one, the 6 percent figure is not entirely fair; a vast share of historical texts also use contemporaneous media as sources. One advantage to these scholarly historical works, however, is that they are more likely to properly vet and contextualize news reports that are more irregular, myopic, or incorrect. Moreover, I use scholarly sources to supplement daily-level news. No war in my data solely relies on concurrent news reporting.

Defining and Coding Negotiations

I define *negotiation* as direct or mediated communication between active belligerents with the ostensible aim of reaching a mutually acceptable agreement. As mentioned in chapter 1, this definition is largely based on that of Fred Iklé and his well-known book *How Nations Negotiate*.[5]

I further unpack and operationalize this general definition on three dimensions. First, communications must involve an exchange and/or assessment of offers that are related to the settlement of hostilities. I make no distinction regarding whether these communications produce tangible agreement or whether the parties are working in good faith. The inclusion of the word *ostensible* in the definition reflects this decision. Indeed, a key element of my argument is that one benefit to negotiations is exploiting them for insincere ends unrelated—if not antithetical—to ending conflict. According to this criterion, shuttle diplomacy by a third party, such as Secretary of State Alexander Haig's travels between the United Kingdom and Argentina during the Falklands War of 1982, is a form of negotiation. Discussions hosted by a third party that involve the belligerent states, such as the Organization of African Unity's emergency summit regarding the war over Angola in 1975, are also negotiations. On the other hand, mediation attempts that fail to get the consent or participation of the belligerents do not qualify.

Second, communication must take place between officially appointed representatives of at least one belligerent nation from each side who, as outlined by the previous point, make and/or assess bargaining offers. Such activity can be either publicly known or performed in secret. Formal exchanges that take place at a summit or conference, whether direct or mediated, clearly satisfy this requirement. The unsuccessful London Conference of 1864, which was organized to address the Second Schleswig-Holstein War between Prussia and Austria on one side and Denmark on the other, is one example. Moreover, informal negotiations may also qualify, conditional on explicit offers being exchanged by appropriate representatives. For example, during the Russo-Finnish War of 1939–40, the first round of communication took place via notes secretly exchanged between Alexandra Kollontai (the Soviet Union's ambassador to Sweden) and Hella Wuolijoki (a feminist leftist playwright and outspoken Finnish Communist) at the Grand Hotel in Stockholm. A passing conversation that takes place in the hallways or corners of the United Nations, on the other hand, does not reach the necessary threshold.

Third, and related to the question of timing, short recesses between talks are still considered days with communication as long as parties expressly agreed to reconvene at a specific later date. The Korean War presents a useful illustration. Between July 27 and October 8, 1952, the United Nations Command and Communist delegations transitioned from meeting on a daily basis to convening on a weekly basis and ended each meeting by agreeing to continue their discussion over how to repatriate prisoners of war the following week. It would be misguided to consider each weekly meeting to be a new round of discussion. I consider this entire span of time to be an uninterrupted phase of communication.

Using these criteria, I create a binary negotiation variable that takes the value 1 on war-days that have negotiations and 0 on days that do not. Each sequence of uninterrupted 1s in a war can be considered a negotiation period. In sum, the ninety-two interstate conflicts feature 189 negotiation periods that occur over 6,332 war-days. This represents 17 percent of the total 36,834 war-days in the overall dataset.

Third-Party Initiatives

One of the challenges to assessing my theory using quantitative data is that we cannot adduce belligerents' true intentions when they choose to negotiate. We may safely say that any talks that lead to the termination of conflict are likely sincere in nature. Approximately one-quarter of negotiations fall into this category. But this is a determination we can make only in retrospect. In what other manner can we plausibly ascertain whether talks are more likely to be sincere or insincere before we are able to observe their ultimate outcome?

My theory suggests that negotiations that are borne of significant third-party pressure are more likely to be insincere, as they take place in conditions that lessen the costs of negotiating and increase actors' liberties to talk with no intention of settling. These acts of diplomacy should therefore have different consequences for war compared to those that are initiated by the belligerents themselves at high costs. If a period of negotiation occurs in large part due to a third party's initiative, we can expect these talks to have a lower likelihood of producing a diplomatic settlement.

For each of the 189 negotiation periods in my data, I ascertain whether talks were the result of third-party pressures or initiatives. I call talks sought by the belligerents themselves *internal negotiations*, while I call talks primarily borne of outside diplomatic pressure *external negotiations*. The unrelenting mediation efforts during the Falklands War, discussed in the introduction, are a clear example of external negotiations. That said, it is important to note that external negotiations are not synonymous with mediation.[6] President Theodore Roosevelt's mediation efforts in the Russo-Japanese War of 1904–5—touched on in the introduction—serves as an instructive case. The peace conference held in Portsmouth between August and September 1905, which successfully ended the conflict, led to widespread praise of Roosevelt and culminated in his receiving the Nobel Peace Prize in 1906. But these talks transpired only because Japanese officials quietly asked Roosevelt to offer his services back in April 1905.[7] Roosevelt never proactively attempted to press either side to negotiate. In fact, he never went to Portsmouth to attend talks.[8] This conference is therefore an internal negotiation.

Although my data include this measure of whether negotiations were the product of third-party pressure, they do not contain information regarding which specific belligerent made the first actual request to initiate negotiations. Historical sources make it very difficult to ascertain the responsible actor in a consistent manner. Nevertheless, my theory is not dependent on identifying which specific belligerent initiated negotiations. I instead focus on whether talks took place at all and, in some cases, whether they were external or internal in nature.

Examples

Figure 2.1 summarizes negotiations in several conflicts that span the temporal scope of my negotiation data. Briefly describing the key diplomatic events of each war will help elucidate the overarching coding process.

The Austro-Sardinian War began on March 24, 1848, when Charles Albert, King of Sardinia, declared war against Austria. After some initial victories, Sardinia suffered a nearly constant string of defeats. The first and only negotiation period to take place spanned from March 26 to March 30, 1849, when Victor Emmanuel—who took power in Sardinia on March 23 after his father went into exile—requested and struck an armistice with Austria. This internal negotiation ended hostilities.

The Third Central American War started on May 27, 1906, between Guatemala on one side and El Salvador and Honduras on the other. The United States almost immediately urged all belligerent states to consider peace. Mexico later joined the United States in this diplomatic press. After receiving constant offers to mediate, the three warring parties accepted the joint United States–Mexico overture. Talks began on July 19 and brought the conflict to an end the next day. The negotiation period is coded as being external. Note that this classification is made based on the fact that the talks were prompted by third parties, regardless of the fact that the meeting did lead to conflict termination.

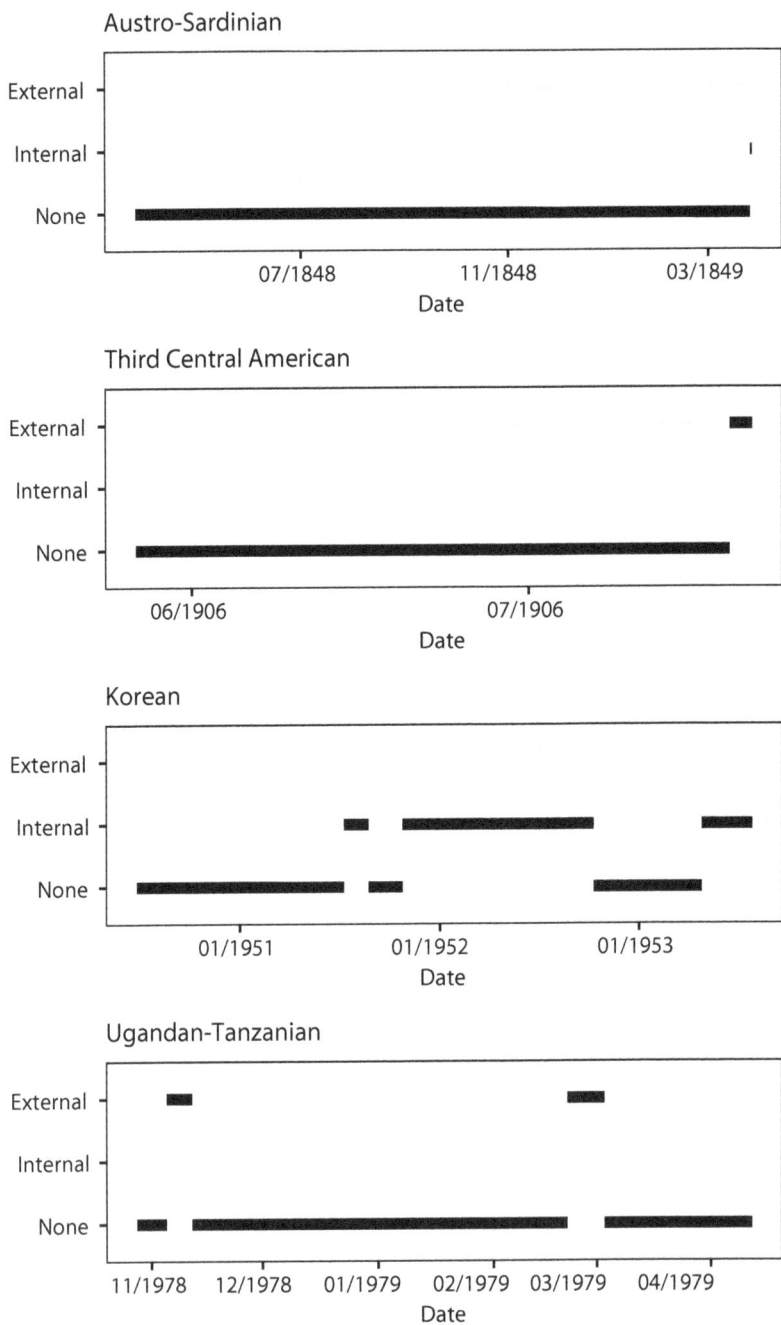

FIGURE 2.1. Negotiations in four wars.

The Korean War is the subject of deeper scrutiny in chapter 6. Hostilities began on June 25, 1950, and continued violently for a year. Negotiations to establish an armistice in the Korean War began on July 10, 1951, between the United Nations Command (UNC) and the Communist delegation of North Korea and China. Talks were halted by the Communists on August 23, 1951, over accusations that the UNC permitted bombings in the neutral zone around the negotiation site. The second negotiation period started on October 25 of the same year and lasted until October 8, 1952—the day that the UNC suspended talks indefinitely due to seemingly irreconcilable differences about how to deal with prisoners of war (POWs). Between July 27 and October 8, the delegations transitioned from near-daily meetings to weekly meetings. Harking back to my third criterion, I count this whole span of time as part of the same negotiation period, as each meeting concluded with an agreement to speak again the following week. The third and final negotiation period began on April 26, 1953, and ended the conflict on July 27 after both sides overcame their impasse regarding POWs. Notably, I do not count a brief period of discussion in February 1953 when the delegations worked out a deal to exchange some sick and wounded POWs. Even though the talks did involve POWs, they did not involve an exchange or assessment of offers related to the original POW issue that precluded a negotiated settlement. While a variety of states encouraged both sides to settle their differences through diplomacy, the negotiations were not directly spearheaded, orchestrated, or led by an external party. All three periods of negotiation are therefore coded as being internal.

Last, the Ugandan-Tanzanian War presents a case where (external) negotiations took place but hostilities ended through a military victory. Fighting broke out on October 28, 1978, as Ugandan forces attempted to annex several hundred square miles of Tanzanian territory. The first negotiation period began on November 5 when a delegation led by Philip Obang (Sudanese ambassador to the Organization of African Unity, or OAU) and Peter Onu (assistant secretary general to the OAU) arrived in Kampala to speak with Ugandan president Idi Amin, who agreed to a withdrawal plan. The effort fell flat on November 11, when the Tanzanian government rejected the OAU's proposal.[9] A second negotiation period started on February 21, 1979, when the OAU convened an ad hoc Mediation Committee prior to its Council of Ministers conference. Representatives from Uganda and Tanzania both participated in this meeting but reached no agreement.[10] The OAU declared this effort a failure on March 2, 1979. Both negotiation periods are clear cases of external diplomacy where outside actors took the initiative to force open channels between the two warring states. By April 11, Tanzanian forces took the city of Kampala and deposed Idi Amin, ending the war.

Trends and Patterns in Negotiations

Below, in table 2.1, I report top-line numbers on the frequency of negotiations across all war-days in my data. As mentioned in chapter 1, 17 percent of war-days feature negotiations. Approximately two-thirds of the time spent talking involves internal negotiations orchestrated by the warring parties, while the remaining one-third is a product of external negotiations pressed on belligerents by third parties.

Table 2.2 disaggregates the 189 negotiation periods by whether they are internal or external. To reiterate, whether talks are driven by outside pressures does not perfectly predict the settlement of hostilities. Even so, the table also shows a distinct pattern where negotiations sought directly by belligerents are more than twice as likely to terminate conflicts as those that are externally imposed on the belligerents. Diplomacy that takes place at the behest of the belligerents themselves thus tends to indicate a more sincere interest and ability to reach a negotiated settlement.

Recall that figure 0.1 in the introduction uses my new data to display the occurrence of all forms of negotiation across the universe of wars included in my study. Figure 2.2 uses kernel regression smoothers to further disaggregate and explore negotiations over the course of war. First, the black line reflects the average propensity for negotiations across time. We see that approximately 10 percent of wars feature negotiations almost immediately after hostilities begin. The rate of negotiations gradually increases over the course of war, reaching a local

TABLE 2.1   Frequency of negotiations across war-days

NEGOTIATIONS	NO. WAR-DAYS
None	30,502 (0.828)
All	6,332 (0.172)
Internal	4,139 (0.112)
External	2,193 (0.060)

Note: Proportions in parentheses.

TABLE 2.2   Results of wartime negotiations

NEGOTIATIONS	MEDIAN (DAYS)	WAR ENDS	WAR CONTINUES
All	9.0	49 (0.259)	140 (0.741)
Internal	8.0	38 (0.336)	75 (0.664)
External	9.5	11 (0.145)	65 (0.855)

Note: Row-wise proportions in parentheses.

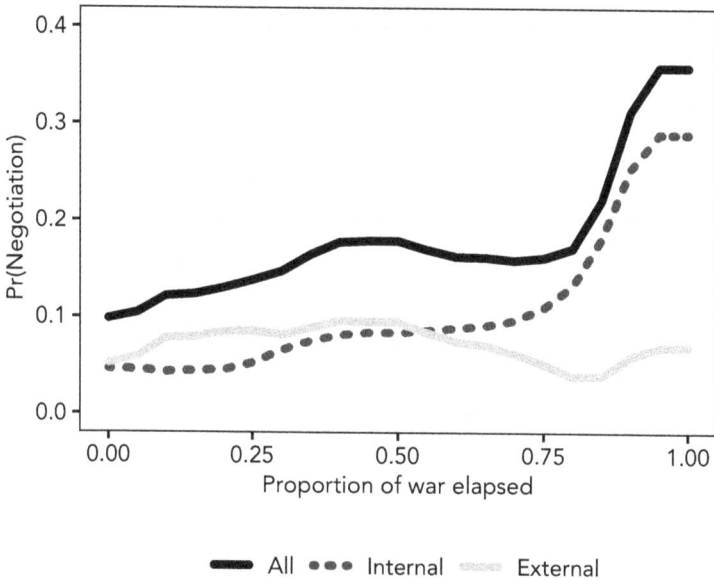

FIGURE 2.2.   Average trajectory of negotiations.

maximum around the time the conflict reaches what will become its halfway point. The sudden upswing in negotiations at the right-hand side of the figure indicates that a healthy share of wars come to an end based on negotiations that immediately preceded the cessation of hostilities.

The gray and dashed lines on Figure 2.2 reveal a striking breakdown in terms of which forms of negotiation contribute to the overall trend captured by the black line. Through the first half of the figure, negotiations that take place are mostly under duress and spearheaded by third parties. At some point in the middle of an average conflict, external talks are supplanted by internal ones. It is highly telling that the vast majority of negotiations associated with the settlement of hostilities are internal. This pattern is consistent with my theory's expectation that when talks are initiated by the belligerents themselves, at least one side believes that reaching an agreement is preferable to the costs of continued conflict or the potential benefits of any side effects from insincerely motivated discussions.

It is worth emphasizing that my core argument speaks to the existence of latent third-party pressures. The distinction I have made between internal and external negotiations is one way of measuring the manifestation of these pressures. We should expect more external negotiations to take place in environments that feature higher levels of latent third-party pressure. I will return to and substantiate this point in chapter 3.

Battle Data

My theory joins many others in claiming that information gathered from hostilities plays a crucial role in allowing belligerents to revise their beliefs regarding how the war will play out, which in turn clarifies the potential acceptable bargaining range for a negotiated settlement. An open question is how to reliably and systematically measure this information across a multitude of wars. The measure should not only be intuitively understandable but also rely on a unit of analysis that has substantive meaning in the context of war.

Battles are a critical lens through which leaders plan and interpret the trajectory of military activity.[11] As Carl von Clausewitz states, wartime strategy "must often be based . . . on the actual outcome of battles."[12] Given the central place that battles hold in understanding conflict, enormous value exists to collecting systematic data on battles across multiple wars and using these as the basis for a measure of battlefield information. This undertaking is not insignificant and requires a clear set of definitions and standards to ensure that the event is recorded in a consistent manner.

Defining and Justifying Battles

While the notion of a "battle" feels familiar, it is not necessarily straightforward to define. For my purposes, I synthesize extant definitions and consider a battle to be a clash at a specific time and location between organized state-level forces over a contested strategic objective.[13] A contested strategic objective can be a hill, fort, city, or any other unit that the belligerents each hope to claim or defend, that can exchange hands, and that affects each side's ability to continue to prosecute the war.[14]

No battle-based data can capture all war activity that fits these criteria. Work by Alex Weisiger—one of very few past endeavors to quantify intrawar hostilities—cites this fact to justify the use of casualties instead of battles to measure battlefield activity.[15] There are nevertheless several reasons why casualties are not a direct or preferable substitute for battles. First, as already mentioned, battles are an undeniably important unit of analysis and a standard lens through which leaders often view military activities. Differences between reference materials concern depth of coverage and not fundamental debates about what constitutes a battle. Second, many battles also do not have reliable or accessible measures of troop strength on each side. For example, historians' casualty estimates for the battle of Tuyutí during the War of the Triple Alliance (or Paraguayan War) range from seven thousand to sixteen thousand. Estimates for the battle of Manila in the final months of World War II span an enormous range from one hundred thousand to five hundred thousand.[16] Third, contemporary theories of war often focus on the exchange of "forts," or military objectives, over the course of fighting.[17] Battles are a much closer approximation to the concept of a "fort" than casualties and thus allow for a more proper test of these ideas. Fourth, casualties often represent a concerted decision by leaders to gain or defend strategic objectives that they feel are vital to bargaining. States may be entirely willing and ready to suffer immense costs if they believe those potential losses to be worthwhile.[18] Casualties are a less convincing proxy for exogenous information than the observed gains and losses of military objectives.

None of this suggests that casualty data are unimportant or not worth further research. My battle data simply provide an alternative and complementary path to understanding wartime activity in a manner that plausibly reflects the information in leaders' minds as they navigate wars.

Coding Battles

I thus create a dataset of battles in interstate wars. The foundations of this dataset are built on an encyclopedia of battles created by Tony Jaques.[19] I supplement and verify the initial list of battles from this volume using several additional reference guides from other military history scholars.

Each reference book contains brief narratives about individual battles or a longer description of an entire conflict that contains mentions of particular clashes. All of these narratives are qualitative and must therefore be converted into quantitative measures. Given the complexity of battles, I lean on the side of caution and create measures only on battle characteristics that can be consistently coded for every battle using the raw qualitative data. The process that I describe below produces a final dataset of 1,708 discrete battles that took place during interstate wars listed in the COW Inter-State War dataset.

ACTORS

The main goal when defining actors is to determine which belligerent was the attacker (in other words, the one initiating the battle) and which was the defender. To accomplish this task, as well as that of identifying the victor of a battle, I rely on two conditions: occupation and movement.

In many battles, one party occupies a contested strategic objective that is the central object of battle. Recall that the term *strategic objective* refers to objects such as forts, cities, bridges, and related units that can be possessed or lost and are influential in determining a belligerent's ability to accomplish its broader goal in the war.[20] The side that initially controls the strategic objective prior to the battle is labeled the defender. The opponent, which plans to take control of the strategic objective that it does not occupy prior to the battle, is deemed the attacker. Two examples may prove useful here. During the 1947–49 Kashmir War, Pakistani forces spent six months laying siege to the city of Skardu, which was protected by Indian soldiers. Pakistan and India are deemed to be attacker and defender, respectively, in this encounter. On November 1, 1964, the Viet Cong attacked a US facility located in Bien Hoa, destroying or damaging dozens of aircraft. The Viet Cong are attackers, while the United States is the defender. This standard of occupation is sufficient to address approximately 90 percent of battles in my dataset.

In the remaining set of battles, neither belligerent occupies or seeks to claim a clearly defined objective of interest. This generally involves situations where military units have incidental encounters or are both mobile. The battle of Jutland from May 31 to June 1, 1916, during World War I, is an example of these two conditions occurring simultaneously; a British fleet coincidentally happened on a German scouting squadron in the North Sea.[21] For such cases, I look to each side's movement on the battlefield. If both sides are on the move, the belligerent that is in pursuit is the attacker, and the one being pursued is the defender. If only one party is moving, I consider it the attacker; the stationary party is the defender. Returning to the battle of Jutland, German ships were the first to open fire and then pursued the British vessels, which had turned away to head toward Britain's main fleet, the Royal Navy Grand Fleet. The Germans are considered to be the attackers, while the British are the defenders.

OUTCOMES

Attackers are considered to win a battle if they seize possession of the objective. This generally involves the ejection, surrender, or destruction of the defending forces. Defenders win a battle if they manage to maintain possession of the objective. This minimally requires the repulsion of attacking forces but can also include instances where defending forces subsequently launch a counterattack and begin to pursue their opponent. In battles that do not feature a self-evident object to be taken or guarded, victory is defined using the criterion of movement; the belligerent that retreats or flees first is considered the loser of the battle. A small set of battles where neither dimension proves sufficient to identify a victor are coded as being inconclusive.

My approach focuses on tactical criteria to define the outcomes of battles. An alternative method would be to code victory based on strategic factors regarding whether the battle created a longer-term advantage for the winner and disadvantage for the loser in their overall war prospects. While tactical and strategic notions of victory often lead to similar classifications, some divergences do arise. Emphasizing the tactical angle is valuable because it reflects considerations that belligerents can contemporaneously observe during the war itself and thus use to revise their future behavior and beliefs. The strategic angle, on the other hand, often requires knowledge of belligerents' prior expectations, which are essentially unobservable; relies on historical hindsight that is impossible for leaders to possess during the conflict; and is a fundamentally political question.[22]

The first battle of Kiev, which took place in 1941 during World War II, embodies this contrast well. In late August, German troops barreled across the eastern front, tearing through Soviet defenses as they advanced toward a poorly protected Moscow, when they encountered a significant Red Army presence in Kiev. Opting to engage in Kiev, German forces almost completely encircled the Soviets and pummeled the city for the next month. By September, Kiev had fallen and the Germans claimed to have killed over six hundred thousand Red Army soldiers. This loss was unprecedented for the Soviets and was easily one of the most catastrophic tactical losses for the Soviet Union—and, equivalently, one of the biggest tactical victories for the Germans. But by stalling his opponents in Kiev, Stalin managed to create time to build new defenses around Moscow and to remobilize his forces. The "delays" caused by the battle of Kiev were also responsible for forcing the Germans to suffer one of the harshest Russian winters in decades, ultimately nullifying their ability to press forward and take Moscow. This would be essential in shifting the momentum of war in the Soviets' favor and leading to a victory years later.[23] Only a retrospective lens reveals that the first battle of Kiev was a massive strategic loss for the Germans. My data therefore code this battle as a German victory.

DATES

A battle begins on the day when hostilities over a strategic objective commence. Since this is a relatively straightforward standard, most historical references report similar start dates for battles. Different standards, however, such as the last advance or the last day of active hostilities, do lead to mild disagreements about end dates. My data define the end of a battle as the day when the outcome of the battle as previously defined becomes readily apparent.[24] In cases where multiple bouts of conflict take place in a single location, battles are identified using periods of sustained combat. As an example, during the Greco-Turkish War of 1897 (explored more in chapter 3), Turkish forces attempted to push Greeks out of a key city called Velestino. I disaggregate this effort into two battles, one on April 30 (a Greek victory) and one on May 5–6 (a Turkish victory), as each clash was separated by a period of inactivity. Note that these battles were not delineated by the fact that each had a different victor.

In practice, these discrepancies make little difference. One-third of recorded battles last a single day, and three-quarters are shorter than two weeks in duration.

I use both military history reference materials and war-specific books to resolve remaining inconsistencies as best as possible. My main analyses of these data also use varying temporal windows to measure battlefield activity, and these adjustments do not unduly impact the results.

Examples

Two battles may prove enlightening in demonstrating how the qualitative accounts of battles are converted into quantitative measures. First, I consider the battle of Plevna from the Second Russo-Turkish War of 1877–78. Russian forces led by Grand Duke Nicholas faced little resistance as they swept down toward the Danube River. Approximately 30,000 Ottoman forces took defensive positions in the town of Plevna to fend off the approaching Russians, who numbered between 90,000 and 110,000. Between September 10 and 12, 1877, the Russians engaged in a major assault to overtake Plevna but failed at the cost of approximately 20,000 casualties.[25]

Briefly stated, Russian forces took the offensive against a Turkish stronghold but were repulsed, suffering a humiliating loss that received enormous international attention. In terms of the individual battle at Plevna, Russia was the attacker and the Ottoman Empire was the defender. These designations do not factor into the score given to the battle but help define the criteria used to determine which belligerent won the battle. At the level of the entire war, Russia was the initiator and the Ottoman Empire was the target. Since the battle resulted in a victory by the war target, the assault on Plevna receives a score of –1.

Second, consider the battle of Ouadi Doum during the Libyan-Chad War of 1986–87, also known as the War over the Aouzou Strip or the Toyota War. On March 19, 1987, Libyan forces stationed at a major air base at Ouadi Doum headed toward the city of Fada with the intention of reclaiming it from Chadian forces, who had gained control in a battle on January 2. The decision proved immensely costly for Libya. Chad's army trounced the Libyans, diverting them back to Ouadi Doum and eventually taking the air base for themselves. On March 22, Chad declared victory and announced that its forces had killed upward of 1,200 Libyan soldiers and captured approximately 450. Libya's loss of the Ouadi Doum air base marked the end of Libya's hold on northern Chad.[26]

Libya started the battle by sending its forces against Chad but faced a terrible defeat. Libya was thus the battle attacker, while Chad was the battle defender. More broadly, Chad was the initiator of the overall conflict, while Libya was the target. The battle at Ouadi Doum was therefore a victory for the war initiator and is assigned a score of +1.

Table 2.3 summarizes the distribution of battles based on actors and outcomes for all 1,708 events. The data indicate that actors who start individual battles tend to have a significant advantage, winning approximately two-thirds of all clashes.

Two caveats merit mention here. First, as table 2.3 intimates, my data treat all battles as being equivalent in magnitude. On one hand, this is a limitation of data; current information on all of these individual battles is not sophisticated enough to create a reliable system that weighs events differently according to forces deployed, casualties suffered, or the like. On the other hand, this property of my battle data parallels how many well-known formalizations of war treat "forts," the object of individual battles, as identical units.[27] My analysis therefore reflects a relatively direct assessment of the learning dynamic featured in these models.

Second, wars vary substantially in the number of battles recorded. Perhaps most prominently, the two world wars account for approximately 47 percent of my data. Much of this variation likely captures real differences in the intensity and frequency of conflict, yet I cannot eliminate the possibility that uneven coverage also plays a role. For example, the Saudi-Yemeni War of 1934, which lasted two months, is reflected by only one battle. English-language documentation for the conflict is relatively limited and piecemeal.[28] The battle data for the Vietnam War contain only fifty entries over a dozen years of hostilities—an apparently low number that may reflect the difficulties of tracking and quantizing guerrilla warfare.

Regardless of whether every single conceivable battle is captured, the more relevant question is whether the current data present a faithful portrayal of the broader trends and changes on the battlefield. The figures presented below suggest that my data do satisfy this more elemental condition.

TABLE 2.3 Distribution of battle victories

	BATTLE ATTACKER	INCONCLUSIVE	BATTLE DEFENDER	TOTAL
War initiator	550 (0.322) +1		243 (0.142) +1	793 (0.464)
Inconclusive		74 (0.043) 0		74 (0.043)
War target	595 (0.348) −1		246 (0.144) −1	841 (0.492)
Total	1,145 (0.670)	74 (0.043)	489 (0.286)	1,708 (1.000)

Note: Proportions in parentheses.

Measures of Battlefield Activity

I use these raw data regarding 1,708 battles to create daily-level measures of battlefield outcomes. For each day t in war w, $s_{w,t}$ is the sum of the outcomes for any and all battles that concluded on that war-day. If three battles came to an end on some war-day, the basic form of $s_{w,t}$ could range in value between –3 (three victories by the war target) and +3 (three victories by the war initiator).

Several of my hypotheses scrutinize the effect of clear battlefield information on negotiation. There are multiple plausible paths we could take to measure the concept of "clear information" based on these daily sums. Previous research suggests that distinct battlefield trends supply the most overt information regarding the future trajectory of conflict and also create conditions for a self-enforcing agreement. For those reasons, some studies find that distinct battlefield trends are predictive of war termination and the resilience of postconflict peace.[29] I will therefore generate and rely on measures designed to track the outcomes of recent fighting.

My first measure, which I call *momentum*, calculates the sum of all battles that have ended in the previous d days of the conflict (or all days of the conflict—whichever is closer). I use $d = 60$ as my default window of time. This variable represents recent battlefield trends and reverts to 0 if no new battles end in the next d days. Formally,

$$\text{Momentum}_{w,t} = \sum_{j=\max\{1, t-d\}}^{t} s_{w,j}$$

Note, however, that my hypotheses are agnostic as to which particular belligerent wields an advantage or disadvantage while fighting. As such, much of my analysis of battlefield trends relies on a measure called *recent imbalance*, which is simply the absolute value of momentum.

$$\text{Recent imbalance}_{w,t} = \left| \sum_{j=\max\{1, t-d\}}^{t} s_{w,j} \right|$$

Although we have reasons to focus on recent battle trends, some may justifiably believe that the entirety of hostilities influence decision-making and that events in the more distant past do not fade in importance.[30] I account for the accumulation of all battle outcomes using a measure called *position*, which is a running total of all daily sums for the entire war up to the given war-day:

$$\text{Position}_{w,t} = \sum_{i=1}^{t} s_{w,t}$$

I then take the absolute value of this measure to reflect the *overall imbalance* observed from the battlefield:

$$\text{Overall imbalance}_{w,t} = \left| \sum_{\max\{1, t-d\}}^{t} s_{w,t} \right|$$

Regardless of the specific trends on the battlefield, we would also want to gauge the overall intensity of hostilities. To do so, I count the number of *active battles* taking place on each day of war.

Figure 2.3 illustrates these measures for World War I.[31] The data align well with our qualitative understanding of the conflict. The Central powers initiated the war and are thus represented using positive values, while the Allied powers' victories are captured with negative values. Early German offensives found success in invading Luxembourg, Belgium, and parts of France. By September 1914, however, British and French troops were able to blunt German momentum at the first battle of the Marne. This is reflected by the small shift from positive to negative values in both position and momentum in the opening months of the war. The somewhat middling values observed in the first several months of the conflict reflect the stalled nature of trench warfare, which led to a back-and-forth exchange of victories and losses on the western front.

The Central powers began accumulating significant victories in April 1915. Many of these occurred on the Gallipoli peninsula, where Allied forces arrived in late April hoping to seize control of the Turkish straits from the Ottomans. The offensive was a disaster for the Allies,[32] leading to a withdrawal in late 1915. Much of early 1916 featured victories by the Ottomans against Allied forces in Mesopotamia and numerous failed Russian offensives against the Germans, both of which are reflected by significant upward movement in position and momentum.

The war entered a significant shift in the middle of 1916. The battle of the Somme in the summer, despite its enormous costs and somewhat inconclusive outcome, was a turning point in favor of the Allies.[33] Figure 2.3 exhibits a downward shift around this time. The German loss at the battle of Verdun later in the year severely blunted German initiative. The entry of the United States on the side of the Allies in April 1917 only worsened Germany's situation.

Seeing the window of opportunity for victory close, the Germans launched several last-ditch offensives in early 1918. While these saw some partial success, these efforts did not make any significant breakthroughs. The second battle of the Marne in 1918, which would be Germany's last major offensive, was countered by the Allies and was the start of an implacable Allied advance. The sudden and aggressive changes in battlefield trends starting in the middle of 1918 capture this shift and continue until the war ends in favor of the Allies on November 11, 1918.

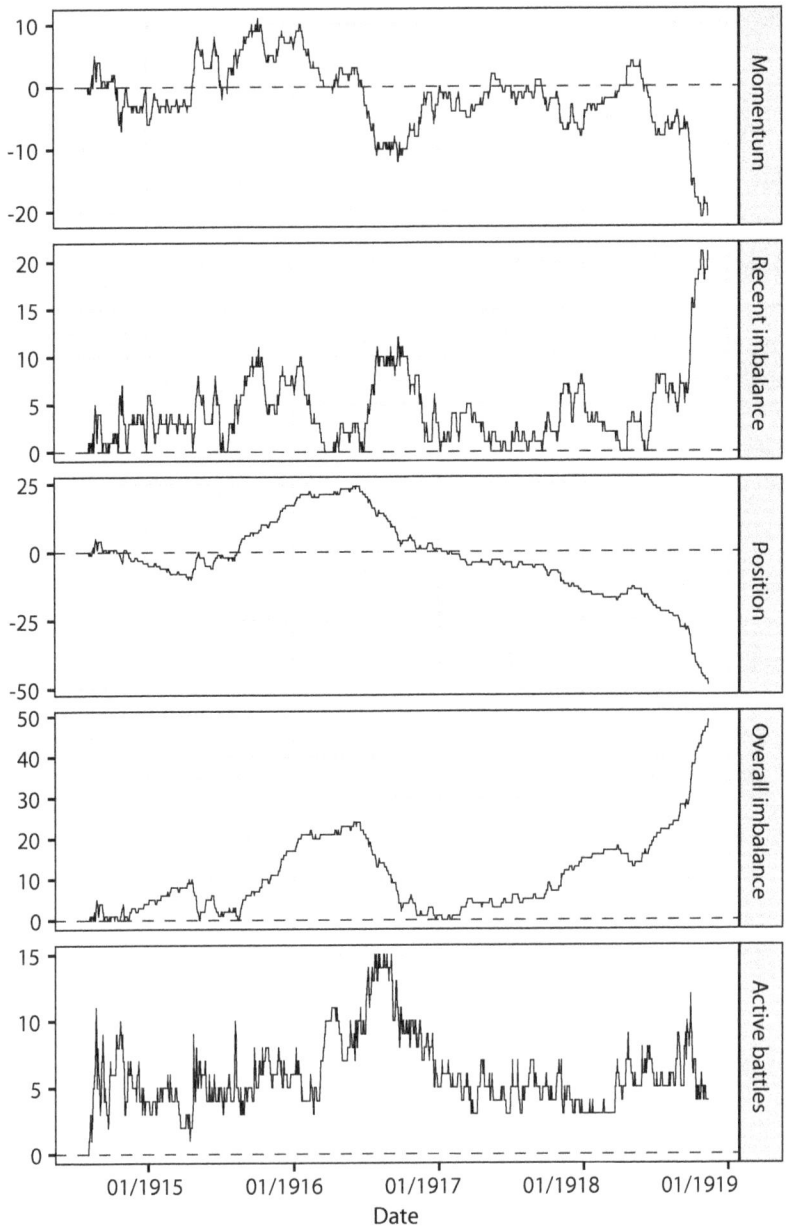

FIGURE 2.3. Five measures of the battlefield in World War I.

Opening the Black Box of War

No data effort on phenomena that take place during the chaos of war can ever be comprehensive. Little doubt exists that these new datasets have their shortcomings. Throughout this chapter, I have discussed several of these possible limitations and potential ways to address them.

In this case, however, perfect is the enemy of good. For any and all limitations these data harbor, they represent an enormous step forward in our ability to capture the tumultuous activity that comes to pass within individual conflicts. These two resources exceed the leverage of coverage offered by extant sources of quantitative intrawar diplomacy or battles.[34] Any useful insights that emerge from analyzing these data should only encourage further attempts to expand, refine, and improve them. Even the surface-level analysis of negotiations and battles in this chapter has revealed considerable levels of fluctuations that are not predicted or explained by extant theories of war or conflict resolution. Neither fighting nor negotiating follows a monotonic path toward victory or peace.

My theory presents a framework that seeks to explain the variation exhibited in the negotiation data and to demonstrate that negotiations play a much more complex role in shaping conflicts than previous scholarship has assumed. The next two chapters apply statistical methods to the new data to realize these two objectives.

FIGHTING TO TALK

My theory produces several interrelated predictions about when negotiations will happen during war and when those negotiations will succeed in their ostensible goal of settling hostilities. These predictions are conditional on the level of latent third-party pressures that can be easily activated and placed on belligerents, as well as the degree of information revealed from fighting on the battlefield. Each of these factors influences the relative costs and benefits to negotiating either sincerely or insincerely.

This chapter uses a combination of statistical methods and two comparative case studies to assess the validity of these claims. My negotiation and battle data, described in the previous chapter, offer an opportunity to analyze negotiation and battlefield behavior across two hundred years of interstate wars. To test the impact of latent external pressures for peace, I make the case for using the year 1945 as a critical source of empirical leverage. Numerous scholars have observed and demonstrated that the liberal international order established in the aftermath of World War II has produced multiple institutions and connections aimed at preserving international peace and opposing the use of force. These compounding forces facilitate the activation of diplomatic pressures on belligerents in contemporary wars. A series of statistical tests indicate that the year 1945 indeed marks a turning point in the frequency of negotiations. Additional models based on this finding show firm support for my theory's predicted implications. Wars before 1945 involve far fewer negotiations, but negotiations that occur are responses to a clear battlefield trend and promptly end wars. In contrast, wars after 1945 have a much higher propensity for negotiations regardless of the battlefield and frequently fail to end hostilities, but talks in response to distinct battlefield trends are more likely to produce peace. I provide greater context for this finding by differentiating negotiations borne of direct external pressure from those sought by the belligerents themselves. This exercise shows that post-1945 negotiations are far more frequently products of third-party endeavors, and talks spearheaded by third parties are far weaker predictors of war termination than talks launched by the belligerents.

While the year 1945 is objectively important to understanding the changing character of wartime negotiations, it is a blunt instrument to assess the effects of latent pressures on negotiation behavior. I therefore also leverage whether or not belligerents are major powers. I show that minor powers are far more likely to be pushed into negotiations that amount to nothing. Additional data on third-party interventions reveal that outside actors initiate more diplomatic appeals in post-1945 wars when major powers are not directly involved in the war itself.

I supplement my quantitative analysis with a qualitative comparison of two wars that feature the same sets of belligerents, separated by almost eighty years: the Greco-Turkish War of 1897 and the Turco-Cypriot War of 1974. In an environment featuring relatively few external pressures to negotiate, Turkey and Greece did not negotiate in the former conflict until the battlefield solidly demonstrated the Turks' superiority. In contrast, the heavy presence of third-party diplomatic pressures in the latter conflict resulted in constant but largely unsuccessful talks. It was only once Turkey made major territorial advances that a diplomatic settlement brought hostilities to an end. Across both the quantitative and qualitative evidence, the coalescence of latent pressures and information from recent battlefield developments defines not only when negotiations take place but whether they accomplish their professed aim of reaching a mutually acceptable agreement.

1945 and the Explosion of Latent Pressures

The theory I have established highlights the importance of latent external pressures for peace in explaining wartime negotiation behavior. Domestic actors, individual states, and international organizations may have varying degrees of interest in promoting peace in active conflicts, depending on specific circumstances regarding the identity of the belligerents, the nature of the disputed issue, and the like. But the ability to quickly and effectively direct these diplomatic pressures against warring parties depends on the size and strength of an infrastructure designed to facilitate such activity. The baseline degree of pressure that auxiliary actors can harness depends on how many actors can immediately be deployed to try facilitating dialogue, what connections already exist between states to allow them to communicate with each other, and what institutions exist that foster and promote peaceful dispute resolution. I argue that one historical change most effectively captures a change in these latent pressures: the establishment of the post-1945 international order.

Numerous pieces of scholarship have pointed out the myriad enormous shifts that redefined the international system following World War II. In the words of the political scientists Gary Goertz, Paul Diehl, and Alexandru Balas, "World War II constitutes the tipping point in the international system's movement toward more peace."[1] Various works have extensively scrutinized several features of this post-1945 liberal international order, some of which emerged in inchoate form after World War I, and how each has affected the nature of international conflict. By extension, these features influence the number of sources of diplomatic pressure, as well as their potency. Three are particularly notable.

First, the rules of conflict changed on both normative and legal fronts. The trauma of World War I raised questions about the legitimacy of war,[2] but the experience of World War II consolidated a broader aversion to conflict.[3] Norms on sovereignty and territorial integrity became vital sources of stability designed to preclude the territorial disputes and conquests that fueled World War II.[4] Laws of conflict also attempted to punish and stem inhumane acts of violence during war. Early steps were taken with the Hague Convention of 1899, but a broader global framework came into being with the 1949 Geneva Conventions and postwar trials in Nuremberg, Tokyo, and Manila. Contemporary research has not yet produced a clear consensus about whether states comply with laws of war due to self-interest or international enforcement, but these laws do appear to effect changes in state behavior.[5]

Second, the weapons that could be used in conflict became cataclysmic in their destructive power. The bombings of Hiroshima and Nagasaki violently heralded a new era of warfare where ruinous destruction required only mere seconds. Widespread acknowledgment of this danger may help to explain why wars since 1945 have been relatively limited in nature.[6] Belligerents that possess nuclear weapons may have incentives to seek moderation and increase contact with their opponent to avoid cataclysmic outcomes, and nonnuclear actors would also highlight these concerns.

The third dimension, which is built on the previous two, is the advent of fixed institutions. While international institutions have existed for centuries, they rose to real prominence after World War II. The Charter of the United Nations, signed by fifty original member states on October 24, 1945, epitomized the desire for an international order that strove "to maintain or restore international peace and security."[7] A multitude of additional fixed institutions have been created to promote the same cause.[8] Over time, these institutions have fostered a growing community of professional negotiators that embody a set of increasingly legitimized norms and procedures that promote the peaceful resolution of conflict.[9]

The post-1945 international order therefore establishes an array of tools and ideas that attempt to promote peace and stability. Third parties, many of whom now work as career officials for these fixed institutions, are buttressed by a normative and legal framework and can urge states to engage in diplomacy. The pre-1945 world therefore features far lower levels of latent external pressure than the post-1945 one. Consequently, the 1945 line can be exploited to test the impact of latent external pressures on negotiations.

The Validity of the 1945 Line

While existing literature suggests that the 1945 line represents a tenable proxy for low or high latent external pressures for peace, we must first address whether this assumption holds up to empirical scrutiny. Two findings strongly suggest that the year 1945 indeed marks an inflection point in the frequency of wartime negotiations. Importantly, both pieces of evidence identify the 1945 line on their own, based solely on the nature of my negotiation data.

The first assessment is a structural break test. For each year between 1823 and 2003, I calculate the total number of war-days that feature negotiations, as well as the total number of interstate wars and war-days. This produces a time series to which I apply a structural break test that identifies the years in which the frequency of negotiations systematically shifts, accounting for the total number of wars and war-days. The test with the best fit in terms of the Bayesian information criterion (BIC) identifies two inflection points: 1945 and 1972.[10] The break in 1972 represents the significant drop-off in negotiations after the United States negotiated its withdrawal from the Vietnam War. If I restrict the test to identifying only one structural break, it identifies the year 1947. Given that no wars take place between the end of World War II in 1945 and the start of the First Kashmir War in 1947, this is effectively indistinguishable from 1945 and merely identifies the fact that the First Kashmir War marks a sudden increase in rates of wartime diplomacy.

The second test uses a battery of bivariate logistic regressions. For each year Y ranging from 1824 to 2002 (the years immediately following and preceding the limits of my war data), I regress the binary negotiation variable on an indicator variable that takes the value 0 on all war-days up to year Y and the value 1 on all war-days after the year Y. This exercise produces 179 separate models, each of which fits the negotiation data to varying extents. The BIC again offers a direct way to compare fits across these 179 iterations. The two models with the lowest

BICs, and thus the best fits, are those in which Y equals 1945 and 1946.[11] We therefore have evidence that the 1945 line is indeed associated with a meaningful change in belligerents' negotiation calculus and is thus a useful source of leverage in the statistical analyses to follow.[12]

Basic descriptive statistics about the binary negotiation variable bolster these findings. Consistent with the implications of my theory, there are clear signs that the rate of negotiations distinctly jumps upward in an environment with higher latent pressures. While 11 percent of war-days in wars before 1945 involve negotiations between belligerents, more than double that—28 percent—do so in wars following 1945. Note that the overall statistic of 17 percent across the entire dataset, which I have mentioned in preceding chapters, masks this distinct change in frequency between the two historical eras.

The descriptive statistics I have shown here are informative, easily interpretable, and entirely consistent with the broad implications of my theory. They do not, however, account for the impact of battlefield information or a host of other factors that could influence states' negotiation strategies. For that, we move on to a more complete and thorough statistical analysis of wartime negotiations.

Modeling Wartime Negotiations

In order to properly assess my hypotheses regarding the frequency of negotiations and their impact on peace, I require a model that simultaneously accounts for the onset of talks and the impact of these talks on the termination of conflict. The ideal model would permit explanatory variables to have different effects on both phenomena and capture the entire sequential process through which wars eventually come to an end.

The most effective tool for this endeavor is the multistate model. Multistate models have had a longer history in the field of health, where they have been used to study individuals' transitions between different stages of disease.[13] The method has received far less attention in political science, despite how useful it would be in analyzing complex dynamics that are common to political affairs.[14] Multistate models allow a researcher to capture a process that may go through multiple stages along any pathway that the researcher defines as being possible. Once a subject undergoes a transition from one state to another, the subject remains in the data, and the model then estimates the subject's likelihood of transitioning to another state from this new state.

This feature not only permits us to study wars that feature multiple periods of negotiation but provides insights into why wars may transition out of negotiations and back to only fighting. Perhaps more importantly, multistate models also allow covariates to have varied impacts on the likelihood of different state transitions.

Figure 3.1 depicts how a multistate model would be applied to my theory's setting. On any given day of war, the conflict may be in one of three states: no negotiations taking place, negotiations taking place, or the termination of hostilities. Note that, throughout the conflict, the war can repeatedly transition between having no talks and having talks. The move from either of these states to termination, however, is final and marks the end of the war. Coincidentally, this is also known as the "terminal" state.[15] To facilitate a more natural discussion of transitions between these states, figure 3.1 also includes names for each of the four possible transitions that can take place within this structure. I will use these names throughout the remainder of the quantitative analysis in this chapter.

The numbers in figure 3.1 also show the frequency of transitions between these three states at the daily level. Unsurprisingly, the vast majority of war-days feature no negotiations and remain in that state the following day. In all, 187 negotiation periods begin following a day without talks.[16] The figure also shows that when negotiations take place, they often continue into the next day. But discussions fall apart in 137 cases and produce peace in the remaining 52. A multistate model will help reveal which factors influence each of these transitions between the three different states of war.

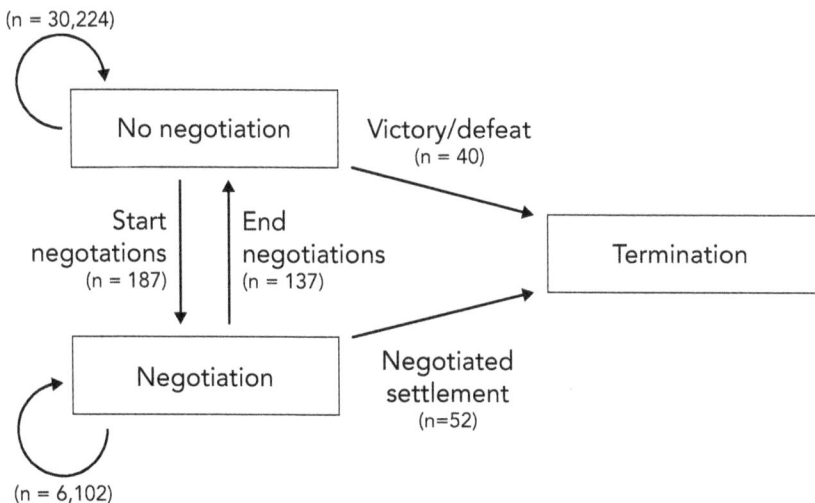

FIGURE 3.1. Three states and four transitions of war.

Design

According to my theory, battlefield information should have different impacts on the occurrence and outcomes of negotiations depending on whether high levels of latent third-party pressure exist. Environments with low latent pressures should feature fewer negotiations overall, but talks should become more likely as fighting reveals a clear trend in one side's favor. The high costs of negotiating lead most of these talks to be sincere and thus more likely to end the conflict. In contrast, environments with high latent pressures decrease the costs of negotiating. Wars in this context should exhibit a much weaker relationship between battlefield outcomes and the onset of negotiations, but any talks that do occur will be increasingly sincere and likely to end the conflict if fighting exhibits a trend.

I assess this general claim by applying separate multistate models to wars before 1945 and after 1945. As I have shown, systemic changes following the end of World War II provide a source of leverage to test the impact of latent third-party pressures for peace. The key explanatory variable in each model is *recent imbalance* in fighting over the previous sixty days.[17]

A variety of factors may confound our ability to identify the relationships between these central variables throughout my tests. I therefore include several control variables common to war literature that could simultaneously affect battle outcomes, negotiating behavior, and conflict resolution.

First, belligerents may be more willing to fight harder when a conflict involves existential threats, which are often linked to wars with serious credible commitment issues. I account for *issue salience* using a three-level classification scheme developed by Holsti and extend it to cover more recent wars.[18] I add together the issue salience scores of both sides to produce the final measure included in the analysis.

Second, wars between more distant belligerents may be difficult to supply or manage.[19] Conflicts between neighboring states may not only be easier to prosecute but involve more familiar parties and difficult issues such as territorial claims. I use the Correlates of War Direct Contiguity dataset to create a dummy variable of *contiguity*, indicating whether belligerents share a land or river border.[20]

Belligerents with greater capabilities are likely to have an upper hand over their opponent.[21] Using the Composite Index of National Capability (CINC) measure from the National Material Capabilities dataset,[22] I add together the annual CINC measures for all active belligerents on each side in the war. I divide the war initiator's total score by the sum of both sides' scores, with adjustments made when individual states in multilateral wars enter and exit. For this *CINC ratio,* values near 1 represent a far more capable war initiator, while those near 0 indicate a more capable war target.[23]

A trove of literature expects democratic war initiators to be more discernible, credible, and effective—yet impatient—belligerents.[24] A binary measure based on the Polity dataset tracks whether the initiating side of the conflict features at least one state that is a democracy. In other words, this variable reflects the involvement of a *democratic initiator*.[25]

The threat of nuclear warfare is often considered a vital reason why post-1945 wars have maintained a limited nature.[26] Not only may the presence of nuclear weapons incentivize states to seek peace, but nuclear states at war may also wield greater coercive capabilities while bargaining because of their ability to resort to a nuclear option. In analyses involving post-1945 conflicts, I include a variable for *nuclear* states, which tracks whether any belligerent has successfully tested a nuclear weapon on or after the war-day in question.[27]

The number of states actively involved in conflict may complicate how one side of a conflict engages in hostilities or determines its negotiation strategy. Coalitions of states fighting a war on the same side often enjoy higher prospects of victory but may harbor concerns about individual members abandoning the conflict, leaving the remaining states to manage with fewer resources.[28] I thus include a variable for the total *number of states* involved in the war on a given war-day.

It is also natural to believe that negotiations would occur more readily or be more efficient between belligerent countries that already have standing diplomatic representatives before the outset of war. I thus use the Diplomatic Exchange dataset to determine whether any diplomatic representation exists between states that are on opposing sides of a conflict.[29] This binary variable reflects *opponent diplomatic representation*.

While international institutions, norms, and organizations may lay the foundation for latent external pressures for peace, belligerents' alliances may create conflict-specific forces for or against diplomacy. If a war features states that are allied with major powers, belligerents and their powerful allies may be concerned about the risk of entrapment or escalation and thus see the appeal of diplomacy. Conversely, having powerful allies that could potentially intervene on one's behalf could decrease the appeal of exploring a diplomatic exit.[30] I account for these possibilities by creating a measure called *major allies*. This variable indicates whether any active belligerent has an alliance with a major power (as defined by the Correlates of Wars State System Membership dataset) in pre-1945 wars or one of the two superpowers—the United States or the Soviet Union—in post-1945 wars.

Finally, while my theory is consistent with other scholars' arguments that recent battlefield trends weigh more heavily on decision-makers' minds, the total accumulation of past hostilities may still remain relevant. I therefore include a measure of *overall imbalance,* which captures the cumulative outcomes of all battles throughout the entire war. I also add a running count of the logged number of *completed battles* by a particular war-day, based on my battle data.[31]

Results

Figures 3.2 and 3.3 summarize the results of models applied to pre-1945 and post-1945 wars, respectively. Overall, the results directly reflect the expectations of my theory.

We begin with pre-1945 wars, where latent third-party pressures for peace are systematically lower compared to the post-1945 world. The positive and statistically significant coefficient for the transition into negotiations indicates that the initiation of talks becomes more likely as recent battlefield activity firmly moves in one side's favor. Moreover, a similarly positive and statistically significant effect appears for the transition from negotiations into war termination—in other words, negotiated settlement. This indicates that when negotiations do take place, discussions that take place alongside a heavily slanted battlefield are more likely to produce diplomatic settlements. By dint of ending the conflict, these negotiations have shown themselves to be sincere. We therefore see strong evidence that a clear battlefield trend both triggers negotiations and leads negotiations to be successful in resolving the conflict.

We can compare these results with those from post-1945 wars, where latent pressures for peace are significantly higher and where I have demonstrated that negotiations become more frequent. The findings for recent imbalance are telling. There is no longer a significant relationship between battlefield trends and the initiation of talks; however, negotiations that do take place are still more likely to produce a negotiated settlement if recent imbalance trends consistently in one side's favor.

A more intuitive way to interpret these models is through hazard ratios. A hazard ratio is the ratio of the hazard rates (the rate at which an observation may transition into a new state) between two groups that experience different levels of an explanatory variable. All else being equal, if the hazard ratio for the recent imbalance variable is 1.35, a war where recent imbalance has a value of 1 is 35 percent more likely to undergo a transition compared to a war where recent imbalance has a value of 0; a war with a recent imbalance of 2 is 35 percent more likely to experience a transition than a war with a recent imbalance of 1; and so on.

Table 3.1 uses the multistate models to derive hazard ratios for transitioning into negotiations as well as negotiations leading to settlement, conditional on latent external pressures and battlefield trends. The first row shows a distinct

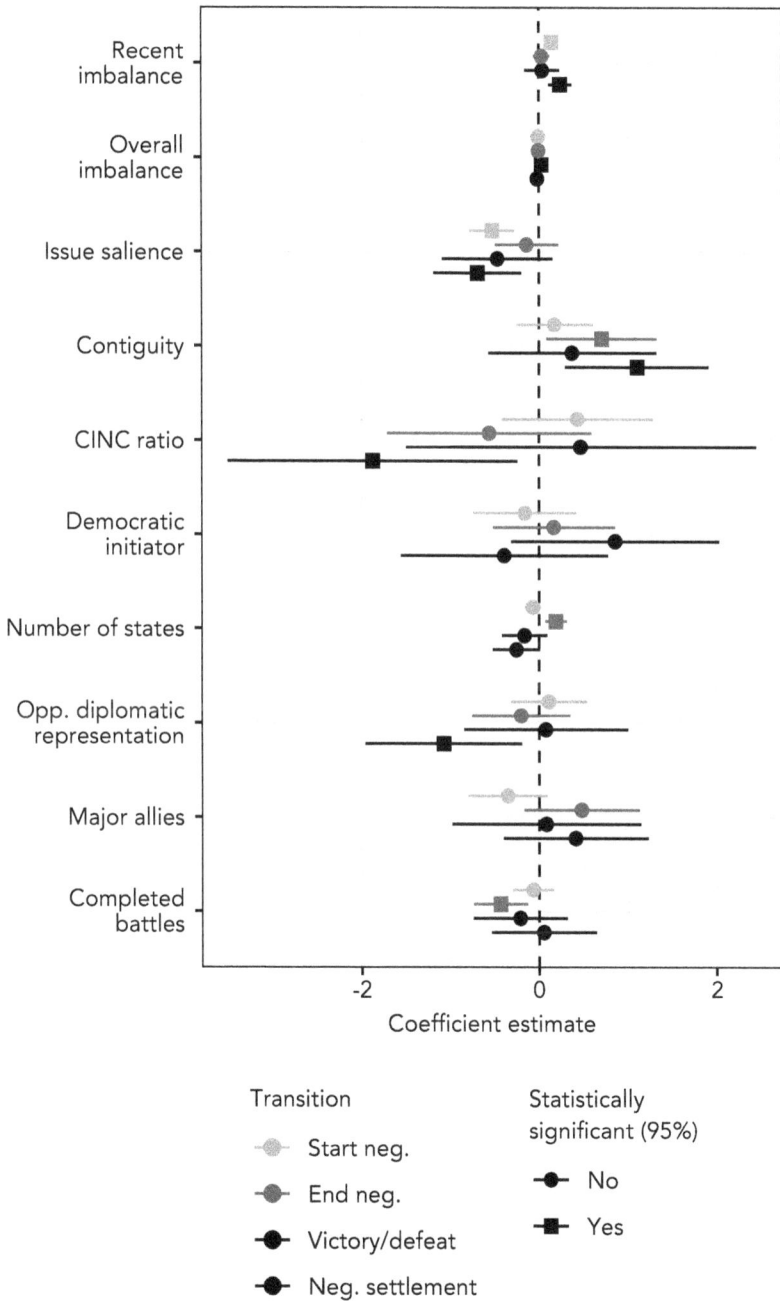

FIGURE 3.2. Coefficient plots for multistate models of negotiation in pre-1945 wars. Bands represent 95 percent confidence intervals (*N* = 23,711).

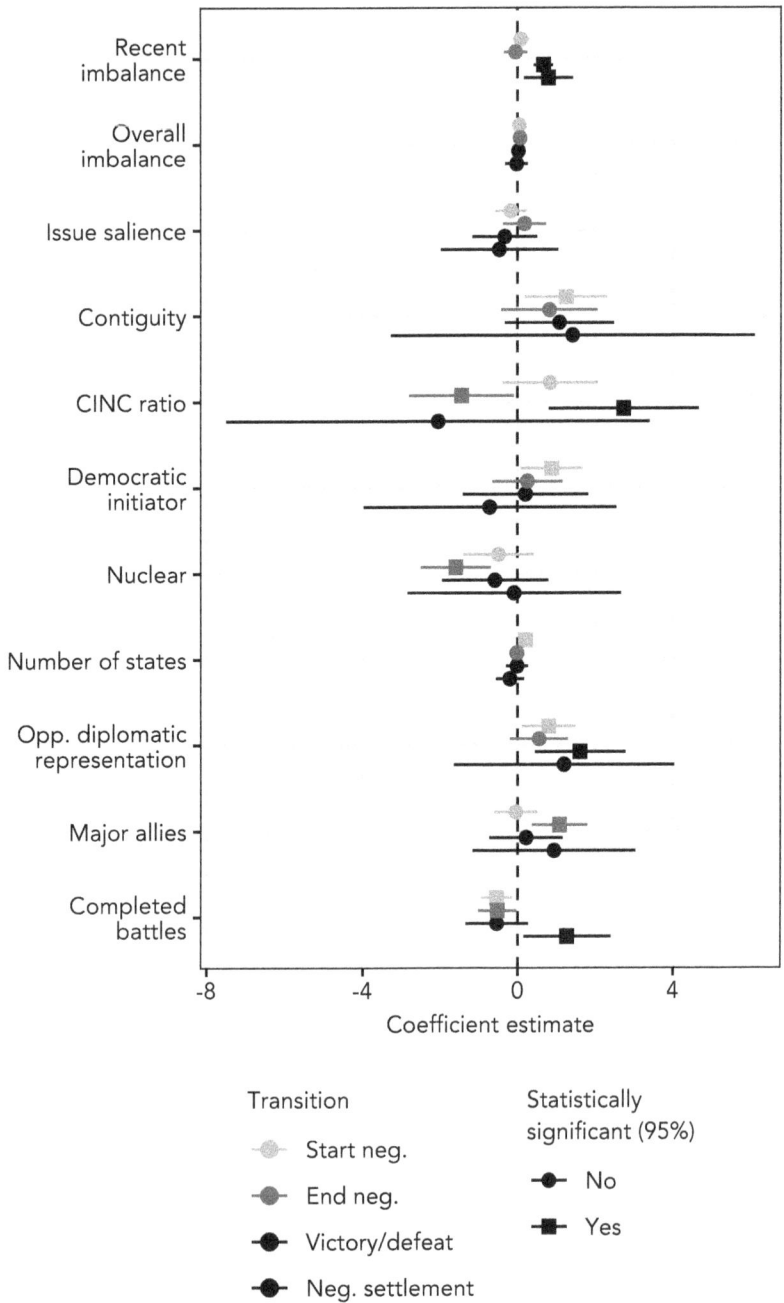

FIGURE 3.3. Coefficient plots for multistate models of negotiation in post-1945 wars. Bands represent 95 percent confidence intervals (*N* = 13,123).

positive relationship between recent imbalance and the likelihood of negotiations in pre-1945 wars, where latent external pressures for peace are relatively low. Across all nonzero values of recent imbalance, the lower bound of the 95 percent confidence interval is higher than 1, indicating that battlefield trends indeed expedite the onset of negotiations. The hazard ratios themselves indicate that these changes are substantively meaningful. According to the model, increasing one side's recent battlefield trend by one unit increases the chances of negotiations by 15 percent over the baseline. Matters look different in post-1945 wars, which feature higher levels of latent external pressure. The positive relationship between recent imbalance and negotiation onset is also approximately 9 percent, but the 95 percent confidence interval around the hazard ratio includes the value 1. No statistically significant relationship exists between recent battlefield trends and the start of talks.

The second row of Table 3.1 displays corresponding hazard ratios for the transition from negotiations into a diplomatic settlement. The result for pre-1945 wars looks largely similar to what I find for the initiation of talks. For a one-unit increase in recent imbalance, the likelihood of negotiations leading to settlement increases by 27 percent. Increasingly obvious battlefield trends therefore engender talks, and these talks are more likely to successfully settle conflicts. This provides evidence that negotiations become more sincere as fighting becomes more obviously tilted in one side's favor. In contrast to what we saw for negotiation onset, post-1945 wars also exhibit an extremely positive and statistically significant relationship between fighting and the propensity for negotiations to produce peace. Increasing recent imbalances by one unit augments the chances of negotiations forging settlement by more than 120 percent. Put together, these results strongly align with my theory's predictions.

Before moving on, it is also worth mentioning that many covariates have differing results according to historical era. Issue salience is a useful case in point. In pre-1945 conflicts, the negative and statistically significant coefficients for transitions into negotiations and into negotiated settlements indicate that belligerents fighting over existential issues are less likely to conclude wars through diplomatic means; wars simply last longer because the stakes are so high. After 1945, issue salience has no bearing on whether negotiations start. This is further suggestive

TABLE 3.1   Hazard ratios of transitions in wartime diplomacy

TRANSITION	PRE-1945	POST-1945
Start negotiations	[1.068, 1.151, 1.241]	[0.883, 1.092, 1.350]
Negotiated settlement	[1.114, 1.269, 1.447]	[1.181, 2.216, 4.158]

Note: Each triplet represents the lower bound, estimate, and upper bound for 95% confidence intervals.

evidence that latent external pressures for peace may be activated without as much regard for the underlying nature of the dispute itself.[32]

Similarly, the belligerents' relative capabilities have different effects over time. In pre-1945 wars, the CINC ratio variable has a negative and statistically significant relationship with negotiated settlements, indicating that any diplomatic talks that occur are less likely to forge peace when the war initiator is relatively strong compared to the target. After 1945, the ratio exhibits a negative relationship with the end of negotiations and a positive one with military victory/defeat. The negative coefficient for the transition out of talks suggests that negotiations end more quickly when the war initiator is much more powerful than its opponent, while the positive coefficient for military victory/defeat shows that relative capabilities are a useful gauge of whether post-1945 wars end via military means.

Alliances with major powers also have some differential effects across time. No meaningful effects appear to exist between these powerful allies and any of the transitions during pre-1945 wars. After 1945, being allied with a superpower appears to hasten the end of any negotiations that come to pass. This result suggests that belligerents that have backing from superpowers feel less need to make compromises or to continuously allay externally generated pressures for peace. At the same time, note that the relationship between nuclear belligerents and the ending of negotiations is negative and statistically significant in post-1945 wars. Put together, these results suggest that the threat of nuclear escalation may push warring parties to keep talking with one another if at least one side actually possesses nuclear weapons, but having allies with massive nuclear arsenals on the sidelines undermines the chances of diplomacy successfully reaching an agreement. Nuclear weapons thus offer a mixed bag with respect to their contribution to conflict management.

Notably, overall imbalance on the battlefield does not offer much leverage to understand negotiation behavior. Battlefields that are more slanted in one side's favor increase the chances of military/victory defeat in pre-1945 wars, but this is the only statistically meaningful effect found across all models. This bolsters the argument that recent fighting is more relevant than all fighting.[33]

Finally, the effect of enduring more battles differs across historical eras. Talks are less likely to end and are therefore longer in pre-1945 wars. Meanwhile, in post-1945 wars, talks are less likely to begin but are also more likely to produce peace when they do occur. The negative coefficient for the transition into negotiations in post-1945 conflicts intimates the possibility that external diplomatic pressures are applied most readily in the early stages of conflict, before many battles have allowed any actors to update their beliefs about the future trajectory of war. Evidence in the next section also supports this claim.[34]

Manifestations of Pressure

The main results I have just presented show the prominent impact that the post-1945 international environment has on wartime negotiation behavior. Given the significance of these core findings, it is worth gathering additional evidence that the observed changes in negotiation frequency following 1945 are actually a consequence of third-party pressures.

If latent pressures for peace are indeed responsible for changing how negotiations occur, then we should expect to see more negotiations that are direct consequences of external pressure in the post-1945 world. The data prove this to be the case. Out of 116 negotiations in pre-1945 conflicts, 89 (77 percent) are orchestrated by the belligerents themselves, and the remaining 27 (23 percent) are products of third-party missions. In wars after 1945, 49 out of 73 negotiation periods (67 percent) are products of external pressure—a nearly threefold increase in the rate of outside influence.

Figure 3.4 visually summarizes trends in negotiations over the duration of pre-1945 and post-1945 wars.[35] The solid black lines represent rates of all talks across both periods. The breakdown of negotiations by type reveals significant differences across historical eras. Most negotiations during pre-1945 wars are internal, and almost all negotiations that end wars are also internal. A small wave of external talks occurs in the middle of many wars but does not amount to much. In contrast, in the post-1945 world, where negotiations are much more common over the entire conflict, external talks occur most readily at the outset of conflict and gradually fade as wars continue. Meanwhile, internal talks gradually rise in frequency, and both forms of negotiation contribute roughly evenly to war termination.

An even more striking contrast between these two time periods is the composition of internal and external negotiations. Most negotiations in pre-1945 conflicts are internal, and the vast majority of diplomatic settlements that terminate conflict are based on internal negotiations. The mixture of internal and external negotiations is much more varied and seemingly uninformative in explaining when or why wars would end. That said, one conspicuous aspect of figure 3.4 is that almost all negotiations that occur at the outset of post-1945 conflicts are external; the belligerents are given little opportunity to seek diplomacy on their own or to avoid the issue. Internal negotiations gradually increase in prevalence as the war proceeds, but these talks do not have the same relationship with settlement as what we see in pre-1945 wars. In short, negotiations that occur in wars after 1945 and that are external have weak connections to conflict resolution.

To more rigorously test whether negotiations based on external pressure differ in their effects on settlement, I turn to hazard models where the outcome of interest is war termination. Figure 3.5 displays the results of two models designed

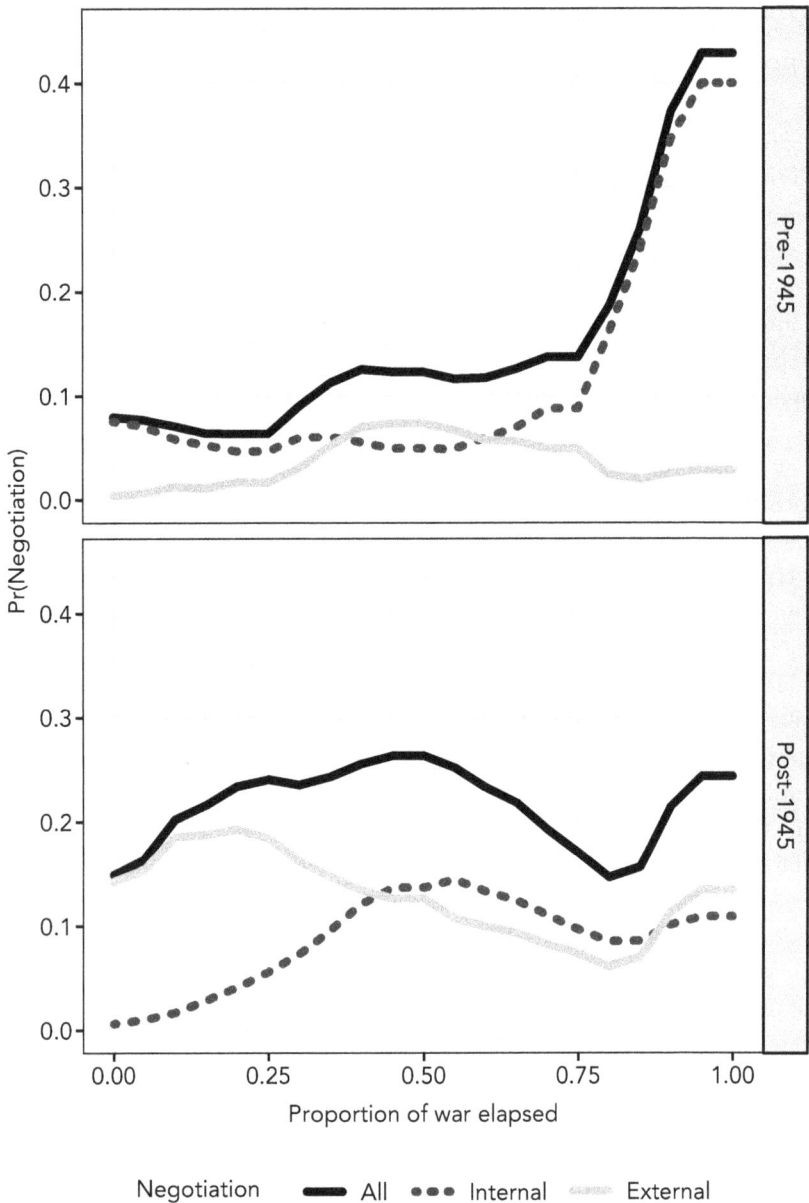

FIGURE 3.4. Smoothed plots of propensity to negotiate over the course of wars.

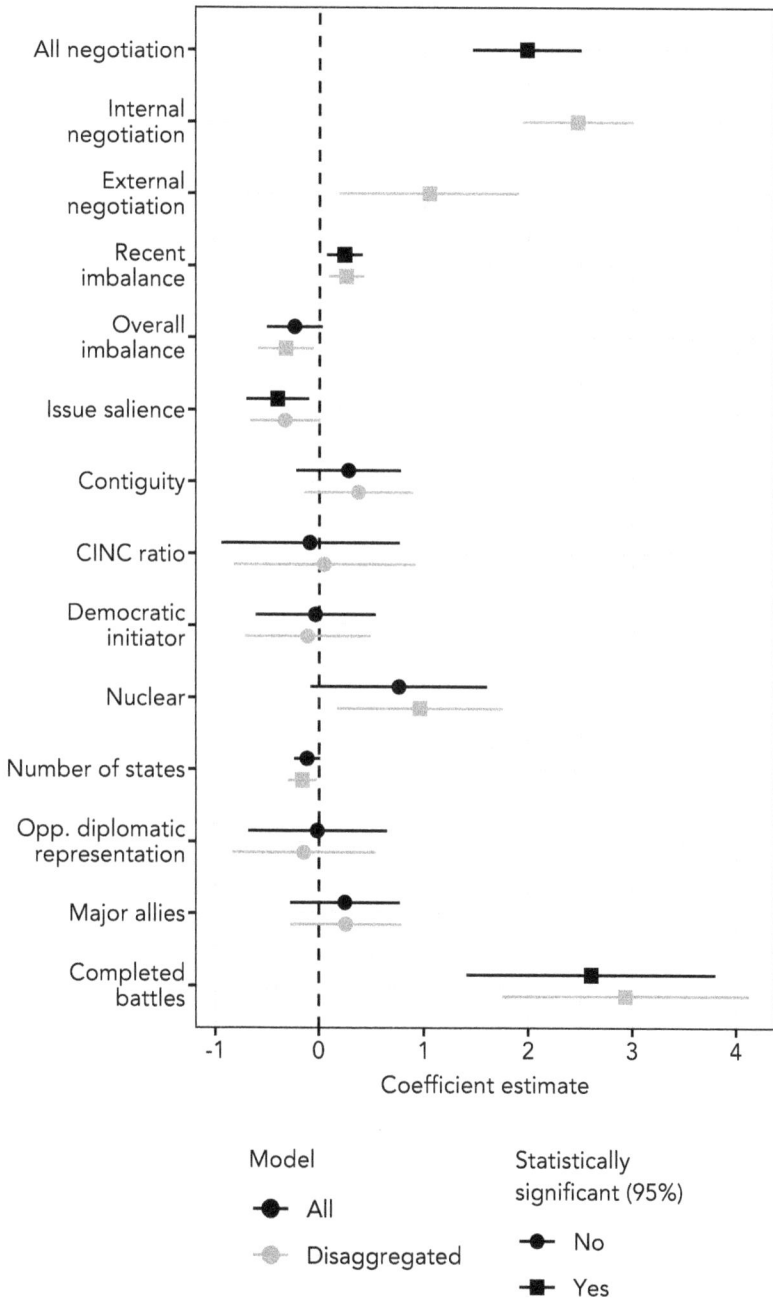

FIGURE 3.5. Hazard models of war termination. Bands represent 95 percent confidence intervals ($N = 36{,}834$).

for this purpose. As a point of reference, the first model features the original binary negotiation variable I have used thus far in my analysis. The second model includes two separate binary variables that track whether negotiations were internal or external. We see that negotiations as a whole have a highly positive and statistically significant impact on prospects for the cessation of hostilities. All else being equal, a day with negotiations is more likely to end on the following day compared to a day where belligerents are not speaking with one another, by a factor of 7.2.[36]

The model that disaggregates internal and external negotiations, however, demonstrates that much of this hastening effect is dictated by diplomatic bargaining that the belligerents themselves pursue without direct outside interference. Internal negotiations increase the odds of war termination by a factor of 11.8 relative to the baseline rate. External negotiations augment the odds of war termination only by a factor of about 2.8. A linear hypothesis test indicates that the coefficient estimates for internal and external negotiations are statistically different from one another ($p < 0.01$). External negotiations as a whole thus have a meaningful and positive effect on war termination, but this effect is meaningfully lower than that for internal negotiations. This supports the logic of my theory that diplomacy under duress is much less likely to involve sincere or successful efforts at peace.[37]

When combined, these results suggest that one of the main reasons the 1945 line drives much of my findings is that modern-day external actors have become far more vocal and successful in getting belligerents to negotiate with each other during war. Yet the nature of these talks allows belligerents to engage in diplomacy even when they have no genuine desire to stop fighting. Third-party efforts certainly do not guarantee failure, but they more frequently permit settlement-averse actors to still talk to one another (perhaps for side effects) without feeling as many negative repercussions for doing so. In short, outside pressure to negotiate may lead to more insincere forms of diplomacy.

Minor Sources of Pressure

The shift in negotiation behavior around 1945, while significant, captures an average effect. It is an admittedly blunt approach to capturing changes in latent pressures. Peace-forward institutions certainly existed before 1945, and not all conflicts after World War II have been inundated with conflict management efforts. Are there any other more refined ways we can test for the impact of latent external pressures that do not rely on this historic shift?

Past literature offers one potential alternative: the distinction between major and minor power belligerents. Across time, a limited and evolving group of states have had the material means to project their power and to shape world politics in ways that suit their own interests. These states are known as major powers. Major powers may frequently clash with one another as they jockey for supremacy,[38] but they have also frequently served as guarantors of peace for smaller warring states.[39]

Major powers are able to influence behavior because they have the resources to incentivize parties' bargaining positions—either by withdrawing existing streams of support or by offering new resources to compensate for any perceived losses from a potential agreement.[40] This leverage has had tangible influences on conflict management. Smaller states that rely on external support are more likely to accept third-party diplomatic efforts and the terms laid out in subsequent discussions.[41] Conversely, major powers frequently elude or resist third-party conflict mediation efforts.[42] Even lower-level rivalries involving major powers have attracted far fewer outside diplomatic efforts because potential third parties realize they do not possess the clout to influence major powers' incentives.[43]

It also bears emphasis that major powers not only wield significant power on their own but are often the architects of international institutions that formalize their own interests and control. The Congress of Vienna in 1814 and 1815, organized to restructure Europe after the fall of Napoleon, is a seminal example of how major powers (at the time, Austria, France, Great Britain, and Russia) created a framework favorable to themselves that would stabilize the continent for the next century. Today, the United Nations Security Council is a prime example of how major powers (as understood in the middle of the twentieth century) define the parameters of discussion in affairs regarding international peace and security, all while nullifying proposals they do not like. Major powers can therefore mobilize a large infrastructure and peace lobby against actors that infringe on the major states' own interests.

A logical conclusion to these arguments and evidence is that wars featuring only states that are not major powers—what we could call minor-power wars—are subject to greater degrees of latent external pressure than conflicts that include at least one major power as an active belligerent. To be clear, this does not suggest that major powers are wholly immune from outside pressures; Margaret Thatcher's lamentations about being forced into mediations during the Falklands War, mentioned in chapter 1, attest to that. Indeed, the fact that the United Kingdom could feel obligated to negotiate only underscores how much more weight minor powers may perceive when diplomatic efforts are set on them.

To assess whether minor power wars offer another proxy for latent pressures to negotiate, I create a new measure for each war that tracks whether a major power participated in the conflict. I use the Correlates of War State Membership dataset to determine this information. According to the data, forty-five out of ninety-two wars feature only minor powers. Minor-power wars indeed undergo fundamentally different pressures than wars with at least one major-power belligerent. When major powers fight, only eighteen of ninety (20 percent) negotiations that occur are directly attributable to a third party's efforts. When only minor powers fight, the rate almost triples; fifty-eight of ninety-nine (59 percent) talks are results of outside pressure.

Figure 3.6 investigates this relationship more rigorously using a multistate model. In this model, wars can transition between fighting and internal negotiations or between fighting and external negotiations. I exclude transitions to war termination, as it is necessary to reduce the number of states in the model in order to produce proper estimates.[44] But the results on war termination in figure 3.5, which use internal and external negotiations as their main explanatory variables, provide the ideal complement to this model. The findings in figure 3.6 are consistent with my general argument. Conflicts with minor powers appear much more prone to entering periods of external negotiations, more than doubling the likelihood of such talks starting on any given day compared to wars with at least one major-power belligerent. The involvement of major or minor powers bears no meaningful connection with the onset of internal negotiations. Given that I have shown external talks to be much weaker predictors of war termination than their internal counterparts, we see that minor powers are more easily press-ganged into negotiations and that these discussions have a somewhat weak track record of producing sufficient concessions to settle the war.

Based on these results, some may conclude that the post-1945 effect is simply a consequence of more wars being between minor powers after World War II. This is not the case; roughly half of wars feature only minor powers across both periods.[45] The effects related to minor powers are relevant across two centuries of fighting.

Determinants of Third-Party Pressure

My analysis of internal and external negotiations reveals valuable insights about the effects of latent pressures for peace. In particular, I produce evidence that higher latent pressures for peace from third-party actors create ideal conditions for negotiations that are likely to be insincere. Yet we must remember that third-party efforts to promote peace are not randomly assigned. States and international organizations outside a conflict are strategic actors that decide whether and when to apply pressure in hopes of spurring negotiations.[46] Previous research by Jacob Bercovitch and Scott Gartner finds a negative relationship between mediation efforts and their success. Bercovitch and Gartner suggest that this initially discouraging assessment is the product of a selection effect where mediators

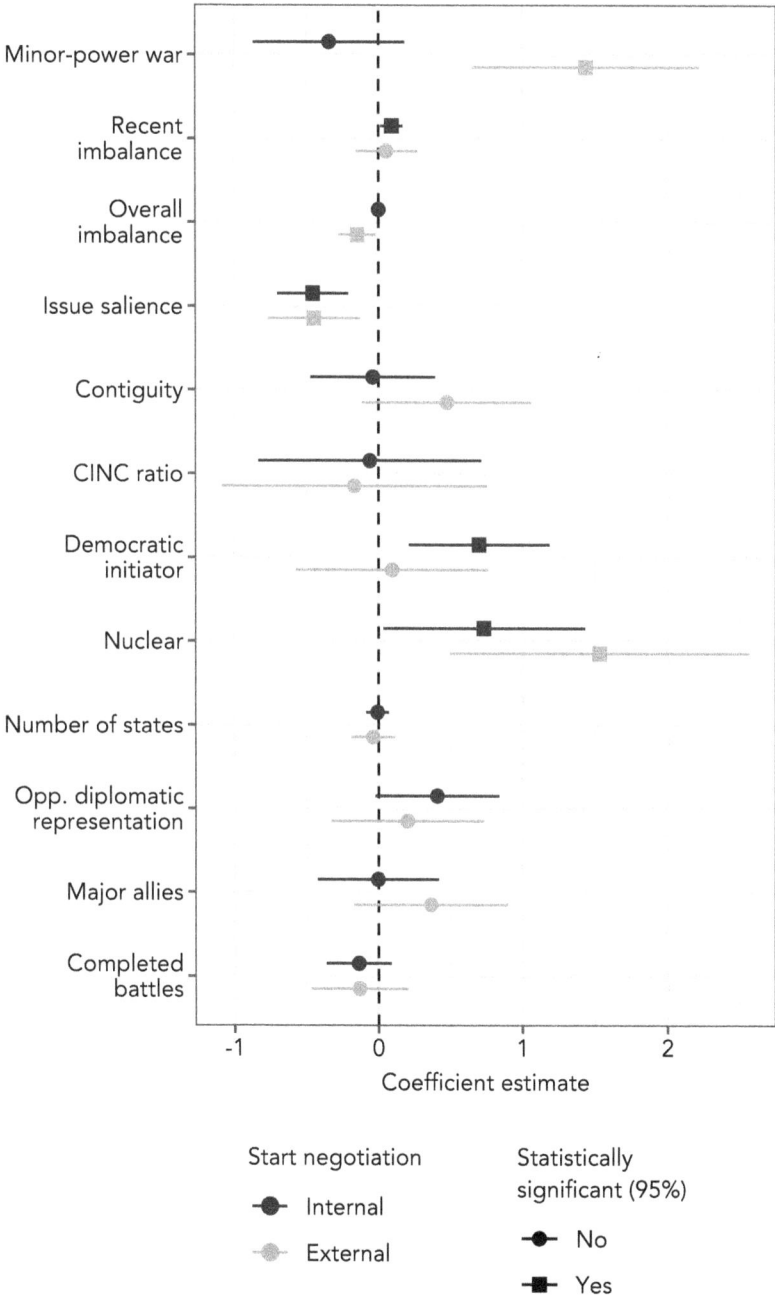

FIGURE 3.6. Coefficient plots for multistate models of negotiation onset, disaggregated by third-party pressure. Bands represent 95 percent confidence intervals (*N* = 36,864).

involve themselves in the most challenging cases where chances of long-term peace are already low.[47] If this argument regarding mediation is true, then my results regarding negotiations more broadly could be an artifact of third parties applying pressure in conflict scenarios that are relatively hopeless, leading to negotiations that simply have dim prospects regardless of belligerents' sincerity. The existence of a selection effect would not wholly nullify my argument; third parties may involve themselves in more difficult conflicts while also contributing to the higher failure rate of the talks that they spearhead. Nonetheless, it is worth addressing this potential issue directly.

An ideal quantitative test that would address the possibility of a selection effect would involve data that track all third-party diplomatic efforts to encourage negotiations, and not only ones that came to pass. Such data would shed light on what factors are responsible for the actual activation of external pressures in war and whether they are correlated with the intractability of a war. I can approximate such a test for post-1945 conflicts using the International Conflict Management (ICM) dataset.[48] The ICM dataset is a large-scale quantitative effort by Jacob Bercovitch to document all acts of conflict management around the world between 1945 and 1999, regardless of whether they had any success.[49] The dataset contains information on the first day that a conflict management effort began, as well as whether that effort ultimately produced any negotiated concessions.

The ICM dataset provides evidence that third-party diplomatic intervention attempts frequently took place in the early stages of overall conflicts. Of 151 total diplomatic interventions, 75 (49.7 percent) occurred in the first third of wars' eventual durations, and 61 of these 75 attempts either failed to convince belligerents to negotiate or did not generate any concessions. The remaining 14 resulted in some concessions but not enough to stop hostilities. This trend of early interventions followed by a drop-off in efforts stands in tension with the selection effect story, which would predict that more diplomatic efforts should occur as a conflict lengthens.[50]

Figure 3.7 applies a hazard model to the daily-level data to explore what factors affect the likelihood of third parties launching diplomatic efforts. Multiple results contradict the idea that third parties choose to intervene in the bleakest moments. Tellingly, we see more evidence that wars involving minor powers—which are more susceptible to external pressure than wars involving major powers—invite far more frequent intervention attempts. The point estimate suggests that the likelihood of such an attempt is higher by a factor of 7.4 for minor-power wars relative to the baseline rate.

Meanwhile, we find no statistically significant effect for issue salience, nuclear belligerents, the total number of belligerents, or the number of completed battles—all four of which would increase complexity and thus decrease prospects for peace.

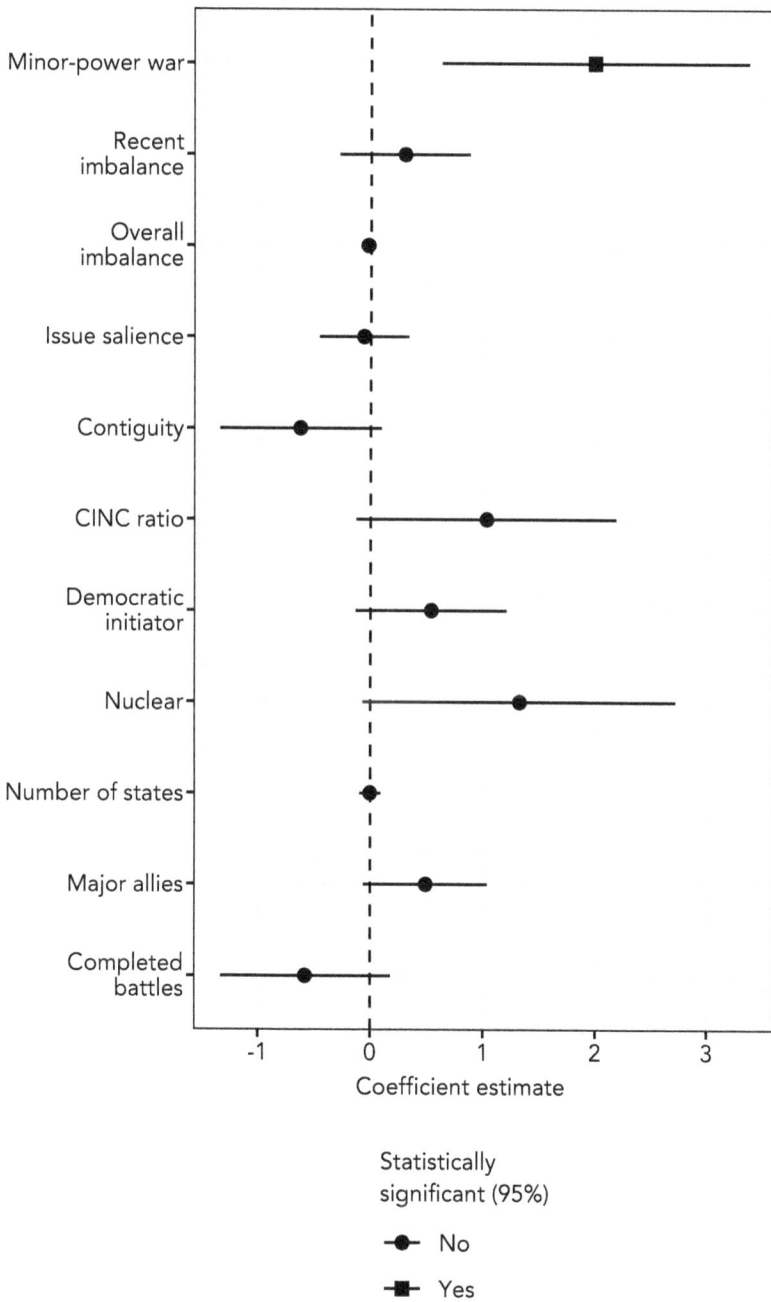

FIGURE 3.7. Coefficient plots for survival model of third-party diplomatic interventions in post-1945 wars. Bands represent 95 percent confidence intervals ($N = 11{,}398$).

The result for battlefield outcomes is also noteworthy. Third-party diplomatic efforts do not appear to be informed by recent or overall levels of imbalance. This is consistent with my theory's expectation that the relationship between the battlefield and the bargaining table becomes loosened in an environment with high levels of latent pressures for peace.

Outside appeals for diplomacy appear to be more frequent in minor-power conflicts and perhaps before belligerents have a meaningful chance to fight—and thus exchange information—to the best of their abilities. It should be unsurprising that talks borne of these efforts are, at best, a weak predictor of conflict termination and liable to be abused in service of the conflict. These trends indicate that external negotiations prompted by third-party diplomatic pressures are not systematically associated with intentional intervention in the toughest cases. At least after 1945, selection effects are not responsible for my findings.

As a whole, the array of results I have presented show that outside diplomatic pressure, captured using the post-1945 liberal international order as well as distinctions between major and minor powers, is associated with higher rates of negotiations but also a lower rate of success in formulating a mutually acceptable settlement. The political, institutional, and normative environment that surrounds the belligerents plays a meaningful part in shaping belligerents' incentives to engage in diplomacy during war. Critically, my theory and findings emphasize that the choice of whether to talk to the enemy is distinct from the choice of whether to seriously attempt to make peace with the enemy.

Two Wars between Greece and Turkey

My quantitative results, which use new data at the war-day level of analysis, reveal novel and systematic patterns regarding the strategic logic of negotiating during war. At the same time, these patterns are broad, and they are identified using coarse variables that serve as proxies for key concepts. One may wonder the extent to which external pressures are truly responsible for the occurrence and outcomes of wartime diplomacy. I buttress this claim by briefly comparing the story of negotiations in two conflicts: the Greco-Turkish War of 1897 and the Turco-Cypriot War of 1974.

I choose these cases for three reasons. First, they exist on opposite sides of the year 1945, which plays a prominent role in my empirical tests to this point. Second, the conflicts involve the same set of key states: Greece on one side and the Ottoman Empire, or Turkey starting in 1919, on the other. While three other pairs of wars also satisfy these two criteria, they also involve multiple states on at least one side in at least one war, which inhibits clean comparisons.[51] Third, both wars were sparked by disputes over the control of an island with significant historical and ethnic connections to the opposing parties. The two islands central to the two conflicts are also roughly similar in size. Holding the belligerents and issues roughly constant mitigates concerns that any observed differences in negotiation behavior exist because I am comparing different pairs of states with distinct pasts, areas of disagreement, or other dyadic attributes.[52]

The Greco-Turkish War of 1897

For years, Greece and Turkey disagreed over the fate of Crete. An island roughly three times the size of Rhode Island, Crete rests about 150 miles southeast of mainland Greece and 200 miles southwest of mainland Turkey. Figure 3.8 illustrates the geographical relationships between the two disputants and their object of dispute.

The proximate origins of the war arose in the 1878 Congress of Berlin, which was arranged to address outstanding issues following the Russians' victory in the Russo-Turkish War of 1877–78. The congress was led by six major European powers: Austria-Hungary, France, Germany, Great Britain, Italy, and Russia. As one outcome of the diplomatic gathering, Crete, which had been under Ottoman rule since 1669, was to remain in Turkish hands but also be granted some limited political autonomy.

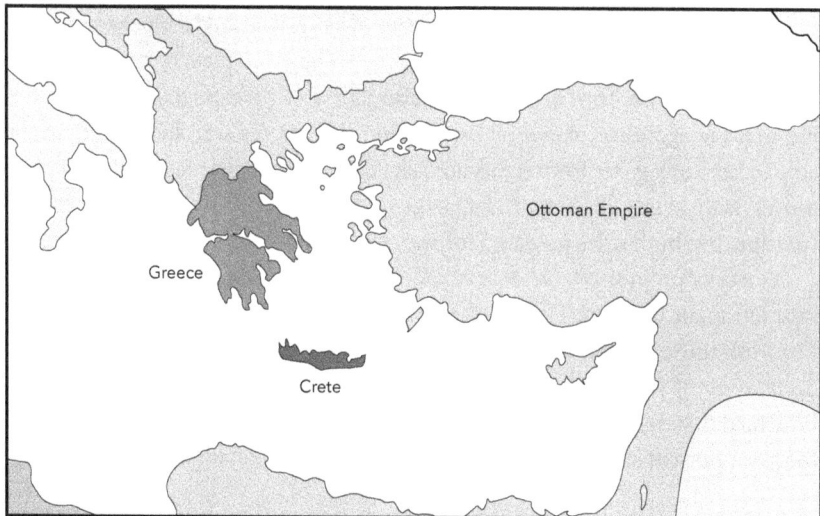

FIGURE 3.8. Map of Crete in 1895.

Crete had deep historical roots in the Greek and Roman empires, and the majority of its population was ethnically Greek. This majority had expressed its opposition to Ottoman rule on numerous occasions, staging at least eight revolts. Being granted autonomy, many Greek Cretans sought to be unified with Greece—a state that had declared independence from the Ottoman Empire in 1830 after a yearslong war of independence. Indeed, many ethnic Greeks in Europe spent the second half of the nineteenth century fixated on the "Megali Idea" (or "Great Idea") of liberating Greeks from Ottoman rule and restoring the Byzantine Empire.[53] The Ottomans were unwilling to allow this irredentist movement to make any progress.

Over the following two decades, the Turks dragged their feet on instituting meaningful reforms.[54] By early 1897, tensions between Greek Cretans and the Turkish regime reached a state of crisis. A local revolt in Canea, the island's capital, led to an alleged massacre where Ottoman troops killed numerous civilians. Greece soon deployed warships to patrol the waters around Crete, and by February, a Greek corps numbering 1,500 under Colonel Timoleon Vassos was sent to Crete with orders to take control of the island.[55] On February 14, Vassos landed at Canea and unilaterally declared that Crete was now taken in the name of Greece.[56]

The great powers, responsible for upholding the terms of the 1878 Congress of Berlin, were alarmed by these developments and attempted to defuse the situation. The powers sent a joint note to both the Greeks and the Turks stating that, in accordance with existing agreements, Crete could not be annexed. Greece had to withdraw its forces from the island, and in exchange, the Ottomans had to move forward with Cretan autonomy.[57] By March 21, a naval squadron comprising warships and personnel from the great powers established a blockade around Crete to stop further Greek reinforcements.[58] The great powers attempted one last-ditch effort on April 6, when they submitted a verbal note to both states stating that the aggressor would be held responsible for the war and would not be able to keep any gains from fighting.[59] The Ottoman Empire responded to these moves with highly diplomatic language and expressed a desire for a peaceful solution, but both sides prepared for war all the same.

As weeks progressed, Greek irregular forces were repeatedly found crossing into Ottoman territory. Despite the Greek government's denial of any association with those forces, the Porte had had enough. The sultan approved a formal declaration of war on April 17.[60] The Greek ambassador at Constantinople was informed that diplomatic relations were severed, and both the general public and the great powers learned of these developments the following day.[61]

A WINDING ROAD TO DIPLOMACY

The opening days of the conflict seemed auspicious for Greece. While limited hostilities occurred in Crete itself, the main campaign took place in the region of

Thessaly, a northern area of Greece that the great powers had transferred from the Ottomans in the 1881 Convention of Constantinople. Upon declaring war, the Ottoman Empire deployed troops, under the command of Edhem Pasha, into Thessaly. Edhem Pasha would soon encounter Crown Prince Constantine of Greece, who commanded Greece's troops. Between April 17 and 18, Turkish forces were temporarily repulsed by approximately 1,200 Greeks situated in the mountains near the village of Nezeros.[62] Two days later, once Crown Prince Constantine received reinforcements, he moved north and managed to reclaim the town of Vigla from Turkish forces by launching a heavy artillery bombardment.

But these victories would not last. The Greek army was poorly organized and equipped, and it was managed by substandard officers who tended to retreat from hostilities.[63] On April 18, Turkish forces had taken control of the Meluna Pass, which was essential to north–south movement. On April 22 and 23, Edhem Pasha amassed his forces near the town of Mati (in the northern part of Thessaly) and defeated the Greeks. Between the twenty-third and twenty-fifth, both Greek soldiers and civilians fled from the town of Tyrnavos and the city of Larissa, which was Constantine's headquarters during the war. Greek forces were eventually forced to retreat further south to the towns of Velestino and Pharsalus.

Reports on these developments caused alarm in Athens and also among the great powers, which were all taken aback by Greece's disastrous military prospects. Around the time Mati fell to the Turks, Greek officials relayed to the powers their interest in talks but refused to make this request on their own. Some form of external pressure would thus be necessary to instigate talks. Officials from France, Great Britain, and Russia discussed the possibility of offering terms of peace and mediation services to the belligerents. But the great powers did not fully agree on what preconditions they would require of the belligerents in order to move forward with diplomatic intervention. A week and a half passed between the first internal discussions on a mediation offer and the making of the actual offer itself. Emperor Wilhelm II of Germany created the highest barriers to diplomatic outreach, insisting that Greece had to admit defeat, withdraw all forces from Crete, and, in the emperor's own words, "throw herself at the mercy of the Powers."[64] The great powers excluding Germany signed a démarche offering to mediate on May 6.

While the great powers had discussed the terms for mediation among themselves for almost two weeks, Greece's military prospects cratered further. A total of 13,000 Turkish soldiers encountered a less well-equipped collection of 9,000 Greeks in Velestino on April 30.[65] The Turks were initially repulsed after an ill-fated cavalry charge that cost at least 1,200 casualties.[66]

In the brief lull after this attack, Greek officials—growing increasingly anxious about their battlefield fortunes—privately informed the great powers on May 3 that Greece was interested in talks, but that they "would like the initiative to be taken by the Great Powers" in order to provide political cover for the government in Athens.[67] The Greeks would have to wait three more days for the great powers to make this offer.

This waiting period came at a significant cost. On May 5, Turkish forces initiated a new assault at Velestino. The clash was costly for both sides but also depleted the Greek soldiers' ammunition. Contemporaneous to this second attack, the Ottoman army launched a major assault in Pharsalus. The simultaneous battles were overwhelming for the Greeks, who on May 5 and 6 were forced to abandon both Velestino and Pharsalus and head further south to Domokos.[68]

It was now evident that Greece's fortunes were doomed. On May 8, the government in Athens agreed to the great powers' demands, including Germany's additional requirement that all Greek troops be withdrawn from Crete.[69] Two days later, Greece also distributed a statement that pledged to recognize Crete's autonomy—yet another precondition added by Germany at the last second. Greece's willingness to accept these increasingly humiliating terms was a testament to how hopeless the military cause had become. The great powers presented these updates to the Ottomans on May 12 and requested Turkish assent to mediation. Five days later, Constantine staged one last battle against the converging Turkish forces in Domokos. Edhem Pasha forced the Greeks into one final retreat before the Ottomans agreed to a ceasefire and great-power mediation.

Greece's fervor and enthusiasm over the Megali Idea was ultimately not matched by Greece's military capabilities to realize it. On May 20, thirty-two days after hostilities began, Greek and Turkish representatives met to negotiate near Lamia, only a handful of miles south of the final battle in Domokos. An armistice was immediately signed that day, formally ending hostilities and the war, which had taken the lives of approximately two thousand soldiers across both sides.[70] The preliminaries of peace were signed in Constantinople on September 18, and the official Treaty of Constantinople was signed on December 4.[71] Over the coming months, the great powers used their weight to shape specific terms regarding territory, indemnities, and political arrangements in Crete. All were unfavorable to Greece. A small portion of Thessaly was given to the Ottomans, and Greece was ordered to pay a large indemnity to the Turks. An international commission would be created to manage the Greek economy and ensure that this indemnity was paid.[72] In exchange, the Turks would grant authority over Crete to an internationally supervised protectorate.

LITTLE CHOICE BUT TO ACCEPT DEFEAT

The Greco-Turkish War of 1897 offers a useful illustration of an environment with relatively weaker latent external pressures for peace. This is not to argue, however, that a peace lobby did not exist in the pre-1945 era. The great powers viewed themselves as guarantors of a fragile order in Europe, and they made efforts both to prevent the war and to mediate a diplomatic resolution between Greece and Turkey. Given how reticent the Greeks were to make a request for peace, it is quite possible that the war would have continued beyond May 20 if the great powers had not become involved. Indeed, the sultan appears to have stopped hostilities following the battle at Domokos because of an urgent entreaty by Tsar Nicholas II of Russia.[73] Turkish troops may have kept marching toward Athens if not for great-power pressure.[74]

Yet at the same time, the process the great powers navigated to determine the terms for mediation was slow and fractured. The powers were all uneasy about the "Eastern question" of how the European order would be revised if the waning Ottoman Empire eventually collapsed. Seeking to avoid a new crisis in southeastern Europe, but also deeply suspicious of one another's motives, the great powers moved deliberately and in hopes of maintaining a consensus diplomatic position.[75] In that light, Germany's constant insistence on imposing more onerous preconditions on Greece delayed the powers' ability to relay a unified offer of mediation. The official démarche eventually agreed on by the five other powers was circulated on May 6, which was almost 60 percent of the way into the war's eventual duration.

Greece's diplomatic behavior attests to the perceived costs that belligerents face when considering peace talks. News of battlefield losses in late April were so politically costly that Prime Minister Theodoros Deliyiannis was pushed into resigning on the twenty-seventh.[76] The new government led by Dimitrios Rallis was eager to stop the war and arguably had a mandate to do so.[77] Nevertheless, newly appointed Greek foreign minister Stefanos Skouloudis could send the aforementioned message only on May 3, and he mentioned that domestic tumult disallowed the government in Athens from making the first move and that the powers had to publicly intervene first. When Edhem Pasha's forces overtook Domokos and pushed toward Athens, the Rallis government still did not publicly announce an interest in negotiations. Officials instead pleaded with the great powers to intervene on May 19, which likely led Tsar Nicholas II to help stop the Turkish advance.[78] The fact that the Greeks had to implore the great powers to push for diplomacy—as opposed to a hypothetical world where the Greeks constantly refused the great powers' appeals for diplomacy—indicates the relatively weak pressures for peace that the great powers were placing directly on the belligerents, as well as the urgency that Greece felt to end a futile war.

Hypothesis 1 derived from my theory suggests that when external pressures are relatively low, negotiations should be infrequent but also sincere and likely to end hostilities when they do take place. Moreover, Hypothesis 3 predicts that negotiations should be more likely to end hostilities when the battlefield trends in one side's favor. Both implications are borne out in this war. The armistice talks on May 20 almost immediately ended hostilities because Greece saw no other options at that point. Even though Greece managed to maintain the facade that the great powers had imposed diplomacy on both parties, the military circumstances for Greece were dire. The terms did not pose any existential threat to Greece and exchanged very little territory, partially because the great powers did not want to rattle the status quo ante bellum. Greece's punishments were mainly financial, economic, political, and reputational. The fact that the Athenian government accepted these embarrassing and repentant conditions was a visible testament to its desperate situation. Negotiations were perceived by the belligerents as highly costly to initiate on their own and required a very clear battlefield trend that overshadowed the risks inherent to seeking diplomacy. Talks were therefore slow to start, but because such acute circumstances were necessary for negotiations to occur in the first place, they also brought the war to a swift end.

The Turco-Cypriot War of 1974

Seventy-seven years after a war over the island of Crete, Greece and Turkey found themselves in another struggle over another island: Cyprus. That island, about 3,500 square miles in size, is slightly larger than Crete. Although figure 3.8 is primarily meant to identify Crete, Cyprus is the other large island to the east. Figure 3.9 provides a more detailed view.

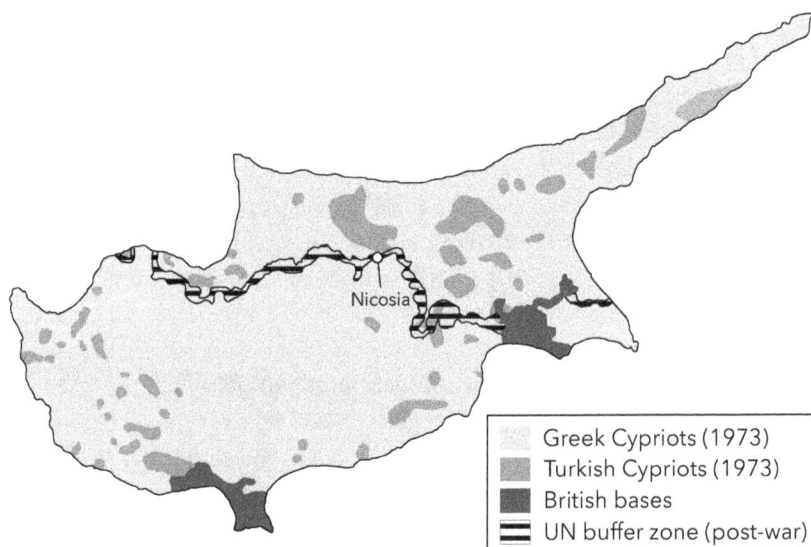

FIGURE 3.9. Map of Cyprus.

Cyprus was settled by Greeks several thousand years ago, and numerous empires took control of the island over the centuries. Between 1571 and 1878, Cyprus was part of the Ottoman Empire. The same Congress of Berlin in 1878 that set the stage for the 1897 Greco-Turkish War in Crete played a significant role in Cyprus as well. In a secret agreement during the congress, the British obtained administrative control of Cyprus in exchange for establishing military bases to defend the Ottomans from the Russian Empire.[79] The United Kingdom would subsequently annex the island from the declining Ottoman Empire, abrogating the agreement, in 1911.

As a consequence of Cyprus's history, the vast majority of the island's population was Greek. Many Greek Cypriots sought to unite Cyprus with Greece—an idea known as *enosis* ("union" in Greek). In 1955, some Greek Cypriots formed a nationalist paramilitary organization called EOKA (the Greek acronym for National Organization of Cypriot Fighters) to realize this goal. Turkish Cypriots, many of whom had sought to divide Cyprus between Greece and Turkey (*taksim*, which means "division" in Turkish), became worried that enosis would turn them into a highly vulnerable minority group. Growing concerns about the risk of war led Greece, Turkey, and the United Kingdom to agree that the best solution would be to allow Cyprus to become its own state.

The resulting 1960 Treaty of Guarantee between Cyprus, Greece, Turkey, and the United Kingdom prohibited Cyprus from uniting with any other state, guaranteed the integrity and security of Cyprus, and assigned the three non-Cypriot parties as guarantors of this arrangement.[80] The Republic of Cyprus came into being on August 16, 1960, and the nation's first president was Archbishop Makarios III—a fervent and influential champion of enosis.

Continuing ethnic tensions posed an immediate challenge to the new state's stability. Upon independence, approximately 78 percent of the population was Greek, and 18 percent was Turkish.[81] The Cypriot constitution of 1960 attempted to divide power between these two groups to ensure that each had a voice in government. Turkish Cypriots were given 30 percent of all government positions and would make up 40 percent of the army. The vice president would be a Turkish Cypriot, and both the president and vice president were granted wide-ranging veto powers.[82]

Pro-enosis Greek Cypriots grew increasingly frustrated by inhibitions to their dreams. In December 1963, Greek Cypriots attempted to push through a series of constitutional amendments that would strip the Turkish Cypriots of their political rights. A civil conflict erupted between the end of 1963 and the summer of 1964. The United Nations established a peacekeeping force in Cyprus (UNFICYP) as well as a buffer zone known as the "Green Line," which divided the island into northern and southern regions, in an attempt to strike a ceasefire in December 1963. These efforts had limited effects. Many Turkish Cypriots were pushed into the Turkish quarter of Nicosia (the capital city), and others lost or abandoned their property. In June 1964, the Greek Cypriots in government unilaterally established the National Guard in an attempt to consolidate all military power on the island under Greek control.

Makarios's government spent the next few years uninterested in enosis. Several factors contributed to this apparent reversal in policy preferences. First, a sudden economic boom for Greek Cypriots set them on a better trajectory than citizens in Greece.[83] Second, Greece was overtaken by a military dictatorship under Georgios Papadopoulos between 1967 and 1973. Third, Makarios appeared to enjoy being president and was loath to give up this role, which he would have to do if Cyprus was incorporated into the Greek state.[84]

Extreme Greek nationalists banded together with elements of the military junta in Greece and guerrilla organizations in Cyprus to effect unification by force. Several unsuccessful assassination attempts failed to eliminate the archbishop, who continued to seek harsher measures against the Turkish Cypriots while making no steps toward enosis. Many of these attacks were staged by members of the armed organization EOKA B, a revival of EOKA that was created in 1971 by General Georgios Grivas, another influential figure in the enosis movement, who died in 1974. On November 25, 1973, Papadopoulos was tossed from power in Greece during a military coup by Dimitrios Ioannidis. Ioannidis and his compatriots had more direct connections to Cyprus and had served under Grivas in the past. The new military regime in Greece took action to remove Makarios from power and to press forward with enosis. On July 15, Ioannidis used the Cypriot National Guard to stage a military coup d'état that caused Makarios to flee the island. The Guard installed Nikos Sampson, a journalist and radical proenosis nationalist, as president of the new regime.

Turkey had watched developments in Cyprus over the last thirteen years with great consternation, but Makarios's lack of interest in unification had kept the Turks from interfering in Cypriot affairs. The July 15 coup was a bridge too far. Turkish prime minister Bülent Ecevit conferred with British prime minister Harold Wilson, invoking the obligations of the 1960 Treaty of Guarantee to convince the UK to help restore the Makarios regime. Ecevit requested that Turkish forces be allowed to use the existing British bases to enter Cyprus and protect the Turkish Cypriots. The UK declined—an outcome Ecevit fully expected. A day later, on July 18, Ecevit spoke with US officials and enumerated Turkey's demands: a withdrawal of Greek officers from Cyprus, the admission of Turkish troops in Cyprus, and equal rights for Greek and Turkish Cypriots. The Ioannidis government refused to consider such terms.[85] Exhausting its diplomatic options, Turkey took unilateral military action.[86] Around six o'clock in the morning on July 20,

Turkish forces initiated their first military operation, landing near Kyrenia on the north shore of the island. The Turkish government informed the UN, US, and UK of its intentions to honor the Treaty of Guarantee by intervening on Turkish Cypriots' behalf.[87] Turkish troops faced significant resistance from both Greek and Greek Cypriot forces. Realizing an invasion was at hand, Greece mobilized within hours and moved some troops to the Greek-Turkish border. The war for Cyprus had begun.

HIGH PRESSURES, CONSTANT DIPLOMACY

External pressures to end the conflict and return to diplomacy were both immediate and sizable. The day the war began, the United Nations Security Council unanimously adopted Resolution 353, demanding the withdrawal of all foreign military personnel and calling on the belligerents to "enter into negotiations without delay for the restoration of peace."[88] For weeks, Secretary of Defense and National Security Adviser Henry Kissinger had been concerned with developments in Cyprus. He frequently corresponded with British foreign secretary James Callaghan to discuss diplomatic strategies to manage the conflict. With President Nixon fixated on political fallout from the Watergate scandal (which would lead to his resignation on August 9, in the middle of the war), Kissinger deployed Under Secretary of State Joseph Sisco to join Callaghan and meet Ecevit with the intention of offering a four-point request to cease further hostilities.

Collective efforts by Sisco and Callaghan were significant enough to push both Greece and Turkey to accept a nominal ceasefire while representatives met to start negotiations in Geneva. When the ceasefire came into effect on July 22, the Turks had captured only about 3 percent of Cyprus. Attempting to place more weight on diplomacy, NATO officials staged a ninety-minute emergency meeting immediately following the ceasefire and publicly urged Greece and Turkey to bring fighting to a halt and enter "prompt and successful discussions" to prevent matters from "threaten[ing] the existence of the alliance."[89] A coup in Greece on the same day, as well as the removal of Nicos Sampson from power in Cyprus a day later, delayed the start of talks by three days.

The Geneva conference commenced on July 25. Diplomats from Greece and Turkey—led by Greek foreign minister George Mavros and Turkish foreign minister Turan Güneş, respectively—were guided through mediation by Callaghan. With hostilities somewhat paused, Callaghan attempted to forge a more permanent peace. As talks proceeded for several days, however, it became obvious that the two sides' positions were far apart and unlikely to appreciably change. The three states could not even agree on whether the Geneva talks were taking place because those states were the guarantors of the 1960 Treaty of Guarantee or because they had been pushed into talks by Resolution 353. Greece sought an immediate cessation of Turkey's military activities and the withdrawal of troops to prewar positions. Turkey had no intention of reversing its gains. On the eve of talks, Ecevit publicly declared that "Turkish presence on the island is now irrevocably established."[90] Turkey frequently violated the ceasefire based on the claim that Turkish Cypriots and Turkish soldiers were being attacked.[91] Ecevit's government demanded that all Turkish Cypriot enclaves be reverted back to the prewar status quo, that Turkish troops should be allowed to remain on the island with no limits on further reinforcements, and that Turkish Cypriots should be granted full autonomy.[92] A request by the Greeks for a map of a provisional ceasefire line was also rejected.

Nevertheless, by July 30, the Geneva conference ended with a joint declaration among all parties and shaped by both the UK and the US, calling for a ceasefire, security zones, exchange of military prisoners and civilians, a gradual reduction of armed forces on the island, and further negotiations to begin on August 8. Critical questions regarding the size of the security zone and the responsibilities of the UNFICYP in administering this peace were not resolved and were instead pushed to the second round of talks. Greek Cypriot and Turkish Cypriot representatives would be invited to the next negotiations. Even though the declaration was meant to be only preliminary and tentative in nature, it still contained some noteworthy language. Importantly for the Turkish Cypriots, the declaration "noted the existence in practice in the Republic of Cyprus of two autonomous administrations." The document emphasized that this observation would not bring "any prejudice to the conclusions to be drawn from the situation," but it was clear that enosis was likely off the table.[93]

Turkey's ability to dictate many terms in Geneva was a testament to its superior military position. An initial contingent of 750 Turkish soldiers in Cyprus, placed there in the past, was first reinforced with 8,000 more soldiers and ultimately expanded to a final total of 40,000 troops with two hundred tanks.[94] The Greeks mustered approximately 14,000 men but were unable to properly reinforce or resupply them when their ships were intercepted and destroyed by Turkish vessels. Turkey pressed this advantage over the course of negotiations. The five days of talks in Geneva had quieted the battlefield, but the ceasefire was repeatedly violated by the Turks. The Turkish army made numerous advances between July 25 and 29. On the twenty-ninth, Turkish troops warned UN peacekeepers to leave their camps near Kyrenia. Between July 29 and August 1, Turkey took its time in demarcating the front line as required by the joint declaration, using the opportunity to make more territorial gains without much Greek resistance.[95] S. J. L. Olver, British higher commissioner in Cyprus, noted on August 1 that it was "clear that until we get a cease fire line demarcated and properly policed, the Turkish military will go on extending their area."[96] Olver and other observers were not wrong. Between the two Geneva conferences, Turkish forces pressed westward with minimal resistance. The demarcation committee, which was tasked with determining the demarcation line mentioned in the July 30 declaration, found significant differences between lines as they stood on July 30 and where they stood during the committee's first meeting three days later. Turkish troops also began to forcibly evict and relocate Greek Cypriots from newly "liberated" areas on August 3. Greek Cypriots were firmly told that they would never return.[97] These efforts, which were human rights violations on their own, were also paired with other atrocities such as kidnapping, rape, forced starvation, and murder of civilians.[98]

When a second round of talks began on August 8, Turkey had increased its territorial control of Cyprus from 3 percent to about 15 percent.[99] A confident Turkish delegation returned to the language of the July 30 declaration and proposed that Cyprus become a republic with two administrative autonomous regions. The northern region would be Turkish, the southern region would be Greek, and all Cypriots would need to relocate to these respective areas. A new constitution would be necessary for this arrangement. The Greek delegation refused this idea and insisted on reverting back to and potentially amending the 1960 constitution. On August 11, with the indirect prodding of Henry Kissinger in Washington, Turkey made a new proposal involving the establishment of several autonomous Turkish Cypriot cantons around Cyprus. Since both the partition and canton plans granted about 30 percent of the island to the Turkish Cypriots, the Greeks balked at both proposals.[100] The same day, the Greeks also noted with concern that Turkish aircraft and military appeared to be mobilizing.[101] Desperate mediation by both Callaghan and Kissinger on August 13 and 14 produced no further compromises. According to Glafcos Clerides, the temporary president of Cyprus after Nico Sampson's removal, no Greek Cypriot could accept the Turks' terms "in 15 days or even in 15 years. The geographical limits were inconceivable."[102]

At 2:25 on the morning of August 14, the Geneva talks failed. Turkish air fighters began bombing the capital city of Nicosia hours later.[103] Reinforced Turkish troops proceeded to make a largely unopposed advance down Cyprus until they reached the buffer zone (the Green Line) that the UN had established in 1963. The northern half of Cyprus, or about 38 percent of the island's total area, was effectively under Turkish control.[104] On August 16, Security Council Resolution 360 formally disapproved of Turkey's actions and urged all parties to comply with Resolution 353. By that point, Turkey had obtained its objective of securing an autonomous region for Turkish Cypriots, and the government in Ankara therefore agreed to the ceasefire mandated in Resolution 353. The war ended twenty-seven days after it began, with at least six thousand Greek Cypriots, one thousand Turkish Cypriots, and three hundred Turkish soldiers dead.[105] In the coming weeks and months, about fifty thousand Turkish Cypriots were displaced to the north, while two hundred thousand Greek Cypriots fled south.[106]

NEGOTIATION THEATER

In contrast to the Greco-Turkish War of 1897, the Turco-Cypriot War shows what happens in an environment with strong latent external pressures for peace. Serious diplomatic force was triggered on the first day of the war. The United Nations immediately launched into action by adopting Resolution 353, which called for the territorial integrity of Cyprus, the withdrawal of foreign military, a ceasefire, negotiations by the three guarantor states, and cooperation with the existing peacekeeping mission on the island. While Turkey did not accede to Resolution 353 until August 16, the resolution's existence loomed over talks at Geneva. One of the first joint press releases distributed during the Geneva conference explicitly mentioned all three parties' commitment—however genuine it may or may not have been—to upholding Resolution 353.[107]

Regardless of the resolution, the largest direct sources of diplomatic pressure came from the United Kingdom and the United States.[108] The Geneva talks occurred on the sixth day of the war, 22 percent of the way into the conflict's overall duration, and one-third of the total conflict would involve formal talks between the belligerents. A prominent feature of the Anglo-American diplomatic effort was its lack of coordination. Both parties eagerly sought peace but had differing views on the scale and nature of that peace. Callaghan, serving as the official mediator, aimed to produce a stable ceasefire in order to allow the Cypriots to determine their own political solution. Kissinger, who was communicating with the belligerents directly from outside the Geneva talks, believed no peace was possible without a broader agreement that included a long-term constitutional arrangement that would grant Turkey some protections and concessions.[109] Though Kissinger introduced the idea of a cantonal arrangement to Ecevit on August 11, Callaghan learned of this proposal only when the Turkish ambassador to the UN mentioned it later that day. Callaghan angrily called the State Department, saying he "was not prepared to be a dummy in the middle."[110] Callaghan favored a plan that cleanly separated Greek and Turkish Cypriots. He therefore addressed the cantonal idea when other delegations mentioned it but made clear his fear that numerous cantons scattered around the island would increase the likelihood of conflict. Unlike in the 1897 war, however, policy differences between the third parties did not stop them from pressing the belligerents to settle, even if in slightly different directions.

In retrospect, the policy rifts that emerged during the Anglo-American push for a negotiated peace were immaterial in that they did not acknowledge a fundamental truth: Turkey had no interest in a diplomatic settlement. Talks in Geneva took place before the belligerents reached a common understanding of how the war would unfold. The Greeks, British, and Americans did not observe sufficient information to realize Turkey's serious ability and willingness to accomplish its goals by unilateral force. During a meeting on July 21, one day before both belligerents agreed to a ceasefire and talks, and at the point when Turks controlled only 3 percent of the island, Kissinger suggested that the Turks were "doing lousy militarily."[111] Weeks later, the Greeks still appeared to have a weak understanding of Turkey's military capabilities. Officials balked at the Turks' cantonal proposal on the basis that it would grant too much of the island—34 percent—to the Turkish Cypriots.[112] This Turkish proposal came with an ultimatum, which neither the government in Athens nor the one in Washington appeared to take seriously. The fact that Turkey ultimately seized almost 40 percent of Cyprus shows that most actors did not fully grasp what Turkey could accomplish. Negotiations that took place at this point in the conflict, before belligerents could fully activate their military capabilities, were unlikely to produce any self-enforcing peace.

My theory predicts that when external pressures are high and amounts of information from recent fighting are somewhat limited, negotiations will be relatively frequent but also used insincerely to further belligerents' war aims; such is the synthesis of Hypotheses 2 and 3. The Turco-Cypriot War bears this out. Constant diplomatic efforts by the United Kingdom and United States made it difficult for Greece and Turkey to sidestep negotiations. Efforts to avoid being pressured by third parties, which included a Turkish attempt to not grant clearance to a plane that was transporting Under Secretary of State Sisco to Ankara,[113] were not successful. On multiple occasions during the Geneva talks, Callaghan and Kissinger also persuaded both sides to stay at the bargaining table longer than they originally intended.

Although Kissinger and many in the State Department sought negotiations, others in Washington feared that diplomacy would only exacerbate the war. Secretary of Defense James Schlesinger, in particular, opposed the first round of Geneva negotiations due to concerns that the Turks would "bring in more troops under a ceasefire, reinforce here and there. That would change the whole picture."[114] The Turks not only reinforced troops in Cyprus but made significant territorial gains in violation of the ceasefire.

At the same time, Greece attempted to drag its feet during the July session in Geneva. Greek officials knew that the issue of Cyprus would go to the United Nations in early August. Consequently, Mavros's delegation chose to offer very few concessions, instead hoping that they could use late July and early August to reinvigorate their military while going on an international campaign to frame Turkey as a military occupier. The Greeks hoped that global disapproval of

Turkey would produce a new Security Council resolution that might force Turkey to pull back.[115]

The second round of negotiations in Geneva exhibited even more insincere behavior. Greece continued to use talks to reshape public sentiment against Turkey. Indeed, by early August, reports of Turkish atrocities were swiftly souring global support for Turkey.[116] Güneş expressed concerns that the new iteration of Geneva talks were being used by the Greeks to, in the *New York Times'* words, "stall for time, to wall in the Turkish force with barbed wire and to diminish its effectiveness."[117]

Turkey's accusations toward Greece may have been a form of projection. Political observers at the time suspected that Turkey was worried that protracted talks would enervate its bargaining position (which it knew was worsening due to international condemnation of Turkish troops' human rights violations) while allowing the Greeks and Greek Cypriots to recover both militarily and diplomatically.[118] Critically, Turkey also entered talks with an exit option in mind.[119] In the first week of August, Ecevit told Güneş that the military would be fully prepared for its next offensive in the next two or three days.[120] As such, if the Greeks and British did not accept Turkey's demands, Ecevit would furtively inform Güneş that troops were ready to go and that negotiations could continue but that the Cyprus affair would be resolved militarily. When Güneş was told on August 11 that Ecevit said "Ayşe [Güneş's daughter] should go on vacation," the encrypted message was sent.[121] Talks would continue, but mainly to go through the motions of diplomacy and to allay suspicions about Turkey's increasingly obvious troop mobilizations. Callaghan would later write in his memoir that Güneş constantly used stall tactics to gain time for Turkey to engage in military activity.[122] The government in Ankara therefore used discussions in Geneva to improve its reversion outcome. Once talks were terminated on August 14, Turkey was fully prepared to realize military victory.

The war would have likely proceeded differently in the absence of diplomatic pressure. Greece and Turkey would have been far less inclined to negotiate and may have refused to talk completely. The vast policy differences between Athens and Ankara during the first Geneva round further suggests that neither side would have reasonably sought to negotiate with the other only days into the war. Both Mavros and Güneş informed Callaghan that the highly unstable domestic environments in their respective countries (including the collapse of the military junta in Greece on July 23) prevented them from making significant concessions.[123] The ceasefire and negotiation between late July and mid-August were highly unlikely to have emerged organically without pressures from the UN, UK, and US. Despite numerous Turkish violations, the ceasefire significantly quieted the battlefield and gave both sides an opportunity to regroup.

To be sure, Greece and especially Turkey could have managed to replenish their military forces in the absence of negotiations. Turkey almost assuredly would have accomplished its objectives by force without spending any time talking to the UK or US. Nevertheless, the relative decline of active hostilities gave Turkey more breathing room to expand and organize its military presence to forty thousand men on its own terms, enabling more brutal and systematic atrocities against Greek Cypriots. Negotiations also had political consequences. Floating proposals and having Turkey reject them helped contribute to Greece's campaign to publicly vilify Turkey and pressure Ecevit's government to potentially pull its troops back. Greece did not succeed on this front, but that does not negate the fact that an attempt was made. Turkey was afforded the opportunity to (somewhat erroneously) justify its ceasefire violations as responses to Greek Cypriot aggression and to suggest that military action was reluctantly chosen as a last resort because Greece and the United Kingdom refused to compromise.

It is worth noting that Turkey's war objectives did not appreciably change during the entire conflict. On August 10, the Turkish government outlined its bargaining demands in an article in the newspaper *Milliyet*. The proposal involved a united republic with two autonomous regions and an allocation of 30 percent of Cyprus to the Turkish Cypriots. These terms were essentially the same as what British intelligence officials had reported on July 19 before the invasion began.[124] Turkey was thus highly unlikely to have tried seizing a larger portion of Cyprus if mediation never occurred. In sum, negotiations during the Turco-Cypriot War likely inflamed political animosities, prolonged the conflict, and worsened humanitarian suffering without changing the war's ultimate outcome. Wartime diplomacy, when deployed at inopportune moments, may have hurt more than it helped.

Placing Excessive Pressure on the Wound

This chapter has painted a multifaceted picture of wartime diplomacy. Factors both beyond and within an individual conflict have consequential effects on the initiation of negotiations as well as their likelihood of resolving wars.

My quantitative analysis has demonstrated that latent pressures for peace, embodied by the bevy of peace-centric institutions and the relationships that belligerents have with outside actors, broadly define how the act of negotiating can damage or improve a party's reversion outcome. Those pressures thus shape a belligerent's willingness to talk to the enemy. Wars that take place after 1945, as well as wars featuring only minor powers, undergo more frequent but unproductive negotiations. The day-to-day developments on the battlefield, which sculpt expectations about the trajectory of hostilities, further modulate whether diplomacy is sought sincerely or insincerely. Quiet and indeterminate phases of fighting offer little incentive for belligerents to settle using their words. It is when recent fighting reveals a clear trend in one belligerent's favor that any diplomatic interactions that do take place are more likely to be sincere and promptly lead to a settlement. New data, which capture conflicts at a level of granularity not yet seen in quantitative studies of war, were necessary to identify and explore these dynamics across two hundred years of conflict.

Comparisons of two wars between Greece and Turkey illustrate the importance of latent external pressures and the battlefield in more vivid terms. When third parties do relatively little to push belligerents toward diplomacy, as was the case with the great powers during the Greco-Turkish War of 1897, the states do not start talking until hostilities have provided enough information to change the diplomatic calculus. Greece overcame its concern about looking weak only when a series of battles made its weakness self-evident. Talks hastily brought the war to an end in the Ottomans' favor. In contrast, in the Turco-Cypriot War of 1974, the same two states were subjected to constant pressures to negotiate. Mediation in Geneva was hurried and persistent and brought the belligerents to the table long before any parties had a clear understanding of the war's likely trajectory. The talks, as well as the pockets of peace they helped create, enabled both Greece and Turkey to adjust their political and military strategies in hopes of improving their reversion outcomes when diplomacy foundered. These machinations failed to stop Turkey from achieving its original goal of creating an autonomous Turkish region in Cyprus.

My findings both reinforce and counter existing strands of conflict scholarship. When it comes to determining whether wars continue or conclude, the battlefield remains supreme. Bargaining models of war have consistently made the case that fighting provides the information necessary to resolve wars. My results reinforce that existing branch of scholarship while standing in contrast to ripeness theory, which would predict the opposite relationship between trends from fighting and negotiation onset. At the same time, my theory and analysis identify conditions in which negotiations are likely to occur yet are simultaneously unlikely to accomplish their professed objective of ending hostilities. Bargaining models of war would suggest that when a round of negotiations fails, the conflict resumes on the same path it had followed before talks began. Negotiations are presumed to have no impact on how the remainder of the conflict unfolds. Ripeness theory provides little insight into whether diplomatic talks are more or less likely to succeed in achieving peace, often implicitly assuming that negotiations presage settlement. I have shown that the frequent disjuncture between talking and settling indicates how negotiations are a much more complex and irregular activity than extant theories often presume. Diplomacy can worsen one's reversion outcome, and the combination of this concern with latent external pressures often helps to explain belligerents' unwillingness to talk to the enemy.

My analysis of the Turco-Cypriot War touches on the second half of my argument: whether negotiations, used insincerely and failing to produce peace, can instead produce side effects that improve an actor's reversion outcome and the subsequent trajectory of the conflict. While the 1974 conflict provides evidence in favor of this claim, we must address it more systematically and thoroughly. This is the task of the next chapter.

TALKING TO FIGHT

In the previous chapter, I provided evidence that a combination of latent external pressures and battlefield trends explains a great deal of negotiation strategy. I found consistent evidence that higher latent pressures for peace lead to more frequent negotiations, regardless of belligerents' actual desires to either stop or continue fighting. Simultaneously, a more distinct battlefield trend in one side's favor increases the likelihood that any negotiations that do take place are sincere efforts to resolve conflict. These findings support Hypotheses 1, 2, and 3 as characterized at the end of chapter 1.

While chapter 3 analyzed how battlefield activity can influence negotiation behavior, this chapter explores how negotiations can reshape the battlefield. Hypotheses 4 and 5 speak to these dynamics. This is an important test of my theory. If the only consequence of unsuccessful peace negotiations is that war continues on the same path as before talks began, then it is easier to dismiss diplomacy as a mechanical reflection of the battlefield. A core innovative claim I have made is that insincere negotiations not only fail to end hostilities but can be exploited to reshape the subsequent trajectory of conflict. Evidence that talks can affect the nature of fighting itself is therefore essential to painting a more complete picture of my conception of wartime negotiation.

This chapter provides that evidence. I first return to my quantitative data to substantiate the remaining two hypotheses derived from my theory. In support of Hypothesis 4, I confirm that periods of negotiation are associated with lower levels of active hostilities on the battlefield. The effect is especially pronounced for internal negotiations organized by the belligerents themselves. My theory suggests that these moments of relative quiet on the battlefield are natural for belligerents that sincerely want to stop fighting but also necessary for belligerents that merely want to abuse negotiations to improve their political and military position. On that note, I demonstrate that negotiations that do not result in peace are followed by battlefield trends that systematically differ from the state of fighting prior to the onset of talks. This result, which is consistent with Hypothesis 5, is novel and underscores the importance of viewing negotiations as a very real extension of war.

In the latter half of the chapter, I walk through a brief qualitative analysis of the relationship between fighting and negotiating in two conflicts: the War of the Roman Republic of 1849 and the Cenepa Valley War of 1995. Both support Hypotheses 4 and 5 but also more fully depict how belligerents can use diplomacy to directly sculpt the political and military battlefields in their favor.

Quantitative Analysis

Chapter 2 described the negotiation and battle data I have amassed to analyze ninety-two interstate conflicts between 1823 and 2003. I now use these data to investigate the relationship that negotiations have with both contemporaneous and subsequent battlefield activity.

A Quieter Battlefield

Hypothesis 4 as described in chapter 1 avers that negotiations should be associated with a lower level of active hostilities on the battlefield. I can use my quantitative negotiation and battle data to test this claim across dozens of interstate conflicts. To do so, I treat the number of active battles per war-day as the primary outcome of interest. This is a count variable, which is most appropriately analyzed using a Poisson model.[1] The key explanatory variable is the occurrence of negotiations on a given war-day. Standard errors are clustered by war.

Many of the control variables I include in these models are identical to those described in chapter 3, so they will not be repeated here. Three new variables, however, become relevant when considering the impact of negotiations on active hostilities. The first is my measure of *recent imbalance*. My own theory and analysis suggest that it is appropriate to account for contemporaneous battlefield trends when analyzing how diplomacy affects the state of the battlefield.

The second is the existence of a formal ceasefire. Many periods of negotiation also feature ceasefires that hold alongside diplomatic bargaining. For example, during the final phases of the Saudi-Yemeni War of 1934, Ibn Saud announced a ceasefire on all fronts when also indicating his willingness to negotiate with Yemen. Saudi Arabia had the upper hand on the battlefield at the time, and talks that took place alongside a ceasefire promptly forged an agreement filled with concessions by Yemen.[2] Ceasefires, by definition, are designed to pacify the battlefield. It is important to ensure that any effects I find regarding diplomacy are not simply consequences of ceasefires. I therefore include a binary variable for whether a *ceasefire* was active on a given war-day.

The third is the trend in the number of recent battles. One may be concerned about reverse causation: instead of negotiations leading to reduced hostilities, perhaps reduced hostilities precede negotiations. To account for this possibility, I take the number of battles that have taken place over the previous sixty days of war (or the entirety of the war to that point, whichever is closer) and determine the slope of the best-fitting line across those data. The estimated slope is a measure of an *active battle trend*.

Figure 4.1 reports the estimated effects from two models of active battles. The first model analyzes negotiations as a whole. The negative and statistically significant coefficient for the negotiation variable makes clear that periods of diplomacy feature quieter battlefields. Stated in more intuitive terms, the occurrence of talks is associated with a 30 percent decrease in the number of contemporaneous battles.

Other important patterns emerge upon disaggregating negotiations by whether they are internal or external. The disaggregated model shows that much of the pacifying effect of negotiation is driven by internal negotiations. Internal talks have a markedly negative and statistically significant effect, while external negotiations are associated with an estimated coefficient that is close to zero and is not statistically significant. Moreover, external talks are associated with a 6 percent decrease in the number of active battles from a baseline rate, while internal talks are associated with a much larger 43 percent decrease—a sevenfold jump. A linear hypothesis test verifies that this difference between the two coefficient estimates is statistically significant as well ($p \ll 0.01$). Negotiations primarily pursued by belligerents are more likely to be reflections of sincere intentions to stop fighting. Meanwhile, talks resulting from third-party efforts will create some drawdown in hostilities but reflect a more hollow effort to find a lasting peace. This is a natural implication of my theory.

Active battle trends over the previous sixty days exhibit a positive and statistically significant relationship with the number of active battles on a given war-day. This is hardly unexpected, yet recall that the purpose of including this variable was to address concerns of reverse causality. Even after adding this measure to the regressions, we still see that negotiations have a meaningful impact on contemporaneous levels of fighting.

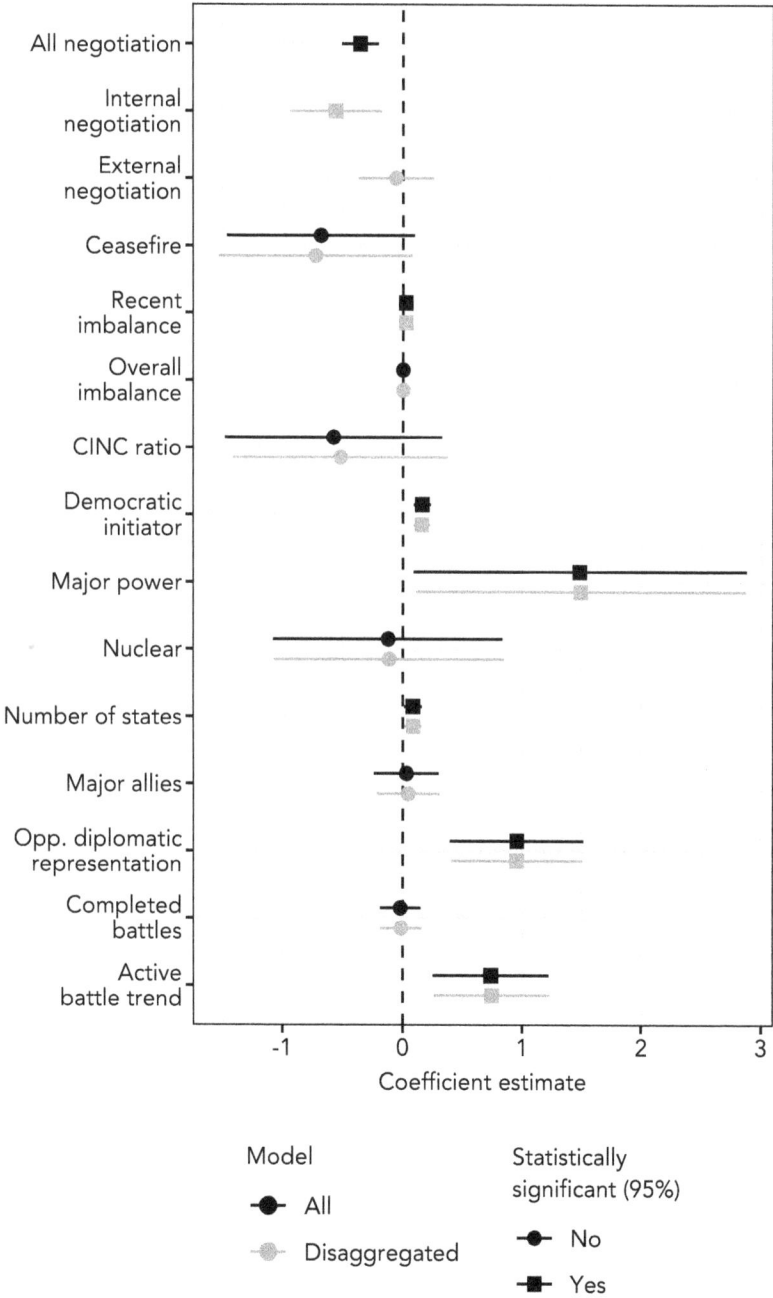

FIGURE 4.1. Coefficient plots for Poisson models of active battles with war fixed effects. Bands represent 95 percent confidence intervals ($N = 36{,}834$).

The coefficient for ceasefires across both models is negative and slightly larger in magnitude than what I find for internal negotiations, but it is statistically significant only at the 90 percent level. Even if ceasefires were to exhibit a highly statistically significant effect, the fact that negotiations can have an impact on fighting that is comparable to that of ceasefires—agreements explicitly made to pause hostilities—merits attention. Notably, despite the common belief that negotiations are tethered to ceasefires, my data suggest that the two are only weakly related across two centuries of war.[3] About 9 percent of negotiations include ceasefires, and only 30 percent of ceasefires include negotiations.

The pacifying impact of negotiations on the battlefield could be construed as evidence that the back-and-forth construct of fighting and negotiating in bargaining models of war is reasonable.[4] There are three reasons this conclusion is not completely justified. First, the effect identified in my models represents a decrease in fighting rather than a complete cessation. Second, the differential effects I find for internal and external negotiations are not captured by formal models. Third, the alternation process assumes that no other aspect of the war could change during or as a consequence of a negotiation period. A core contention of my theory is that negotiations can change a belligerent's reversion outcome even when negotiations do not yield agreement. This leads to my last set of statistical tests.

Changing Battlefield Trends

Negotiations that lead to conflict settlement reveal themselves to have been sincere efforts to forge peace. A fair share of negotiations that do not end conflicts may also be sincere, albeit misguided, efforts, but it is also likely that many of these talks are insincere ploys to buy time and revitalize one's political and military fortunes. If insincere negotiations generally help to realize these cynical goals, then we should see evidence that the trajectory of the battlefield changes before and after talks that do not lead to war termination. This prediction is at the heart of Hypothesis 5.

To assess this prediction, I focus on a subset of my data that analyzes only war-days surrounding the 143 negotiation periods that do not terminate conflict. For each of these negotiations, I extract the sixty days prior to the start of the negotiation period and the sixty days following the end of the negotiation period.[5] I compare battlefield trends on the prenegotiation days with those on postnegotiation days to see whether the battlefield has systematically changed trajectory. My main explanatory variable is a straightforward indicator for whether a war-day occurs in the sixty-day *postnegotiation* window following the cessation of talks.[6] Since I am making direct comparisons of temporal windows within wars, it is not necessary to include a complete battery of controls. I do, however, add two. The first captures any *concurrent negotiation* taking place within a sixty-day window. The second is a simple linear *time trend* variable, which accounts for the possibility that some changes on the battlefield are simply consequences of time. I return to this point later in this section.

Figure 4.2 displays the results of several regression models that analyze differences in battlefield activity on the sixty days before and after all negotiations that do not end a conflict. For now, I focus on estimates depicted in black, which represent models that include all negotiation periods. The first model, which looks at differences surrounding all negotiations, exhibits a positive and statistically significant coefficient for the postnegotiation period. This is consistent with Hypothesis 5. If I calculate the variance of the recent imbalance measure within each war, I find that the median value of these variances is 0.594. As such, the coefficient for the postnegotiation period, 0.225, represents a sizable shift on the battlefield.

The fact that negotiations have this prominent effect on subsequent hostilities is conspicuous. If this dynamic indeed exists, it has significant theoretical and policymaking implications and thus demands further investigation. We can better understand this relationship and how it is manifested on the battlefield by replicating the analysis using two alternate measures of battlefield activity. Each provides additional insight into precisely how fighting changes after talks end.

THE WAR TARGET'S RALLY

The first is my measure of momentum. Recall from chapter 2 that this is simply the recent imbalance measure before taking its absolute value. Momentum takes a positive value when recent battlefield trends favor the war initiator and a negative value when trends favor the target. The second model in figure 4.2 indicates that the upswing in recent imbalance is reflective of battlefield trends that tilt toward the war target's advantage. The point estimate for the postnegotiation period is –0.232. For reference, the median value for momentum within wars is 0.805.

The fact that battlefield trends undergo a reversal of fortune for the target dovetails with an array of research on the importance of the first-mover advantage in war. By having the ability to select the time, place, and manner in which to begin hostilities, war initiators have a vital chance to choose conditions that optimize their likelihood of success.[7] Targets may not expect to fight, or they may be unable to predict when, where, or how an initial attack will occur. Initiators can exploit this window of opportunity during which their opponent is not fully prepared or mobilized.[8] Clausewitz highlights the importance of initially waylaying the opponent through "plans and dispositions, especially those concerning

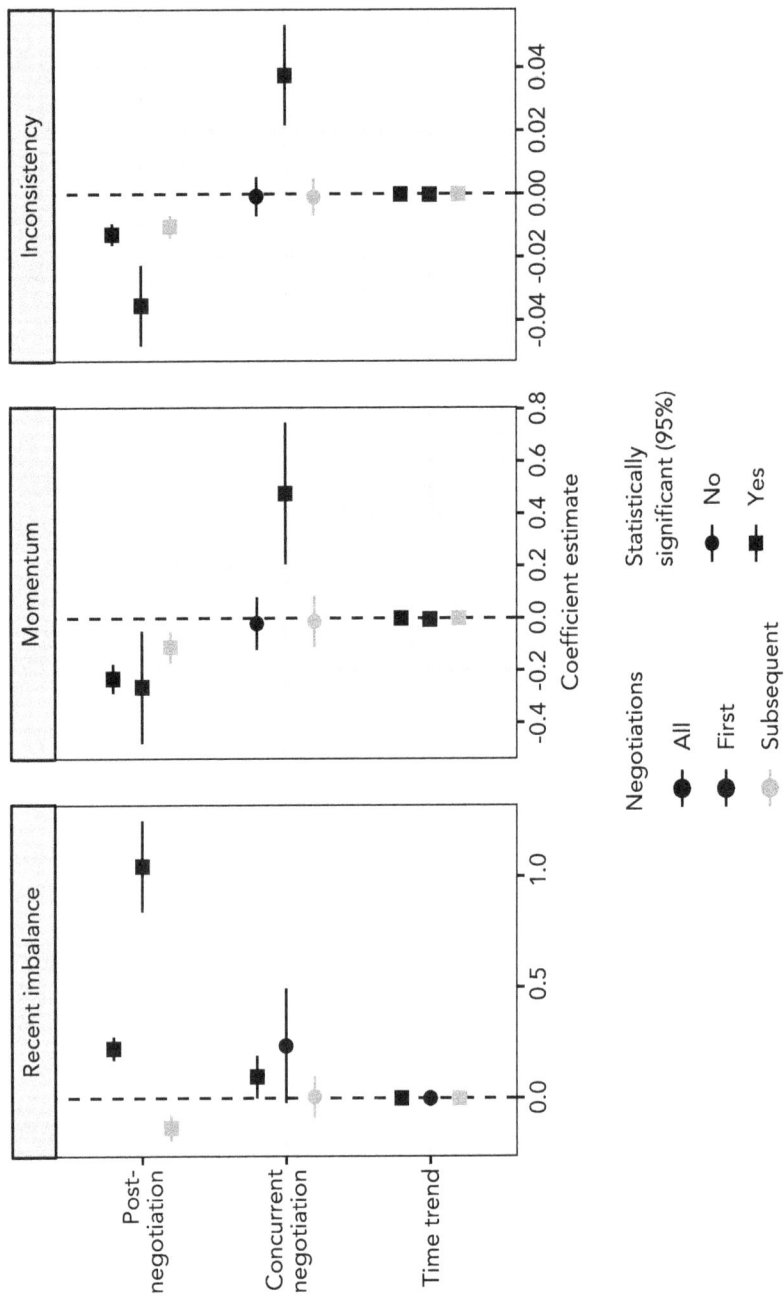

FIGURE 4.2. Coefficient plots for OLS models of changes in battlefield outcomes after failed negotiations, using a sixty-day temporal window. Bands represent 95 percent confidence intervals.

the distribution of forces" so that opening combat "confuses the enemy and low-ers its morale."[9] Sun-Tzu makes a similar point in *The Art of War*: "Whoever is first in the field and awaits the coming of the enemy, will be fresh for the fight; whoever is second in the field and has to hasten to battle will arrive exhausted. Therefore the clever combatant imposes his will on the enemy, but does not allow the enemy's will to be imposed on him."[10] In other words, the first-mover advan-tage exploits the initial and temporary disparity between an opponent's potential capabilities and its mobilized capabilities. Negotiations can therefore play a cru-cial role in allowing some war targets to mitigate their second-mover disadvan-tage by buying time to more fully mobilize their military forces and adjust both their political and military strategies.

LINING UP WITH PREWAR EXPECTATIONS

Results based on recent imbalance and momentum show that the battlefield tends to shift in one side's favor following failed negotiations. Another factor we may want to consider is the extent to which the outcomes of fighting are consistent with belligerents' expectations from before the war began. Scholars frequently note that actors' strategic choices are influenced by prewar beliefs.[11] My ability to gauge this consistently across dozens of interstate wars is limited, but one plausible measure is the CINC ratio, which I use as a control variable in the previous chapter. Recall that the CINC ratio is based on the Composite Index of National Capability measure from the National Material Capabilities dataset.[12] I sum the annual CINC measures for all active belligerents on each side in the war, accounting for the entry or exit of individual states. I then divide the war initiator's total score by the sum of both sides' scores. Values close to 0 reflect wars with more capable war targets, while values close to 1 indicate more capable war initiators. To be sure, actors do not have complete information regarding all parties' material capabilities, but we can at least assume that there is enough commonly observable information for both sides to have a somewhat similar understanding of each side's relative strength.[13]

These values must then be compared to a measure of observed battlefield outcomes. To produce this, I use my battle data to calculate what proportion of battles have been won by the war initiator up to that day in the conflict. As with the CINC ratio, proportions close to 0 or 1 reflect fighting that favors the war target or war initiator, respectively. By taking the absolute value of the difference between the CINC ratio and observed proportions from fighting, I can mea-sure the degree of *inconsistency* between expected and observed outcomes. When inconsistency is close to 0, the proportion of battles won by each side perfectly aligns with what we might expect based on their material capabilities. Increas-ingly higher values suggest a widening gap between expectations and reality.

The third model in figure 4.2 reflects how levels of inconsistency change around failed negotiations. The results are noteworthy. Talks are followed by battlefield developments that decrease the level of inconsistency. In other words, fighting becomes *more* consistent with prewar expectations. The average variance in the inconsistency measure within wars is 0.005. The estimated coefficient of –0.013 for all negotiations, despite sounding small, is substantively significant.

These findings underscore the importance that material capabilities indeed have on the consequences of fighting. Pauses from diplomacy allow more of the belligerents' dormant abilities to be realized, which leads subsequent battlefield activity to more closely reflect each side's underlying strength. The average level of my inconsistency measure on the last day of war, however, is 0.318—a sizable number on a 0-to-1 scale. Many conflicts end on the back of fighting that does not align very closely with the material resources each side can bring to bear. This discrepancy could reflect the fact that the CINC measure is a flawed predictor of war outcomes.[14] It may also indicate how the bargaining range expands due to the costs of fighting, permitting agreements that are not directly aligned with prewar expectations. Yet this still provides evidence that a costly lottery approach to understanding war may not be sufficient. The ebbs and flows of intrawar activity are highly influential in determining whether and why conflicts come to an end.

NEGOTIATION'S FADING EFFECTS

The results to this point have treated all negotiations equally, assuming that their potential effect on the battlefield remains constant over time. My argument offers at least two reasons we may want to differentiate between negotiations over the course of hostilities. First, any first-mover advantage that a war initiator wields at the beginning of hostilities should eventually diminish. Past studies have found that war initiators tend to fare worse the longer a conflict lasts, pointing to the weakening of their initial strategic and operational advantages.[15] Beyond the advantage that war initiators often enjoy when starting wars, both sides should also be able to narrow the gap between their underlying capabilities and their ability to mobilize those capabilities for war. Second, the more frequently negotiations fail to end conflict and are instead followed by a shift in battlefield trends, the more likely it should be that at least one belligerent would avoid negotiations until it feels more confident that talks will be sincere.

Returning to figure 4.2, I now focus on the results depicted in gray, which disaggregate negotiations by whether they were the first failed negotiation in a war. The first period of negotiations appears to drive much of the postnegotiation effect for all three measures of battlefield activity. This distinction is especially prominent for momentum and inconsistency; the estimated coefficient for the postnegotiation effect for these first rounds of talks is between double and qua-druple the magnitude of the estimates for all subsequent negotiations.

The strength of these postnegotiation effects may raise two connected con-cerns. One is that these changes on the battlefield are simply a function of time and would occur regardless of whether negotiations ever took place. Another is that my finding is a statistical phenomenon based on a reversion to the mean. A couple of considerations settle these matters. First, the models reported in fig-ure 4.2 include a variable for a linear time trend, and these do not undermine the main finding. Second, I perform a series of placebo tests where I create random periods of negotiation in the data and assess whether the postnegotiation effect appears in these simulated analyses. All of my placebo tests produce no evidence of a meaningful effect.[16] These null results lend further support to my argument that negotiations share a nontrivial relationship with belligerents' reversion out-comes and thus with their abilities to regather themselves and redouble their efforts on the battlefield. The rebalancing of the battlefield certainly requires the passage of time, but time on its own does not sufficiently identify the moments in which battlefield trends actually change. Negotiations provide the mechanism through which these shifts occur.

Put together, the quantitative results tell a coherent story about how negotia-tions that do not end conflicts can instead shape belligerents' abilities to pros-ecute the continuing war. Negotiations provide a moment of relative quiet and opportunity for belligerents to better mobilize their forces and harness their underlying material capabilities, which may not be used as fully or efficiently at the outset of hostilities. A main effect of failed negotiations is that they bring battlefield outcomes closer in line with prewar expectations, which are defined by each side's observed material capabilities. In many but not all cases, the side that benefits more from this respite is the side that did not have as much time to prepare for the conflict: the war target. These stabilizing effects are most salient in the earliest rounds of negotiation but become less prominent as wars proceed.

Talks and Fights in Two Wars

Despite the strength and stability of my statistical findings, one may believe they capture an average effect that does not reflect changes actually seen in any individual war. The quantitative analysis also captures only the effect that failed negotiations have on the battlefield, but my theory also suggests that diplomacy has political ramifications as well.

To address this, I now turn to two extended cases that more clearly illustrate how negotiations are used to influence the state of the battlefield in a manner consistent with my large-N quantitative results. Both conflicts offer meaningful evidence in favor of Hypotheses 4 and 5.

The War of the Roman Republic of 1849

The War of the Roman Republic presents an archetypal example of how a state can use negotiations to reshape the battlefield for its own benefit. In this particular conflict, insincere negotiations were important and successful enough not only to defeat a belligerent but to functionally terminate its existence as a political entity.

THE FALL AND RISE OF ROME

The year 1848 was a tumultuous one for the Italian states. Revolutionaries in several Italian states in the North, including Lombardy and Venetia, sought to wrest themselves free of the Austrian Empire's rule and to create a unified, independent, and liberal Italian republic. King Charles Albert of Piedmont, receiving the apparent support of Pope Pius IX, declared war against Austria in March 1848. This revolutionary war, however, proved unsuccessful against Austria's superior forces.

The failed revolution did not discourage the underlying cause. Indeed, many nationalist Italians directed their ire at Pius IX, the ruler of the Papal States (see figure 4.3). Upon his election as pope in 1846, Pius IX—an Italian himself—was hailed by those in Italy as a liberal champion of reform, republicanism, and progressive causes. Yet during the revolutions two years later, Pius IX reversed course, embracing conservative values and refusing to confront the Austrian Empire.[17]

Enraged nationalists orchestrated the assassination of the prime minister of the Papal States, Pellegrino Rossi, on November 15, 1848. Days later, the Swiss Guard was replaced by the "Civic Guard," and Pius IX was effectively imprisoned in the Papal Palace. He managed to escape on November 24 by dressing as a priest and fled to the port of Gaeta in Naples, itself the capital of the Kingdom of the Two Sicilies.[18] With the pope gone, liberals claimed power over the Papal States, taking control of the center of the Italian peninsula. The new government instituted a bevy of desired political reforms, including the establishment of a democratic government, religious freedoms, the abolition of the death penalty, and key social reforms to help the poor and unemployed. The ascendant liberals also sought to declare war against Austria once more.

On February 9, 1849, a republican government backed by a new constitution declared itself the Roman Republic. Modeling itself after the governing structure of ancient Rome, the new republic was led by a triumvirate: Carlo Armellini, Aurelio Saffi, and Giuseppe Mazzini. Of these three, Mazzini—a politician,

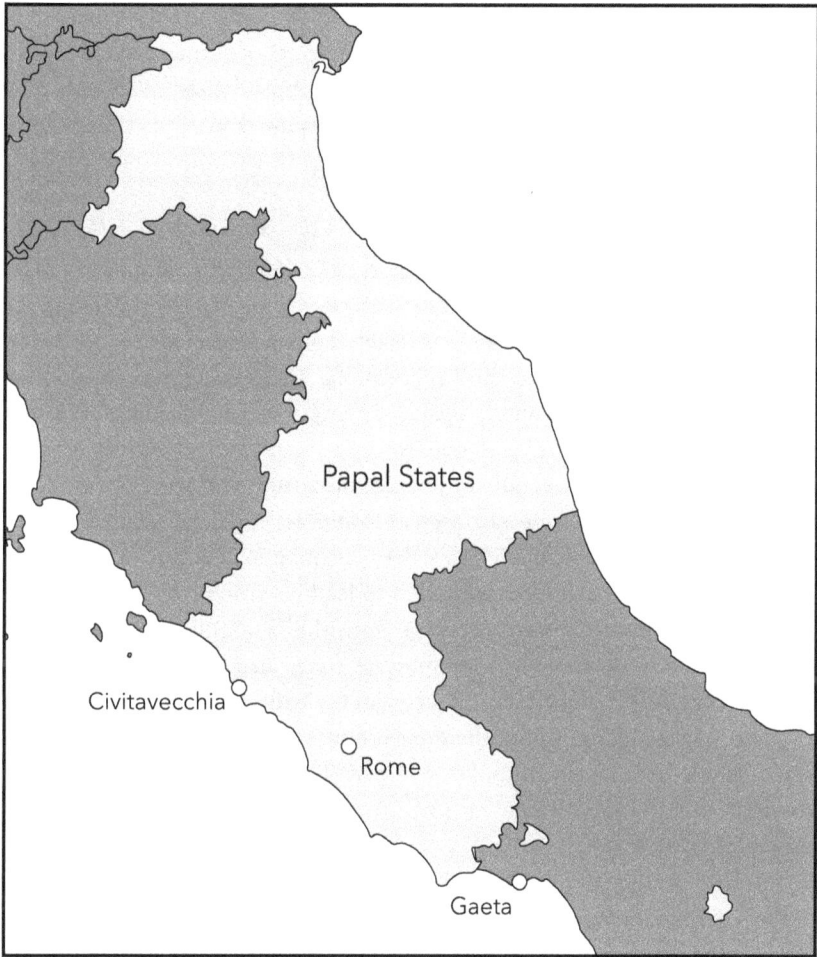

FIGURE 4.3. Map of the Papal States in 1849.

activist, and leader of several failed uprisings—arguably wielded the most influence in the Italian revolutionary movement and the broader democratic campaign to take hold across Europe. The armed forces of the Roman Republic were
commandeered by Giuseppe Garibaldi, who himself was a follower of Mazzini
and a fierce proponent of a unified Italian republic.

Exiled in Gaeta, Pius IX sought the military assistance of other states that were
sympathetic to Catholicism. One of these was France, where Louis Napoleon had
been elected the first president of the Second Republic on December 20, 1848.[19]
Louis Napoleon was caught between two difficult crosswinds. On one hand, he
had personally participated in an insurrection against the Papal States in 1831

and personally supported the republican project in Rome. On the other hand, his recent electoral victory rested heavily on the votes of French Catholics, who obviously desired a restoration of the pope and Papal States.[20] Napoleon ultimately chose to prioritize electoral politics and deployed an expeditionary force to reclaim Rome for the papacy.

FIGHTING, TALKING, AND SEEKING THE HIGH GROUND

French troops landed at the city and seaport of Civitavecchia, about forty miles northwest of Rome, on April 25. Led by General Nicholas Charles Oudinot, the forces, numbering between seven and eight thousand, headed toward Rome, believing they would be welcomed as liberators. Anticipating the arrival of the French, Garibaldi and his men prepared defenses on the Janiculum—a hill in western Rome—between April 27 and 29.

Hostilities, and the overall war, began in earnest on April 30. Oudinot and the French Army were not prepared to meet much, if any, resistance. They were misinformed, and in more than one manner. Oudinot's map of the Janiculum was out of date, causing him to lead his troops to a gate that had been closed. A daily cannon that fired from the Janiculum at noon, meant simply as a way to publicly communicate time, alarmed the French, who thought they were being attacked. Garibaldi took advantage of these deficiencies and successfully repulsed the French attackers, inflicting approximately 850 casualties and diminishing 11 or 12 percent of the French troops' overall strength.[21] Oudinot withdrew his forces to Civitavecchia and requested further reinforcements.[22]

Garibaldi sought to press this advantage and pursue the French all the way to the sea. Mazzini, however, decided to avoid further confrontation, hoping to instead establish a relationship with the French. Mazzini believed that the French Republic was fundamentally sympathetic to the Roman Republic's liberal cause and that it would also be willing to fight against the Austrians.[23]

France's loss at the Janiculum was deeply humiliating and politically precarious for Louis Napoleon. French officials had not expected Roman resistance, much less to be driven back by an outnumbered opponent. Napoleon feared that news of this loss would tarnish his reputation as a military leader. Oudinot and Napoleon went as far as to egregiously misrepresent the events at the Janiculum, informing the French Assembly that the "affair of April 30 is one of the most brilliant in which the French troops have taken part."[24] Oudinot also bragged that no French troops had been taken prisoner, conveniently leaving out the fact that the Romans had freed all their French prisoners as a sign of goodwill.[25] But the actual outcome could not be concealed; news of the loss at the Janiculum spread in Paris by May 7.[26] Citizens and members of the French Assembly were upset to have been misled but ultimately seemed uninterested in further hostilities. Public sentiment bent toward peace with the Roman Republic.

These developments on their own were already troublesome, but another complication loomed: French legislative elections, meant to elect the first National Assembly of the Second Republic, were scheduled for May 13 and 14. The Party of Order, which had been instrumental in Louis Napoleon's electoral victory the previous year, had only 23 percent of seats in the Constituent Assembly that had created the new republic. A larger loss against the Roman Republic would sink Louis Napoleon's chances of obtaining a favorable assembly.

He therefore had two significant reasons to initiate negotiations. The first was that based on battlefield developments, the relative costs of unabated fighting were high. Another assault on the Roman Republic in the current state of affairs would likely be a failure, and any move by Garibaldi to counterattack could prove dangerous. Additional French losses not only would be harmful militarily but would ripple through upcoming legislative elections. The second was that the costs of negotiating were quite low compared to the potential benefits from extracting side effects. By stalling for time, Louis Napoleon—belatedly realizing the broad support for the new republic in Rome—could send reinforcements to Oudinot and mount a much more serious attack, all while satisfying the general public's desire for a suspension of hostilities during the election period. The French government would have much to gain from insincere negotiations.

On May 8, Louis Napoleon charged the career diplomat Ferdinand Lesseps with a mission to go to Rome with the ostensible aim of forging a ceasefire. We now know, however, that the French government had no intention of negotiating a meaningful peace agreement and that Lesseps was unaware of this ploy. On the exact same day, Louis Napoleon quietly sent a message to Oudinot, stating that "our military honor is at stake. I will not suffer it to be compromised. You may rely on being reinforced."[27] It was also around this time that Austria and the Two Sicilies involved themselves in the war, sending their own troops to Rome.

Lesseps left Paris on May 9 and arrived in Rome on May 15. Despite Mazzini's interest in speaking with the French government, it appears that France initiated the actual negotiations that began on this date. Lesseps received an enthusiastic welcome and was enraptured by Mazzini's affability and warmth.[28] By May 17, Lesseps and Mazzini arranged a two-week armistice during which the two sides would continue negotiating to forge a more permanent agreement.

This two-week ceasefire and negotiations proved critical for France. In that brief time, the Party of Order won an outright majority of seats in the first National Assembly, and Louis Napoleon's promised reinforcements arrived. During talks, Oudinot had asked Lesseps to request permission for French troops to occupy several hills overlooking the city. Oudinot promised that this was only for the health of the troops and would in no way endanger the Romans. The triumvirate granted permission, believing that discussions with Lesseps were going well.[29] But Oudinot and others in Paris had made this request in order to prepare for additional hostilities once reinforcements arrived. Seemingly earnest diplomatic bargaining had thus allowed Oudinot to place his troops, now including Austrian soldiers and numbering twenty thousand, on advantageous high ground just two to four miles outside Rome.

On May 31, as the ceasefire period came to a close, the Roman triumvirs and Lesseps signed the Treaty of Peace and Alliance. The agreement stated that the French would become allies with the Roman Republic against Austria and Naples. French troops would remain outside Rome and aid in its defense, but they would not join any offensives against the Austrians or Neapolitans. Lesseps, perhaps realizing that he had ceded more than he should have, insisted on adding a clause saying that the treaty had to be ratified by the French Republic.

When Lesseps returned to the French camp with the agreement in hand, Oudinot refused to sign. He instead gave Lesseps a note from Paris: "The Government of the Republic has put a stop to your mission. You will be good enough to start upon your return to France as soon as you have received this despatch."[30] Lesseps soon learned of rumors spread by his own government that the mission had "affected his brain."[31] Louis Napoleon's government had successfully used diplomacy—and Lesseps—to buy time. Now wielding far greater political and military power than he did mere weeks earlier, Louis Napoleon immediately nullified the treaty and initiated a siege against Rome on June 3. French forces eventually peaked at 34,000, while Garibaldi could collect a maximum of only 18,600 less well-trained and less well-equipped men.[32]

The Roman Republic was unable to mount a proper defense against such a tightly orchestrated siege. By the end of June, the Roman Assembly gathered to discuss their next steps. Three options became part of the discussion: they could surrender, they could continue fighting, or their government and troops could withdraw from Rome and continue their resistance from the Apennine Mountains. The Roman Republic ultimately settled for the first option. A truce was negotiated on July 1, and the Roman Republic was disestablished, allowing for the reinstatement of Pope Pius IX the following year. While Garibaldi and some of his forces opted to fall back to San Marino and fight another day, the present war and the Roman Republic were finished.

TALKING ONE'S WAY TO VICTORY

The events of the War of the Roman Republic offer a direct example of the strategy and potential of insincere negotiations. Louis Napoleon faced an unexpected loss at the Janiculum and recognized that continued fighting would be perilous not only in a militaristic sense but also in a political one. As such, Louis Napoleon foresaw relatively high costs to continuing hostilities without making any changes. His government thus made an initial offer to open negotiations. In support of Hypothesis 4, which predicts that periods of negotiations should be linked with lower levels of active hostilities, the battlefield was dramatically quieter over the two weeks during which negotiations took place. Lesseps the diplomat was unaware that his own government was using talks to create a reversion outcome that was far more favorable to the French Republic when negotiations would be intentionally sunk. The war target, fully capable of mobilizing itself to fight more effectively and to adjust strategy, used the veil of diplomacy to facilitate that process. This case also vividly illustrates Hypothesis 5, which anticipates that negotiations that do not result in settlement will be followed by a battlefield trend that differs from what existed prior to talks. The striking reversal of fortune in France's favor following the abandonment of peace negotiations forced an end not only to the war but to the Roman Republic.

One may believe that the war would have unfolded in the exact same manner even if no negotiations had taken place. The Roman Republic largely accepted the French diplomatic overture because it had few other options. Its primary goal was not only to defend its new existence but to garner the French Republic's political and military support, especially against the Austrian Empire. The victory at the Janiculum was, in the triumvirate's view, a necessary step for the Roman Republic to defend itself. But every choice the republicans made from that point was designed to ingratiate themselves with the French. The triumvirate took the necessary gamble of negotiating with France in hopes that Louis Napoleon would agree to defend the Roman Republic. They knew that the agreement they had made with Lesseps was risky, but all they could do was hope that France would fulfill it. In the moments before Mazzini took the proposal to the Roman Assembly for approval, he told Lesseps, "The positions with regard to which we are about to facilitate your occupation, and the privilege which you reserve for yourselves of only repulsing our foreign enemies if they come directly in contact with yourselves, leave our political existence at the mercy of your good faith."[33] It was also clear that Garibaldi's forces would not win an outright war against the French, and Oudinot's military forces would have been reinforced even in the absence of any diplomatic interactions between the two sides. Recall that both Lesseps and military reinforcements were deployed on the same day. Perhaps the war would have ended in exactly the same manner whether or not Lesseps and Mazzini engaged in diplomatic discussions.

This conclusion, however, overlooks several benefits that Louis Napoleon could not have accrued if he had adopted a strategy based solely on military force. By opening diplomatic channels, he created an opportunity for General

Oudinot's forces not only to be reinforced but to relocate themselves to a strategically advantageous spot. This relocation process could have faced armed resistance and created undue costs for the French military if it were not permitted by the Roman Republic over the course of negotiations. Moreover, due to the apparent success of negotiations, Garibaldi's forces were directed to return to Rome, and they did so between May 31 and June 2—immediately before France would renege on its agreement—even though they had the ability to continue fighting. The fact that Garibaldi's men were concentrated in Rome made General Oudinot's task of neutralizing the Roman Republic considerably easier. The republican army would resume their armed resistance once the siege began, but their efforts were curtailed by their disadvantageous position. Consistent with the findings from the quantitative analysis, the battlefield tilted more dramatically and in the war target's favor and became more consistent with prewar expectations after negotiations were halted. The occurrence of talks also quelled domestic opposition to the war in France on the eve of legislative elections. Louis Napoleon managed to deflect political pressures for peace by engaging in the theater of diplomacy but with the ultimate intent of stalling for time until his political fortunes were more secure. These benefits outweighed any costs Napoleon may have perceived from being willing to negotiate with a largely unrecognized state.

Mazzini's writings after the war indicate his indignation over being betrayed. A letter he wrote on August 7, 1849, two months after the Roman Republic dissolved, bemoaned that "France had been guilty of falsehood" and that the Roman Republic had been a "victim [who] was then on the ground, with a dagger in her throat."[34] Regardless of whether members of the Roman Republic were deceived, two facts remain. The first is that the republic had no other tractable option but to negotiate and hope that the other party would agree to the triumvirate's requests. The second was that one belligerent strategically used negotiations to promote and redirect its war aims rather than settle them.

In sum, France would have ultimately prevailed in this conflict, and the Roman Republic had very little chance of survival. Yet the costs and outcomes of war are not binary. Louis Napoleon used diplomatic talks to create a more favorable reversion outcome that mitigated both political and military liabilities. By saving some French lives and resources, the French Republic accomplished an easier victory, and Louis Napoleon more effectively navigated complicated political waters. None of these would have been possible without the exploitation of negotiations.

The Cenepa Valley War of 1995

The Cenepa Valley War was a brief but sharp struggle between Peru and Ecuador.[35] By the war's peak, approximately five thousand troops were deployed to an area of jungle approximately twenty-seven square miles in size.[36] The conflict offers an effective illustration of how belligerents on both sides can use diplomacy to strategically manipulate not only battlefield activity but also the broader political environment. Through negotiations, both Peru and Ecuador extracted side effects that enhanced their gains from conflict.

A WATERSHED MOMENT

The dispute had roots in the administrative borders drawn by the Spanish Empire in the eighteenth century. Many of the lines drawn at the time were somewhat arbitrary, as they were all under Spanish dominion and often ran through uninhabited swaths of jungle. But as South American states began to claim independence in the early 1800s, questions about territorial control became more pressing. Peru and Ecuador had political and economic reasons to determine a clear boundary line between them. Between 1802 and 1936, both states engaged in at least thirteen concrete but failed diplomatic efforts to define a border.[37] Some of these discussions involved third-party assistance, with the United States and Spain being the most active mediators. None of these projects succeeded in determining a mutually acceptable line of demarcation.[38]

After more than a century of deepening dissatisfaction and nationalistic fervor, the dispute came to a head in July 1941, when Peru and Ecuador fought a monthlong war over their border.[39] The conflict quickly revealed Peru's superiority; its military was thirteen times the size of Ecuador's,[40] and its invading force was five times larger than the Peruvian contingent it faced on the battlefield.[41] In light of the decisive Peruvian victory, four nations—Argentina, Brazil, Chile, and the United States—helped the two countries arrange a settlement. The eventual agreement, called the Rio de Janeiro Protocol, more commonly referred to as the Rio Protocol, was signed on January 29, 1942. Peru was to ultimately withdraw from Ecuadorian territory. In exchange, Ecuador was to acknowledge that seventy-seven thousand square miles of disputed land would be granted to Peru, and Ecuador would end its claim for direct land access to the Amazon River. The four states that helped forge the protocol cosigned as guarantors of the agreement.

The protocol quickly resolved about 95 percent of existing territorial disputes between Peru and Ecuador. In 1946, the US Army Air Corps attempted to map the disputed area to help finalize a territorial arrangement. The aerial survey sparked a new and unexpected controversy: the Cenepa River, previously thought to be short and inconsequential, was actually 120 miles long and created two watersheds. The Rio Protocol spoke of only a single watershed, and its description of the revised border no longer applied properly to approximately fifty miles of disputed territory in the Cordillera del Cóndor (Condor Mountain Range).[42] Ecuador claimed this meant the protocol was not executable and that a new deal had to be made. Peru argued that the protocol could remain intact because the boundaries had already been determined, regardless of the number of watersheds. With neither side being willing to cede ground to the other, Ecuador withdrew from the demarcation process in 1948. By 1960, Ecuadorian president-elect José María Velasco Ibarra adopted a hard-line stance that the entire Rio Protocol was null and void because it was signed under duress following the 1941 war and because it could not be fully executed due to the discovery of new geographical features not addressed in it. Subsequent Ecuadorian governments all perpetuated this claim.

Disagreements regarding this territory continued for decades, and both states gradually increased their military presence in the Cenepa Valley (see figure 4.4). Armed forces briefly clashed in another limited conflict in January 1981. This dispute is often called the Paquisha War, named after the Ecuadorian base that Peru claimed was established in Peruvian territory.[43] Peru was again quick to demonstrate its military superiority and seized the Paquisha outpost in two weeks. Due to Ecuador's unwillingness to recognize the Rio Protocol, the Organization of American States (OAS), rather than the guarantor states, oversaw an agreement where both states pulled their forces back to clearly defined territory. Further bloodshed was avoided, but the underlying issue was left unresolved.

At the start of the 1990s, Ecuador began to deploy military units near the Cordillera del Cóndor and Cenepa River. Ecuadorian forces built three new bases—named Tiwinza, Base Sur, and Cueva de los Tayos—on high ground in the disputed territory. These outposts were heavily fortified and surrounded with numerous land mines. Peru's internal struggles with the Shining Path party and guerrilla organizations led the government in Lima to do little in response to these developments. Once President Alberto Fujimori managed to capture the Shining Path's leaders in 1992, however, he began to focus more on Ecuador's activities in the Cenepa Valley. Peruvian forces had a few minor encounters with Ecuadorians in 1994. January 9 and 11 saw two brief incidents between the two sides' troops, during which troops were captured and sent back to their commanding officers.[44] The gradual increase in the number of run-ins between soldiers raised concerns for Ecuadorian forces, who believed the Peruvians were lurching toward a larger offensive.

With these concerns in mind, on January 26, Ecuador launched a surprise attack on a Peruvian helipad. The rocket and mortar fire killed three Peruvian soldiers and forced the rest to flee into the jungle. Ecuadorian troops renamed the helipad Base Norte.[45] Armed hostilities were underway.[46]

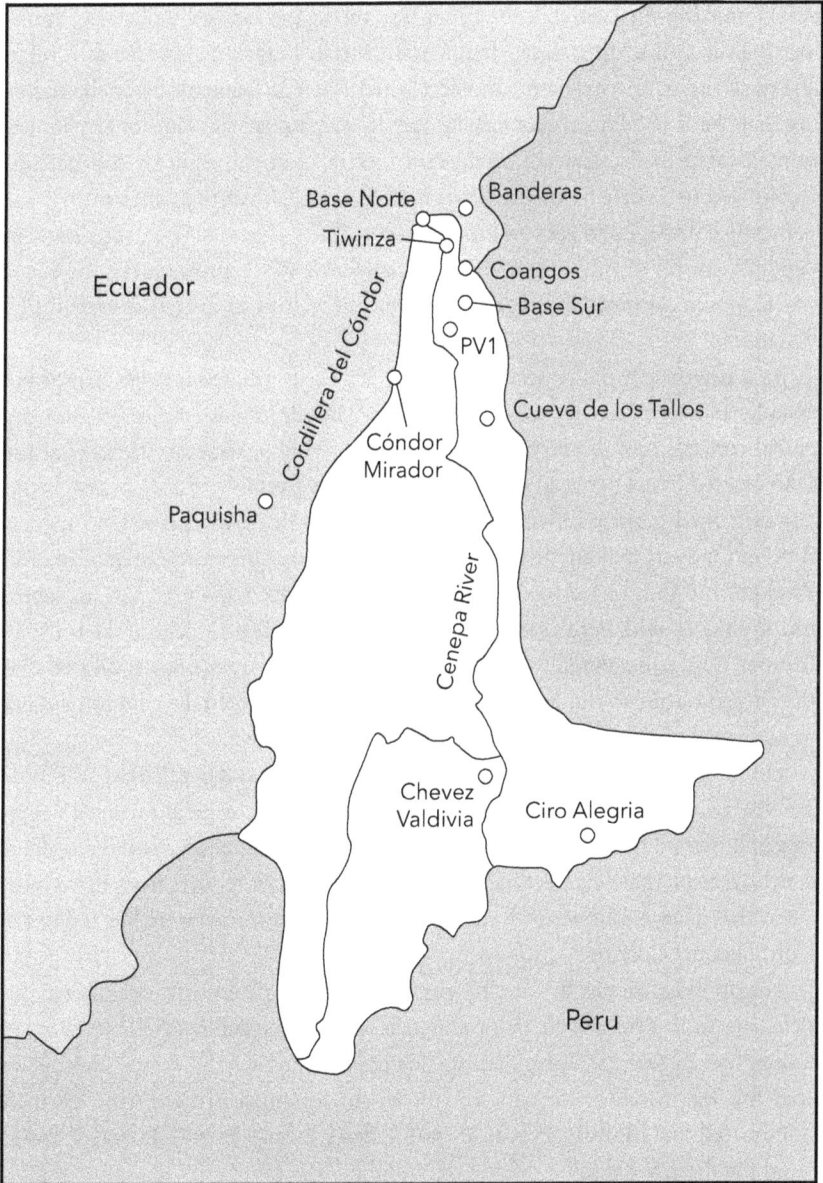

FIGURE 4.4.   Map of the disputed Cenepa Valley area.

MULTIPLE "GUARANTEES" OF PEACE

Third parties cast a large shadow over Peru and Ecuador. Knowing the international community would likely disapprove of conflict, both belligerent states quickly and readily attempted to argue the justness of their cause to third-party actors, making the case that the other was the aggressor and violator of international law. In a letter dated January 27, the Ecuadorian minister of foreign affairs wrote to the president of the United Nations Security Council, claiming that "Peru had launched military operations against Ecuadorian army positions located in Ecuadorian territory. In exercise of the right of self-defence recognized in Article 51 of the Charter of the United Nations, my country was naturally compelled to respond to Peru's attacks."[47] One day later, the Peruvian deputy minister of international policy also wrote to the president of the Security Council, claiming that Peru "has been the victim of armed aggression by Ecuador."[48]

As a response to its retreat on January 26, Peru initiated a series of ground assaults between January 28 and 31. These developments triggered growing global concern. On January 29, César Gaviria Trujillo, secretary general of the OAS, started flying between Quito and Lima to try to resolve the dispute.[49] Ecuador expressed interest in working with the OAS, but Peru refused OAS mediation on the basis that any mediation needed to follow the framework of the Rio Protocol and thus be led by the guarantor states. Indeed, the international community agreed with Peru's stance. Ernesto Cardenas, the president of the Security Council (and coincidentally the UN ambassador from Argentina), indicated that the United Nations would stay out of the matter and directed the guarantor states to address the crisis.[50]

On January 31, representatives from the guarantor states gathered in Rio de Janeiro, two days after the fifty-third anniversary of the original protocol's signing, and invited both Peru and Ecuador to come discuss peace. Both belligerent states agreed to participate. One day before talks began, reports from Lima indicated that a large number of well-equipped Peruvian troops were headed to the Cordillera del Cóndor.[51]

Negotiations at Rio de Janeiro initially appeared promising. By February 1, delegates from Peru and Ecuador announced that they had reached the terms of a ceasefire. Argentinian president Carlos Menem publicly expressed confidence that the war would soon end, and President Fujimori of Peru even publicly announced that his military would "immediately begin the withdrawal of tanks" from the disputed land.[52]

But this optimism did not last. The ceasefire declared on February 1 appeared to fail within one or two days, and the guarantors were unable to develop a written agreement that satisfied both belligerent states. The primary disagreement involved the size and scope of military drawdowns. Peru asked for a limited withdrawal that would create a demilitarized zone approximately five miles wide. Ecuador, fearing that this would allow Peruvians to later retake any disputed outposts, sought an unconditional ceasefire and complete demobilization of troops.[53] Talks were ended on February 5, with the guarantor states planning on another round of mediation in Brasilia on some undetermined date.

Two days before the Rio de Janeiro negotiations officially ended, Peruvian helicopters began a new round of attacks that bombed Ecuador's outposts in Cueva de los Tayos and Base Sur.[54] Despite Ecuador's insistence that it had not lost any posts, Peru appeared to take these two bases within a handful of days.

Hostilities continued in bursts over the next week. Because the thick jungle environment made ground operations difficult, an increasing amount of fighting took place from the air.[55] Ecuador shot down three Peruvian planes, while Peru shot down two Ecuadorian warplanes.[56] At least one Peruvian helicopter was also taken down during an attempted attack on the Coangos outpost.[57]

The outpost at Tiwinza, which was one of the disputed positions closest to Ecuador, became a focal point for both sides.[58] Ecuadorian forces had secured the area with mines, artillery, and other traps prior to the war and made significant efforts to maintain control over it. One notable aerial photograph shows Ecuadorian troops at Tiwinza; they had used stones to write out a phrase that Ecuadorian president Sixto Durán Ballén would popularize during the war: "ni un paso atrás" (not one step back). Multiple Peruvian assaults against Tiwinza had failed to make headway.[59] On February 12, Fujimori stated on national television that additional Peruvian forces were headed toward Tiwinza, which he claimed was the last outpost on Peruvian soil that remained in Ecuadorian hands.[60] A large-scale Peruvian assault began in the early hours of February 13.[61]

Fujimori was quick to declare victory that evening, proclaiming on television that "the Peruvian flag waves in Tiwinza" and declaring a unilateral ceasefire that would come into effect the next day at noon.[62] Ecuadorian officials denied Peru's claim and invited both the media and the Red Cross to come visit Tiwinza, Base Sur, and Cueva de los Tayos to see that they remained in Ecuadorian hands.[63] We now know in retrospect that Peru had already taken Base Sur and Cueva de los Tayos earlier in the month but that their latest assault on Tiwinza failed.[64] Fujimori likely made his announcement to mislead his public in order to increase his standing before elections would take place in April. In any case, Ecuador agreed to reciprocate Peru's ceasefire, but this arrangement collapsed within hours.[65] Between the fourteenth and sixteenth, the two sides continued fighting but failed to appreciably change the situation on the ground.

On February 17, the four guarantor states brought Peru and Ecuador back together for talks, leading to the Declaration of Itamaraty. The agreement called for a ceasefire, gradual withdrawal, and creation of a demilitarized zone that would allow military observers from the guarantor nations—designated as the Military Observer Mission, Ecuador Peru (MOMEP)—to monitor the withdrawal. The agreement left some key questions unanswered. For one, it did not specify when the two sides would begin their troop withdrawals. Moreover, it did not address the actual border dispute. The demilitarized zone was meant only to stop the fighting and not to define new boundaries.[66] The primary issue of demarcation would be saved for talks, which would happen at some point in the future.

Both sides violated the ceasefire repeatedly, with most infractions taking place around Tiwinza. Peruvian battalions staged an attack on Tiwinza on February 18 but were thwarted by mines and artillery fire.[67] Some of the heavier fighting of the conflict took place on February 22, with Peruvian forces attempting to penetrate Tiwinza yet another time. This was the one and only moment Peruvians reached the outpost, but they were soon pushed back out.[68] Ecuador's military command indicated that fourteen soldiers died as a result of this successful defense.[69] Despite the fact that Ecuador successfully repulsed the Peruvian attack, this clash was the country's worst day in terms of casualties, leading Ecuadorians to call February 22 "Black Wednesday."[70] These continuous flare-ups prevented the team of approximately twenty MOMEP military observers called on by the Declaration of Itamaraty from entering the disputed areas.[71] During a visit to the Cueva de los Tayos outpost on February 24, Fujimori briefly came under mortar fire, with one mortar exploding about 150 feet from his group of soldiers and reporters.[72]

Yet over the next few days, skirmishes faded away, and the guarantor states pressed Peru and Ecuador to adhere to the Declaration of Itamaraty. On February 28, the six parties gathered once again in Montevideo, Uruguay. As part of the inauguration ceremony of incoming Uruguayan president Julio María Sanguinetti, Peru and Ecuador signed the Montevideo Declaration. According to the declaration, the belligerents "reiterate[d] their commitment to the immediate and effective cease-fire established in the Declaration [of Itamaraty]," and the "Guarantor Countries reiterate[d] their commitment to continue to carry out their obligations under the Rio de Janeiro Protocol."[73] Both countries' military forces began withdrawing from the area at the end of March, and MOMEP verified that the process was completed by the middle of May.[74]

The monthlong war in the Cenepa Valley was estimated to have cost a total of $500 million across both states.[75] Ecuador lost and could not recover control of the outposts at Cueva de los Tayos or Base Sur. Fujimori would claim that "there was not an Ecuadorean soldier left on Peruvian soil,"[76] but Ecuadorian troops did manage to hold Tiwinza, some other bases slightly in the periphery of the disputed area, and the Cóndor Mirador base further south where they had successfully infiltrated the Peruvian rear.[77]

Peru, Ecuador, and the guarantor states eventually formulated the Act of Brasilia on October 24, 1998. The agreement designated some limited territorial allocations to each side, guaranteed Peru the right of free navigation on the Amazon River, and established an ecological park that would be co-operated by both nations. The agreement was not too dissimilar from the Rio Protocol fifty-six years before, but it also granted Ecuador a small patch of land at Tiwinza (in Peruvian territory) to recognize Ecuador's human losses there.[78]

EXCHANGING FIRE AND ACCUSATIONS

Militarily speaking, the war in the upper Cenepa Valley represented a form of reserved victory for Ecuador. The Peruvians' significantly larger military, as well as Peru's history of easily subduing Ecuador on the battlefield, would have suggested an easy win for Peru. Ecuador's ability to keep control of Tiwinza, despite Fujimori's claims, represented the first Ecuadorian military triumph over Ecuador since the battle of Tarqui in 1829.[79] Peruvian political observers also expressed disappointment about the conflict's outcome, noting that this was Peru's "worst defeat since 1879" (alluding to Peru's loss against Chile in the War of the Pacific of 1879–83) and that "anything less than a swift annihilation of Ecuadorean forces represents a first-ever defeat."[80]

Ecuador's successes in claiming Base Norte on January 26 and maintaining control of Tiwinza rested on its first-mover advantage. The Ecuadorian military enjoyed a series of strategic benefits, many of which were accrued by learning lessons from its embarrassing loss in 1981, professionalizing its military, and engaging in long-term preparations for a potential conflict.[81] Ecuador's outposts, which had been constructed starting in 1991, were on high and familiar ground that would limit the effectiveness of Peruvian aircraft. Short supply lines and a system of footpaths facilitated the movement of soldiers, supplies, and information. Thousands of land mines and guns defended Ecuador's outposts.[82] Ecuador also picked an "ideal" time and place to start the fight. Peru had so little expectation of an international conflict that it redirected much of its military and intelligence apparatus to deal with the Shining Path and the Túpac Amaru Revolutionary Movement at home.[83] Even when Peru started paying more attention to events in the Cenepa Valley in the months before hostilities began, it did not fully understand Ecuador's military presence or capabilities, assuming little had changed since the 1981 dispute. As a result, Peruvian forces were few in number, deeply undersupplied, and not prepared for a surprise attack anywhere near the Cenepa Valley. Logistical operations were poor and Peruvian roads in the area were terrible, forcing Peru to use helicopters to transport supplies and support to its inadequately prepared soldiers—all in airspace that Ecuadorians more effectively controlled.[84] But Peru also had the ability to alleviate some of these handicaps if it could find more time to prepare.

Thus, when talks began in Rio de Janeiro on January 31, neither side was ready to settle. The belligerents had not yet exchanged or learned enough information to consider a lasting settlement. Peru wanted to reverse these unfavorable conditions, while Ecuador wanted to capitalize on them. Insincere diplomacy played a significant role in both belligerents' attempts to promote these goals. The need and latitude to extract side effects from negotiations were facilitated by the immense pressure that the guarantor states placed on Peru and Ecuador to engage in discussions. Diplomats from the guarantor countries did not appear to understand this situation, believing that Peru and Ecuador would easily accept peace. When the first round of talks formally ended on February 5, Alexander Watson, the chief US representative in Rio de Janeiro, admitted that he originally "was planning to be here only six hours."[85]

For Peru, talks created a chance to mobilize more of its forces and send them to the Cenepa Valley. Discussions for a potential ceasefire agreement were active on January 31 but began to fall flat. By February 2, diplomats indicated there were "slim hopes" of any negotiated solution. But later that evening, the two sides presented new proposals and spent the night attempting to consolidate them into a single document. On February 3, Durán Ballén of Ecuador announced a willingness to accept a ceasefire on these terms. That same day, however, Peru asked for a series of changes to the proposed agreement. Importantly, a report on February 4 noted that "some analysts here [in Rio de Janeiro] say Peru is prolonging the peace negotiations to give its troops time to advance on disputed borderlands."[86] Peru thus focused on using negotiations insincerely to regroup and reorganize more of its military potential.

For Ecuador, where many were riding a wave of nationalistic fervor and optimism, negotiations were an opportunity to curry international favor for its cause while directing ire toward Peru. Durán Ballén reportedly told his National Security Council that he would request the guarantor countries' diplomatic assistance because Ecuador would gain an advantage by apparently acting in good faith while Peruvian forces repeatedly attempted to take Tiwinza and the other bases by military means.[87] Indeed, Durán Ballén widely communicated that Ecuador had accepted the guarantors' ceasefire proposal on January 31, only for Peru to ask for numerous unacceptable modifications that sank the deal.[88] Ecuadorian communications secretary Enrique Proano also spoke to the press on February 5, claiming that Peru was attempting to look accommodating in negotiations "to make it appear that Ecuador has taken an intransigent position, and to justify the escalation of an armed aggression against a pacifist country."[89] Durán Ballén also went on series of trips to the South American guarantor states between February 6 and 7 to show Ecuador's professed interest in peace and to seek a general demobilization (instead of Peru's request to create a temporary demilitarized zone).[90]

Hypothesis 4—that periods of negotiation co-occur with lower intensity of battlefield activity—finds partial support here. Levels of fighting settled slightly at the outset of Rio talks when both sides were initially discussing the possibility of a formal ceasefire, as well as when the belligerents' delegates claimed to have reached a ceasefire on February 1.[91] Yet Peru bombed both Cueva de los Tayos and Base Sur on February 3, two days before talks ended. Notably, these attacks all used aircraft; ground forces were not involved, as they were still waiting to be reinforced.[92] Regardless, consistent with the theoretical basis for Hypothesis 4, Peru and Ecuador frequently declared a willingness to halt fighting over the course of the war, blamed their opponent for any violations, and used these activities to further both their political and their military causes.[93]

For whatever caveats exist with respect to Hypothesis 4, the Cenepa War illustrates Hypothesis 5 well: conditions on the battlefield became markedly different following the end of failed negotiations at Rio. The additional time allowed both sides to activate more of their latent military power and send it to the Cenepa Valley. Approximately 1,500 troops were in the valley at the start of the war, and this number quadrupled to 6,000 by the end.[94] As a result, most of the overall hostilities and casualties during the war took place in the last two weeks. This delayed uptick shows how much the chance to mobilize mattered, as well as how much early fighting may not have been sufficient to convince either belligerent to revise its beliefs or strategies.[95] This opportunity was especially useful for Peru, which seized Cueva de los Tayos and Base Sur in the immediate aftermath of the Rio talks falling apart. These battle victories significantly undermined Ecuador's position in the Cenepa Valley and better reflected the reality of Peru's overall military capabilities. By early February, these military realities pressed President Durán Ballén to publicly acknowledge that the Rio Protocol was in force but to argue that it was not executable in the disputed area due to its inaccurate description of the geography there.[96] His government also began to call Argentina, Brazil, Chile, and the United States "guarantors" instead of "friendly countries."[97] The Itamaraty and Montevideo Declarations were both built on top of the Rio framework. Ecuador's recognition of the 1942 Rio Protocol after three decades of deeming it null and void was a major policy victory for Peru.

Consistent with the quantitative evidence for Hypothesis 5, the first round of talks had the greatest impact on changing the battlefield's trajectory. The additional negotiation that produced the Declaration of Itamaraty on February 17 was followed by additional fighting, including Peru's deadliest attempt to take Tiwinza on February 22, but none of these efforts appreciably changed the states' control over the outposts. Both countries had already mobilized much of what they would mobilize to fight the war.

One may argue that the war's ultimate outcome would not have been very different in the absence of negotiations. Ecuador almost certainly could not have clinched a swift or total military victory against Peru, and Peru would have eventually mobilized more troops to fight Ecuadorian troops in the upper Cenepa Valley. It is nonetheless notable that Peru's battlefield turnaround took place right at the tail end of the first talks in Rio—and that similar shifts did not occur at any other moment. Moreover, recall that insincere negotiations produce, beyond the battlefield, other side effects that are not captured by my quantitative analysis. Both belligerents engaged in public posturing after negotiations in order to frame themselves as the peace-seeking party and their opponent as the aggressor. Ecuador's government was especially adept at manipulating the public's understanding of the conflict. Durán Ballén's trips to Argentina, Brazil, and Chile following the Rio talks were widely reported and drew sympathy to Ecuador's cause. Some days later, Peru also started sending former ambassadors and other notable people across Latin America and the United States to make the Peruvian case. A report from that time stated that this action "was launched partly in response to the belief that Ecuador was ahead in the public relations war."[98] Ecuador's diplomatic offensive, which projected an aura of strength and confidence based on the military's successes, may have helped Durán Ballén acknowledge the Rio Protocol—which significantly expedited a settlement—while also creating conditions for the guarantor states to recognize Ecuador's control over Tiwinza.[99]

Tiwinza notwithstanding, Ecuador fell short of an ideal outcome. The Ecuadorean plan in the Cenepa Valley essentially involved a fait accompli: seizing the disputed territory and forcing the international community and guarantor states to accept the reality of Ecuador's de facto control.[100] This goal was partially realized at best. Yet the fact that both sides could celebrate some measure of success rested on how they used the guarantors' diplomatic efforts to reshape the military and political battlefields in their favor.

Externally motivated negotiations had cross-cutting impacts on the war's outcome. In one respect, guarantors may have facilitated insincere negotiations that furthered each side's war aims. Both Ecuador and Peru realized political and military victories, as limited as they may have been, by exploiting the guarantors' diplomatic endeavors. Yet in another respect, the high latent pressure the belligerents felt to settle the conflict may have allowed them to back out of fighting and enter negotiations more easily. Neither state wanted the war to escalate dramatically,[101] but it was not clear whether the war would remain limited. Over one hundred thousand men were mobilized by the two nations to potentially fight for their country.[102] The war claimed only hundreds rather than thousands of lives, and diplomacy likely limited this fallout.

Words Can Kill

Few would deny that fighting, in some form or another, helps dictate when and why belligerents choose to talk to one another during war. Yet far more people may be more resistant to the idea of that story in reverse: talking can directly influence the nature of fighting.

In this chapter, I have presented both quantitative and qualitative analysis attesting to the effect that wartime negotiations have on the subsequent trajectory of the conflict. My quantitative study of interstate wars between 1823 and 2003 shows that periods of diplomatic bargaining between the belligerents are consistently associated with lower levels of hostilities on the battlefield— even when we also account for formal ceasefires. This pattern is consistent with Hypothesis 4 in chapter 1. But my findings go one step further in showing that these temporary lulls in fighting provide moments of opportunity for belligerents that can and want to fight more effectively. In the immediate aftermath of negotiations that do not resolve conflicts, the battlefield swings in one side's favor more dramatically than was the case before talks began. Additional tests show that these shifts are directly tied to negotiations and are not simply statistical artifacts where the battlefield inevitably changes over time. These results lend strong support to Hypothesis 5.

The War of the Roman Republic in 1849 and the Cenepa Valley War of 1995 illustrate how these dynamics play out in individual conflicts over discrete negotiation periods. In the former case, France used talks with the Roman triumvirate to arrange a deal that Louis Napoleon immediately nullified as soon as his troops had relocated to more advantageous high ground and once his party had prevailed in legislative elections. The republicans, who had been unsure of France's intentions, paid the price of losing their inchoate nation while Louis Napoleon minimized his own nation's losses. In the Cenepa conflict, both belligerent states leveraged the enormous diplomatic pressure that outside states placed on them to extract benefits for themselves. Peru used the slowdown in hostilities during mediation to reinforce woefully unprepared troops in and around the battlefield. Ecuador used talks to play the role of the peace-seeking party and went on a diplomatic offensive afterward to continue appealing to international audiences. Both countries profited, in slightly different manners, from negotiating insincerely with one another.

These results stress the importance of viewing negotiations as a strategic act that, in specific circumstances, belligerents exploit in service of their war objectives. Scholars and policymakers frequently think of negotiations as producing one of two outcomes: the war ends, or the war proceeds as if nothing meaningful had happened. Neither ripeness theory nor the bargaining model of war fully acknowledges or furnishes a theoretical explanation for whether, when, and why diplomacy is leveraged to produce side effects that change belligerents' reversion outcomes and the dynamics of the subsequent hostilities. Such a binary form of thinking reflects an overly restrictive view of how diplomacy can affect conflict, potentially producing dubious and possibly harmful policy prescriptions about how to bring wars to a peaceable end.

Put together, this and the previous chapter present a comprehensive empirical case in support of the five primary hypotheses underlying my theory of wartime negotiations. But the four brief historical case studies across these two chapters each speak to separate parts of my argument. The next chapter delves into a war—and, specifically, its diplomatic activity—that illustrates and substantiates the entirety of my theory.

FIGHTING WORDS IN THE FIRST ARAB-ISRAELI WAR

The mood in Tel Aviv on the afternoon of May 14, 1948, was celebratory. A private gathering of numerous officials would take place inside the Tel Aviv Museum at four in the afternoon, but people in the streets had all heard rumors of the meeting's purpose. Inside the museum, David Ben-Gurion, leader of the Jewish community in Mandatory Palestine, would declare the establishment of the new and independent State of Israel. Ben-Gurion's proclamation spoke of a potential world where this Jewish homeland could coexist with its surrounding Arab states: "We offer peace and amity to all neighboring states and their peoples, and invite them to cooperate with the independent Jewish nation for the common good of all. The State of Israel is ready to contribute its full share to the peaceful progress and reconstitution of the Middle East."[1]

Such a world was the stuff of dreams. Within a day of Ben-Gurion's speech, military forces from Egypt, Iraq, Jordan, Lebanon, and Syria descended on Israel with the intention of eliminating it. So began the Arab-Israeli War.

This conflict is important with respect to wartime diplomacy for at least three reasons. First, it was only the second interstate war to erupt following the establishment of the United Nations in October 1945.[2] Analyzing the moments right after the UN's creation can help reveal the immediate impact, if any, of the high latent external pressures created by the post-1945 environment. Second, and on a related note, this conflict was the first to involve direct mediation efforts mandated by the nascent organization. As we will see, the advent of the United Nations mediator in Palestine represented an innovation in global affairs wherein the international community's diplomatic heft and desire for peace were embodied in a single individual. The UN mediator could thus bring not only substantial but also sharp diplomatic pressure to bear. Third, this war between the Arab states and the State of Israel, while the first, would certainly not be the last. Tensions between Israel and its Arab neighbors continue to be one of the more volatile situations for international affairs. Understanding the dynamics in play in fighting and negotiating in this past war thus has significant implications not only for conflict in general but also for modern-day manifestations of these violent rivalries in the Middle East.

Over eight months between May 1948 and January 1949, the Arab-Israeli War underwent three distinct phases of fighting that were punctuated by three UN mediation efforts. The first bout of hostilities proved difficult for the new State of Israel, as it struggled to fend off an assault on all fronts using a sparsely equipped paramilitary force. The second round, however, saw the battlefield decidedly tilt in Israel's favor, and the third saw the Arab states suffer sizable territorial losses before Egypt became the first Arab state to negotiate a peace with Israel. This sequence of events raises three questions: What helps to explain Israel's remarkable ability to turn the tides of favor in the conflict? Furthermore, why did the mediation efforts begin and end—and, thus, repeatedly fail—when they did? And what explains why the Arab states and Israel were finally willing to negotiate an end to the conflict?

My theory indicates that the answers to these questions are deeply intertwined. The combination of very high latent external diplomatic pressures and battlefield developments explains the timing and motivations behind each negotiation period, as well as the impacts each had on the subsequent trajectory of conflict. The opening phase of conflict saw a somewhat disorganized coalition of Arab states fight an inadequately equipped Israel, with both sides' fighters quickly becoming exhausted. The intense and perpetual pressures produced by the UN mediator permitted both Israel and the Arab states to engage in diplomacy with insincere ends. Both sides exploited the first mediation effort to rest, rearm, and regroup in order to continue fighting more capably once negotiations ended. But as we will see, Israel had more to gain from stalling for time through diplomacy, as this allowed it to absorb a large influx of troops and weapons into its military. In other words, insincere negotiations gave Israel a chance to mobilize more of its latent military capabilities into actual power on the battlefield. These enhancements gave Israel an upper hand during the remainder of the war.

By the second mediation effort, the embattled Arab states became more sincere negotiators that harbored real, though still highly reluctant, desires to stop fighting. Conversely, Israel was buoyed by its recent successes and continued negotiating insincerely with the intention of planning military operations to definitively defeat the Arab states. It was only when Israel faced threats of intervention from

Britain that it also saw poor prospects to continued fighting and chose to accept a diplomatic settlement. In sum, the Arab-Israeli War shows how changes on the battlefield produce different forms of negotiation in a setting with high latent pressures for peace. Side effects extracted from diplomacy helped the belligerents achieve goals and reshape the battlefield in ways that would have been far less tractable without third-party pressure to negotiate.

The remainder of the chapter expands on this argument. I first provide some background information on the "Palestinian Question" that was the precursor to the Arab-Israeli War, as well as a brief summary of the conflict itself. I next scrutinize the war in more discrete stages, highlighting connections with my hypotheses as appropriate. I then review the diplomatic strategies that played out over the course of the war and how they align with my theory of wartime negotiations.

Prelude to War

The end of the First World War brought many changes to global affairs. One distinct development was the dissolution of the centuries-old but waning Ottoman Empire. The Turks suffered painful losses to the Russians in two wars—the first between 1768 and 1774, and the second between 1877 and 1878.[3] The Ottoman Empire officially collapsed with the conclusion of World War I. As European powers split the former empire up for themselves, the territory of Palestine, which the Ottomans had held for four centuries, was placed within a protectorate under Great Britain. This allocation fulfilled the terms of the Balfour Declaration of 1917, in which the British government voiced its support for the creation of a "national home" for the Jewish population in Palestine.[4] The League of Nations formalized this arrangement in 1923. Disagreements quickly arose between the members of the Arab majority in Palestine, who had nationalist beliefs and hopes of an independent Palestinian and Arab state, and members of the Jewish minority in Palestine, who sought a Jewish state on the same land. Animosity only grew as Zionists continued to immigrate to Palestine in hopes of establishing this Jewish state. Internal strife tore Palestine apart multiple times over the next two to three decades and signaled that the British Mandate did not provide a long-term solution.

The rise of antisemitism prior to the Second World War, as well as the Holocaust during the war itself, resulted in a surge of Jews fleeing persecution and heading for Palestine. The 1930s alone saw Palestine's Jewish population, or Yishuv, skyrocket from about 205,000 to 475,000.[5] The British government attempted to prevent large influxes of Jewish immigration during the war itself, concerned that Arabs would further destabilize Palestine out of fears that they would soon become a minority. This decision attracted widespread opposition and condemnation. A notable source of international opprobrium was President Harry Truman, who supported the notion of allowing 100,000 Jews to immigrate to Mandatory Palestine. A growing contingent of disaffected Zionist insurgents also began orchestrating terrorist attacks against British government officials. On September 26, 1947, Britain declared that it would end its mandate over Palestine. The specific end date by which point British forces would exit was later announced as May 14, 1948. The monumental task of figuring out who or what would replace the British Mandate was then placed on the shoulders of the United Nations, which by that point was less than two years old.

The UN General Assembly passed its compromise proposal, Resolution 181 (II), on November 29, 1947. The resolution called for the partition of Palestine into two separate and independent states, one of which would be Jewish and the other Arab. The leftmost map in figure 5.1 depicts this proposal. The Holy City of Jerusalem, central to followers of both the Jewish and Muslim faiths, would be placed under an international regime. While members of the Jewish community were somewhat supportive of the proposal, leaders in the surrounding Arab states were highly dissatisfied with the idea of dividing territory and argued that it infringed on individuals' rights to self-determination. The terms of Resolution 181 (II) did not come to pass. Palestine fell into a civil war shortly thereafter, pitting Arab militants in Palestine against the Haganah, the primary paramilitary organization of the Yishuv. Furthermore, Great Britain refused to enforce a deal that did not have the backing of both concerned parties.

Thus, by the last day of the British Mandate on May 14, Palestine faced a power vacuum. The vacuum was partially filled that afternoon when leaders of the Yishuv came together at the Tel Aviv Museum and declared that the new independent state of Israel would come into being at midnight on May 15. David Ben-Gurion, a renowned Zionist leader, would be both the first minister of defense and prime minister.[6] The creation of a Jewish state was wholly unacceptable to the Arabs in Palestine as well as those in the Arab states, who were founding members of a regional organization called the Arab League, surrounding it. Foreseeing an imminent conflict, the UN General Assembly had passed a resolution on May 14 appointing Folke Bernadotte—a Swedish diplomat and former vice president of the Swedish Red Cross—as the United Nations mediator in Palestine. The role that Bernadotte assumed was the first of its kind, and he would face a significant challenge that erupted soon after this appointment. Hours after Israel came into being, the armed forces of Egypt, Jordan, Iraq, Lebanon, and Syria simultaneously sprang into action and engaged in an attack on all fronts.

	Arab control
	Jewish control
	Jerusalem district

Proposed
1947 partition   June 1948   January 1949

FIGURE 5.1.   Maps of changing control of Palestine.

The War Itself

Bernadotte officially assumed his official capacity as UN mediator on May 20 and relentlessly attempted to open channels of communication between Israel and the Arab states. The UN and Bernadotte were able to establish two truces during the war, each of which was intended to allow for mediation to change the belligerents' reversion outcomes and find a suitable settlement regarding the fate of Palestine. The first period was from June 11 to July 8, and the second began on July 18 and ended on October 15. Both diplomatic endeavors ran into significant resistance from the belligerents, neither of which was willing to accept the proposals made by the UN mediator.

Prior to the first mediation effort, battlefield activity firmly tilted in the Arab League's favor. But in the moments following the first truce, Israeli forces seized the initiative and made significant territorial gains. The Jewish state's battlefield advantages only mounted in the aftermath of the second truce. On January 7, 1949, Israel and Egypt agreed to an initial ceasefire agreement, paving a path to a more formal peace that they would sign on the Greek island of Rhodes by February 24. Agreements with the other Arab states would subsequently materialize and be signed through the rest of 1949. Each of these settlements would establish terms that were favorable for the state of Israel.

A notable aspect of the Arab-Israeli War is that Israel's reversal of fortune began in the aftermath of the first failed mediation effort. My theory suggests that this is no mere coincidence; diplomacy was critical to explaining Israel's ability to reshape the trajectory of battlefield activity. As I will demonstrate, strong and unrelenting international pressure for peace, generated by the incipient United Nations and personified in the role of the UN mediator, created an opening for both the Arab states and Israel to transition into more peaceful periods of diplomatic bargaining when it suited their strategic interests as dictated by the battlefield, and to do so without suffering the degree of political disadvantage they would face from seeking diplomacy without external motivation. The belligerents thus had greater liberties to exploit periods of mediation to further promote their war aims rather than search for a meaningful negotiated settlement.

Israel ultimately had more to gain from bouts of insincere diplomacy. By buying pockets of time, Israel secured valuable opportunities to translate more of its latent war-fighting potential into actual force that could be used against the Arab states. Each period of relative calm afforded a moment to rearm, reorganize, and regroup for hostilities. These respites paid off, enabling the new Jewish state to win the very begrudging acknowledgment of—and indirect right to exist alongside—its Arab neighbors.

To elaborate on this argument, we must walk through the war once again but in greater detail, elucidating the strategic environment in which the conflict began.

Israel's Initial Disadvantages

In terms of raw troop strength, Israel and the Arab states were roughly even at the outset of hostilities. Israel wielded approximately nineteen thousand fighters against the Arab League's twenty-three thousand regular military troops.[7] Israeli forces had relatively better training and quicker lines of communication. Yet on most other dimensions, Israel began the war at a significant disadvantage against its rivals. Jewish leaders in Palestine had long realized that a declaration of statehood would invite Arab attacks, but the new State of Israel was remarkably underprepared for the assaults that began on May 15. Several factors contributed to Israel's handicapped position.

First, the Arab states wielded the element of surprise in the opening stages of conflict. Arab forces also began on high ground, while much of the Jewish population was in the lowlands.[8] The Haganah also had poor intelligence capabilities, precluding it from learning valuable information about its Arab rivals or their imminent plans.[9]

Second, serious discussions about preparations against the Arabs began only on May 11, mere days before the planned declaration of statehood.[10] Ben-Gurion disagreed with his military leaders about overarching strategy. The prospective prime minister and defense minister wanted to throw all possible force into overtaking the area that linked Tel Aviv with Jerusalem, while military officials sought to keep some forces in reserve as reinforcements that would be deployed only once Israel observed how the Arab states would respond. While initial plans largely followed Ben-Gurion's desires, both overall proposals were preoccupied with offensive plans to claim territory and said startlingly little regarding the establishment of any defenses against Arab invasions.

Third, the Haganah and other Jewish fighters had continuously fought a civil war against Arabs in Palestine since November 1947, leaving them both physically and materially exhausted compared to the Arab troops that were engaging in hostilities for the first time. To be sure, this meant that Israeli forces—many of whom had also fought for the Allies in World War II—had far more combat experience than the Arab states' militaries, none of which, except for Iraq's forces, had fought in the war.[11] But this experiential advantage was materially outweighed by Israel's lack of arms and heavy weaponry. Their fighters had no field guns, a couple of old tanks, a handful of modest planes, and a disorganized assortment of rifles and machine guns. Only three-fifths of all fighters were armed,[12] and ammunition supplies were so low that, on average, each rifle was allocated fifty rounds and each machine gun had only seven hundred.[13] In mid-April, Ben-Gurion noted that the Yishuv remained "quite far from having the force we need to meet the 15th of May. We lack almost half the necessary manpower, we lack 80 percent of the transport, and we lack the rest of the [necessary] equipment in no small measure. . . . There is no food, there is no fuel, and a thousand other things."[14] On the other hand, the Arab states' lack of combat experience was offset by substantial weaponry that included at least 150 field guns, twenty tanks, and fifty fighter aircraft.[15] On top of this, the Haganah was a decentralized paramilitary force, and one of many. Arab opponents had more traditional command structures. The unified Israel Defense Forces (IDF) was established only on May 28, thirteen days after the war began.

These deficiencies had a concrete impact on Jewish assessments of the imminent conflict. On May 12, Yigal Yadin, the director of Israeli military operations, was asked to provide an assessment of the military situation. His response was unpropitious: "I would say not that the chances are quite even. If I want to be frank I would say that their advantage is greater."[16]

Yadin's pessimism was not unjustified. The nearly simultaneous assault from every front was overwhelming. Troops from Lebanon and Syria would come in from the north, either to take the Sea of Galilee or to split Israel into pieces; those from Iraq and Jordan would come in from the east and move toward the city of Haifa; and those from Egypt would enter from the south toward Tel Aviv. Two days into the conflict, Ben-Gurion openly told his cabinet that "the situation is very grave. There aren't enough rifles. There are no heavy weapons."[17]

Opening Hostilities and Exhaustion

Israel's plans of a heavy offensive against the Arab states were instead transformed into painful efforts to repulse numerous attacks with limited resources. On May 19, a group of individuals responsible for defending the kibbutz of Degania Alef from Syrian invasion arrived in Tel Aviv to request reinforcements in advance of an imminent attack. Ben-Gurion's response reflected how grim the material situation remained: "There are not enough guns, not enough planes; men are lacking on all fronts. The situation is very severe in the Negev, is difficult in Jerusalem, in Upper Galilee. The whole country is a front line. We cannot send reinforcements."[18] On May 28, after about ten days of intense fighting, Jordan's military forces managed to overtake the Jewish Quarter of Jerusalem and force the evacuation of all remaining Jews from the area. Teddy Kollek, who would become mayor of Jerusalem from 1965 to 1993, later called this day "the blackest event in Israel's War of Independence."[19]

Meanwhile, attempts to take the offensive had limited success. This was certainly the case near Latrun, an area designated as part of the Arab state in the UN's partition plan. It also included the old road that linked Tel Aviv with Jerusalem. Ben-Gurion believed Latrun to be so strategically important to Israel's defense that he overrode his generals and ordered attacks on Arab troops there.[20] In May and once in early June, Israeli forces attempted to take Latrun. They were repeatedly repulsed at great cost by well-prepared Jordanian forces and experienced the worst losses on a single battlefield that they would suffer until 1973.[21]

By early June, the Arab states had gained control over much of the territory that the United Nations partition plan had granted to Palestine. Israelis managed to push away a fair share of assaults, but about a third of the territory allocated to the Jewish state, most of which was in the Negev desert, was still occupied by Arab forces. Israel had managed to hold the Arab states at bay, but its forces were exhausted. Access to Jerusalem and the Jewish population there was incredibly tenuous, leaving people without reliable access to food, water, or medicine, and the Arab states continued to pose serious threats on basically every front.[22] The middle map of figure 5.1 reflects the Israelis' dire situation at this time.

The Arab states' military forces were also deeply strained, and despite some successes, military leaders began to confront the reality that they were unlikely to eliminate the Jewish state wholesale. Politicians in the Arab League (with the exception of Jordan) continued to see decent prospects for gaining some advantage over Israel that could be framed as a victory, but the last month of fighting had left their soldiers and supplies drained. Jordan's forces, the Arab Legion, faced significant issues. Having deployed all of its troops in the previous month, Jordan had no personnel reserves and had dwindling arms supplies.[23]

The First Mediation: Bernadotte's Blitz

As the first phase of conflict intensified, the United Nations mediator sprang into action. Bernadotte received his official designation on May 20 and embraced the role with enormous devotion. UN Security Council Resolution 50, adopted on May 29, called for a four-week truce and made Bernadotte the key negotiator to lead this endeavor. Bernadotte had arrived in Cairo the previous day and began his mediation effort on May 30.

What followed was a furious week and a half of shuttle diplomacy, during which time Bernadotte and his staff traveled to Cairo, Tel Aviv, Amman, and Beirut to speak with each respective government. Collecting their thoughts, he attempted to identify key areas of disagreement and to offer proposals for truces in a take-it-or-leave-it format.[24] A significant breakthrough took place on June 5, when Bernadotte essentially presented an ultimatum regarding terms of a truce; discussions had come to a standstill over definitions of "military personnel" and "men of military age," both of which were part of Resolution 50. The belligerent states accepted the proposal, and a formal arrangement of a four-week truce was completed by June 9. The four-week ceasefire, which would be spent engaging in further mediation efforts to reach a more durable agreement, officially came into effect on the morning of June 11. While the ceasefire certainly reduced the intensity of hostilities compared to the previous month, compliance was inconsistent. Upward of five hundred ceasefire violations were reported during the first truce.[25] Given the highly limited number of UN observers that were available to supervise the belligerents' adherence to peace, many other infractions were likely not documented. This truce nonetheless opened the door to more substantive discussions that would ideally result in a mutually acceptable agreement regarding Palestine.

It is important to note that this mediation effort and associated drawdown in hostilities would likely not have occurred without the direct interposition of the United Nations and the mediator in Palestine. Both were critical to lowering the relative costs of negotiation for all belligerents. In early June, the Arab states were exhausting their military reserves but were unwilling to directly interact with Israel, as doing so would confer legitimacy to a state that it not only refused to recognize but hoped to eliminate.[26] The government in Tel Aviv, seeking international recognition, was more open to diplomacy for the exact same reason, but it also could not freely make direct offers to negotiate for fear of looking weak.[27] As such, one month into the war, both sides wanted to temporarily stop fighting but could not reasonably initiate a unilateral ceasefire without emboldening the enemy, sparking furor at home, or inviting the imposition of an unfavorable arrangement by the United Nations. Outside diplomatic pressure from the UN, major powers, and Bernadotte himself provided each side the necessary justification and political cover to pause hostilities without triggering as much blowback.[28] In support of the ideas behind Hypothesis 2 (and, implicitly, Hypothesis 1), increased external pressure to negotiate played a critical part in getting parties to come to the table.

Substantiating Hypothesis 4, the period of mediation featured lower levels of hostilities compared to moments without diplomacy. Of course, this was a consequence of the formal truces imposed by the UN, but we also see evidence that the ceasefires were constantly violated. These repeated infractions attest to the external nature of the truce and mediation, which occurred when neither side harbored a genuine desire to strike a negotiated agreement.

Exploiting a Respite

My theory predicts that low costs to diplomacy will enable belligerents to engage in insincere negotiations that are not meant to terminate hostilities and may even attempt to extend them. The sequence of events that occurred during this first ceasefire and mediation confirms this claim. A weeks-long respite was exactly what both sides desired by early June, and each party was given a chance to extend and reshape hostilities compared to a situation where the war continued with no formal interruption.

A central tenet of the truce, and one that Bernadotte stressed, was that it would not be used to change the state of military affairs or grant either side a military advantage.[29] The four weeks were meant to create room for dialogue that could lead to a more permanent peaceful arrangement. While both Israel and the Arab states entertained Bernadotte's diplomatic efforts, it is now clear that neither side expected or really wanted a diplomatic peace. Each belligerent instead seemed more interested in exploiting negotiations and the associated lull in battlefield hostilities to promote the aims that triggered the war in the first place.

For the Arab states, the four-week period provided valuable time to resupply themselves with varying degrees of success. According to a secret commission of inquiry in Iraq, the government managed to ship substantial arms and ammunition to forces in Jordan and Palestine by disguising these shipments as food and clothing. Iraqi forces at the front had been boosted to ten thousand. Egypt reinforced its troops, replenished its ammunition (though Arab forces continued to face issues on this front), and repaired its planes for further combat. Both Egypt and Syria launched a massive recruitment effort to increase their numbers as well.[30]

Yet the party that had more to gain from the pause was Israel. In a document dated June 11, 1948, a British official stationed in Haifa argued that the first truce "would certainly be exploited by the Jews to continue military training and reorganization."[31] Iraqi chief of staff General Salah Saib al-Jaburi also reported to his own government that Israel would be much more militarily capable following the truce.[32] These assessments proved to be correct. Moshe Carmel, a military commander who would later become minister of transportation, called the military pause "dew from heaven."[33] The four weeks were vital for reorganizing the new IDF force, replenishing supplies, giving soldiers time to rest, and addressing grievances that troops had about the lack of support for their families.[34]

Beyond refreshing the forces already on the ground, having extra time would also allow Israel to gain additional troops and weapons that would significantly augment the country's military power. The continuing influx of Jews, many of whom were veterans of World War II, into Israel provided a significant boost to recruitment efforts. While Israel had approximately thirty thousand fighters at the war's opening, the number expanded to sixty-five thousand by the middle of July.[35] Israelis eventually had a three-to-two advantage in terms of troops in Palestine.[36]

Israel's most critical weakness—its comparatively paltry supply of weapons—was also addressed during this lull in hostilities. The United States had imposed an embargo on arms sales to Palestine and neighboring states in December 1947 as part of its commitment to the partition plan laid out in UN Security Council Resolution 181 (II).[37] Resolution 50, which had sought a four-week truce, instituted a global arms embargo against all belligerents during the ceasefire. Zionist leaders failed to change the Truman administration's policy despite Truman's support of the Jewish cause, and the global embargo appeared to be generally upheld.[38] Yishuv leaders, however, had made numerous large orders of weapons, aircraft, and ammunition from Latin America, Western Europe, and Czechoslovakia in the months immediately following the partition plan and before the first truce. Illegal purchases in the United States also boosted Israel's capabilities.[39] A steady stream of fifty million bullets, twenty-five thousand rifles, five thousand machine guns, and numerous tanks arrived in Israel and were incorporated into the IDF before the global arms embargo began.[40] The Israeli Air Force also came into being in late May but obtained more modern aircraft only as the conflict progressed. Ben-Gurion was eager to take advantage of this respite to engage in more war planning. Flouting the terms of the truce, he demanded that military production increase and that Israelis establish new stronghold settlements (*yishuvei mishlat*) that would consolidate Israel's control over its newly won territory.[41]

Conspicuously, Bernadotte was oblivious to the dramatic expansion of Israeli military capabilities over the truce period. He and his team intensified their interactions with the belligerent governments, but these efforts occurred under the misguided presumption that both sides' forces remained relatively even.[42] Some of these misconceptions may have made their way into the initial proposal he made to the concerned parties on June 28, 1948. A central provision of this plan was the creation of a "Union, comprising two Members, one Arab and Jewish," each of which would have political autonomy but share an economic union. The document offered several suggestions about how territory that was in dispute during the war would be allocated between the two autonomous territories.[43] Bernadotte also proposed an extension of the truce by an additional month to create more time for his proposal to elicit dialogue. UN Security Council Resolution 53, adopted on July 7, reiterated this appeal for "the prolongation of the truce."[44] Despite Bernadotte's assurances that these ideas were only preliminary and offered in hopes of extending the truce for further dialogue, both sides were extremely displeased with the proposal and perceived it to be too concrete for comfort.[45]

On June 30, while discussing Bernadotte's first plan, Ben-Gurion and his cabinet considered but subsequently rejected the idea of launching a premature attack. Ben-Gurion believed that the Arab states would reject the deal and refuse to keep talking, thus creating an opening for Israel to launch its offensives after setting up the Arab states as the recalcitrant party.[46] In general accordance with Ben-Gurion's prognosis, the Arab League took public actions that appeared more belligerent. The Israelis dismissed the specific terms in his proposal but expressed openness to a longer truce. On July 6, the Arab states unanimously declared their opposition to both the proposal and a ceasefire extension.[47]

Renewed Hostilities

The Egyptians ended the truce a day early on July 8, hoping to exploit the element of surprise for an advantage on the battlefield. The hostilities that unfolded in the second phase of violence are retrospectively called the "Ten-Day Battles," reflecting the relatively brief bout of violence before another ceasefire and mediation effort came into effect. The nature of combat fundamentally changed compared to the more indeterminate state of hostilities before the first truce: the strengthened Israeli military now seized the initiative. In the North, Operation Dekel (July 8–18) captured a series of Arab villages, including the symbolically significant town of Nazareth.[48] On the central front, Operation Dani (July 9–19) claimed territory near Tel Aviv and created a vital bridge to the Jewish soldiers and civilians who were isolated in Jerusalem. Consistent with the implications of Hypothesis 5, hostilities immediately following failed negotiations resulted in a battlefield that reduced levels of imbalance on the battlefield by neutralizing many of the Arabs initiators' gains in the first month of hostilities.

Israel's new offensives did not accomplish all of Ben-Gurion's goals. For example, Operation Dani fell short of its objective of securing Latrun—a constant struggle for the Israelis. An effort to retake Jerusalem also did not materialize. Nontrivial resistance by Arab forces inflicted significant losses on the IDF, leading it to adopt more limited territorial aims.[49] Leaders in the Arab states were nonetheless startled to see how dramatically their fortunes had turned. Over ten days, Israel gained nearly four hundred square miles of territory, while the Arab states had cobbled together only about thirty.[50] The Arabs' defenses in key locations such as Latrun and Jerusalem had held, but only barely and with few resources left to repeat the process.

The Second Mediation: Bernadotte's Demise

Eight days into fighting, on July 15, the UN Security Council adopted Resolution 54, which ordered all belligerent states to cease fire and resume cooperation with Bernadotte. Unlike the first truce, this demand was not predicated on the idea of negotiations leading to a quick agreement, nor did it come with a finite time limit. The ceasefire and mediation were intended to continue indefinitely until a deal could be made, but such an arrangement would be conditional on the parties' continued cooperation.[51]

The Arab League collectively informed UN secretary-general Trygve Lie of their acceptance of a truce on July 17, with numerous conditions attached. Even the initially hawkish politicians now realized that they had likely achieved all they could and that future hostilities would probably lead to losses. In a meeting of Arab League leaders, the prime minister of Jordan reported that his country's military had completely run out of ammunition.[52] Negotiations therefore presented the only practical path to consolidate the gains made thus far from fighting and to attempt to impel Israel to make a deal before it managed to take more ground. Even if Arab leaders recognized that talks could prove unsuccessful, they saw the costs of uninterrupted fighting as too high to simply accept.

In a testament to how the UN Security Council lowered the relative costs of negotiation, the Arab League also took clear advantage of Security Council Resolution 54 to create political cover for themselves. Local media lambasted Western states and the Security Council for imposing a truce and mediation efforts, simultaneously broadcasting false stories about Arab victories to placate their citizens.[53] Foreign officials in these states became victims of attacks on the streets. Diplomats surmised that the Arab governments had steered public outrage toward the West in order to deflect criticism from their own shortcomings in Palestine and their voluntary accession to the truce. Iraq publicly rebuffed the truce proposal but privately admitted to the British that the Iraqi prime minister had simply "seized an opportunity for increasing his political stature in Iraq, where public opinion was strongly in favor of continuing the fighting."[54]

The Israeli government, very aware of international pressure for peace, accepted the ceasefire a day before the Arabs did. But their underlying motivation for doing so was markedly different. Seeing success on the battlefield, Israeli leaders wanted to use this second round of diplomacy as yet another break in advance of renewed hostilities. Ben-Gurion's lack of interest in a negotiated settlement was almost immediately apparent, at least behind closed doors. On July 19, only one day into the truce, Ben-Gurion met again with Director of Military Operations Yigal Yadin to ask when Israeli forces would be prepared to resume fighting. Ben-Gurion then spent a cabinet meeting on August 1 making the case for the eventual resumption of hostilities.[55] He also mandated that each soldier undergo at least one month of training and be discharged to get rest before having to fight again. While Israel had enjoyed new victories in the ten days of hostilities, Arab forces had not been driven out of Palestine and appeared unwilling to take any action—a situation that Ben-Gurion found unacceptable for Israel's longer-term security. The prime minister thus started reviewing plans to stage offensives that would lay waste to the Arab states and obliterate their interest in any future hostilities.[56] Military decisions made in Tel Aviv were not responsive or connected to diplomatic activities taking place simultaneously, largely because officials concluded that the Arab states would never withdraw troops from Palestine of their own accord.[57] As such, Israel entered the new mediation effort with truly insincere intentions. Ben-Gurion did not expect or want agreement, but rather sought time to prepare for an assault that would break the Arab states' backs.

Between late July and mid-September, Bernadotte resumed another aggressive round of shuttle diplomacy between the belligerent states. Discussions mainly revolved around issues of territorial control—with special emphasis on Jerusalem, the Negev, and ports in Haifa and Lydda—and the status of Arab refugees who had been driven out of their homes during the conflict. Notably, leaders in each Arab government now begrudgingly accepted the existence of an independent Jewish state, even if they would refuse to formally recognize it.[58] This was a significant political concession, but it did not translate into an acceptable deal. Egypt indicated that it would accept only a peace settlement that reverted to the military situation from early June, which would negate all gains Israel had made after the first truce was prematurely ended by Egyptian forces.[59]

Bernadotte released his second plan on September 16, 1948. The revised proposal now recognized the existence of an independent and fully autonomous State of Israel. Rather than placing Jerusalem in Arab Palestine, the new plan put the Holy City under UN control, much as was outlined in the UN resolution from November 29, 1947. The disputed ports in Haifa and Jaffa were to be freely accessible to Arab states—an idea the Israelis could not accept. The Negev, which the 1947 partition plan had designated as part of a Jewish state, was now to be allocated to the Arabs. While these represented improvements from Israel's perspective, the proposal outlined an Israel that would constitute only one-fifth of the original Mandatory Palestine.[60] Finally, the plan's stipulation that Arab refugees would have the right to return to their homes meant that hundreds of thousands of Arabs would be allowed to freely reenter the small Jewish state.

On September 17, Bernadotte was assassinated by Zionist militants from a group called Lehi. The so-called "second plan" would become Bernadotte's final act and testament. Ralph Bunche, Bernadotte's highly trusted assistant and adviser, assumed the role of acting mediator from this point forward. While Bernadotte's death placed additional weight on the proposal, both Israel and the Arab states voiced objections to it in the following week.[61]

The Third Phase and Mediation: Bunche's Peace

By early October 1948, the Israeli government grew impatient with foundering mediation efforts. The time had come to take action and employ the forces that had been renewed and replenished over the last three months. While the first truce permitted Israel to grow to sixty-five thousand troops, this number had now ballooned further to more than ninety thousand.[62] A cabinet meeting on October 6 coalesced around a plan to break through on the southern front against Egypt with the apparent aim of opening the road to the Negev.[63] The desert as a whole was largely uninhabited, but Ben-Gurion saw the vast open space as being necessary for Israel's growth. The Israelis would try to make as many gains as possible in a few days before the Security Council could press for another ceasefire. This would proceed through separate campaigns, and Operation Yoav would be the primary assault.

Operation Yoav (also known as Operation Ten Plagues), from October 15 to 22, was ruinous for the Egyptians. After provoking Egyptian forces into firing shots that could serve as a pretext for a broader response, Israeli planes destroyed Egyptian airfields while ground forces split Egyptian troops into smaller clusters that could not support one another or receive reinforcements. Israeli forces were able to overtake a series of Arab villages, as well as the city of Beersheba, which was the largest city in the Negev and the key to controlling the rest of the desert.[64] A large contingent of four thousand Egyptian forces was isolated in the village of al-Faluja.[65] Conspicuously, the other Arab states were weary of fighting and did not offer any support to Egypt.[66] On October 19, the Security Council passed a resolution calling for a ceasefire. After a day of delay, Ben-Gurion decided to accept this appeal and also believed that doing so would help to prevent an Egyptian counterattack.[67] A localized ceasefire went into effect on October 22.

Operation Yoav succeeded in claiming Beersheba by the time the latest ceasefire began. Yet much of the Negev still had to be secured. The good news from Operation Yoav encouraged Israel to continue pushing out Arab forces and claiming territory as expeditiously as possible before international pressure would tie its hands. On October 28, Israeli forces initiated Operation Hiram, engaging in sixty hours of fighting against Arab forces situated in Galilee. Approximately eight hundred Arab casualties were killed or captured, and the Upper Galilee was seized by Israelis before another local truce was established. On November 4, the Security Council adopted Resolution 61, which called for all sides to withdraw back to positions held on October 14 (before Operation Yoav) and to work with the UN mediator to establish "permanent truce lines."[68] Israel continued its attacks regardless of this resolution, attracting a wave of criticism and building momentum for Resolution 62, which would reiterate the appeal for an armistice and negotiations.

When Resolution 62 was adopted on November 16, Israel had not yet completed its objective of securing the Negev. Moshe Sharett, the first minister of foreign affairs, demurred and bided his time by offering a series of insubstantial concessions regarding control over the coastal strip, all with the intention of buying more time for Israel to consolidate its control.[69] Israeli diplomatic activity in the face of high international pressures and low relative costs of fighting were insincere—explicitly designed to delay in hopes of advancing Israel's war aims rather than end them.

Resolution 62 also went unheeded but bought political time and space for Israel to press the war slightly further. One additional and final major Israeli effort, Operation Horev, began on December 22 with the intention of pushing all Egyptian forces out of Israeli lands. By New Year's Day 1949, international opposition to the Israelis' campaign became significant, but IDF forces made one final push to take the town of Rafah, which would grant them high ground and also trap many Egyptian forces. On January 6, the Egyptians relented and declared their willingness to enter mediation to forge an armistice with Israel. With the British applying some pressure on Ben-Gurion, Israel accepted a January 6 ceasefire and brought hostilities to an end.

Delegations from Israel and Egypt met in Rhodes on January 12. The two parties, with the assistance of Ralph Bunche, signed a formal armistice agreement on February 24, 1949. The settlement established a temporary demarcation line that tabled the ultimate question of what to do about Palestine. Israel would have to withdraw troops from several cities and allow Egyptian troops trapped in al-Faluja to go back home, but these concessions were not too significant compared to Israel's gains. Beersheba and the Negev, both part of the proposed Arab state in the 1947 partition plan, would now go to the Israelis. Over the next several months, Israel would sign a series of armistice agreements with the remaining Arab states, largely on terms that recognized the state of the battlefield and Israel's military superiority. As seen in the right-most map in figure 5.1, the new state came to possess almost four-fifths of the former Mandatory Palestine,[70] which was about 22 percent more than what the partition plan had originally envisioned.[71]

Reviewing Wartime Diplomacy

The Arab-Israeli War underwent two periods of mediated and external negotiation before Israel and Egypt undertook steps to sign an armistice agreement in a third mediation.[72] The first negotiation period ensued when both Israel and the Arab states were exhausted from initial hostilities but saw value to fighting as long as they could have an opportunity to reorganize and replenish themselves. The UN mediator, backed by a series of Security Council resolutions, decreased the relative costs of negotiation and thus enabled all belligerents to participate in diplomacy more freely. As both parties believed they could find success on the battlefield after a brief respite, they acceded to the efforts of Folke Bernadotte but harbored very little interest in making any concessions to their opponent. Nearly all states instead focused on rearming and recruiting more soldiers to join the war. The first mediation effort therefore proved to be borne of insincere intentions on both sides, and each belligerent realized that its opponent would use these inorganic talks to improve its military capabilities.

The strategic calculus changed slightly during the second truce and mediation. Israel continued to believe—and had now seen evidence—that it could amass more territory with limited resistance if it kept fighting. With the relative costs of negotiation being low but the relative costs of future fighting being even lower, Israel sought to stall for time through negotiations and to rearm yet again for another series of offensives to claim the Negev. Ben-Gurion entered talks with insincere motives. On the other hand, members of the Arab League began to see that future hostilities would yield grave outcomes and sought to lock down their battlefield gains through a negotiated settlement before Israel could wrest away those gains militarily. The Arab states' willingness to acknowledge Israel's existence marked a significant shift that was reflective of their updated beliefs. All the same, the Arab states were not yet ready to make major policy concessions regarding Palestine and indeed offered proposals involving a return to prewar conditions, which did not get much traction. With the relative costs of future fighting being high, the Arabs states' negotiation strategies were now more sincere.

By late 1948, Egypt knew its fortunes were grim and wanted to stop the conflict. Indeed, in the early days of 1949, King Farouk of Egypt had his personal plane standing by in case he needed to flee Cairo.[73] Diplomatic documents suggest that Egypt had in fact made numerous peace overtures in the late months of 1948, only to be ignored by the Israelis.[74] The combination of low relative costs of negotiation and high relative costs of fighting resulted in a more sincere negotiation effort from Egypt. Even so, the government did its best to minimize public ire by dissembling and portraying the decision as an accession to international pressure. Prime Minister Ibrahim Abdel-Hadi was quoted in the January 27, 1949, issue of the state-owned magazine *Al-Musawar* as saying that Egypt had ceased hostilities "because the Security Council so decreed," even though the nation's "armed forces were at their zenith in discipline and strength"[75]—a patently false claim.

While Israel continued to enjoy military success on the battlefield, Ben-Gurion saw two reasons why future fighting would not be profitable. First, at the domestic level, the Israeli public was sick of the war and largely felt they had been successful against the Arabs.[76] Second, at the international level, Britain threatened to intervene militarily in accordance with the 1936 Anglo-Egyptian Treaty if Israel refused to withdraw its forces from Egypt. A concurrent message from Washington, DC, on December 30 warned Ben-Gurion that this British threat was serious.[77] Ben-Gurion interpreted these signals as ultimatums, which would be deeply unfavorable for Israel if triggered.[78] With discouraging prospects from continued fighting, Israel ordered its IDF units to pull out of the Sinai, and Israeli representatives entered talks at Rhodes days later.

The mediation at Rhodes was difficult and almost came apart at least once. Nonetheless, both parties were now sincere in their negotiation behavior and made concessions regarding the division of Palestine. Unlike the two previous diplomatic efforts, which had invited insincere motivations, the discussions at Rhodes succeeded in codifying a set of concrete proposals regarding the demarcation and demilitarization of the former Palestinian mandate.[79] The demarcation lines and demilitarized zones were meant to be temporary arrangements that would lead the way to more formal talks within the next year. But as we have seen, these developments did not come to pass, and the hundreds of thousands of Arab refugees created by the conflict would have significant ramifications that resonate to this day.

It is worth noting that ripeness theory does not provide an effective explanation of diplomacy during this war. Scholars have written about the utility of ripeness theory in addressing the more protracted multidecade conflict between Israel, Palestine, and the Arab states,[80] but far less is said about this particular war in isolation. The three rounds of talks during this inaugural conflict took place in periods of high battlefield movement—not moments of costly stalemate. Intense third-party efforts to facilitate negotiations and identify ways out of fighting instead enabled belligerents, who still had not had sufficient opportunity to ascertain the bounds of a viable bargaining range, to buy time and extract side effects that they hoped would improve their war-fighting prospects. Ripeness theory does not systematically recognize this possibility, nor does it address the conditions in which negotiations are more likely to be exploited insincerely. The argument and evidence I have presented do address the causes and effects of these critical diplomatic maneuvers that, in the end, actualized Israel's existence.

The Limits of Diplomatic Pressure

Over the course of the war between May 1948 and January 1949, the UN Security Council adopted at least eleven resolutions related to "the Palestine Question," many of which explicitly called for ceasefires and diplomacy. Israel selectively acceded to only two resolutions, resulting in two mediation efforts, and did so when it suited its strategic interests. The new Jewish state thus demonstrated a definite awareness of how third-party diplomatic pressures could be exploited for additional gains.

Israel faced existential trouble in the first month of its war against neighboring Arab states.[81] Considered on their own, the inauspicious results from the battlefield could have compelled Israel to consider terminating hostilities. But Prime Minister Ben-Gurion and other decision-makers around him knew that having more time would prove crucial to translating more of their latent capabilities into actual force on the battlefield. The four-week mediation period in June and July 1948 afforded such an opportunity. The UN's intense diplomatic pressure campaign decreased the relative costs of negotiation. As Hypotheses 1 and 2 together suggest, such pressure enabled negotiations at higher rates than would have occurred without outside intervention, but these talks did not facilitate settlement. Both belligerents instead engaged in insincere diplomacy aimed at preparing for additional combat. In line with Hypotheses 4 and 5, talks were associated with reductions in active hostilities, and the end of failed mediation was quickly followed by sudden changes in battlefield trends. Israel may have continued bolstering its military capabilities even in the absence of UN mediation, but the historical record shows that the monthlong diplomatic undertaking created an indispensable avenue for Israel to ready itself for conflict. Commander Moshe Carmel's description of this period as "dew from heaven" underscores the importance of the pause for Israel's military fortunes. The more Israel's advantages materialized on the battlefield, the more both sides were willing to contemplate settlement. The context and consequences of the three rounds of negotiations during this war are consistent with expectations derived from Hypothesis 3.

Both Israel and the Arab states believed that the first mediation would help them fight more effectively in the near future. Yet ultimately, we see that Israel had more to gain from buying time, and this advantage only grew over the course of hostilities. The Israeli government's activities throughout the war illustrate an awareness of how much international opinion and pressure could be obstacles but also assets in accomplishing its overall goals. At the terrible cost of six thousand deaths, or about 1 percent of the population at the time, Israel secured its existence and grew by approximately 2,500 square miles compared to the hypothetical Jewish state that the United Nations had proposed in November 1947.[82] Insincere negotiations helped realize these accomplishments.

Diplomacy remains deeply relevant in the contemporary iteration of the Israeli-Palestinian conflict. Since the turn of the twenty-first century, numerous peace initiatives have been launched to devise a long-term resolution to the territorial dispute, which was exacerbated by Israel's significant gains in the 1967 Six-Day War. A common theme across the majority of these efforts, however, is that they have been spearheaded by external actors that often cajoled Israeli and Palestinian representatives to even come to the table. For instance, direct talks that took place sporadically throughout 2010 were the result of President Barack Obama's address in Cairo in June 2009, as well as intense monthslong pressure by Secretary of State Hillary Clinton.[83] An additional round of negotiations in 2013 and 2014 was championed by the next secretary of state, John Kerry, who met with Palestinian president Mahmoud Abbas and Israeli prime minister Benjamin Netanyahu approximately one hundred times over nine months.[84] My theory emphasizes that talks borne of such pressures are likely to fail or even be abused. Indeed, both Netanyahu and Abbas eventually agreed to participate in (and later abandoned) renewed dialogue in 2013 and 2014 only because they worried about

hurting their long-term relationships with the United States and facing international ire for rejecting diplomacy outright.[85] As a *New York Times* article concerning Kerry's relentless diplomatic mission noted, third parties "cannot force an
agreement if the parties are unwilling."[86] Tragically, whatever diplomatic efforts
do occur to address this conflict, their likelihood of success in forging a somewhat stable peace will hinge not simply on the prudence of outside actors but also
on the degree to which all parties absorb terrible truths from carnage.

6

THE "TALKING WAR" IN KOREA

Through much of the evidence I have presented thus far, I have treated periods of negotiation as a single unit of analysis. Quantitative models in chapters 3 and 4 have shown that negotiations that are the product of third-party pressures are generally less likely to terminate conflicts and to pacify the battlefield compared to talks sought by belligerents themselves. My qualitative case studies have also characterized entire uninterrupted stretches of negotiation as being sincere or insincere. But if negotiation is a truly strategic act that helps to navigate hostilities, belligerents' decisions to talk sincerely or insincerely could be fluid within individual rounds of diplomacy. My theory explicitly predicts that, if all else is held equal, periods of fighting that provide more information should incentivize belligerents to negotiate more sincerely. Does this prediction hold for other conflicts, and can it be measured in a more systematic and hands-off manner that reduces the likelihood of cherry-picking evidence?

This chapter addresses these questions by exploring a single case: the Korean War of 1950–53. Known as the "Forgotten War" due to its timing between World War II and the Vietnam conflict, as well as its relative irrelevance and obscurity to the American public at the time, since the late 2000s, this war has received far more attention in scholarly literature on international relations.[1] A defining feature of the Korean War is that the final two years featured extensive and difficult negotiations between the United Nations Command (UNC), which fought on behalf of South Korea, and the Communist states of North Korea and China. Over seven hundred separate meetings took place before the conflict came to an end with an armistice agreement on July 27, 1953.

Three key findings emanate from my analysis of the circumstances surrounding and within these extensive talks. First, third-party pressures loomed large over the belligerents' decisions concerning negotiations. Both sides were keenly aware of the political and military implications linked to negotiating with the enemy. Concerns over looking weak by asking to negotiate lingered in all warring parties' minds. The United Nations and several states played crucial roles in applying pressure and offering political cover, which facilitated the start of talks in July 1951. The fact that the United States and China were both major powers did not fully insulate them from external pressures or a desire to curry favor with the international community. I provide qualitative evidence to substantiate these claims.

The next two results speak to what happens within negotiations themselves. The tools and resources I use to explore these two final points are new to the study of conflict: computational analysis of large sets of archival documents that chronicle the battlefield and bargaining table over the whole war. Full transcripts of armistice negotiations, totaling several thousand pages, record every word uttered between the delegations from July 1951 through July 1953. Daily military reports filed by the UNC provide granular data on battlefield movements. These resources permit me to develop precise and dynamic measures of the battlefield in terms of both movement and casualties, as well as negotiation behavior over the final two years of the war.

By applying a combination of text and supervised learning methods to the negotiation transcripts, I systematically gauge the degree to which each delegation's verbal statements were sincere or insincere. This leads to my second central result: the two sides did not slowly and surely converge on an agreement over time. Delegations fluidly moved between periods of relatively sincere and insincere negotiations. At points, delegates spoke at great length about substantive issues that would make concrete progress toward an armistice agreement. The transcripts feature many instances of "failed" sincere negotiations where the two sides did not reach an agreement despite exchanging meaningful views about their opposing stances regarding the technicalities of an armistice. At other points, the negotiators launched into caustic accusations, diatribes, and other hostile language that were clearly designed to paralyze talks and create propaganda that would publicly malign the adversary and frame it as the recalcitrant party uninterested in peace. Such activity could make no meaningful contribution to peace, and if anything could pull the process backward.

I then use text analysis methods for the daily military reports to create precise measures of battlefield movement and imbalance, which reflect information from fighting. Statistical analysis of the battlefield and negotiation data produce the third and perhaps most important result: fluctuations in negotiation behavior were tightly tied to recent developments on the battlefield. Both belligerents adopted policies where military force would be employed to convince the other side to yield and make concessions at the bargaining table. When recent fighting tilted in one belligerent's favor, both delegations were more likely to negotiate in a more substantive and ostensibly sincere manner. When recent fighting became indeterminate, however, negotiators engaged in more propagandistic, obstinate, and insincere negotiation behavior. Even during talks that are broadly considered to be difficult and exploited, I find meaningful and predictable variation in how seriously or not seriously a belligerent discussed ideas that could lead to a diplomatic settlement of hostilities. Negotiations were therefore always valuable, but the nature of the value derived from them—whether helping to reach peace or helping to support the war effort—varied depending on the state of hostilities. My theory therefore not only predicts whether entire negotiation periods are more or less likely to be sincere but also addresses shifting negotiation behavior *within* individual rounds of talks. My argument and evidence do not contradict conventional wisdom regarding the reasons why the Korean War ended but rather show that the frustrations of negotiation also followed a consistent logic. Importantly, these findings were made possible by the methodological innovation of analyzing archival documents using computational methods.[2]

A Review of the Korean War

Prior to introducing any computational analysis of Korean War negotiations, it is first useful to provide some background information on the conflict and the environment in which negotiations took place. This review has three interrelated benefits. First, the historical context is valuable in its own right. Second, several key moments leading up to negotiations, which I will explore qualitatively, also dovetail with implications of my theory. Third, knowledge about the war is essential for assessing whether the quantitative measures I create using archival documents align with our qualitative understanding of the conflict.

Fighting in the First Year

The Korean War erupted after years of escalating tensions following World War II. Under Japanese occupation since 1910, the Korean peninsula was mutually occupied and divided by the Soviet Union and the United States in 1945. The two states split the peninsula along the thirty-eighth parallel and took control of the territory north and south of this line, respectively. Figure 6.1 depicts the peninsula and its geographic division. By 1948, both sides established their own

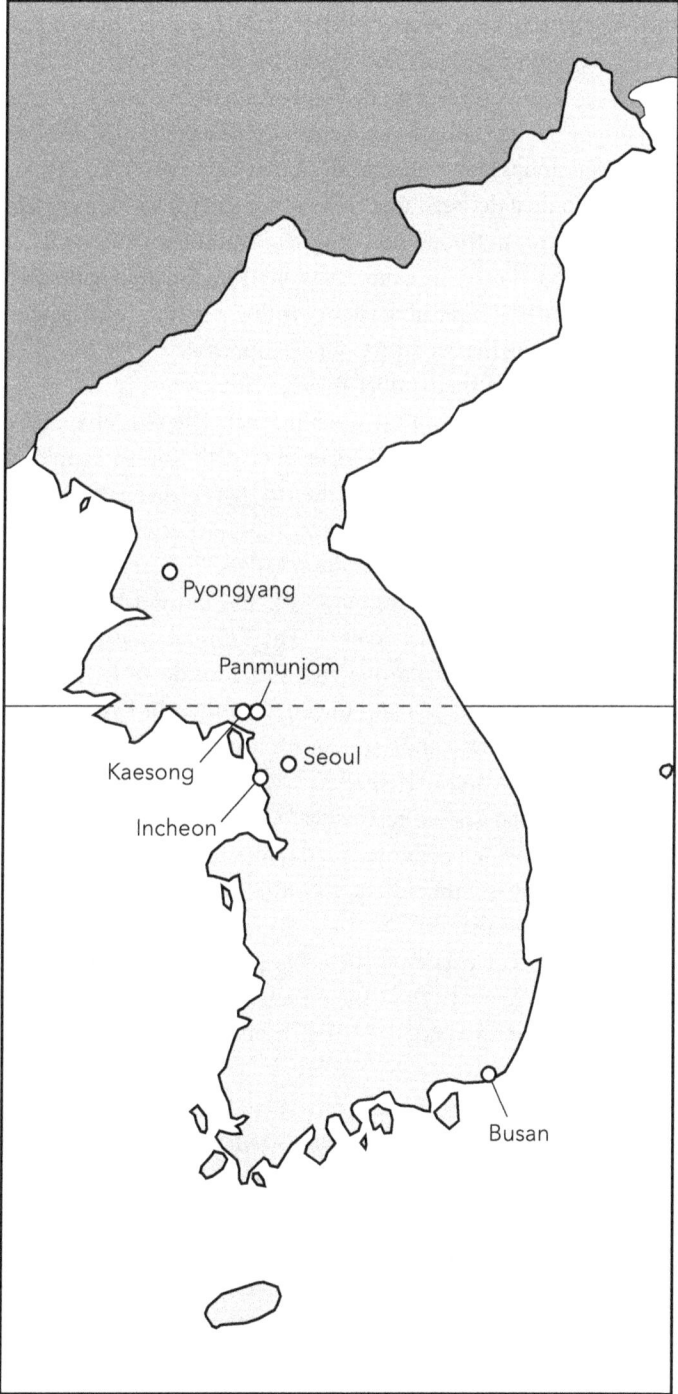

FIGURE 6.1. Map of the Korean peninsula.

governments. The Democratic People's Republic of Korea (DPRK, informally North Korea) took root in the North, while the Republic of Korea (ROK, informally South Korea) was established in the South. Each regime had the support of a different superpower and claimed to govern the entire peninsula.[3] On June 25, 1950, North Korean troops launched a sudden offensive across the entire parallel. The UN Security Council declared this an invasion and called for a ceasefire on the same day. North Korean troops did not observe this request. Beyond harboring a fundamental suspicion of the United Nations, Kim Il-sung, chairman of the DPRK, had anticipated accomplishing victory within a month,[4] and he therefore had no interest in heeding the Security Council's appeals.

Historical treatments of the conflict divide it into four distinct phases, of which the first three took place in the opening year. The first phase occurred between June 25 and September 14, 1950, as the North Korean People's Army (KPA) engaged in a relatively swift southward sweep down the peninsula. Troops of the Republic of Korea were poorly equipped and had no means to deal with the tanks or heavy artillery at the invaders' disposal. US troops, few in number, were also unprepared for an attack and did not have the appropriate weaponry to stage a proper defense. The Truman administration had placed far more of its focus on Europe and also considered Japan to be the critical factor to containing China and the Soviet Union in East Asia. Unable to quickly recover from these handicaps, South Korean and US forces were in a state of constant retreat and driven all the way down to Busan, a port city on the southern tip of the Korean peninsula.[5] On July 7, the Security Council adopted Resolution 84, which recommended that member states provide military forces for a "unified command" that would be led by the United States.[6] The United Nations Command (UNC) was formally established on July 24, 1950. One week later, ROK president Rhee Syng-man transferred operational command of the ROK Army to the United States and hence the UNC. Given that South Korea was not a member of the United Nations at that time, this was a significant decision.

The second phase began on September 15, 1950. The UNC, under the command of General Douglas MacArthur, was tasked with restoring the prewar status quo. This effort started with a surprise amphibious landing in Incheon, a town near Seoul and the thirty-eighth parallel. As a result, the UNC cut off supplies and communication between the North Korean government and KPA troops that had moved into the South. The Incheon landing greatly exceeded the UNC's expectations. The KPA fled back to the thirty-eighth parallel in only two weeks and offered very little resistance as the battle front swung back up the peninsula. The UNC revised its original goal of restoring the prewar status quo, instead opting to eliminate the DPRK altogether. UNC forces thus continued to press their advantage by moving toward the Yalu River, which was on the border of the People's Republic of China (PRC), by late October, under the belief that Kim Il-sung's regime in the DPRK would surrender while China would stay out of the conflict. Riding high on optimism, the UNC planned and initiated a "Home-by-Christmas" offensive on November 24.[7]

The UNC was incorrect and unknowingly entered the third and most tumultuous phase of conflict.[8] At the instruction of Mao Zedong, Chinese forces had clandestinely infiltrated the peninsula in October and November before staging their first major offensive on November 25.[9] The sudden introduction of over three hundred thousand People's Volunteer Army (PVA) troops reshaped the battlefield. Over multiple battles culminating in the massive New Year's Offensive in January 1951, UNC forces were impelled to cede control of Seoul and withdraw to the thirty-eighth parallel, engaging in some of the worst retreats in US military history.[10] By March, the UNC reclaimed the initiative by launching Operation Ripper, which was designed to eliminate as many Communist forces as possible from the vicinity of Seoul and to get UNC troops back to the thirty-eighth parallel. The operation successfully reclaimed Seoul and reached the thirty-eighth parallel but did not take down many Communist forces, who had rapidly retreated. In April and May, the PVA responded with the large Spring Offensive that pressed against the entire front. Chinese forces pushed UNC forces back but were also spread too thin to complete their objective. The UNC's bombing campaign and counterattack, called Operation Strangle, began on May 20 and reversed the PVA's gains. By mid-June, lines of control had started to stabilize around the thirty-eighth parallel.

Losses during the first year were severe. Counting all those killed, captured, wounded, and sick, the United States amassed 73,600 casualties, while South Korea sustained about 180,000. The Communist states, however, suffered upward of 1,100,000.[11] Facing a clear disadvantage in armaments and air power, North Korea and China compensated through greater willingness to withstand heavier costs than their enemy. Yet by this point, leaders of both sides privately realized that neither side could land a decisive blow that would lead to total victory and thus sought some form of restoration of the prewar status quo.[12]

The Path to Negotiations

Both the United States and the Communist states had contemplated negotiations several months before mid-1951. As my theory highlights, however, all belligerents were deeply concerned that showing interest in talks would create perceptions of weakness, which in turn would embolden the adversary to push harder at both the negotiation table and the battlefield.

During the United States' darkest moments in the war in December 1950, the Truman administration contemplated whether to start ccasefire talks.[13] In a memorandum submitted on December 3, George Kennan and Secretary of State Dean Acheson argued vociferously against diplomacy, concluding that any attempt at a negotiated ceasefire "would probably be taken by [Communist] leaders as a bid for peace by us on whatever terms we can get. They would regard this as confirmation that we were faced with the alternative of capitulation, on the one hand, or complete rout and military disaster on the other. . . . Any approach we make to them without some solid cards in our hand . . . may simply be exploited by them for purposes of spotlighting out weakness and improving their own position."[14]

During a meeting the following day, additional officials, including Dean Rusk, agreed that this was "the poorest time possible for any negotiations" on the basis that talks would make the United States look like it was suing for peace.[15] Around the same moment, Mao and Chinese prime minister Zhou Enlai conferred with the Soviets about prospects for negotiations. Stalin stridently opposed talks, arguing that they would help the UNC to feel that conditions were improving and to "win time" to fight more aggressively.[16]

Third-party pressure to negotiate weighed heavily on all belligerents' minds during the first year of the war. UN secretary-general Trygve Lie made numerous attempts to initiate talks between the warring parties—talks that were complicated by the fact that the UN was technically an active participant in the war. At the same time, the Nehru government in India exerted significant diplomatic pressure. The first Indian attempt at peace began in July 1950 but ultimately went nowhere. By December 7, India led a coalition of thirteen Arab and Asian states to submit a proposal to begin peace talks. The proposal was soon adopted by the UN General Assembly and led to the creation of a three-party ceasefire committee involving representatives from the UN, India, and Canada. These diplomatic moves concerned both the Communist states and the United States, neither of which wanted to stop fighting in late 1950.

The fact that the two sets of belligerents made efforts to deflect blame, rather than to ignore peace proposals outright or refuse them without explanation, shows that third-party pressures were indeed salient. On December 7, the PRC stated that one of its preconditions for talks was the immediate withdrawal of all foreign troops from the Korean peninsula. This demand, which was formulated in consultation with the Soviet government, was made under the belief that the United States would not agree to it despite how reasonable it would sound to the international community.[17] In a meeting with Lie on December 9, Chinese representatives stressed that China wanted peace and that any blame for continued conflict rested with Washington's unwillingness to make any useful proposals.[18]

In mid-January 1951, the three-party ceasefire committee established a month earlier submitted a report and proposal for peace talks. While the United States accepted the proposal's terms, China mistakenly believed that global sentiment was still behind the Communists and thus rejected the deal. China's refusal was a political windfall for Washington.[19] Riding a new swell of international frustration with the PRC, Truman's administration went on a public diplomatic offensive, culminating with the passing of UN General Assembly Resolution 498, which accused the PRC of aggression and unwillingness to reach peace. Communist leaders were outraged by the development and openly argued that the resolution, which was pushed by the United States, was responsible for killing any prospects for talks. Notably, at the same time that Washington was working to pass this resolution, UNC forces initiated a major counteroffensive called Operation Thunderbolt, which brought Seoul back under UNC control for the remainder of the war.

The emerging and shared reality of a military standoff in June 1951 marked the start of the war's fourth phase. In the face of a mutually costly stalemate, and reverting back to lines of control that hovered around the thirty-eighth parallel, both sides privately decided that outright military victory was beyond their reach and that negotiations were necessary.[20] Oriana Skylar Mastro avers that the costly military stalemate around the thirty-eighth parallel may have demonstrated that any appeal to negotiate should not be interpreted as weakness.[21] While this may be largely true, a letter written by Mao in June 1951 stated that China ought to wait for the UNC to make the first appeal for talks.[22] The White House, while publicly shifting its rhetoric on Korea to a more limited scale, had no immediate plans to make such an offer.

A third party of sorts proved critical to providing political cover and moving the process forward. On June 23, 1951, during a broadcast of the United Nations' weekly radio program, *The Price of Peace*, Soviet deputy foreign minister and United Nations delegate Jacob Malik made remarks encouraging both sides to consider "a cease-fire and an armistice providing for the mutual withdrawal of forces from the thirty-eighth parallel."[23]

Tellingly, each side's response to Malik's appeal highlights the extent to which all states sought to distance themselves from any interpretation of this proposal being their own idea. Two days after Malik's radio statement, the *People's Daily*, the official newspaper of the Chinese Communist Party, coolly endorsed the Soviet proposal. North Korean radio broadcasts followed suit two days later.[24] The United States' response came after almost a week of internal discussions about how to accede to the negotiation offer without looking weak or generating raw material for Communist propaganda.[25] On June 29, General Matthew Ridgway—who had assumed command of all UNC forces after Douglas

MacArthur was relieved of command—broadcast a highly vetted message to the Communist states: "I am informed that you may wish a meeting to discuss an armistice providing for the cessation of hostilities. . . . Upon the receipt of word from you that such a meeting is desired I shall be prepared to name my representative."[26] The Chinese government waited until July 2 to officially agree to talks.[27] The two sides soon agreed to meet at Kaesong—a historical capital of the Goryeo dynasty, which was the first kingdom to rule over a unified Korean peninsula between the tenth and fourteenth centuries. At this point in the war, Kaesong was in territory under Communist control but was deemed a neutral zone for purposes of negotiations.

To be sure, third parties may not have been necessary for talks to eventually occur. Both belligerents privately expressed interest in peace multiple times throughout the war, and each would have likely agreed to talk of their own accord due to exhaustion. Truman began to reconsider negotiations in March 1951, and the administration became more interested in a ceasefire over the following months.[28] Meanwhile, both Zhou Enlai in the PRC and Kim Il-sung in the DPRK privately noted in 1951 and 1952 that negotiation was necessary because their respective states could not bear the economic and human costs of indefinite war.[29] Yet it is very likely that the talks that did come to pass began prematurely, before the two sides learned enough information to reach a common set of expectations about the war's future. Two pieces of evidence are consistent with this conclusion. First, in preliminary discussions to set up negotiations, both parties agreed that hostilities would continue alongside talks. Neither the UNC nor the Communists trusted that their opponent would truly stop fighting while discussing an armistice, and each harbored significant concerns that the war could tip away from their favor if they inadvertently engaged in a unilateral ceasefire. Even though the costliness of the military stalemate made the warring parties more open to negotiations, it was clear that both sides still had the capability and at least some political will to keep fighting and change the state of the battlefield.

Second, and as will become evident in the next section, the two sides quickly realized the enormous gaps that existed—and would exist to varying degrees for two additional years—between their bargaining positions. In accordance with Hypothesis 2, talks that emerge from heavy third-party pressure occur relatively frequently but often do little in terms of reaching peace.

Fighting and Negotiating in the Second and Third Years

Each set of belligerents assembled a team of individuals with military credentials to negotiate in Kaesong. On the UNC's side, Vice Admiral C. Turner Joy, commander of the US Naval Forces, Far East, was appointed as the senior delegate.[30]

He was backed by an array of US officers, as well as Major General Baek Son-yeop from the ROKA. Tellingly, no ROKA official, including Baek, spoke on behalf of the UNC during talks.

The Communist delegation comprised military officials from both China and North Korea. Unlike their UNC counterparts, the Communist representatives also had pasts in civilian politics. Lieutenant General Nam Il of the KPA, who had been deputy minister of education before moving to the Ministry of Defense, was the chief negotiator for the Communists during meetings with the UNC. But the true head of the Communist delegation was Li Kenong from the PRC. Li had rich political and military experience from the Chinese Civil War several years prior. His effectiveness and loyalty to the Chinese Communist Party earned him positions as both vice minister of foreign affairs and director of the army's Military Intelligence Department by the time the Korean War began. He was thus granted wide authority to coordinate battlefield and negotiation strategy during armistice talks. He managed the Communists' diplomatic strategy, never entering the negotiation tents himself but supervising day-to-day affairs from a separate tent and reporting to Mao and Zhou in Beijing.[31]

Formal negotiations to arrange an armistice began in Kaesong on July 10, 1951. The UNC delegation was not fully prepared for how the Communists would immediately exploit the trappings of negotiation for propaganda. Because Kaesong technically remained behind Communist lines, the Communist states' media widely distributed pictures of the UNC delegation entering the city in a car bearing white flags as evidence that the UNC was suing for peace.[32] Early flare-ups regarding seating arrangements, the presence of news media, freedom of movement within the neutral zone, and the like typified the constant struggle to control the tone and momentum of talks.

The first order of business was determining the items to be discussed during negotiations. The Communist delegation sought a more politically charged docket, while the UNC delegation wanted to limit talks to strictly military affairs. By July 25, the delegations agreed on the following five agenda items:

- Adoption of the agenda
- Fixing a military demarcation line between both sides so as to establish a demilitarized zone as a basic condition for a cessation of hostilities in Korea
- Concrete arrangements for the realization of a ceasefire and an armistice in Korea, including the composition, authority, and functions of a supervising organization for carrying out the terms of a ceasefire and armistice
- Arrangements relating to prisoners of war
- Recommendations to the governments of the countries concerned on both sides

The delegates then moved on to Item 2. The Communists hoped to designate the thirty-eighth parallel as the demarcation line for an armistice, which was the prewar status quo. The UNC, however, had pushed the actual line of contact between military forces slightly past this point and thus refused to revert to the thirty-eighth parallel.

In August, armistice negotiations began to adopt a tiered structure that would become commonplace for the remainder of talks. Facing a deadlock on Item 2, both delegations sought a different environment where they could be more candid and less performative—in other words, more sincere. Negotiations to this point had all taken place at the plenary level, featuring a formal and more scripted tone that was aimed at public messaging. On August 15, Joy suggested moving talks to a "subdelegation" level that would exclusively address Item 2 in a less stilted setting. The Communists agreed to this proposal. According to the historian Walter G. Hermes, the first subdelegation meeting seemed somewhat promising: "The first subdelegate discussion took place on 17 August, and although no concrete progress resulted, the atmosphere was more relaxed. General Hsieh seemed to like this type of exchange. He spoke frequently and acted as a moderator when the comments became sharp. As the talk flowed back and forth around the small table, there was even a tendency on the part of the Communists to consider the demarcation line on the map."[33] This shift is very interesting, especially since the same individuals often attended different levels of talks. Discussions continued at the subdelegation level until August 23, when the Communist delegation accused the UNC of flying planes over the neutral zone around Kaesong—an erroneous accusation—and suspended negotiations. The Communists likely did this to express their dissatisfaction with the UNC's unwillingness to use the thirty-eighth parallel as an armistice line, as well as to nullify the international media's coalescing view that the Communist delegation was anxious and constantly backing down.[34]

Consistent with Hypothesis 4, the first period of negotiations was notable for how it temporarily muted the battlefield. In his opening remarks on July 10, C. Turner Joy affirmed what both sides had already accepted: "Hostilities will continue in all areas, except in those neutral zones agreed upon, until such time as there is an agreement." On July 30, General Nam Il of North Korea reiterated that "hostilities would continue during negotiations." Yet despite this mutual understanding, hostilities slackened substantially over the first several weeks. This was true for two reasons. First, neither side wanted to needlessly lose lives or resources while assessing whether a peace deal was possible. General Ridgway stated this in his memoir: "While both sides had immediately agreed that hostilities should continue during negotiations, it seemed to me, with a cease-fire faintly visible on the horizon, that I should do all I could to keep our losses at a justifiable minimum. I notified our commanders therefore that we would conduct no major offenses."[35] Second, and at the same time, all sides remobilized and rearmed their troops to address two possible contingencies: that the opponent would exploit talks to prepare a new offensive if negotiations failed and that troops could no longer be moved or replenished if an armistice was reached.

These preparations were brought into action once the Communists suspended talks. The weeks between late August and late October featured several significant UNC offensives, which were designed to force the Communists to return to the bargaining table. Writing about the state of affairs on September 12, General James Van Fleet, commander of the US Eighth Army (which was the commanding formation of the US Army), reported that the Communists "were in bad shape, and we are hurting them more and more. They will want peace before winter before we are through with them."[36] While the UNC suffered significant casualties during these two months, the manifold higher losses the UNC inflicted on the Communists proved crucial to the resumption of talks on October 25.[37]

Subsequent discussions were moved to a more neutral location—a precondition the UNC demanded for any talks to resume. After some exchanges, the newly chosen site was Panmunjom, which was in decidedly neutral territory several miles southeast of Kaesong. By late November, Item 2, regarding the establishment of a demarcation line, was settled via a series of mutual compromises. The Communists gave up their demand of using the thirty-eighth parallel as the demarcation line. A demilitarized zone around the line of contact at the time, which crept significantly north of the thirty-eighth, would instead be established.[38] As a concession, the UNC proposed that the line of contact would be used as the demarcation line for an armistice if the Communist delegation agreed to an overall agreement in the next thirty days; it would be renegotiated if no armistice was struck within one month. As some US officials (including Joy) feared, however, Communist forces merely used this thirty-day period to reinforce their positions and resupply their forces.[39] All subsequent fighting became positional in nature, involving limited but strategically and symbolically important changes in territorial control.

Discussions on Item 3, which involved matters regarding the ceasefire, began on November 27. Questions revolved around three main issues: what countries would be part of a Neutral Nations Supervisory Commission (NNSC), what ports of entry and airfields would be permitted for use after the war, and what number of troops would be allowed to rotate in and out of the peninsula on either side. Multiple impasses led the delegations down to the subdelegation level on December 4, and talks moved to another rung that was newer, lower, and more congenial—the staff officer level—on December 20.

The issue of the NNSC vividly demonstrates how progress at the bargaining table not only stalled at points but was even steered backward, standing at odds with the notion of negotiations following a convergence or war-of-attrition dynamic. On February 16, 1952, after almost three months of discussion on the matter, the Communist states abruptly nominated the Soviet Union as one of their choices for a neutral nation that would oversee an armistice. The proposal stunned the UNC. It was no secret that the Soviets were providing material aid and that Stalin was constantly conferring with Mao and Kim about wartime strategy. But by 1951, the Truman administration also knew that Soviet pilots were secretly fighting on behalf of the Communists.[40] The UNC immediately rejected the nomination of the Soviet Union, surmising that the Communists were trying to stall talks and gain bargaining leverage.[41] This allowed the Communist delegation to counter that "opposition on your part will only inevitably lead to show that your side is attempting not to resolve the question."[42] This fabricated deadlock, which would eventually be resolved once the Soviet Union was replaced by India in early May 1953, was soon overshadowed by the next agenda item.

Negotiations ground to their most severe halt in early 1952 over disagreements about how to repatriate prisoners of war (POWs), which fell under Item 4.[43] Many POWs detained by the UNC were Nationalist Chinese who had been coerced into serving in the PVA, as well as South Koreans who had been pushed into the North Korean People's Army when Communist forces had overtaken the southern half of the peninsula. The UNC argued that these POWs would face grave consequences if repatriated to Communist China or North Korea, presented evidence that many POWs did not wish to be sent back,[44] and thus supported a policy of voluntary repatriation. For his part, President Truman opposed the notion of forced repatriation not only on strategic grounds but also on moral ones.[45] The Communist delegation angrily refused, accusing the UNC of violating the 1949 Geneva Convention—which mandated that POWs should be repatriated once hostilities end—and brainwashing the prisoners.[46] Two uprisings of Communist POWs at a camp in Koje-do in February and March resulted in several dozen North Korean deaths, which caused great embarrassment for the UNC. The Communist delegation would spend the next several months vociferously accusing the UNC of wanton slaughter. On April 28, with talks returning to the plenary level after months of stagnation at the subdelegation and staff officer levels, the UNC proposed what it stated was its "final and irrevocable" package proposal for an armistice, which offered to repatriate only a fraction of Communist POWs. The Communist delegation flatly refused the offer, and talks devolved further. After numerous fruitless exchanges where the repatriation question remained the one outstanding issue, the UNC unilaterally ceased negotiations on October 8, 1952.

Historians identify two key factors that may have led both sides to return to the negotiating table in April 1953. One was the January inauguration of President Dwight D. Eisenhower, who as a candidate had openly mentioned the possibility of introducing atomic weapons to the conflict.[47] The second was the death of Stalin in March 1953. The Soviet Council of Ministers, more concerned with their grip on power than with a proxy war, directly called on North Korea and China to announce their interest in resolving the deadlock.[48] The UNC and Communists agreed to an exchange of some sick and wounded POWs in late March and performed the exchange in April. Formal talks at the plenary level resumed in Panmunjom on April 26. After a month of ineffectual discussion, the UNC stated its (truly) final position on May 25, offering some concessions to the Communists but ultimately adhering to its refusal to repatriate all POWs.[49] After expressing vehement objections, the Communist states accepted the offer on June 4. The path to an armistice was temporarily and forcefully derailed on June 18, when ROK president Rhee Syng-man, who was upset with any arrangement that left Korea divided, released about twenty-five thousand anti-Communist POWs from the camps.[50] The Communist states expressed their anger in Panmunjom and launched a last-minute offensive in mid-July to punish the ROK and make some final territorial gains before agreeing to still move forward with peace. The war came to a close once the final armistice agreement was signed on July 27, 1953.

A Deeper Strategy to Negotiations

Numerous studies of the Korean War have effectively argued that the onset of stalemate in mid-1951 helped both sides choose to come to the bargaining table. The arrival of Eisenhower and the exit of Stalin were critical reasons why negotiations, which had ended in October 1952, resumed in April 1953. I do not dispute these existing claims.

These findings, however, have also invited a relatively cursory analysis of the final two years of the conflict. Reviews of Korean War diplomacy often end or greatly accelerate once they reach the start of talks in July 1951, suggesting that both sides gradually eked out mutual concessions until leadership changes in the United States and Soviet Union propelled talks across the finish line.[51] Moreover, the fact that fighting on the battlefield became more geographically limited over the course of negotiations compared to the dramatic swings over the first year has further encouraged scholars to heed less attention to the impact of fighting on the two sides' diplomatic behavior. Such characterizations of the war and its associated negotiations may not be wrong in the aggregate, but they still assume away the highly strategic and dynamic manner in which battlefield activities influenced belligerents' negotiation behavior, as well as the benefits to analyzing it.[52] Such choices, implicit or not, shortchange our understanding of conflict.

The fact that fighting became more geographically limited after talks began does not mean that it became unimportant or subdued. Both sides actively fought over specific battlefield objectives that had significant strategic or symbolic importance, all in hopes of shaping a diplomatic agreement in their favor.[53] Even though clashes became narrower in the spatial sense, they involved significant casualties and thus effort from both sides. Almost half of the fifty deadliest days for the UNC occurred after negotiations began,[54] and China amassed half its casualties during the same time frame.[55]

Moreover, both sides' attitudes toward diplomacy and settlement were complex, nonlinear, and not indicative of either a convergence or war-of-attrition dynamic. The Communist delegation's nomination of the Soviet Union to the NNSC, where progress on Item 3 was intentionally backpedaled, is a case in point. The deadlock regarding POW repatriation also did not trend in a single direction. Even though the issue was not fully resolved until June 1953, the two sides held numerous negotiation sessions that ranged between substantive policy disagreements and acrimonious mudslinging.

This mudslinging was meant not only to attack the opposing delegation but to steer international public opinion regarding the war and the belligerents. The vast majority of negotiations were not private and were thus fair game for media reporting. Each side exploited this situation to frame itself as the magnanimous party interested in peace while portraying its adversary as the real enemy of peace. For example, in the *New York Times* on June 13, 1952, an article reporting on deadlocked negotiations quoted both delegations at length. The Communists accused the UNC of having an "outrageous attitude in negotiations conducted by both sides on an equal footing," while the UNC responded that the Communists' "daily insistence on 'negotiations' is nothing but a reiterated demand for further concessions by our side. . . . When we meet you have nothing to say you haven't said before."[56]

Emotional, psychological, and other situational factors must have certainly influenced the approach that delegates took at Kaesong and Panmunjom. Nevertheless, both the UNC and the Communist states committed significant time and effort to sculpting the words they would use during negotiations, as well as how those words would be said. Records indicate that statements made during negotiations—as truculent and bombastic as they would eventually become—

were the product of collective decision-making and had a keen awareness of recent battlefield activities. Admiral Joy emphasized this point in his memoir:

> The United Nations Command delegation followed a practice of "staffing" all formal statements uttered in an armistice conference by delegates. Each day staff officers prepared a number of proposed statements for use by the delegates. These were considered and discussed by the delegates and staff officers in meetings at our camp in Munsan, before proceeding to [the negotiation site] for the day's events. The statement finally worked out was almost never the work of any one individual. It was the product of careful editing by all delegates and final approval by the Senior Delegate. Thus the benefit of all the fine intellects to the delegation was used to the fullest.[57]

The Communist delegation had an analogous approach to working out its diplomatic stance. Each night at ten o'clock, Li Kenong and other members of the delegation gathered to discuss the day's talks, learn about updates from the battlefield from radio operators who were part of the delegation, and determine subsequent negotiation strategies in light of these developments.[58]

The negotiators themselves were also fully aware that armistice talks were not necessarily meant to resolve the conflict but could also help encourage it. In describing the Communist delegation's tactics, the UNC's chief psychological warfare adviser, William Vatcher, provided a description of negotiations that my theory would consider to be insincere:

> Having been unsuccessful in attaining their objectives on the Korean field of battle, [North Korea and China] turned to the conference table as a means of achieving their ends. Their use of the conference table was obvious indeed: to gain precious time while they rebuilt and strengthened their forces, to obtain every possible benefit from the UNC, and to serve as a sounding board for their propaganda. This they attempted to achieve by haggling over the agenda, demanding the UNC withdraw to the 38th Parallel, manufacturing incidents and pointing to the UNC as instigator, maliciously injecting propaganda into the substance of the meetings in order to create a false impression of UNC perfidy, presenting irrelevant issues for stalling purposes, and frequently acting in a very discourteous and arrogant manner.[59]

Vatcher's view of Communist intentions could be understandably biased, but archival evidence indicates that the Communists indeed sought to exploit negotiations for political gain. Chinese and Soviet sources released decades after the war indicate that China went into talks in 1951 with the overarching objective of stalling for time in order to bolster the Communist troops' battlefield positions.[60] Additionally, until his death in March 1953, Stalin spent the entirety of negotiations encouraging the Communist delegation to adopt a stiff bargaining position because any prolongation of the war would drain US resolve, strain the United States' relationships with its allies, allow the Soviets to spy on the US military, and give the Communists an avenue to publicly accuse the US of war crimes for its intense bombing of North Korea.[61]

The UNC was also guilty of engaging in foot dragging and pursuing side effects.[62] During a visit to the peninsula in late 1951, Chairman of the Joint Chiefs of Staff Omar Bradley and State Department chief adviser Charles Bohlen discussed the pros and cons of attaining a peaceful settlement. Both concluded that the UNC was doing well on the battlefield and that there was no urgency to reach an agreement with the Communist states. Even so, they also believed that the ongoing talks should continue, largely with the goal of placating the numerous allies of the United States that urged for diplomatic dialogue.[63] Private correspondence between Mao and Stalin in November 1951 also observed that "the Americans are dragging out the negotiations" in order to perpetuate "a policy of an advance in the course of negotiations."[64]

Despite these tactics, the two delegations managed to arrange an armistice agreement that remains in effect to this day. How did the opposing parties ever soften their bargaining positions and exert any diplomatic effort to make an agreement? The belligerents' answer was simple: gaining leverage by fighting. Both sides commonly understood that changing fortunes on the battlefield, even if slightly more limited and positional, were critical to sculpting bargaining positions and extracting concessions from the other side. Immediately before talks began, Li Kenong told his delegation to constantly pay attention to the battlefield in order to adjust negotiating tactics.[65] While discussing Item 2 among themselves, Chinese elites argued that the primary way to get more favorable terms was to make gains on the battlefield to generate leverage at the bargaining table.[66] In accordance with the recommendations of the Joint Chiefs of Staff, the UNC simultaneously planned to amass battlefield successes in order to place pressure on the Communist delegation to more seriously consider an armistice.[67] Many battles were fought and even more lives were lost during negotiations with these goals in mind.

The summary above reflects the fact that many historical reviews of and anecdotes from the Korean War have already described the general ebbs and flows of hostilities on the peninsula and negotiations at the bargaining table. No study to this point, however, has analyzed the relationship between battlefield activity and bargaining behavior in a fine-grained manner, where one might investigate whether and what developments from fighting on one day were directly followed by any changes in negotiation behavior on subsequent days. Descriptions of negotiation behavior during this war are frequently characterized in terms of phases where the two delegations would or would not engage in insincere behavior. To be sure, talks did undergo stages of sustained acrimony. But times of bitter disdain also featured moments of limited progress; times of productive discussions also featured moments of rancor. These more subtle vacillations can provide tremendous insight into warring parties' diplomatic strategies. Sincerity exists on a spectrum, but our ability to leverage and understand variation on that spectrum relies on the creation of precise data that track not only negotiation behavior but the battlefield activity that informed it.

How can we systematically capture whether negotiations were sincere or insincere in nature, as well as how contemporaneous hostilities interacted with this choice, in an exact manner over the course of these two years? And to what extent do any of these dynamics align with my theory's specific predictions about the role of information in negotiation dynamics? I tackle these questions by turning to a novel technique: computational analysis of archival documents from the war.

Archival Data of the Korean War

To properly test the implications of my theory within individual negotiation periods, I require measures of information collected from fighting as well as both sides' negotiation behavior during talks at Kaesong and Panmunjom. Archival documents provide the raw material necessary to track both.

Data related to fighting come from daily operations reports submitted by the UNC, which include updates about troops' movements as well as casualties suffered. These reports exist and were individually photographed at the Truman Presidential Library in Independence, Missouri; the Eisenhower Presidential Library in Abilene, Kansas; the National Archives II in College Park, Maryland; and the MacArthur Memorial Archives in Norfolk, Virginia. Information on negotiations comes from full transcripts of the armistice talks at Kaesong and Panmunjom, which are available in their entirety at the National Archives II.[68]

Each page of every document was photographed and converted into computer-readable text using optical character recognition software. These raw text data were then converted into meaningful measures of my key concepts. I describe the procedure for each set of documents in turn.

Measuring Battlefield Activity

On practically every day of the conflict, the UNC operations staff submitted reports about the status of each military unit and the overall progress of the

UNC. In many cases, the primary military unit is the regimental combat team (RCT), which was a major infantry unit of the US Army in World War II as well as the Korean War. A total of 1,102 reports were filed, with the majority of reports being between six and ten pages in length.[69]

UNITED NATIONS COMMAND

One practical aspect of the Korean War is that most military movements went up and down the peninsula. Combined with the fact that the military is already a highly bureaucratized body, the daily operations reports use standardized vocabulary to describe the status of individual military units. A small set of terms are consistently utilized to express gains, losses, or stasis that UNC RCTs experienced each day. Table 6.1 supplies several examples of these entries.

The most common terms used to express gains, losses, and stasis from the perspective of the UNC are summarized below.[70]

Figure 6.2 illustrates what proportion of all status terms each day reflects the UNC's gains or losses over the entire conflict. The two lines correspond well with our understanding of the broad ebbs and flows of the war as I have previously described.[71] The first spike in gains reflects the Incheon landing of September 1950. The second and third jumps in gains correspond with Operations

TABLE 6.1 Examples of entries from UNC reports

DATE	ENTRY	TYPE
August 10, 1950	*Advanced* during early daylight hours against light opposition.	Gain
January 8, 1951	*Improved* positions on line D in the area north of ANSONG CR4696.	Gain
September 23, 1951	*Maintained* psns along line CS0492—CS 0794—FS0996 with elms in assy area vic CS0789.	Stasis
October 7, 1952	Outpost elms vic DT0542 received atk from estimated 2 enemy plats at 062200I and *withdrew* slightly.	Loss
June 2, 1953	*No change.*	Stasis

Note: Key terms italicized for emphasis.

TABLE 6.2 Common UNC terms expressing gains, losses, and stasis

GAIN	LOSS	STASIS
Advance	Enemy capture	Assemble
Capture	Enemy occupy	Maintain
Improve	Withdraw	No change
Occupy		Remain

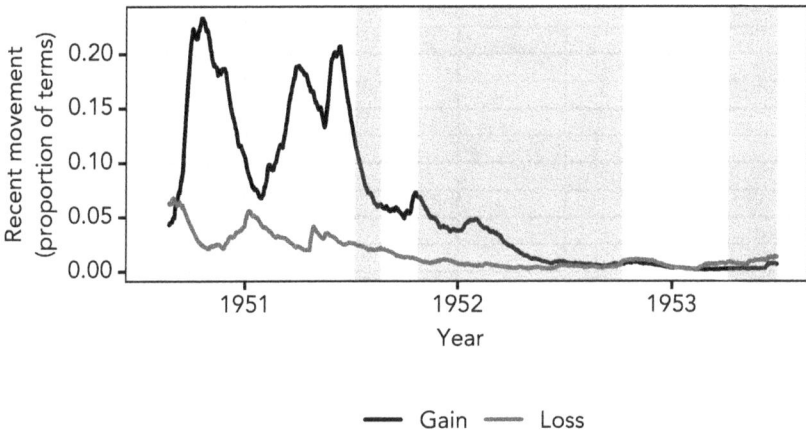

FIGURE 6.2. Gains and losses for the UNC over the course of the Korean War. Regions shaded gray feature negotiations alongside hostilities.

Ripper and Strangle, respectively, which produced significant gains for the UNC across the entire front.

The three most prominent waves of losses also reflect the UNC's grimmest moments during the war. The first surge aligns with North Korea's sweeping offensive down the peninsula from July to September 1950, which met little resistance before the UNC landed in Incheon. The second major loss, from November 1950 to January 1951, reflects the entry of Chinese forces and the massive New Year's Offensive. The third spike, in April and May 1951, captures the Chinese Spring Offensive, which Operation Strangle managed to stem.

It is notable that the UNC operations reports contain far more mentions of gains than of losses. Given that the war started and eventually ended at the thirty-eighth parallel, we may expect the number of terms indicating gains and losses to be roughly equivalent. While this may raise issues regarding whether the UNC underreported the absolute magnitude of its losses, the fact that these measures align with broadly understood characterizations of the Korean War increases our confidence that the measures dependably capture everyday and less dramatic battlefield developments.

The conclusion of each UNC operations report also provides a detailed breakdown of the number of troops supplied by each coalition member state, as well as each country's casualties. Casualties involve three different categories: killed in action (KIA), wounded in action (WIA), and missing in action (MIA). I use these data to create an exponentially weighted moving average of

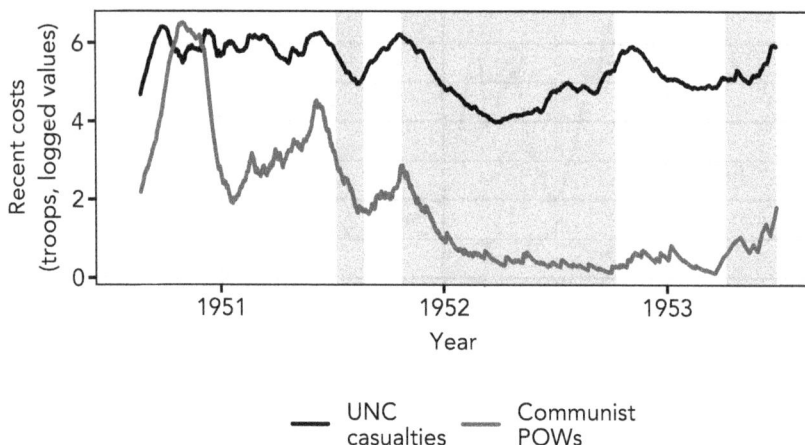

FIGURE 6.3. UNC casualties and Communist POWs over the course of the Korean War. Regions shaded gray feature negotiations alongside hostilities.

the logged number of UNC casualties over the previous two weeks. Figure 6.3 illustrates this measure, which is central to the forthcoming analysis. Despite the overall stagnation in battlefield movement beginning in 1951, we see frequent swings in casualties over the course of the entire conflict. This divergence speaks to the importance of distinguishing different types of battlefield activity.

COMMUNIST STATES

The UNC's daily military operations reports contain far more comprehensive information about the UNC than they do about the experiences of the Communist states. Nevertheless, the reports supply sufficient data to create plausible measures of combat outcomes and casualties for the Communists. Given that much of the battlefield activity was aimed at pushing lines of control up or down the peninsula, the UNC's relative gains arguably mirror the Communists' relative losses and vice versa. This means that my measures of relative gains for the UNC and the Communists are the same in magnitude but with a reverse in sign. While this may be an adequate measure for movement along the battlefront involving the two sides' organized forces, it will not necessarily reflect the activity of Communist guerrilla fighters that infiltrated the southern half of the peninsula. Even so, the UNC estimates these Communist contingents to total no more than a few thousand in 1952 and 1953, compared to the hundreds of thousands of total Communist forces.

A larger challenge exists in tracking Communist casualties. No accurate data on this matter are publicly accessible, and they certainly do not exist at the daily level. That said, the UNC's daily operations reports do offer a glimpse into the Communists' personnel losses by providing a count of the number of Communist soldiers processed as POWs. It bears emphasis that POWs are a highly incomplete measure of overall casualties, which also include those who are killed, wounded, and missing of their own accord. The reports account for approximately 190,000 Communist POWs, but the ROK's estimates suggest that almost 480,000 Communists were also killed over the course of the war.[72] Moreover, the UNC reports do not include POW counts in approximately 18 percent of reports, with most of these omissions in documents between September 1952 and the end of the war. I impute the missing values using a weighted average and then calculate the exponentially weighted moving average over the previous sixty days of hostilities. Figure 6.3 shows that, despite these limitations, the (logged) numbers of POWs processed over the course of the war also align well with our understanding of when the Korean conflict was most intense and active.

Measuring Negotiation Behavior

Stenographers from the UNC were present at all negotiations and transcribed the proceedings. The transcripts total seven thousand pages in length and capture 14,123 statements made by the UNC and Communist delegations over the course of 713 separate meetings. These documents provide the most direct insight possible into both sides' negotiation behavior.

I perform several steps to create measures of how sincere or insincere each delegation is. First, I split long statements into three-hundred-word segments. This is useful to help capture variation in negotiation behavior during more protracted remarks. Second, I apply standard text preprocessing to each segment. This includes removing punctuation, numbers, words shorter than three letters, and stop words (such as *a, the, so, in*, and the like) and converting the remaining words into tokens, which are the basic unit of meaningful text. For instance, words like *discussion, discussed, discuss*, and *discussing* are all converted into the basic token *discuss*. I then identify common multiword expressions in the transcripts (such as *united nations command, unreasonable demand, raise the question*, etc.) and add tokenized versions of these words to the comprehensive list of terms.

Throughout negotiations, 9,639 unique terms are used. Many of these terms are used only once or twice, adding very little to our understanding of talks while inflating the size of the dataset and the intensity of the computation required to analyze them. To make the analysis more tractable without losing much information, I focus on the 1,120 terms that appear most frequently in the negotiations. After removing segments that do not have associated battlefield measures, I end up with a document-term matrix (DTM) with 16,460 rows, each of which reflects a single segment, and 1,120 columns, each of which contains a count of the number of times a unique term was used in a segment. The entire DTM captures about 529,000 words or phrases uttered throughout negotiations.[73] I thus utilize what is often called a "bag of words" approach that does not account for grammar or word order aside from the inclusion of some common phrases; I simply count how many times different terms appear in a segment. As will become evident, even this simplified representation of the speech segments produces informative measures of negotiation behavior.

For each segment, the objective is to create a binary coding for whether the segment likely indicates sincere or insincere negotiation behavior. A segment is considered to be sincere when it solely discusses concrete aspects of an agenda item. A segment is coded as insincere when it also or only exhibits overt hostility or obstinacy. Examples of this latter category include accusations of neutral zone violations; denunciations of propagandizing, lying, or delaying during talks; and allegations of mass illegal violence. Note that speech acts that reflect disagreement can still be coded as sincere as long as they discuss actual policy proposals.

Several examples will help to provide useful context. On November 10, 1951, the UNC representative in the Item 2 subdelegation meeting continued discussions of how to draw a demarcation line between opposing forces. The following quotation is coded as indicating sincere negotiation behavior:

> First I would like to take up the arguments in regard to Kaesong. General Hsieh mentioned some of the arguments and said that they were all refuted. We do not believe they have been refuted. In addition to the arguments he mentioned there is the one of equivalent adjustment. The adjustment in the Kaesong area which we recommended in other parts of the line. They are compensatory adjustments and are approximately equal in magnitude, equal in withdrawal and equal in range. Now I will take up our 8 November proposal and the difference between it and our 5 November proposal, and why these differences exist. We offered the 8 November proposal in the spirit of compromise. We felt that our original proposal of 25 October was fair, but because we do want to negotiate a military armistice, we were willing to compromise in order to attain that armistice as quickly as could be done and still have reasonable terms.[74]

Even though the segment mentions disagreement regarding how to draw this demarcation line, it involves direct discussion of an agenda item. Conversely, during a plenary session on August 3, 1952, the UNC responded to Communist bluster in the following manner, which is coded as reflecting insincere behavior:

> It is noted that you have said nothing new and nothing that can lead toward achievement of an armistice. Some of your language this morning is what we in civilized countries associate with common criminals or persons who through ignorance or stupidity are unable to speak logically and convincingly. In their frustration, they resort to efforts to insult. You should know by now that such talk serves no useful purpose in negotiations and we do not propose to engage in it with you. Therefore, if you expect to conduct discussions, it would be advisable to use more restrained language. As for the issue itself, it is clear. We have nothing to propose.[75]

The Communist delegation's segments also vary widely. During a staff-level meeting regarding Item 3 on February 14, 1952, the Communists spoke in great detail regarding the wording of a specific proposal, which is coded as being sincere:

> Very well. Regarding sub-paragraphs 13c and 13d, and your suggestion in particular to add the phrase "have the right to"—to insert this phrase in the sentence about the conduct of supervision and inspection by the Neutral Nations Supervisory Commission, we still hold that in order to ensure really that the military personnel, and weapons and ammunition, introduced into Korea during the armistice are those permitted by the agreement, the Neutral Nations Inspection Teams shall conduct supervision and inspection, but not just shall "have the right to" conduct supervision and inspection. Regarding sub-paragraph 13i, we have studied your revised draft submitted yesterday. It is our opinion that at present neither side is holding complete data pertaining to the burial of its deceased military personnel in the area of the other side.[76]

On the other hand, during a plenary-level session regarding prisoners of war on June 17, 1952, the Communists began by expressing disagreement on a substantive proposal but quickly veered into vitriol, leading to a statement coded as insincere:

> You have only the obligation to repatriate war prisoners but no right to retain war prisoners. You had better pack up forthwith all your nonsense about screening and re-screening. In your attempt to whitewash your criminal acts of slaughtering war prisoners, you trumpeted on the one

hand about your so-called humanitarian principles, and resorted on the other hand to fabrication and calumny. I tell you that such efforts of yours are futile. There cannot be on this earth humanitarian principles of slaughtering and retaining war prisoners. Your crimes of murdering war prisoners have already been recorded on the pages of history and are not to be deleted.[77]

Manually coding over sixteen thousand segments for negotiation behavior is impractical for a variety of reasons. A fully manual process is more prone to error and inconsistencies as the number of human coders (or the hours they spend on this task) grows. It also does not provide flexibility if codings need to be adjusted, since every single segment would need to be reviewed once again. Such an approach cannot reasonably scale upward for similar tasks that involve many more observations. For those reasons, I instead code the vast majority of speech segments using a supervised learning approach.[78] To do so, I first draw a random sample of four hundred segments from each delegation and manually classify these eight hundred total segments for whether each represents sincere (1) or insincere (0) negotiation behavior as defined and illustrated above. Approximately 30 percent of the segments in my sample were coded as reflecting insincere behavior.

These hand-coded classifications, along with the DTMs of the associated segments, are necessary for the statistical learning process. A majority of the hand-coded segments are chosen at random to be part of a training dataset, while the remainder are part of a test dataset. The training data are inputted into a series of candidate statistical learning models, each of which finds the best predictive relationship between the speech act's composition of tokens and the hand-coded classification. Once these models are trained to predict the relationship between the inputs (token counts) and the outcomes (hand codings of negotiation behavior), they are used to predict the outcomes in the test data. These predictions are then compared to the original hand codings to create an unbiased measure of the model's performance with new out-of-sample data.

Out of multiple models tested, a balanced random forest model featured the best overall out-of-sample performance.[79] A random forest is an ensemble learning method where numerous simpler decision trees, which search for relationships between an observation's features and its target variable, are combined to create a predictive model that can be applied to other data.[80] This balanced random forest is applied to the entire set of speech segment data to produce a prediction of whether each speech act exhibits sincere or insincere negotiation behavior.[81] Finally, I combine the predictions for all segments from the same speech act to create a single measure of sincerity for each statement. The final dataset includes 13,526 statements, of which 8,266 (61 percent) are sincere and 5,260 (39 percent) are deemed insincere.[82]

VALIDATING THE MEASURES

A series of predictive metrics based on cross-validation techniques speak favorably to the balanced random forest's ability to predict sincerity on out-of-sample data not used to train the original model. This is encouraging, but the external validity of these predictions is arguably more important and cannot be assessed using quantitative data alone. Three pieces of evidence indicate that this predicted measure offers a historically credible reflection of negotiations. First, as previously alluded to, qualitative descriptions of the talks suggest that both sides spoke more substantively at lower levels of talks. The most "refreshing" discussions with "an air of serious intent to make progress" on agenda items, as Walter G. Hermes put it, occurred at the staff officer level.[83] My quantitative data also bear out this claim. For each separate meeting, I determine what proportion of each delegation's speeches are sincere. Table 6.3 depicts the distributions of these calculations. The jump in negotiation behavior is most obvious between subdelegation and staff officer meetings. Chi-squared tests show that differences in sincerity between plenary and staff meetings, as well as subdelegation and staff meetings, are highly statistically significant for both the UNC and Communist delegations ($p \ll 0.01$). Liaison, control, and investigatory meetings (presented under the umbrella term *Other*), which were mainly for logistical planning and issues not related to the agenda, are even more agreeable. Importantly, the level of talks was not included as a variable in any of the predictive models. The fact that these differences still appear is compelling evidence that the supervised learning method has created a meaningful measure.

Second, we know that Item 4, relating to POWs, was the largest obstacle to agreement, being the only agenda item left to address between May 1952 and June 1953. The majority of the most embittered days of negotiation should thus

TABLE 6.3 Distribution of sincere negotiation behavior by delegation and meeting level

MEETING LEVEL	UNC	COMMUNISTS
Plenary	0.475	0.358
Subdelegation	0.479	0.469
Staff	0.609	0.587
Other	0.730	0.681

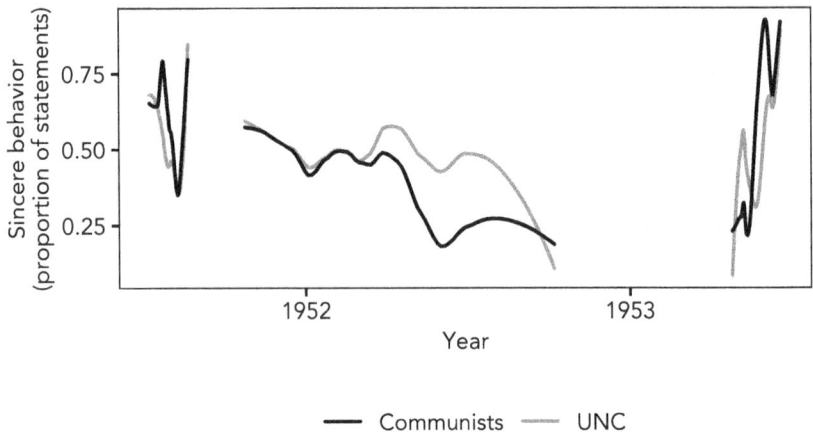

FIGURE 6.4. Smoothed negotiation behavior over the Korean War (excluding control, liaison, and investigatory meetings).

involve this issue. My data support this conclusion. Out of the twenty-four days with the highest average level of insincere negotiation behavior (which represent the worst 5 percent of negotiation days), twenty-two feature discussions of Item 4. Eighteen of these involve only Item 4, while the other four also include thorny discussions of Item 3.

Finally, the general ebbs and flows of negotiation behavior in my predicted data align well with our qualitative accounting of progress made during talks. Figure 6.4 offers a visual representation of the data, tracking what proportion of statements made by each delegation each day were sincere. Three observations are worth mentioning. First, the initial dip and rise in the first round of talks between July 10 and August 23 attest to the delegations' initial litany of bitter exchanges and posturing at the outset of talks, which eventually gave way to more meaningful discussions regarding Item 2 before the Communists accused the UNC of violating the neutral zone and called off negotiations. Second, the next round of talks exhibits a downward drift beginning around March 1952. This aligns with the period during which Item 4, on POWs, became the single— and, as I have explained, most controversial—issue. The lowest values for sincere negotiation behavior emerge in the weeks immediately prior to the UNC's unilateral recess. Third, the dramatic upward swing during the final phase of talks in 1953 indicates the two delegations' ability to reach an agreement regarding POWs by late May. It bears noting again that negotiation behavior does not consistently trend upward in terms of being sincere. While sincerity does not necessarily lead to agreement, the nonmonotonic nature of observed negotiation behavior still undercuts the idea that wartime negotiations inexorably bring the two sides' divergent positions together.

One potential challenge to my coding procedure, illustrated by a couple of pieces of evidence earlier in this chapter, is that actors may make proposals that seem sincere at face value but are designed to be unacceptable to the enemy. This can help actors better feign interest in settlement and thus accrue more beneficial side effects. When read without deeper context or understanding of political circumstances, a speech act containing this type of proposal could be erroneously classified as sincere when it is made with insincere motives. The aforementioned incident where the Communist delegation nominated the Soviet Union as a "neutral nation" to supervise the armistice is arguably the most prominent example of this tactic.[84]

Note, however, that even if one individual speech act such as this may be misclassified, the broader set of speech acts on this topic promptly discern subsequent changes in negotiation behavior. Recall that I code negotiation behavior based on the presence of hostile or intransigent language, not by whether any mentioned policy is acceptable. As long as speech acts discussing these policy proposals contain such language, which they typically do because the parties will recognize and discuss the other side's dilatory intentions, they are coded as reflecting insincerity. I indeed see this in discussions about the topic of neutral nations. Prior to the nomination of the Soviets, approximately 59 percent of all speech acts related to neutral nations are classified as being insincere. The figure soars to 81 percent after the nomination.[85] As such, this act of avoidance bargaining led to insincere behavior, despite the fact that the initial proposal may have been deemed sincere according to my coding criteria and supervised model. Moreover, false negatives like this case are vastly outnumbered by the far more overtly antagonistic statements that the two delegations exchanged, which are more explicit reference points for insincere negotiation behavior.

These correlations between the quantitative data and the historical record bolster the empirical validity of the data, allowing us to proceed to fuller statistical analysis.

Design

My statistical tests focus on battlefield activities and negotiation behavior for the UNC during 473 days of talks in the Korean War between July 10, 1951, and July 27, 1953.

The primary unit of analysis is the speech. The outcome variable of interest is an indicator for whether a speech is predicted to be sincere (1) or insincere (0) by my supervised learning model. I use logistic regression to analyze this binary dependent variable of *sincere negotiation behavior*. Since the (in)sincerity of statements made by each delegation within individual meetings is likely related to that of the other delegation, I cluster standard errors by speaker-meeting-day.[86]

My analysis features two explanatory variables, each of which captures battlefield information. The first, which gauges movement on the battlefield, is *recent imbalance*. This is analogous to the measure central to my quantitative analyses in chapters 3 and 4. For each day, I calculate the total proportion of key status words that indicate either gains or losses in territory on the battlefield. I then generate an exponentially weighted moving average of this daily-level metric over the previous sixty days.

The second, which tracks the material costs of fighting, is *recent casualties*. Similar to recent imbalance, I first determine the sum of all casualties suffered by the UNC and Communist states on each war-day. The UNC's recent casualties include those that are killed, wounded, or missing in action, while the Communists' recent casualties are proxied using POWs processed by the UNC. I then calculate the exponentially weighted moving average of this number over the previous sixty days.

My models include several control variables that address factors that may confound the relationship between battlefield movement and negotiation behavior. First, I capture other battlefield considerations. I account for UNC operation *report length* (in terms of logged number of words) to capture the overall amount of recent military activity. A dummy variable for the *winter* months of December, January, and February reflects the fact that cold, harsh weather had deleterious effects on troops' well-being and ability to fight.[87]

Next are political considerations. I include daily-level indicator variables for the *Eisenhower* administration, which takes a value of 1 starting on January 20, 1953 (inauguration day), as well as another indicator for the *post-Stalin* period, which takes a value of 1 starting on March 5, 1953 (the day of his death). To capture any impacts of the electoral cycle on war,[88] a binary variable for the *1952 presidential election* takes a value of 1 between July 11 and November 4, 1952. These represent the final day of both major parties' national conventions and Election Day, respectively.

Third are variables regarding the negotiations themselves. To account for any systemic differences between the two delegations' degrees of sincerity, I add a dummy variable for statements made by the *Communist delegation*. I absorb the impacts of different levels of discussion by including fixed effects for statements uttered in *subdelegation*, *staff*, and *other* (liaison, control, and investigation) meetings.[89]

Quantitative Results

The black points and segments in figure 6.5 show the key results from my main logistic regression model.[90] As my theory predicts, and consistent with the broad themes of the qualitative analysis I have presented, information from recent hostilities directly informed how the belligerents comported themselves during talks. The estimated coefficients for both recent imbalance and recent costs exhibit positive effects that are statistically significant at the 95 percent level. Experiencing greater amounts of movement or costs on the battlefield led both the UNC and Communist delegations to make more sincere statements during negotiations. This primary finding is consistent with Hypothesis 3, which suggests that negotiations should be more likely to settle conflicts when the battlefield supplies information that obviously favors one side.

To ease the interpretation of these results, I use my regression model to generate the predicted probability that a statement made during negotiations is sincere for the lowest and highest observed values of recent imbalance and recent casualties. I keep the delegation fixed as the UNC and the meeting level as the plenary session, and all other variables are held constant at their mean or median values. The resulting array of probabilities are displayed in table 6.4. The substantive impacts of battlefield information are appreciable. At the lowest levels of both imbalance and casualties, the likelihood that a UNC statement is sincere is approximately 0.382. When both forms of battlefield activity are at their highest observed values, this probability rises sharply to 0.698.

Note that the two sides are making conscious decisions about whether to engage in military activity and thus whether to attempt to gain a bargaining advantage over the opponent. When recent hostilities involve very little imbalance and scant casualties, this indicates that neither side is trying to extract information or inflict pain on its opponent. No additional bargaining leverage is generated, so neither side has a motivation to negotiate more sincerely.

Some control variables also yield noteworthy results. The estimated coefficients for Eisenhower's inauguration and Stalin's death are both statistically significant, revealing the impact that regime change had on the nature of talks. The negative effect of the Eisenhower administration should not be interpreted too deeply or independently of the post-Stalin effect. Only 143 statements, or 1 percent of all things said during negotiations, were uttered in the brief two-month period between the arrival of Eisenhower and the departure of Stalin.[91] The relatively larger magnitude of the post-Stalin estimate compared to the Eisenhower estimate indicates what some scholars have already made clear: Stalin played a crucial role in sustaining North Korea and China's war effort.

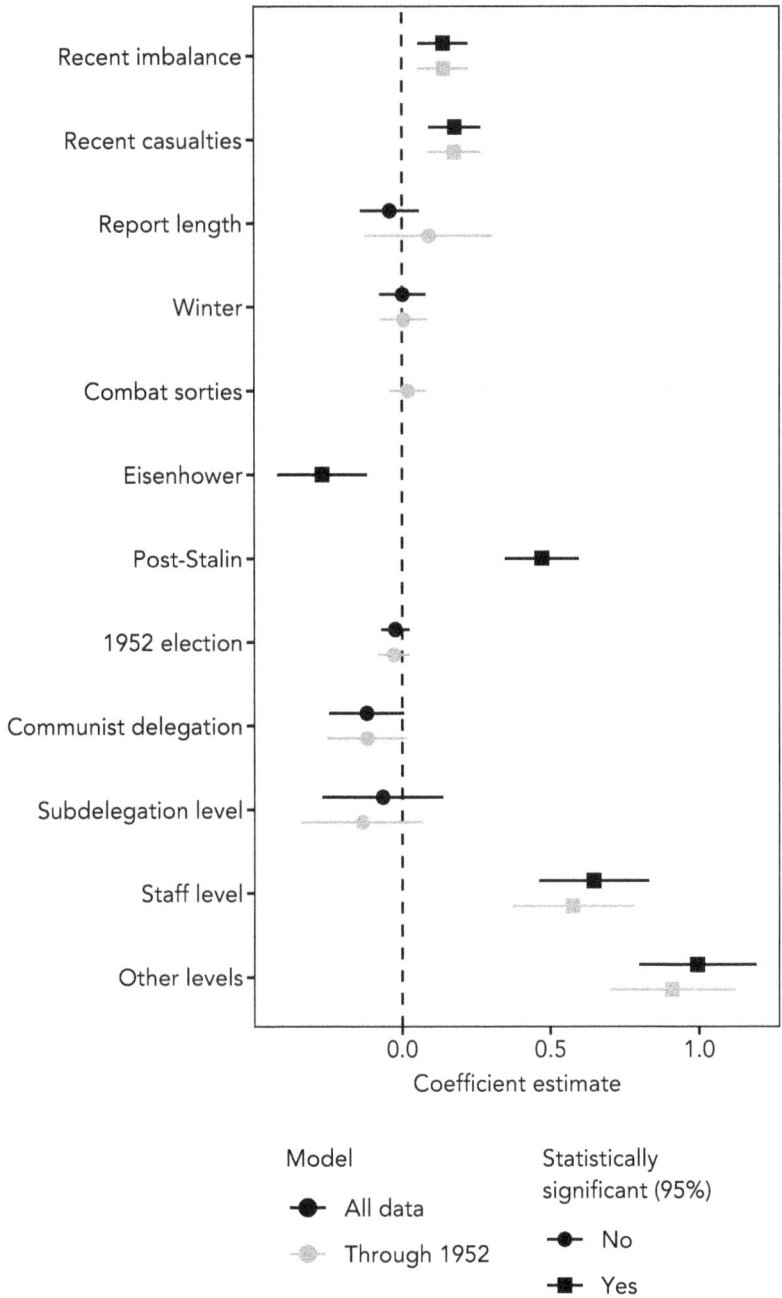

FIGURE 6.5. Coefficient plots for logistic regressions concerning Korean War negotiation behavior. Numerical measures scaled to improve plot legibility. Bands represent 95 percent confidence intervals.

TABLE 6.4   Predicted sincerity of negotiation behavior across minimal and maximal levels of movement and costs

MOVEMENT	LOW COSTS	HIGH COSTS
Low	0.382	0.540
High	0.549	0.698

The length of UNC reports, which serves as a proxy for overall activity, does not produce a statistically significant result. Activity in and of itself does not influence how the delegations behaved; the actual results of such activity in terms of imbalance and casualties are far more relevant.

Two additional sets of results provide additional context for these main findings. The first concerns the use of air bombings by the UNC, and the other involves analyzing each delegation's statements separately.

Once Item 2, regarding the determination of a demarcation line, was largely finalized by late November 1951, ground movement became markedly more limited. The United States increasingly relied on its air superiority over the peninsula to gain military leverage by flying over and past the demarcation line. Fighter planes engaged in numerous combat sorties in order to wear down Communist forces and also to attack civilian population centers.[92] One may be concerned that these air attacks influenced negotiations but are not being reflected by the recent imbalance measure, which focuses primarily on fluctuations around the demarcation line. To account for this, I return to the UNC operations reports. Reports filed between 1950 and 1952 include information on the number of *combat sorties* the UNC flew each day. I add a logged version of this measure to the analysis. Doing so, however, also means dropping all data from 1953, which in turn requires removing the Eisenhower and post-Stalin variables (as they vary only in 1953). The gray elements of figure 6.5 display the results of logistic regressions using these truncated data. My main findings are sustained using this more limited sample. Both recent imbalance and recent casualties continue to bear positive effects on sincere negotiation behavior.

My main findings analyze all 13,526 statements exchanged during armistice talks, using measures of battlefield information that capture overall movements and casualties across both sides. But a more tailored way to test the impact of fighting on negotiating (and to see whether inflicting costs on the enemy actually accomplished its goal of coercion at the bargaining table) would be to see whether and how each delegation responds to its own battlefield losses. To that end, I reanalyze statements made by the UNC and Communist delegations separately. I replace the original measure of recent imbalance with a measure of *ground losses* suffered by each delegation's military forces. The measures illustrated in figure 6.2 are used for this purpose. Naturally, the UNC's ground losses are reflected using its reported losses. The Communists' ground losses around the line of contact are proxied using the UNC's gains. Casualty data are split apart so that UNC negotiation behavior is a function of UNC casualties and Communist negotiation behavior is a function of POWs.

Figure 6.6 reports the results. Notably, different dimensions of battlefield information appear to influence the delegations' diplomatic tactics. The UNC negotiates far more sincerely when it has lost ground in recent fighting; the Communists tend to be more sincere when they have lost personnel to the enemy.[93] Recall that POWs are only one aspect of the Communists' casualties, so this positive finding is somewhat incomplete, but it is telling nonetheless.

The slightly varying results may speak to each side's primary concerns. The Communists were constantly worried about whether they could withstand the human and material costs of war. I have previously cited instances where Zhou Enlai and Kim Il-sung raised these concerns. Mao expressed similar trepidation in November 1951, observing that almost one-third of the PRC's national budget was funneled into the war and that this trend was not sustainable.[94] Meanwhile, the UNC expended its own costs, but its superior military capabilities, deeper well of resources, and lower level of military casualties compared to the Communists (especially because ROK troops suffered the brunt of UNC losses), likely made US officials less sensitive to casualties and more fixated on what final armistice line would be drawn in the peninsula.

Across all four reported models, we see consistent evidence in favor of my argument: When recent hostilities reveal greater amounts of information, belligerents become more likely to engage in sincere negotiations. A quieter and less active battlefield tends to beget less sincere talks, which are highly unlikely to produce peace and may be used to thwart it.

Staggering, Not Drifting, toward Settlement

The Korean War was devastating for Koreans on the peninsula, many of whom bore no responsibility for the conflict. Both Korean states' economies and infrastructure were gutted by three years of battles and bombings. Anywhere between five and six million people—about half of those being civilians—were left dead in its wake. This number exceeds liberal estimates of total deaths inflicted during the decades-long Vietnam War, which would begin soon after.[95] Much of this pain was suffered over the last two years of the war, as delegates from both sides dragged themselves through numerous months of difficult negotiations.

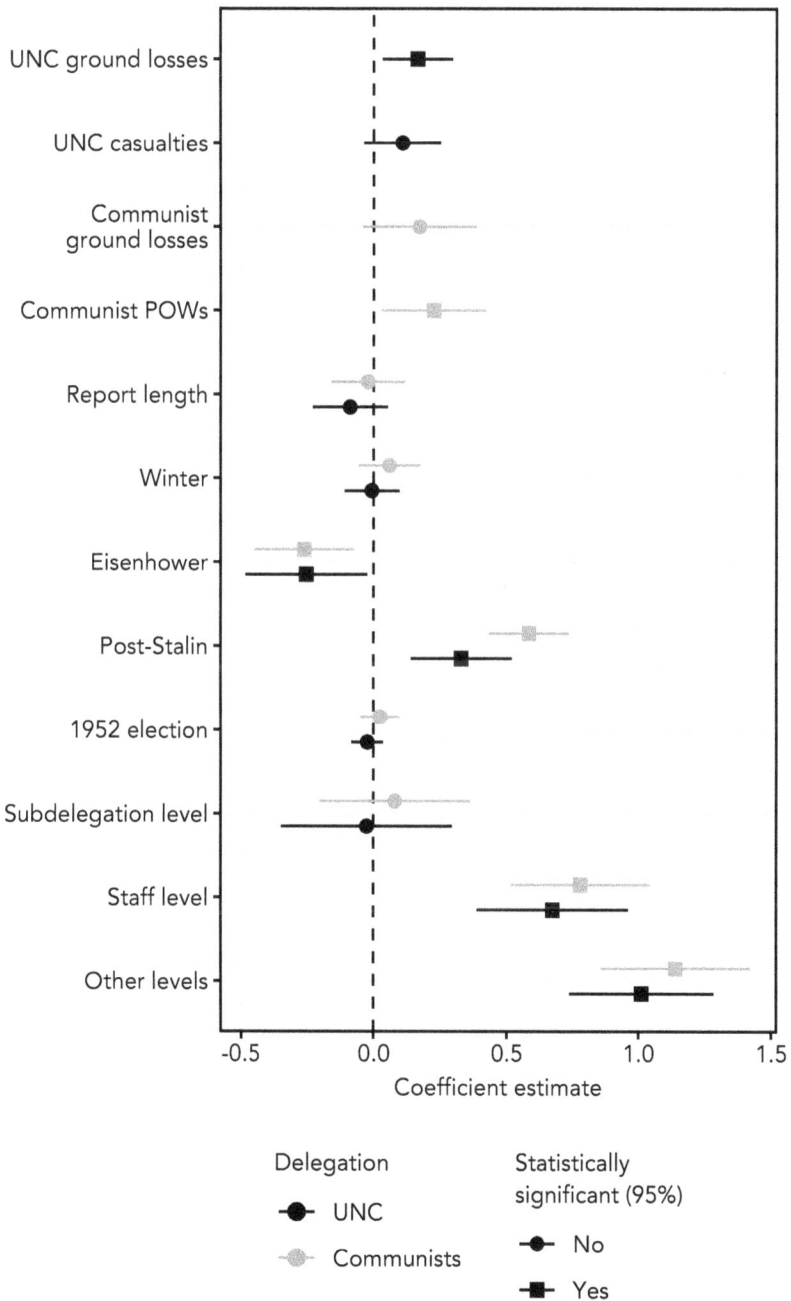

FIGURE 6.6. Coefficient plots for logistic regressions concerning Korean War negotiation behavior, disaggregated by delegation. Numerical measures scaled to improve plot legibility. Bands represent 95 percent confidence intervals.

As interminable as diplomacy seemed to be, the belligerents saw no other way to resolve the conflict. It is perhaps for this reason that US Army officer Mark W. Clark, commander of the UNC from May 1952 through the war's end, called the Korean conflict "the talking war."[96]

This talking war in Korea substantiates multiple aspects of my theory. In the lead-up to negotiations, both the UNC and the Communist states privately contemplated diplomatic overtures but avoided them out of fear of looking weak and vulnerable. As Hypotheses 1 and 2 suggest, the potential costs of negotiation troubled the combatants, even though at least some of them were major powers. Third-party pressures for peace at least partially neutralized some of these concerns and facilitated talks starting in July 1951.

On the surface, Korean War negotiations align well with ripeness theory. A mutually hurting stalemate that emerged around the thirty-eighth parallel in the spring of 1951 created a common belief that complete control of the peninsula by either side was out of the question. The public appeal for peace in June 1951 by Soviet deputy foreign minister Jacob Malik could be seen as a way out of the conflict and a potential opening to the search for a settlement. These two factors helped belligerents start talks in Kaesong. Yet my analysis of negotiation strategies during this war stands in tension with ripeness theory in multiple ways.

First, Malik's call for diplomacy contained little language to suggest interest in settlement. A Central Intelligence Agency assessment at the time characterized the statement as "very vague" and made with the goal of gaining "political and military advantages [for the Communists] rather than because of a military need to end the Korean war."[97] The US government did not see a mutual interest in a way out of the conflict and—in a manner not explained by ripeness theory—recognized that talks might be used to extract side effects rather than settle.

Second, ripeness theory would suggest that the start of talks should indicate a serious effort to find peace. Yet within the first days of negotiations, the UNC and Communist delegations quickly realized the irreconcilable gap between their bargaining demands. This situation was made possible by heavy latent external pressures for peace. Malik, the United Nations, and a coalition led by India offered generic calls for peace or proposals that were far from mutually acceptable, yet they fueled demands for dialogue all the same. Both sides thus came to the bargaining table before they gained a common understanding of how the war would ultimately unfold, which was necessary to swiftly reach agreement. Without a plausible agreement on the horizon, but with the liberty to talk in a tent and reach an international audience, the two sides pivoted to insincere negotiations to accuse their opponent of aggression, deflect criticism, and corral political support.

Third, and on a related note, ripeness theory does not explain changes in diplomatic behavior or attitudes toward peace over the course of negotiations—and certainly not at the level of exactitude permitted by my computational analysis of archival documents. Because belligerents started negotiating before they had obtained enough information to identify a viable bargaining range, they continued to fight. Both sides thought that fighting was the only way to convince their opponent to make concessions. As Joy would later write in his memoirs regarding the war, "Force is a decisive factor, the only logic the Communists truly understand."[98] Communists held similar beliefs about the UNC as well.[99] This idea is consistent with the quantitative and across-war analyses I performed in chapters 3 and 4, which used new data on individual battles to track battlefield information and new data on negotiation periods to track diplomatic bargaining. In this chapter, I have shown that an analogous story holds for the Korean War, and at a much more granular scale. These data belie ripeness theory's emphasis on stalemate and firmly demonstrate the validity of Hypothesis 3: Higher amounts of information gathered from fighting are associated with more sincere attempts at negotiation between the two sides. Stretches of time without such novel information are followed by insincere bargaining.

The Korean War is only one of many conflicts, and we must exercise caution in how broadly we extrapolate findings from this one case to other cases. In particular, the Korean conflict is a limited one where belligerents gave up on the idea of complete victory. The impossibility of a wholly military solution—and a common understanding of this impossibility—is what led the UNC and Communist states to talk extensively with one another, and it is also why they could use more calibrated violence to garner bargaining leverage. Regardless, many contemporary civil and interstate wars fall into this category. Practically no current-day conflict will plausibly end through military means alone. Moreover, the Korean War is not unique in how much of it was spent negotiating. About one-third of the conflict featured negotiations over the key terms of an armistice. This figure is not much higher than the average rate of 29 percent across all interstate wars that have included negotiations since 1945. The findings of this chapter therefore provide useful traction to understand the interplay between war and diplomacy in the modern context. Given the significant pressure that belligerents face to engage in negotiations in our current international order, it is all the more important to understand when, why, and how words can be used as sticks and stones.

CONCLUSION
Time to Stop Talking

Thirty-seven months into the Korean War, the UNC and the Communist delegations were prepared to end hostilities. On July 27, 1953, at 9:57 a.m., head delegates from each side—William Harrison for the former and Nam Il for the latter—walked silently through opposite doors into a building hastily constructed for a signing ceremony. Each individual sat at his own table, on which lay nine copies of the final armistice agreement as well as a small flag representing his side. At precisely 10:00 a.m., Harrison and Nam began to sign all copies of the document that had been painfully forged over two years. The signing ceremony, punctuated by sounds of gunfire in the distance, took all of twelve minutes. Harrison and Nam then walked out without exchanging a single word. The war, which had claimed the lives of several million soldiers and civilians, officially ended twelve hours later.

For readers of the *New York Times*, news about the resumption and productivity of armistice talks starting in April 1953 marked a sudden change of affairs.[1] The negotiations received limited attention in 1952 as fatigue and pessimism regarding diplomacy settled in. Indeed, the front page of the *Times* on October 8—the day on which the UNC unilaterally called off talks after a months-long impasse regarding how to repatriate prisoners of war—included two sentences noting that talks had ended but spent the remainder discussing how the United States' Eighth Army had repulsed a Chinese attack and how "morale has never been higher" for UNC troops.[2] This entire story was placed underneath an article and picture reporting the New York Yankees' World Series victory against the Brooklyn Dodgers. When the *Times* reported on the resumption of negotiations in April 1953, it noted a history of "pointless stalling" by the Communist delegation.[3] Subsequent events seemed to indicate a relatively smooth path to the signing ceremony on July 27. Given this contemporaneous accounting of the conflict, it is not hard to imagine how the American public may have thought that negotiations were immaterial to the conflict until they suddenly brought the war to an end.

Scholarly treatments of wartime diplomacy frequently maintain a similar viewpoint. Seminal models of war initiation implicitly suggest that diplomacy's value for understanding a conflict dissipates once hostilities begin. Subsequent studies that do account for the occurrence of diplomacy presume that the war enters a period of suspended animation while belligerents communicate with one another, with the content of their communications reflecting the realities of the battlefield. If talks do not settle the conflict, the war resumes from the same position that existed before diplomatic bargaining began. This conception of wartime diplomacy perpetuates an important supposition: the reversion outcome to failed negotiations is the continuation of the exact same war, with prospects for victory or defeat unchanged.

My theory suggests that this interpretation of negotiations is shortsighted and does a disservice to our understanding of both conflict and diplomacy. Negotiations, this book has argued, are guided by a deeper strategic logic that is not only a response to the battlefield but an activity that can be used to reshape hostilities and the political climate in which a war takes place. War is a continuation of politics by other means, but diplomacy can also enable a continuation of war by other means. Belligerents can exploit negotiations to help realize the policy objectives at the heart of the original conflict. By quieting the battlefield, mobilizing additional military force, creating political narratives, alleviating pressures to negotiate, and ultimately stalling for time, belligerents can use diplomacy to keep fighting.

Margaret Thatcher, for one, understood this logic well. When, during the Falklands War, she was asked by a BBC interviewer why she was uninterested in talking with the Argentinians, she stated that it "just enables the Argentinians to carry on negotiations on and on and on, a perfectly easy plot. And in the meantime, it will get more and more difficult for us to use a military option. . . . [T]hat would be their plot."[4] Similarly, in the Russo-Ukrainian war begun in 2022, the Zelenskyy government in Kyiv refused the Putin regime's call for the resumption of negotiations and ceasefire in October of that year because it feared that Moscow was seeking to use talks to buy time, conscript more soldiers, replenish supplies, and prepare for a new offensive. Russian sources later confirmed that this was indeed the original intent.[5]

Both Thatcher and Zelenskyy, along with other leaders involved in other conflicts, understood that talking to the enemy had implications for how a war might unfold, and that war and diplomacy should not necessarily be viewed as substitutes but rather as complements. The fact that some negotiations strike peace while others appear to be exploited is not a product of random chance, nor does it suggest that diplomacy is noise. Instead, this variation is a window into belligerents' calculus regarding conflict resolution and their pursuit of desired policies. Tactics such as diplomatic stalling are not, as the *New York Times* suggested in the case of the Korean War, pointless. They may actually be the point.

In presenting this general thesis, I have distinguished between two forms of diplomacy: sincere and insincere. Sincere negotiations involve actors who genuinely seek to reach an agreement (regardless of whether they succeed), while insincere negotiations involve at least one actor who uses diplomacy for ends that are unrelated or antithetical to agreement. While it is intuitive that diplomatic interactions are not always sincere, my theory shows that negotiations during war follow a broadly predictable pattern in terms of their timing, their effects on the battlefield, and their consequences.

Whether negotiations are likely to be sincere or insincere is dependent, as I have argued, on two primary factors. The first is latent external pressure. The more that institutions, norms, and actors embody an environment that promotes diplomacy, the easier it is for any third party to activate forces that push the combatants back to the bargaining table. The second is information from the battlefield. As violent hostilities lay bare the likely trajectory of the conflict, belligerents will develop a common understanding of a viable bargaining range, permitting them to consider a negotiated settlement.

These two factors dynamically influence belligerents' decisions regarding whether and how to negotiate during war. Making an offer to negotiate is costly, as it potentially signals weakness to the opponent, which in turn could embolden them to fight harder. As such, when left to their own devices, belligerents are hesitant to enter negotiations unless the alternative is a ruinous defeat. Diplomatic talks would be uncommon and most liable to occur in the aftermath of battlefield activities that clearly indicate one side's superiority. These negotiations would consequently have a much higher likelihood of being sincere attempts to terminate hostilities. But in the midst of heavy external latent pressures for peace, belligerents may feel not only that the costs of negotiation go down but that the costs of not negotiating go up. Outside efforts to cajole the combatants into diplomacy increase incentives for actors to engage in talks, regardless of whether any actor has a genuine desire for peace. Less fettered by the normal risks of diplomacy, belligerents have greater liberty to use negotiations insincerely in hopes of reshaping the reversion outcome in their favor. In the shadow of latent external pressures, the typically strong relationship between information from the battlefield and negotiations leading to settlement becomes murky. Hostilities that strongly demonstrate one side's advantage will filter out actors with insincere intentions, which in turn increases the chances of talks being sincere, but this relationship is simply not as decisive as when belligerents must make diplomatic overtures on their own.

The preceding chapters drew on diverse evidence to support these claims. New datasets of battles and negotiations across two centuries of interstate wars, which enabled a daily-level analysis of the relationship between bargaining and the battlefield, substantiated my theory. A series of qualitative case studies varying across space, time, levels of latent external pressures for peace, and battlefield activity provided a closer look at specific mechanisms and strategies at work when belligerents chose when and how to negotiate with the enemy. The concerns, ideas, and decisions warring parties had regarding wartime diplomacy reflected key elements of my argument. Finally, hybrid qualitative and quantitative analysis of the Korean War used novel computational methods on archival documents to show that my framework explains not only the (in)sincerity of entire periods of negotiations but also fluctuations in (in)sincerity within a round of talks.

Scholarly Implications

My theory calls for a reassessment of how scholars approach and understand war. As I described at the book's outset, the rational-choice tradition has evolved in a manner such that verbal communication in and of itself is presumed not to carry any costs. Such a conclusion has undercut the motivation to gather separate data on the reality of wartime diplomacy. Consequently, scholarly research tends to see negotiations as a mere mechanism to convert information obtained from fighting into a diplomatic settlement short of military victory or defeat. Any negotiations that do not end a conflict reflect a lack of common beliefs but have few consequences beyond that fact. But even though this view of wartime diplomacy as a mere exchange of words is logically consistent and seemingly reasonable, it does not find much support in the historical record.

This book does not call for jettisoning a rational-choice understanding of war. If anything, it substantiates a critical implication of bargaining models of war: when it comes to forging peace, there is no real substitute for clear battlefield activity. Yet I have also demonstrated that diplomacy is not simply an exchange of words; the act of negotiating implicates far more costs and benefits. Deciding to talk can be perilous in signaling weakness or legitimating an adversary. In other circumstances, deciding not to talk can also be costly. The strength of the post-1945 effect in both my quantitative and my qualitative studies indicates the weight of institutional and normative factors in encouraging belligerents to consider diplomacy. At the same time, engaging in talks can create space to manipulate the military and political environment in order to promote the war effort.

An essential insight of this book is thus that negotiations—particularly during war—can directly affect the reversion outcome that actors will face should talks fall apart. If diplomacy outside war takes place in the shadow of violence, diplomacy during war can be harnessed to increase one's ability to mobilize and apply even more violence. This potential benefit to negotiation has been documented across numerous wars and underscores the importance of grasping more fully the complex calculus that belligerents perform when deciding how to navigate a conflict. Contrary to the suggestions of many studies, bad news from the battlefield does not necessarily engender interest in peace, and diplomacy's value does not suddenly dissipate once weapons are fired. Diplomacy is indeed rational, but a much wider spectrum of considerations helps to explain policymakers' strategies regarding how they talk with the enemy during conflict.

Future bargaining models of war would be well served by accounting for some of these additional strategic considerations regarding the decision to negotiate.[6] But this book also suggests that bargaining models can go only so far on their own, and game-theoretical models may become intractable if too many new parameters or sources of uncertainty are added at the same time. Other lines of inquiry, including the collection and assessment of new data, as demonstrated in this book, may prove necessary to both develop and assess more intricate theories of negotiation.

My argument and evidence also call some aspects of Zartman's ripeness theory—one of the leading frameworks in conflict resolution research—into question. This theory, to recall, argues that "ripe moments" for negotiations arise in the presence of two necessary but not sufficient conditions: belligerents suffering from a mutually hurting stalemate and belligerents simultaneously perceiving the possibility of a diplomatic way out of fighting.[7] The empirical support for ripeness theory and its variants typically relies on qualitative reviews of specific conflicts. Both my broad statistical findings and my individual case studies indicate that distinct battlefield trends, and not periods of stagnation, are a much stronger predictor of negotiations. Ripeness theory also provides no framework to understand or predict insincere diplomacy, instead assuming that negotiation onset presages peace or at least has no negative downstream consequences should talks fail. To the extent that perceptions of a way out are dependent on third-party mediation efforts, my theory suggests that external attempts to pressure belligerents into negotiations may unintentionally generate circumstances that fan the flames of war. Importantly, the battery of quantitative results I produce using daily-level data on fighting and negotiating substantiate my argument and go beyond conventional and anecdotal debates regarding ripeness theory that involve qualitative discussions of purposefully chosen conflicts.

While this book addresses the occurrence of negotiations and belligerents' behavior within periods of conversation, it does not account for the underlying format, topics, or other aspects of the negotiations that may also influence their outcomes. These preliminary interactions that take place in advance of formal talks are often called prenegotiation.[8] Decisions made in this early phase may define what the negotiations can or cannot accomplish before discussions even begin and thus represent a way to control diplomacy through an alternative face of power.[9] For instance, agenda setting is a powerful tool that defines the boundaries of a bargaining interaction. This phenomenon has richer traditions in the fields of American politics and international political economy, where decision-making bodies have much more explicit institutional procedures, but in matters of international conflict, it has received drastically less attention.[10] When Napoleon, for example, sought to win a battle in order to bolster his bargaining position in a negotiation, Charles Maurice de Talleyrand-Périgord—minister of foreign affairs for the First French Republic, Napoleon, and later Louis XVIII—remarked, "Sire, it is not necessary. They have allowed me to set the agenda."[11]

Much as Talleyrand has received acclaim and criticism for his personal prowess as a diplomat, the backgrounds and attributes of the specific individuals sent to negotiate on behalf of a state or organization may also indicate the party's interest in talks or signal any intentional limitations that it seeks to place on the scope of discussions. In the Korean War, the UNC delegation was exclusively populated with military officials who had no background in diplomacy or politics, while more members of the Communist delegation had wider experiences. It is perhaps no coincidence that the first two weeks of negotiations were spent haggling over the agenda, with the UNC seeking to discuss only military affairs and the Communists seeking to also include political questions. Systematically analyzing individual negotiators may thus shed valuable light on how talks in which they participate eventually unfold.

Prenegotiation processes are, as such, consequential and calculated endeavors worth exploring in their own right, both in armed conflict and in other substantive arenas.[12] Indeed, since, as this book underscores, negotiations are a highly strategic activity, the potential value of analyzing negotiations in their more formative stages is all the more evident.

Normative Ideals for Diplomacy

The belief in international relations scholarship that negotiations are a universally desirable and good-faith endeavor without meaningful liabilities is echoed in the policy world. Many experts and practitioners have failed to fully scrutinize the notion of insincere negotiations—largely because of a strong normative belief that diplomacy should not be exploitative.[13] In *Satow's Diplomatic Practice*, Ivor Roberts decries the fifteenth and sixteenth centuries as an era when diplomacy was rife with "the 'Machiavellian' expedients of spying, conspiracy, and deceit" and when "*raison d'état* or what in English is called 'the end justifying the means' took unquestioned precedence over morality."[14] The shift to the notion of diplomacy as a nobler, more honest pursuit appears to have happened only sometime later. For example, in 1604, news leaked of the English diplomat Sir Henry Wotton declaring (after an "Evening in Merriments") that "an ambassador is an honest man, sent to lie abroad for the good of his Country." James I, incensed by this statement, forced Wotton to write two highly public apologies for this perceived impropriety.[15] Some four centuries later, Sir Harold Nicolson—who served as a diplomat for the Foreign Office of the United Kingdom and later became a member of Parliament in the early twentieth century—emphasized the importance of an individual who could adhere to the "truth" when describing the set of criteria he used to "test" whether someone would make an ideal diplomat.[16] But even as the maintenance of longer-term diplomatic relations would thus seem to depend on the honest and fair conduct of individual representatives,[17] it may be shortsighted to believe that diplomacy is always done earnestly—especially during wars in which vital interests are at stake.

Unfortunately, some experts who have recognized that diplomacy can be exploited have inanely concluded that the issue emanates solely from non-Western actors. Following their experiences at Kaesong and Panmunjom during the Korean War, Paris during the Vietnam War, and various other encounters, numerous individuals who interacted with representatives of Communist states wrote books that decried the latter's cynical and time-wasting tactics. Admiral C. Turner Joy's book regarding his time as senior delegate for the UNC, which I quoted at length in chapter 6, is even titled *How Communists Negotiate*.[18] Kenneth Young, who served as US ambassador to Thailand in the early 1960s, published a volume titled *Negotiating with the Chinese Communists* that described his interactions as "annoying and frustrating" because representatives possessed "supreme self-confidence."[19] Implicit in these recriminations is the belief that US representatives were far more sincere and could have realized agreement but for the Communists' bad behavior. Some descriptions of diplomacy with non-Western representatives are imbued with subtle racism; one states that US diplomats had to display "maturity and realism in [their] treatment of non-Western concerns."[20]

This is certainly not to deny the existence of differences in diplomatic behavior across actors. Negotiation scholars have found ample evidence that culture influences how individuals bargain.[21] Nevertheless, even if such concrete differences exist, my empirical analyses show that all actors, regardless of political, geographical, or cultural background, approach negotiations with the same basic underlying motivation: promoting their policy interests, even if it may cut across normative beliefs about the "right" way to conduct diplomacy. Those who research and practice diplomacy should thus be wary of the idea that negotiations cannot cause harm or that only "other" people use diplomacy for cynical ends. As the Indian diplomat Arthur S. Lall once noted, "In defense or promotion of its vital interests, a state has as much latitude in its actions irrespective of the interests of other states."[22] His sentiments are echoed by Secretary of State Dean Acheson, who wrote that we must recognize "negotiation as an instrument of war."[23]

Negotiations in Civil War

Although research focused on interstate war has largely shortchanged the strategic implications of negotiations during conflict, scholars of civil war have arguably made larger strides in recognizing that talking with the enemy is not a costless enterprise. Work by Barbara Walter and Jeffrey Kaplow, among others, has articulated how governments may be resistant to negotiating with rebel groups because doing so could afford these nonstate violent actors an air of legitimacy that bolsters their cause. It could also signal weakness to other potential rebel groups, who may be inspired to wield violence to extract concessions from a seemingly soft government.[24] These potential consequences of negotiation become manifest regardless of whether a state leader strikes a deal with a rebel group. In other words, they are side effects that reshape the reversion outcome—even though most civil war scholars do not use these terms. My theory has taken this astute idea and incorporated it into a more comprehensive framework that enumerates a broader set of risks and rewards that come with negotiating while fighting.

Much of the empirical evidence this book offers has focused on wars between states. But because my core argument bears connections with civil war literature, it is worth reflecting on how my theory of wartime negotiations applies to intrastate conflict. Through much of the twentieth century, civil wars were less likely to end with negotiated agreements compared to their interstate counterparts.[25] Yet the rate of peaceful settlement for intrastate conflicts has steadily grown since the end of the Cold War.[26] These settlements have not come easily. Negotiation efforts to quell violence in Syria, Northern Ireland, Columbia, and Sudan—to name some examples from the early twenty-first century—have all been characterized by suspicions and accusations of parties negotiating in bad faith to prepare for renewed hostilities.

Indeed, there are two reasons to believe that insincere negotiations and the implications of my theory are especially salient when considering civil wars. First, the power imbalances that exist between rebel groups and the government tend to be far wider than gaps in capabilities that arise between belligerent states. One side is the state, which is more organized, resource rich, and partially defined by its monopoly on the legitimate use of force. The other side is a nonstate actor that must overcome deficiencies across these same dimensions. Belligerents on the disadvantaged end of a highly asymmetric conflict have greater incentives to engage in indirect forms of interaction and to wear down the enemy through sustained and costly fighting.[27] Insincere negotiations, which can allow a warring party to stall for time and to reorganize for continued hostilities, accomplish precisely these objectives and increase diplomacy's appeal as a weapon of the weak.

Second, negotiations are more frequent but also more likely to be exploited for side effects when latent external pressures on the belligerents to negotiate are high. My quantitative analysis in chapter 3 demonstrated that interstate wars without any major powers were more susceptible to these talks, which are externally motivated and ineffectual. It is therefore unsurprising that bouts of peace arranged by third parties are inconsistent in how durable they are over the long term.[28] Given that civil wars tend to feature nonmajor states and nonstate actors, third-party countries and organizations wield significantly more political and material leverage to push belligerents into diplomatic ventures.[29]

These two factors suggest that rebel groups in civil wars may see few downsides and significant upsides to engaging in negotiations, even if—or because—they have a meager chance of ending the conflict through pure military might. Quantitative studies of civil war have shown that rebel groups are more likely to request negotiations when the battlefield reaches a period of stalemate, as this demonstrates the rebels' ability to resist the state while also diluting the rebels' optimism about making short-term gains in future fighting.[30] Yet, as I have underscored, an offer to negotiate by one party is not tantamount to the onset of negotiations or the prospects of a mutually acceptable settlement. If anything, my theory suggests that negotiations proposed in the middle of stalemates are most liable to be motivated by insincere intentions that seek to alter the war rather than end it.

Negotiations Not in War

Although this book's proximate goal is to understand the logic of diplomacy during war, it also makes the case that scholars—particularly in the field of international relations—have much more progress to make in studying diplomacy and its practice as a whole, including the quotidian maintenance of relations between nations, institutions, and individuals. Diplomacy can be richly understood as a method to communicate intentions between states,[31] but the interests of a monolithic state and the goal of being credible are only elements of a broader spectrum. Practitioners and historians, on the other hand, have a deeper appreciation of the subtlety, culture, and social dimensions of their craft but frequently discuss the vocation without firm theoretical underpinnings.[32] Stronger connections between these two traditions are essential to helping us develop a more extensive and vibrant understanding of a central institution that holds international society together.[33]

Many of the core insights I have presented also have implications for understanding important diplomatic interactions in settings that are several steps removed from active hostilities. The idea that negotiations can be harnessed to produce side effects is not limited to ceasing conflicts. Any process by which opposing parties attempt to resolve their differences using words can open an avenue for insincerity. Indeed, several examples I have provided throughout this book do not involve active violence.

The United States' diplomatic activities regarding Iran's and North Korea's nuclear ambitions in the twenty-first century may also involve the potential exploitation of diplomacy. In 2018, the Trump administration withdrew the United States from the Joint Comprehensive Plan of Action (JCPOA), the international agreement designed to address Iran's nuclear program that was mentioned at the start of chapter 1. This negotiation process repeatedly stalled over the summer of 2021, and there is suggestive evidence that some of this had insincere motivations. For Iran's part, Supreme Leader Ayatollah Ali Khamenei may have delayed talks through the summer to allow for the new hard-line Iranian president Ebrahim Raisi, a fierce critic of any return to the JCPOA, to take office in August and thus have a stronger hand in any subsequent negotiations.[34] In 2021, the Biden administration worked to shift international public opinion against Iran. Speaking to the press, the State Department official Ned Price decried Iran's "outrageous effort to deflect blame for the current impasse" and claimed that the United States "stand[s] ready . . . to complete work on a mutual return to the JCPOA once Iran has made the necessary decisions."[35]

The United States' actions regarding North Korea's nuclear ambitions also have direct connections with my notion of insincere negotiation. Since the turn of the twenty-first century, North Korea's diplomatic activities—which express a vague interest in some form of denuclearization but typically lead to no new limits on its program—have ultimately allowed the regime to become a de facto nuclear state.[36] Completely understandable international desire for a diplomatic settlement has frequently resulted in very eager attempts to engage in talks whenever North Korea has indicated some interest in diplomacy. This has often created opportunities for the Kim regime to extract side effects, such as the provision of humanitarian aid, that further its survival. Two conspicuous examples were the face-to-face summits between Donald Trump and Kim Jong-un in Singapore in 2018 and Hanoi in 2019, which themselves were partially a product of diplomatic momentum produced by South Korean president Moon Jae-in in 2018. While meant to address nuclear issues, neither summit made concrete progress toward denuclearization, as both sides had differing interpretations of the term. The fact that the two sides had not reconciled their inconsistent definitions of denuclearization in preliminary lower-level meetings, which would be the standard procedure for diplomatic summits, serves as evidence that both leaders were more interested in the public appearance of talks than in making real or difficult progress on the issue. One of the broader consequences and criticisms was that Kim's sitting across from the head of state of the United States, with the two nations' flags intertwined, allowed the North Korean regime to gain both domestic and international status.[37] As the *Washington Post* opined, the first summit "was, without question, a triumph for Kim Jong Un," who could now "parade on the global stage as a legitimate statesman."[38] North Korea's diplomatic maneuvering demonstrates the efficacy of insincere negotiations for weaker parties that can take advantage of international support for engagement.[39]

Accusations of foot dragging have also become prevalent in climate negotiations. With each passing Conference of the Parties (COP) related to the United Nations Framework Convention on Climate Change, highly developed countries and corporations have been criticized for undermining progress in setting or meeting critical goals to prevent disastrous temperature increases. Environmental organizations and activists have warned that the COP has become a forum for states and companies to "greenwash" their activities by touting specific accomplishments to divert attention away from the worst sources of pollution, using the language of environmentalism to disguise lack of concrete action and making seemingly grand commitments that are never fulfilled.[40] As an example, the Copenhagen Accord signed at COP15 in 2009 codified developed countries' commitment to provide $100 billion annually to less developed countries by 2020. This relatively modest target, which will surely rise over time, has never been categorically met in any single year. The Organisation for Economic Cooperation and Development self-reports that contributions rose from $54 billion to almost $90 billion between 2013 and 2021.[41] Other organizations, however, suggest that the numbers are drastically inflated because they include the value of loans and count unrelated forms of aid as being "climate relevant."[42] As another example, the commitment to "net-zero" emissions gained significant attention in 2015, when the Paris Climate Agreement made frequent references to this term.

The concept of "net-zero" sounds promising and has a scientific basis, but governments and corporations often adopt definitions that are not based on scientific principles and omit certain forms of pollution when assessing their own commitments to this goal.[43]

States and companies experience enormous political pressures to come to the bargaining table and discuss solutions to climate change. The rise of climate protests and movements led by young people adds further impetus. Yet so far, many of the actions taken at these talks have allowed high-polluting actors to avoid or delay costly reforms while diverting pressure and blame from themselves, particularly for members of the public who may not follow climate policy in great detail. The fact that a term like "greenwashing" is becoming increasingly common in popular discourse suggests that the general population is more aware of the possibility that climate negotiations are, at least for some actors, conducted insincerely. My theory, considerably extrapolated, would suggest that climate negotiations will become more sincere when trends from the "battlefield" of climate change become stark and feel irreversible. The questions of how painful and absolute the consequences of climate change need to become to spur radical collective action, and whether those changes will be too late to meet the moment, remain open and have existential implications.

When to Give War or Diplomacy a Chance

My book has largely focused on the occurrence of negotiations and their impact on conflict resolution. My empirical analysis, however, does not directly address the welfare implications associated with wartime negotiation. Wars wreak death and destruction, and it is important to understand how diplomacy affects both.

On the one hand, quantitative evidence shows that wars have become shorter and less deadly in the post-1945 environment, where both latent external pressures for diplomacy and observed rates of negotiation have been high. Wars between 1900 and 1945 had a median length of 220 days and 26,700 overall deaths; since 1945, these median numbers have fallen to 157 days and 6,000 deaths.[44] The supposed "long peace" associated with the current international order has also avoided global conflagrations as devastating as the two world wars.[45] If negotiations have been more frequent in this environment, then perhaps efforts to promote diplomacy have been worthwhile regardless of any failures or negative externalities based on insincere negotiations.[46]

On the other hand, some scholars have bemoaned the limited or counterproductive impact that negotiations have had in modern-day conflicts. In the introduction, I made a brief reference to a well-known *Foreign Affairs* piece penned by the historian Edward Luttwak called "Give War a Chance." Written a few years after the Bosnian War of 1992–95, this essay offered a dispiriting assessment of the international community's attempts to promote peace, one that overlaps with themes I have raised in this book:

> An unpleasant truth often overlooked is that although war is a great evil, it does have a great virtue: it can resolve political conflicts and lead to peace. . . . Since the establishment of the United Nations and the enshrinement of great-power politics in its Security Council, however, wars among lesser powers have rarely been allowed to run their natural course. . . . [A] cease-fire tends to arrest war-induced exhaustion and lets belligerents reconstitute and rearm their forces. It intensifies and prolongs the struggle once the cease-fire ends—and it usually does end. . . . Peace takes hold only when war is truly over.[47]

My theory suggests that both "it cannot hurt to negotiate" and "give war a chance" are flawed positions because they adopt unconditional views of negotiation, albeit from opposite directions. Just because wars are more limited today than they were in the past does not mean policymakers can declare diplomatic efforts to be an unalloyed good. The salient question is not whether wars today are less deadly than wars of yesteryear. It is instead whether wars today could be made even less deadly if negotiations were applied more judiciously than they have been. At the same time, just because some negotiations exacerbate violence does not mean diplomacy should be sidelined until one side has fully destroyed the other. These opposing positions are implicitly based on a shared idea that there is no discernible pattern to when and why negotiations succeed in ending hostilities. The argument and evidence I have presented in this book indicate that clear information from the battlefield heavily influences whether third-party pressure is more likely to facilitate peace or to undermine it. The existence of numerous institutions, actors, and avenues that help potential belligerents pursue diplomacy introduces an increased risk of negotiations being abused if they are imposed thoughtlessly. But if applied prudently and in the right circumstances, these same actors and institutions afford a valuable path for belligerents to more quickly arrange peace when they so desire. In the words of the civil war scholar Stephen Stedman, negotiations "should not be offered like buses that come along every fifteen minutes."[48]

My argument and findings offer three suggestions for third parties attempting to quell conflicts. First, external actors could deploy the brunt of their diplomatic pressure when the battlefield has clearly revealed one side's advantage. As we have seen, one prominent method third parties use to create such pressure is organizing mediation efforts. Scholars have produced mixed results about the impact of third-party mediation on conflict. Some works conclude that mediation increases the likelihood and pace of conflict termination, while others produce less promising conclusions.[49] Those in the latter camp frequently analyze mediator bias but yield dissonant findings about whether biased or unbiased mediators are better at terminating conflicts.[50] The effectiveness of mediation also appears to fluctuate as a function of time, with mediation being more productive at early and late stages of conflict.[51] These extant works, whether or not they find positive effects, generally focus on fixed attributes of the actors involved without accounting for battlefield developments and how they dynamically influence the supply of, demand for, and consequences of mediation.[52] For example, wars with quick or decisive outcomes in one side's favor may be readily settled by mediators, while conflicts with less clear-cut trajectories may lead to mediation efforts that are used insincerely. The supply of potential mediators could also be shaped by the state of the battlefield, with more committed mediators offering their services when fighting becomes especially intense or lopsided.[53] While these individual claims require further scrutiny and testing, my theory underscores the importance of considering the future costs of fighting as a motivator for belligerents to not only negotiate but negotiate sincerely. Incorporating this dimension may help to consolidate seemingly disparate judgments regarding mediation's relationship with conflict resolution. When it comes to intrawar diplomacy, nothing is as clarifying as the battlefield.

Second, to further increase a belligerent's interest in negotiating sincerely, outside actors must threaten to impose costs so that whatever benefits could be accrued from negotiating insincerely and improving one's reversion outcome are nullified.[54] While the threat of British military intervention proved useful in stopping Israel during the Arab-Israeli War, actual military involvement by major powers tends to exacerbate conflict by dragging additional actors into hostilities.[55] Sanctions and embargoes that limit the flow of military aid to belligerent states are likely a more efficient manner to reshape the future costs of fighting.[56] The United States' ability to deescalate the 1956 Suez Crisis by threatening the United Kingdom, France, and Israel with economic sanctions lends one important example.

Third, outside parties should be very cautious in promoting ceasefires alongside negotiations. My argument and results demonstrate that sustained and present battlefield momentum expedite diplomacy's ability to settle conflict, while indefinite or quiescent battlefields invite insincere intentions. I have also shown in chapter 4 that both (internal) negotiations and ceasefires are associated with decreased hostilities. If diplomacy has its own independent effect in quelling hostilities, adding formal ceasefires on top of this can further create breathing room for belligerents to remobilize their military forces or to engage in blame shifting.

That said, my point is not that negotiations should be wholly avoided when the battlefield is stalemated or indeterminate, or that ceasefires should never be implemented during war. Having third parties that can rapidly mobilize to facilitate diplomacy may allow belligerents to enter negotiations more quickly and with fewer reservations when they feel interested in talking. This could help prevent wars from escalating needlessly because one or both sides worry about looking weak and being exploited. The Cenepa Valley War, explored in chapter 4, demonstrates this point. But what matters is that belligerents seek negotiations out themselves. The fact that the belligerents in the Cenepa Valley War did so is why that war was resolved so quickly.

Moreover, temporarily dampening hostilities through diplomacy may afford valuable time to conduct humanitarian peace efforts that relieve the suffering of countless individuals affected by a war they did not seek and do not control. Many appeals for ceasefires in contemporary conflicts are framed in precisely this manner. In attempting to ameliorate suffering in the Yemeni civil war, the site of one of the largest humanitarian disasters in modern history, the United Nations and several other states led persistent efforts to broker a ceasefire.[57] Appeals for a ceasefire in the Tigray conflict of 2020–22 emphasized the need for humanitarian deliveries and state parties' obligations to protect Ethiopian civilians in accordance with the Refugee Convention of 1951.[58] Diplomacy and ceasefires can help create critical and short-term moments of relief for innocent civilians.

It is erroneous, however, to believe that negotiations are guaranteed to promote relief even if they do not succeed in ending the overall war. The undeniable benefits of humanitarian aid distributed during moments of quiet must be considered alongside the potential consequences of exacerbating the political and military environment—and thus humanitarian suffering—in the longer term.[59] This is a terrible and morally fraught dilemma. My theory does not provide a straightforward prescription for how to navigate this quandary, but it does highlight the fact that this predicament exists and must be countenanced when shaping conflict resolution policies related to diplomacy.[60]

Some may suggest that a compromise policy would involve organizing talks that are strictly limited to addressing humanitarian concerns, avoiding political matters and broader ceasefires. This idea is not implausible on its face, but policymakers must have their eyes wide open to the reality that the ability to promote humanitarian principles during war is also beholden to belligerents' broader strategic intentions and desire to gain an advantage. Talks held shortly after the onset of the Russo-Ukrainian war, begun in 2022, are illustrative of these pitfalls. In late February and March that year, not long after Russian forces began a "special military operation" that aimed to seize much of Ukraine and realize the so-called "denazification" of the Zelenskyy government, a series of externally motivated peace talks took place—first in Belarus and then in Turkey. These negotiations revealed massive gaps in belligerents' bargaining positions, but both sides agreed to the creation of humanitarian corridors for fleeing civilians.[61] At face value, this was a promising development. But as my argument suggests, and as later events would seem to indicate, such a view is naive. Any artificially constructed pockets of peace, especially when fighting has not provided enough information to create common beliefs between actors, are potential opportunities for belligerents to further their war aims. Indeed, Russian forces were repeatedly accused of intentionally attacking Ukrainian civilians in the humanitarian corridors that the two sides had arranged.[62] To be sure, it was due to these corridors that approximately 125,000 people were evacuated and spared serious injury or death in the first two weeks of the war.[63] But these human rights atrocities indicate that ostensibly peace-promoting activities can be wielded to exact violence.

Brief and abortive negotiations like the ones that took place in early 2022 between Russia and Ukraine can prompt leaders around the world to consider whether they should push belligerents into further talks. The notion that diplomacy could lead to peace in such instances is tempting. But in line with this book's argument, the indeterminate back-and-forth of hostilities over the course of a war, as well as the involvement of major powers on both sides of the conflict, does not produce an environment that is conducive to good-faith diplomacy that begets long-term peace. Diplomatic pushes made in these conditions may not only fail to end the war but also perhaps reinvigorate it. Ultimately, policymakers should both remain wary of diplomacy's potential side effects and avoid applying additional external pressure to artificially accelerate the process, even as—and, indeed, even more so because—peace is at stake.

Final Fighting Words

There is little surprise that war is simultaneously an object of fascination, inquiry, and dread. War represents one of the most overtly destructive processes perpetuated by human civilization. Despite extensive scholarship, including this book, that explains how war is better understood as a strategic activity, war still instinctively feels like the product of irrationality. War is cruel, traumatizing, and catastrophic. Enormous questions about the nature of humans, the fate of individuals and large populations alike, and the state of global affairs hang in the balance because of war.

It is precisely for these reasons that we must appreciate warfare in all of its manifestations, as well as all of the factors that may stymie or enable its continuation. This book has argued that diplomacy does not immediately lose its value once wars begin. The resumption of diplomacy during conflict may trigger optimism among citizens and third-party observers, but it is also not an inevitable sign of progress toward a lasting settlement. Time and again, negotiations have changed belligerents' political and military fortunes regardless of whether they accomplish their professed aim of producing peace. Anyone interested in mitigating conflict must appreciate that distinctions between war and diplomacy are not as binary as we may expect or want them to be. Blood not only is shed by the sword on the battlefield but can also be drawn by the pen at the bargaining table.

Notes

INTRODUCTION

1. White 1964, 245.
2. Kowner 2006, 303.
3. Freedman and Gamba-Stonehouse 1990, 173–81.
4. Finlan 2002, 327; Freedman 1982, 207.
5. My brief overview of the bargaining framework here does not capture the breadth of scholarship on the topic. For cogent reviews, see Jackson and Morelli 2011; Ramsay 2017; Reiter 2003.
6. Morrow 1989; Wittman 1979.
7. Fearon 1995. Fearon discusses a third mechanism called issue indivisibility, but he suggests that most issues are not inherently indivisible and that methods exist to make bargains involving indivisible goods (382). Powell (2006) argues that issue indivisibility is a form of credible commitment problem. I therefore do not discuss issue indivisibility in further detail here.
8. Actors may even be mutually overoptimistic about their chances of success; see Blainey 1988. Fey and Ramsay (2007) and Slantchev and Tarar (2011) offer opposing views regarding the rationality of mutual optimism.
9. Powell 2006. Debs and Monteiro (2014) create a model that allows actors to intentionally choose whether to increase their bargaining power. They suggest that commitment problems lead to war only in the presence of imperfect information. See Geller 2000 and Lemke and Werner 1996 for empirical evidence.
10. Brito and Intriligator (1985) present an earlier formalization of this argument.
11. Bennett and Stam 1996; Goemans 2000a; Long 2003; Slantchev 2004; Weisiger 2013.
12. Wagner 2000.
13. Filson and Werner 2002, 2004; Krainin, Thomas, and Wiseman 2020; Mattes and Morgan 2004; Powell 2004; Slantchev 2003a; Smith and Stam 2003, 2004; Wagner 2000; Wolford, Reiter, and Carrubba 2011.
14. Reiter 2003.
15. This helps to explain why relatively weak actors may still fight overtly stronger opponents. See Arreguín-Toft 2005; Slantchev 2003b; Sullivan 2007.
16. The alternating nature of bargaining models of war is a technical feature that should not be taken literally, but it nonetheless suggests that belligerents are free to communicate at will. Some models suggest that making extreme offers that are sure to be rejected is roughly equivalent to not negotiating; for example, see Powell 2012, 623. But this choice still precludes the analysis of the actual decision to negotiate.
17. Fearon 2013; Krainin, Thomas, and Wiseman 2020; Langlois and Langlois 2009, 2012; Powell 2017.
18. Powell (2004) creates a model that distinguishes wars based on uncertainty regarding the distribution of power from those based on the costs of fighting. The key innovation that enables this distinction in his game-theoretic model is the assumption that multiple bargaining offers can be made with no meaningful time passing between them.
19. Findley 2012; Jones and Metzger 2018; Kaplow 2016.

20. Zartman 1989, 2000, 2001, 2022.

21. Scholarly debate on this topic is active to this day, with special focus on how public diplomatic threats may be more costly to backpedal on and are thus more credible. For some key works, see Fearon 1994; Schelling 1960; Tomz 2007. For dissenting and more conditional views, see Holmes 2013; Katagiri and Min 2019; Kurizaki 2007; Levendusky and Horowitz 2012; Sartori 2002, 2005; Snyder and Borghard 2011.

22. Mastro 2019.

23. Fisher, Ury, and Patton 2011, xxvii.

24. Carnevale and Lawler 1986, 636.

25. Anand, Feldman, and Schweitzer 2009. One exception is Glozman, Barak-Corren, and Yaniv 2015.

26. Acheson 1961, 104.

27. Min 2022, 321; Ponting 2004, 217–20.

28. In her discussion of costly conversations theory (CCT), Mastro (2019, 7) notes that states may still choose to cease discussions after adopting an open posture but that it is no longer credible to say they are unwilling to talk. While it is plausible that the first effort to negotiate marks a turning point with respect to potentially signaling weakness, CCT does not explain when and why actors subsequently negotiate after that point and whether this bears significance for the broader conflict.

29. Nish 1993, 98.

30. Iklé 1964; Pillar 1983.

31. Richmond 1998, 707.

32. Stasavage 2004.

33. Anand, Feldman, and Schweitzer 2009, 1.

34. Wallihan 1998, 258.

35. Lebow 1996, 12.

36. Depledge 2008, 9.

37. Glozman, Barak-Corren, and Yaniv 2015, 671.

38. Schwartz and Gilboa 2021, 1328.

39. Danneman and Beardsley 2020, 190.

40. Kang et al. 2020, 2.

41. Mastro 2019.

42. Beardsley 2009.

43. Gartzke and Poast 2018.

44. Gartner 1998.

45. Luttwak 1999.

46. Downs 1999.

47. Acheson 1961, 103.

48. Adler-Nissen 2015; Roberts 2009.

49. See Reiter (2003, 2009) for further discussion on the promises and pitfalls of developing quantitative data to explore interstate wars.

1. A THEORY OF WARTIME NEGOTIATIONS

1. For example, over seventy additional experts and leaders expressed their support for the pacifying effects of the JCPOA in a letter to Congress; see National Iranian American Council, "73 Prominent International Relations Scholars Say Iran Deal Will Help Stabilize Middle East," August 27, 2015, https://www.niacouncil.org/press_room/73-prominent-international-relations-and-middle-east-scholars-back-iran-deal/.

2. "Press Availability on Nuclear Deal with Iran," US Department of State, July 14, 2015, https://2009-2017.state. gov/secretary/remarks/2015/07/244885.htm.

3. Clausewitz (1832) 1976, 87.

4. *Star Trek: Voyager*, season 4, episode 23, "Living Witness," directed by Tim Russ, story by Brannon Braga, teleplay by Bryan Fuller, Brannon Braga, and Joe Menosky, aired April 29, 1998, on UPN.

5. Iklé 1964. His original definition: "Negotiation is a process in which explicit proposals are put forward ostensibly for the purpose of reaching agreement on an exchange or on the realization of a common interest where conflicting interests are present" (3).

6. Cohen 1991, 8.

7. Cooper 2008; Partzsch 2014; Quessard 2020; Repo and Yrjölä 2011; Wheeler 2011.

8. Schelling 1960. See Downs and Rocke 1990 for a more expansive discussion.

9. Rubinstein 1982, 97.

10. Powell 2002, 2.

11. Rubinstein 1982, 98.

12. Quoted in Roberts 2009, 3.

13. *Oxford English Dictionary Online*, s.v. "diplomacy (*n.*)," accessed April 30, 2024, https://www.oed.com/search/dictionary/?scope=Entries&q=diplomacy.

14. Schelling 1960.

15. See Guilbaud (2020) and Huang (2016) for broader examinations of diplomacy by nonstate actors.

16. Fisher, Ury, and Patton 2011.

17. Birke 2000; Bottom 1998. See also the Harvard Law School Program on Negotiation's Management Report #10, *BATNA Basics: Boost Your Power at the Bargaining Table*.

18. Fearon 1995. Negotiation scholars also call this the "reservation price."

19. White and Neale 1991.

20. Langlois and Langlois 2009; Langlois and Langlois 2012.

21. Fearon 2013; Filson and Werner 2002, 2004; Krainin, Thomas, and Wiseman 2020; Mattes and Morgan 2004; Powell 2004; Slantchev 2003a; Wagner 2000; Wolford, Reiter, and Carrubba 2011. Many models include a discount factor that decreases the value of the disputed good over time, but this is not a function of the war itself.

22. Sebenius 2017, 92–93.

23. Powell 2006. Weisiger (2016b) additionally discusses the dispositional commitment problem, wherein belligerents may be even more convinced that the enemy is inherently aggressive and must be fully destroyed.

24. See chapter 3 of Weisiger (2013) for a very useful study of the conflict. Whigham and Potthast (1999) estimate that between 72 percent and 74 percent of the Paraguayan population perished.

25. Iklé 1971, 85–86; Van Evera 1999; Wittman 1979. Dittman, Kteily, and Bruneau (2021) suggest that actors who seek negotiations may seem less worthy of respect.

26. Epstein and Mealem 2013; Kissinger 1969; Loschelder et al. 2014.

27. "Verbal Message Given to Miss Lisa Howard of ABC News on February 12, 1964 in Havana, Cuba," National Security Archive, February 12, 1964, https://nsarchive.gwu.edu/document/16163-document-07-memorandum-verbal-message-given.

28. President's Daily Brief, February 17, 1970, Central Intelligence Agency document 0005977303. See Carson, Min, and Van Nuys (forthcoming) for more information on and analysis of the President's Daily Brief.

29. *The Office*, season 3, episode 19, "The Negotiation," directed by Jeffrey Blitz, written by Michael Schur, aired April 5, 2007, on NBC.

30. *The Wolf of Wall Street*, directed by Martin Scorsese (West Hollywood, CA: Red Granite Pictures, 2013).

31. Schelling 1960, 53.

32. Mastro 2019, 14.

33. Admati and Perry 1987; Cramton 1992.

34. Mastro 2019; Mastro and Siegel 2023; Pillar 1983; Pruitt and Kim 2004.

35. Laqueur 1980; Spector 1998.

36. Civil war scholars also argue that governments may refuse to negotiate with rebel groups due to fears of looking weak and inspiring other rebel groups to take action. See Kaplow 2016; Melin and Svensson 2009; Pruitt 2006; Toros 2008; Walter 2006, 2009.

37. "Record of Conversation," June 5, 1961, *Foreign Relations of the United States, 1961–1963*, vol. 14, *Berlin Crisis, 1961–1962*, document 34, https://history.state.gov/historicaldocuments/frus1961-63v14/d34.

38. "Telegram from the Embassy in Vietnam to the Department of State," February 15, 1965, *Foreign Relations of the United States, 1964–1968*, vol. 2, *Vietnam, January–June 1965*, document 118, https://history.state.gov/historicaldocuments/frus1964-68v02/d118.

39. "Telegram from the Embassy in Norway to the Department of State," June 14, 1967, *Foreign Relations of the United States, 1964–1968*, vol. 5, *Vietnam, 1967*, document 201, https://history.state.gov/historicaldocuments/frus1964-68v05/d201.

40. Allen and Muratoff 1953, 111–12; Goldstein 1992, 32.

41. Clodfelter 2017, 195; Jaques 2007, 803.

42. Brockett and Bliss 1878, 649.

43. Brockett and Bliss 1878, 649.

44. Iklé 1971, 85–87. Lehmann and Zhukov (2019) make a similar argument regarding battlefield surrender.

45. Fearon 1994; Weeks 2008.

46. Iklé 1971; Sticher 2021.

47. Spector 1998; Tierney 2013, 176. Leaders may become "stuck" in wars due to fears of punishment for losing or exiting wars short of victory. See Croco 2011; Goemans 2000a; Stanley 2009; Weisiger 2016b.

48. Lanoszka and Hunzeker 2015, 682–83.

49. Lukacs 1999, 63.

50. Debo 1992, 122.

51. Beardsley (2009, 280) makes a similar point regarding mediation.

52. Debo 1992, 240.

53. Porter-Szücs 2014, 83.

54. Aggestam 2012.

55. Iklé 1964, 43; Pillar 1983, 51. As the hyphen seems grammatically dubious, I drop it and refer to "side effects" instead.

56. Powell 2004.

57. Anand, Feldman, and Schweitzer 2009; Danneman and Beardsley 2020; Depledge 2008; Glozman, Barak-Corren, and Yaniv 2015; Kang et al. 2020; Olekalns and Smith 2007; Richmond 1998; Schwartz and Gilboa 2021; Wallihan 1998.

58. Noesner 2010, 203–4.

59. Birnbaum and Peters (1990) provide a broader accounting of the CSCE.

60. Lebow 1996, 12–13; Hopmann 2012, 245–46. Substantial evidence also suggests that the United States harnessed arms control negotiations with the Soviets to "offset" the Soviet Union's conventional weapons advantage while boosting its own technological advantages. See John D. Maurer, "The Forgotten Side of Arms Control: Enhancing U.S. Competitive Advantage, Offsetting Enemy Strengths," War on the Rocks, June 27, 2018, https://warontherocks.com/2018/06/the-forgotten-side-of-arms-control-enhancing-u-s-competitive-advantage-offsetting-enemy-strengths/.

61. See sections 8(d) and 8(a)(5) in the National Labor Relations Act, US Congress 1935.

62. Clausewitz (1832) 1976; McMillan 1992, 9–10. The US Army Field Manual No. 3–0 also mentions this concept as one of the nine principles of war; US Army 2017, 6–27.

63. Colosi 1984, 27–30.

64. Corbetta 2010, 2015; Frazier and Dixon 2006; Melin 2014; Regan 2002; Shirkey 2009.

65. Quoted in Colosi 1984, 27.

66. Lebow 2020. See also Montgomery 2013. Hopmann (2012, 243–45) offers an example of this behavior in the lead-up to the Kosovo War.

67. Tal 2004, 395–96.

68. Maureen Dowd, "After the War: The White House; Bush, Urging Wider Peace, Hints at Pressure on Israel to Yield Land for Security," *New York Times*, March 7, 1991.

69. Lebow 1996, 22.

70. Tom Perry, Jack Stubbs, and Estelle Shirbon, "Russia and Turkey Trade Accusations over Syria," Reuters, February 3, 2016, https://www.reuters.com/article/us-mideast-crisis-syria/russia-and-turkey-trade-accusations-over-syria-idUSKCN0VC169.

71. Pillar 1983, 49–50.

72. Filson and Werner 2002, 2004; Powell 2004.

73. Arreguín-Toft 2001; Biddle 2004; Knorr 1956.

74. Freedman 1998; Sullivan 2007.

75. Hanska 2017; Triandafillov 1994.

76. Dahl 2013; Handel 1977; Luttwak 1987; Van Evera 1999.

77. Gray (2018, 7) speaks to the importance of time in conflict.

78. Quoted in Foch 1918, 81.

79. US Department of the Army 1994, 4–8.

80. Beardsley 2011; Regan 2002; Regan and Stam 2000.

81. This advantage may be especially appealing for weaker parties. See McMillan 1992; Tangredi 1985.

82. Sarah El Deeb and Jamey Keaten (Associated Press), "Syria's Warring Parties Spar over Collapsing Cease-Fire," *Seattle Times*, April 20, 2016, https://www.seattletimes.com/nation-world/activists-is-seizes-new-ground-in-eastern-syria/.

83. Maxwell 1970, 376.

84. Goertz, Diehl, and Balas 2016; Fazal 2007, 55; Min 2020.

85. Corbetta 2010; Greig 2001, 2005; Regan and Stam 2000; Wallensteen and Svensson 2014.

86. Aggestam 2006; Pugh 2009. Rubin (1992, 252) vividly remarks that "it is the whip of external pressure and the pain of unacceptable alternatives that drives disputants to the bargaining table."

87. Iklé 1964, 53–54.

88. Michael Goldsmith, "More Fighting as Peace Talks Collapse," Associated Press, March 11, 1987, https://apnews.com/article/13d5f6498fd89991e2454709164b545e.

89. Thatcher 1993, 213.

90. Bjork 1985.

91. Barbara Bibbo, "Analysis: Syria's Peace Process and the Russian and US roles," Al Jazeera, February 28, 2021, https://www.aljazeera.com/news/2021/2/28/analysis-syrias-peace-process-and-the-russian-and-us-role.

92. Beardsley 2011, 38–40; Goldstein 2011, 186.

93. Allee and Huth 2006; Beardsley 2010; Conlon, Carnevale, and Ross 1994; Gent and Shannon 2010; Greig and Diehl 2005; Pruitt 1981; Pruitt and Johnson 1970; Simmons 2002.

94. Werner and Yuen 2005.

95. Wallihan 1998.

96. Ramsay 2017.

97. Slantchev 2003a; Smith 1998a; Smith and Stam 2003, 2004.

98. Blainey 1988, 56.

99. Calahan 1944; Lehmann and Zhukov 2019; Ramsay 2008; Smith 1995.

100. Filson and Werner 2002, 2004; Pillar 1983; Powell 2004; Reiter 2009; Slantchev 2003a.

101. Fortna 2004; Mattes and Savun 2010; Werner and Yuen 2005.

102. Ramsay 2008; Slantchev 2004.

103. Ruhe 2015. Phillipson (1916, 56) also notes that in many (Western) conflicts of the eighteenth and nineteenth centuries, the onset of a temporary armistice before and during talks was almost considered a "well-nigh established rule of international law."

104. Pillar 1983, 41.

105. Substantial literature in military affairs attests to the importance of deception as a "force multiplier" and its use, particularly by weaker parties, to gain a temporary competitive advantage on the battlefield. For a sample, see Daniel and Herbig 1982; Gulsby 2010; Handel 1982; Joint Chiefs of Staff 2006; Lewicki 1983; and Stein 1982. My contention is not that deception is irrelevant in wartime diplomacy, but rather that insincere negotiations can take place even in the absence of deception.

106. Thucydides 1972, 334.

107. Vatcher 1958.

108. Asmussen 2008.

109. Janis and Mann 1977; Jervis 1976.

110. Tversky and Kahneman 1973; Walgrave and Dejaeghere 2017. Lake (2010/11) explores the limits of rationality in explaining the lead-up to the 2003 Iraq War.

111. Jost et al. 2024; Kertzer et al. 2022.

112. McDermott 2004.

113. Kertzer, Rathbun, and Rathbun 2020; Pruitt and Olczak 1995.

114. Lanoszka and Hunzeker 2015.

115. Zartman 1989, 2000, 2001, 2022. Iji and Vuković (2023) curate a compilation of works interacting with Zartman's original argument.

116. Holsti 1966.

117. Pruitt 2005; Zartman and de Soto 2010.

118. Kleiboer 1994; O'kane 2006; Pruitt 2005.

119. Greig 2001; Min 2021.

120. Zartman 2001, 9.

121. Walch (2016) attempts to extend ripeness theory to explain why parties choose to remain in or exit negotiations once they begin.

122. Vuković 2022; Zartman 2008.

123. Kuperman (2022) argues that highly capable third-party actors can engage in "muscular mediation," through which they propose compromises and then coerce the stronger belligerent to accept this proposal. Beyond the general risk of conflict escalation, the theory I establish warns against this tactic, as negotiations borne of intense pressures are more likely to be insincere and abused for side effects.

124. Mastro 2019, 24–25; emphasis in the original.

2. QUANTIFYING TWO CENTURIES OF WAR

1. These conflicts are listed by the Correlates of War (COW) Project, which defines an interstate war as a period of sustained combat involving regular armed forces of internationally recognized states where at least one thousand battle-related fatalities are sustained across all participating states. See Sarkees and Wayman 2010. Reiter, Stam, and

Horowitz (2016a, 2016b) provide a revision of this conflict list. Lyall (2020) argues that the COW list of wars is incomplete and introduces an alternative dataset called Project Mars. Gibler and Miller (2022), however, identify several issues with Project Mars. The two most relevant here are that the dataset's larger set of wars comes from pooling together different types of noninterstate wars that are already captured by other COW resources, and that Project Mars contains four fewer interstate wars than the COW Project does, without justification. Gibler and Miller conclude that the COW Inter-State War list is a highly reliable and comprehensive record.

2. For examples of civil war mediation datasets, see DeRouen, Bercovitch, and Pospieszna 2011 and Regan, Frank, and Aydin 2009.

3. Refer to Min 2020 for more details on sources.

4. Herring 1983.

5. Iklé 1964.

6. The fact that external negotiations are not the same as mediation also serves to distinguish my argument from that of Beardsley (2011).

7. White 1964, 374.

8. Dean 2007, 2.

9. Roberts 2014, 697.

10. Avirgan and Honey 1982, 84.

11. Dupuy 1987; Eggenberger 1985.

12. Clausewitz (1832) 1976, 210.

13. Dupuy (1987, 65) defines battles as "combat between major forces, each having opposing assigned or perceived operational missions, in which each side seeks to impose its will on the opponent by accomplishing its own mission, while preventing the opponent from achieving his." Eggenberger (1985, iv) defines battles as "a general fight or encounter between hostile military forces . . . a confrontation between opposing armed forces that resulted in casualties or in a change in the military position." Jaques (2007, xii) defines battles as "any clash between organised forces of combatants."

14. Smith and Stam 2004.

15. Weisiger 2016b.

16. Reiter, Stam, and Horowitz (2016b) provide other examples of such discrepancies.

17. Slantchev 2003b; Smith 1998b; Smith and Stam 2004.

18. Castillo 2014; Gelpi, Feaver, and Reifler 2009; Hanami 2003.

19. Jaques 2007.

20. Smith 1998a; Smith and Stam 2004.

21. Clodfelter 2017, 425; Jaques 2007, 498.

22. For more on "victory" in warfare, see Bartholomees 2008 and Mandel 2006.

23. Glantz and House 2015, chaps. 4–6.

24. Dupuy 1987, 65.

25. Clodfelter 2017, 196; Eggenberger 1985, 337–38; Jaques 2007, 1943.

26. Collelo 1990, 196; Jaques 2007, 1798.

27. Slantchev 2003a; Smith 1998a; Smith and Stam 2003, 2004.

28. Shirkey and Weisiger 2012, 17.

29. Fortna 2004; Mattes and Savun 2010; Weisiger 2016b; Werner and Yuen 2005.

30. Weisiger 2016b.

31. The online appendix provides a similar overview of the Russo-Japanese War of 1904–5, described in the introductory chapter.

32. Haythornthwaite 2004, 90.

33. Edmonds 1932, xiii.

34. Min 2020, 2021.

3. FIGHTING TO TALK

1. Goertz, Diehl, and Balas 2016, 8. That said, Lee (2020) demonstrates that the decline in overt interstate violence since 1945 may belie the fact that states increasingly engage in strategies of subversion instead.

2. Wright 1924.

3. Mueller 2004.

4. Carter and Goemans 2011; Finnemore 2003; Zacher 2001. Altman (2020) shows that states have adopted to the territorial integrity norm by seizing smaller pieces of territory via fait accompli.

5. Fazal 2013, 2018; Morrow 2007.

6. Halperin 1961; Pauly 2018; Tannenwald 2007.

7. United Nations 1945, art. 39.

8. Pevehouse, Nordstrom, and Warnke 2004; Shannon 2009; Shannon, Morey, and Boehmke 2010; Winham 1977.

9. Hampson, Crocker, and Aall 2007.

10. See the online appendix for full results.

11. Comprehensive results from all models are in the online appendix.

12. The online appendix features more details.

13. See Hougaard 1999.

14. Jones and Metzger 2018; Metzger and Jones 2016.

15. My distinctions between victory/defeat and negotiated settlement are different from classifications that Allan Stam made in his influential book *Win, Lose, or Draw*. Stam (1996, 76) defines draws as situations where "both sides formally agree to cease fighting an internationally recognized and binding treaty," which appears to align with what I call negotiated settlement. But he also codes wars where fighting ends after a long period of time as draws, even if no formal agreement is created. Additionally, any war where one side "benefits in the new territorial status quo after the war" (75) is considered to feature a winner, which means it cannot be classified as a draw even if territorial changes are codified in a diplomatic agreement. My conception of negotiated settlement thus includes cases that Stam may consider either a win/loss or a draw, depending on whether the war was actually concluded through a negotiated settlement and regardless of ultimate changes in territorial control.

16. Two of the 189 negotiation periods are not captured in the figure because the first day of war features negotiations.

17. This measure and the underlying battle data used to construct it are described in chapter 2.

18. Holsti 1991.

19. Slantchev 2004.

20. In wars with more than two states, I consider a war to feature contiguity if any two belligerents on opposing sides share a border.

21. Bennett and Stam 1996; Gartner and Siverson 1996; Reiter and Stam 2002.

22. Singer 1987.

23. Some scholarship has questioned the utility of CINC ratios as a measure of relative power, pointing out that CINC ratios are a poor predictor of dispute outcomes; see Beckley 2018. I nonetheless rely on CINC ratios for three reasons. First, the purpose of the CINC ratio in my analysis is to roughly capture observable prewar capabilities—not to successfully predict the ultimate outcome of the war. Second, some alternative measures, such as the material military power measure by Souva (2023), do not cover as many wars or countries as CINC ratios do. Third, the most comprehensive alternative measure of prewar expectations—the Dispute Outcome Expectations (DOE) score introduced by Carroll and Kenkel (2019)—is not meant to be used in statistical models where the

outcome variable reflects some result of a conflict. Even so, the online appendix replicates all the quantitative analysis in this chapter using DOE scores and shows that my results are largely unchanged.

24. Choi 2004; Reiter and Stam 2002; Schultz 1999; Valentino, Huth, and Croco 2010; Weisiger 2016b. Desch (2002) and Farber and Gowa (1995) are two dissenting voices.

25. Marshall, Gurr, and Jaggers 2016.

26. Halperin 1961; Waltz 1979.

27. Nuclear data come from Jo and Gartzke 2007.

28. Choi 2004; Morey 2016; Min 2022; Weisiger 2016a; Weitsman 2014; Wolford 2017.

29. Bayer 2006.

30. Snyder 1984.

31. Descriptive statistics for all these variables are in the online appendix.

32. The average measure of issue salience in pre-1945 wars is 1.877, and in post-1945 wars, it is 2.229. A t-test suggests that this difference in means is weakly statistically significant ($p = 0.081$).

33. See Weisiger 2016b for a deeper discussion of different views regarding the informational mechanism. My finding is consistent with what Weisiger calls the "informational obsolescence" perspective (351).

34. The online appendix features full statistical tables that correspond with the coefficient plots. It also includes the results from multistate models that use thirty-day and ninety-day windows (instead of the sixty-day window used in the main analysis).

35. This figure is essentially the same as figure 2.2 in chapter 2 but is further disaggregated by historical era.

36. We calculate this by noting that the estimated coefficient in figure 3.5 is 1.977, and $\exp(1.977) = 7.221$. All analogous results mentioned in this chapter are calculated similarly.

37. Similarly, Min (2020) shows that negotiations in pre-1945 wars have a highly positive and statistically significant impact on war termination but that these effects disappear in post-1945 conflicts.

38. Organski 1958; Singer, Bremer, and Stuckey 1972; Wohlforth 2009.

39. Melin 2011, 2014; Wallensteen and Svensson 2014.

40. Greig 2005.

41. Duursma 2018; Frei 1976.

42. Bercovitch 1991.

43. Butterworth 1978; Princen 1992.

44. A model that includes war termination would feature seven possible transitions, including one that is observed only eight times.

45. A simple chi-square test of independence also provides no evidence of a meaningful difference ($p = 0.744$).

46. Regarding the timing of mediation, see Beardsley 2011; Bercovitch 1992; Kleiboer and 't Hart 1995; Melin 2011; Regan and Stam 2000; Ruhe 2015. Note, however, that my argument regarding third parties goes beyond strict mediation efforts.

47. Bercovitch and Gartner 2006; Gartner and Bercovitch 2006; Gartner 2011. Beardsley (2008) and Greig (2005) discuss selection bias in mediation research. Fortna (2008) makes a similar argument regarding peacekeeping missions.

48. Bercovitch 1999; Bercovitch and Fretter 2004; Bercovitch and Jackson 2001; Gartner and Bercovitch 2006.

49. Given that the ICM dataset only covers the years 1945 through 1999, my analysis in this section omits the 2001 invasion of Afghanistan and the 2003 invasion of Iraq.

50. Melin 2014.

51. Egypt and the United Kingdom fought in the 1882 conquest of Egypt and the 1956 Sinai War, but the latter also involved France and Israel fighting alongside the United Kingdom. China and the United States clashed in the 1900 Boxer Rebellion and the 1950–53 Korean War, but several other states joined the United States in the Boxer Rebellion, and both sides were multilateral in the Korean conflict. Finally, Morocco and Spain clashed twice before 1945—once in 1859–60 and again in 1909–10—and then in the 1957–58 Ifni War, but France joined Spain in the Ifni War.

52. One other war involving Greece and Turkey is the Second Greco-Turkish War of 1919–22. I instead focus on the 1897 conflict because the 1919–22 war concerned a much larger expanse of territory and erupted in the immediate aftermath of World War I and the dissolution of the Ottoman Empire.

53. Hatzis 2018.

54. See Dilke and Botassi 1897 for a useful account of these events.

55. Tatsios 1984, 93.

56. Anderson and Hershey 1918, 214.

57. Tatsios 1984, 98–99.

58. Freese 1897, 22.

59. Ekinci 2006, 65.

60. The Correlates of War records the start date of this conflict as February 15, 1897, the day that George I, king of Greece, proclaimed the occupation of Crete. Most treatments of the war, however, use April 17, as this is the day that diplomatic relations were severed and the Ottomans declared war on Greece. For example, refer to Clodfelter 2017, 196; or Phillips and Axelrod 2005, 540. The war is commonly called the Thirty Days' War in recognition of the fact that the war ended on May 19.

61. Ekinci 2006, 73–74.

62. Jaques 2007, 727.

63. Vatikiotis (2014, 29–30) summarizes diary entries written by Ioannis Metaxas, who fought in the 1897 war and later served as prime minister from 1936 to 1941.

64. Tatsios 1984, 217.

65. Showalter 2014, 732.

66. Rose 1897, 173.

67. *Documents diplomatiques* 1897, documents 648 and 649 (pp. 343–44). My translation from the French.

68. Clodfelter 2017, 196–97.

69. Ekinci 2006, 85.

70. Clodfelter 2017, 197.

71. Phillipson 1916, 61.

72. Phillips and Axelrod 2005, 540.

73. Tatsios 1984, 119.

74. Mazower 1992, 895; Miller 2009, 4.

75. Ekinci 2006, 83.

76. Michalopoulos 2013, 73.

77. Croco (2011), Stanley (2009), and Weisiger (2016b) provide broader theories and evidence regarding leadership changes and conflict termination.

78. Vatikiotis 2014, 30.

79. Rosenbaum 1970, 621–22.

80. United Nations 1960.

81. Ker-Lindsay 2015, 19–20.

82. Boroweic 2000, 47; Ker-Lindsay 2015, 20.

83. Markides 1977, 78.

84. Asmussen 2008, 13–14.

85. Dodd 2010, 111–14.

86. Asmussen (2008, 75) notes that Ecevit's diplomatic actions were heavily reported in the Turkish press, perhaps helping to justify the war option.

87. Asmussen 2008, 95.

88. United Nations Security Council (UNSC) Res. 353 (20 July 1974), UN Doc. S/RES/353.

89. UPI, "NATO Urges Parley on Future of Cyprus," *New York Times*, July 23, 1974.

90. Nan Robertson, "Ankara Claiming Permanent Base," *New York Times*, July 23, 1974.

91. Asmussen 2008, 154–55.

92. Asmussen 2008, 161.

93. United Nations (1974, 1277–78) provides the full text of this joint declaration.

94. Clodfelter 2017, 543.

95. Asmussen 2008, 171–72.

96. S. J. L. Olver to A. C. Goodison, July 15, 1974, FCO 9/1907, National Archives of the UK, Kew, Richmond.

97. Hamilton and Salmon 2006, no. 52.

98. Paul Martin, "Villagers Tell of Cyprus Atrocities," *The Times* (London), August 5, 1974.

99. "Transcript of Telephone Conversation between President Ford and Secretary of State Kissinger," August 10, 1974, *Foreign Relations of the United States, 1969–1976*, vol. 30, *Greece; Cyprus; Turkey, 1973–1976*, document 127, https://history.state.gov/historicaldocuments/frus1969-76v30/d127.

100. Kaufman 2007, 207.

101. Asmussen 2008, 194.

102. Hamilton and Salmon 2006, no. 70.

103. "Cyprus Fighting Resumes as Peace Talks Collapse; U.N. Called into Session," *New York Times*, August 14, 1974.

104. Kliot and Mansfeld 1997, 497.

105. Clodfelter 2017, 543; Jaques 2007, 556.

106. Demetriades et al. 1992, 9.

107. Asmussen 2008, 155.

108. On July 21, Kissinger personally called Ecevit, who had been a former student of his at Harvard, and informed him that the United States would take all its nuclear weapons away from the border between Greece and Turkey if Turkey refused a ceasefire. See Warner 2009, 138.

109. Archival evidence suggests that Kissinger was quite inclined to allow Turkey to control one-third of Cyprus. See Mallinson and Fouskas 2017.

110. Hamilton and Salmon 2006, no. 63.

111. "Minutes of Meeting of the Washington Special Actions Group," July 21, 1974, *Foreign Relations of the United States, 1969–1976*, vol. 30, *Greece; Cyprus; Turkey, 1973–1976*, document 110, https://history.state.gov/historicaldocuments/frus1969-76v30/d110.

112. Craig R. Whitney, "Turkish Plan for Cyprus Disrupts Talks in Geneva," *New York Times*, August 13, 1974.

113. Asmussen 2008, 103.

114. "Minutes of Meeting of the Washington Special Actions Group."

115. Asmussen 2008, 162. UN Security Council Resolution 355, adopted on August 1, reaffirmed support for Resolution 353 but did little to subdue Turkey.

116. "Turkey Spoils Her Case," *The Times* (London), August 5, 1974.

117. "Cyprus Fighting Resumes."

118. Polyviou 1980, 159.

119. Constandinos 2008, 268.
120. Birand 1985, 79–80.
121. Asmussen 2008, 191; Kurtulgan 2019, 208.
122. Callaghan 1987, 348.
123. Asmussen 2008, 156–57.
124. Asmussen 2008, 188.

4. TALKING TO FIGHT

1. Overdispersion tests indicate that Poisson models are appropriate for analysis; p-values equal or are very close to 1 across all models.

2. Leatherdale 1983, 155.

3. The Jaccard similarity coefficient is a commonly used 0-to-1 measure that gauges the similarity of two sets of binary vectors. The Jaccard similarity coefficient for my negotiation and ceasefire variables is practically 0.

4. Slantchev 2003a; Wagner 2000.

5. If there are fewer than sixty days before or after one of these negotiation periods, I simply use all observations that do exist.

6. In the online appendix, I show results using the thirty-day and ninety-day windows.

7. Diehl 2004; Gartner and Siverson 1996; Wang and Ray 1994.

8. Luttwak 1987; Van Evera 1999.

9. Clausewitz (1832) 1976, 198.

10. Sun-Tzu 2010, 17.

11. Coe 2018; McMichael 1990; Schub 2020; Sullivan 2012; Weisiger 2016b. Goemans (2000b) and Reiter (2009) explore how prewar expectations and demands evolve in response to information from fighting.

12. Singer 1987.

13. Hegre 2008.

14. Refer to chapter 3, note 23, for further discussion and justification of the use of CINC scores to gauge prewar expectations. Additional results in the online appendix show that a measure of inconsistency using the Dispute Expectation Outcomes scores yields similar findings.

15. Cannizzo 1980; Whitman 1941.

16. I provide more details and full results of these placebo tests in the online appendix.

17. Duffy 1997, 223.

18. Engel-Janosi 1950, 130.

19. Louis Napoleon would soon assume the title of "Prince-President." Upon orchestrating a self-coup and becoming emperor in 1852, he took the name Napoleon III.

20. Trevelyan 1912, 145.

21. Clodfelter 2017, 177.

22. Showalter 2014, 590.

23. Robertson 1952, 372.

24. "Assemblée nationale: Séance du jeudi 10 mai," *Gazette nationale ou le Moniteur universel*, May 11, 1849; translation from Trevelyan 1912, 146.

25. Robertson 1952, 372.

26. Ward, Prothero, and Leathes 1909, 122–23.

27. "Assemblée nationale: Séance du mercredi 9 mai," *Gazette nationale ou le Moniteur universel*, May 10, 1849; translation from Trevelyan 1912, 146. This ruse was not known publicly until June 9, at which point France had begun a siege on Rome. See Dwight 1851, 147–48.

28. Trevelyan 1912, 147–48.

29. Dwight 1851, 147.

30. Quoted in Smith 1895, 35.

31. Marraro 1943, 477. This quotation comes from a message sent to US secretary of state John Clayton. See also Robertson 1952, 375.

32. Clodfelter 2017, 177.

33. Quoted in Smith 1895, 29.

34. Dwight 1851, 149–50. The Roman Assembly went into official adjournment for the first time on May 18, the day the negotiated ceasefire began, based on the triumvirate's belief that hostilities between Rome and Paris were effectively over.

35. While the Correlates of War (COW) Project lists this conflict as an interstate war, it is unlikely that the conflict satisfies the one-thousand-casualty threshold that COW uses to identify interstate wars. Reiter, Stam, and Horowitz (2016b) exclude this war from their dataset for this reason. Nonetheless, I analyze this case because it still represents an important example of a modern-day interstate conflict.

36. Scheina 2003, 125.

37. Palmer 1997, 117.

38. St John 1999, 5–10.

39. Militarized Interstate Dispute 1154; see Gibler 2018, 140–41.

40. Gibler 2018, 141.

41. Marcella 1995, 6.

42. Palmer 1997, 113. See also St John 1996.

43. Militarized Interstate Dispute 2119; see Gibler 2018, 143–44.

44. Sarkees and Wayman (2010, 180) indicate that the war began on January 9, 1995, because of "an exchange of fire" between the two sides. Other sources, however, indicate that the January 9 encounter involved only troop exchanges without violence; for example, see Spencer 1998, 137. Most accounts identify January 26 as the first day of active hostilities. I adopt this latter view in this case study.

45. Spencer 1998, 139.

46. At the outset of the conflict, both civilian governments may not have known what their militaries were doing. See Bonilla 1999, 69; Herz and Nogueira 2002, 45–46; Palmer 1997, 119.

47. Galo Leoro, "Annex: Letter Dated 27 January 1995 from the Minister of Foreign Affairs of Ecuador Addressed to the President of the Security Council," January 28, 1995, United Nations Document Symbol S/1995/87, United Nations Digital Library, https://digitallibrary.un.org/record/167722.

48. Eduardo Ponce, "Annex: Letter Dated 28 January 1995 from the Deputy Minister of International Policy and Secretary General for External Relations of Peru Addressed to the President of the Security Council," January 29, 1995, United Nations Document Symbol S/1995/89, United Nations Digital Library, https://digitallibrary.un.org/record/168790.

49. James Brooke, "Ecuador and Peru against Skirmish over an Old Disputed Border," *New York Times*, January 29, 1995.

50. James Bone, "UN Makes Guarantors Responsible for Peru Deal," *The Times* (London), January 31, 1995.

51. Gabriella Gamini, "War Intensifies as Peru and Ecuador Launch Air Raids," *The Times* (London), January 31, 1995.

52. Reuters, "Peru Vows to Pull Back Tanks," *The Times* (London), February 2, 1995.

53. Mac Margolis and William R. Long, "Mediators Halt Peru-Ecuador Talks," *Los Angeles Times*, February 6, 1995. See also Mares and Palmer 2012, 45.

54. Reuters, "Ecuador Accuses Peru of New Raid," *The Times* (London), February 4, 1995.

55. Some reports indicated that Peruvian soldiers got lost in the jungle and took eight days to meander back to their base. See Gabriel Escobar, "Peru, Ecuador Weigh Peace Terms," *Washington Post*, February 17, 1995.

56. Reuters, "Ecuador Border Dispute Escalates," *The Times* (London), February 13, 1995. Also see Reuters, "Peru 'Shoots Down Two Ecuador Jets,'" *The Times* (London), February 14, 1995.

57. Tincopa 2021, 44–45.

58. Greene (2008) provides a highly enlightening account of the indigenous dimensions to the disputed territory.

59. A separate raid against the Ecuadorian outpost at Coangos that same day also failed; see Spencer 1998, 144.

60. Reuters, "Peru 'Shoots Down Two Ecuador Jets.'" Peruvian troop strengths were indeed increased on this day; see the "What's News—Worldwide" column in the *Wall Street Journal*, February 13, 1995, A1.

61. Fournier Coronado 1995, 169.

62. James Brooke, "Peru and Ecuador Halt Fighting along Border, Claiming Victory," *New York Times*, February 15, 1995.

63. Monte Hayes, "Peru's [*sic*] Declares Unilateral Cease-Fire in Border War," Associated Press, February 14, 1995.

64. Manrique 1999, 9; Spencer 1998, 149. Contemporaneous reporting on control of outposts was unclear for two reasons. First, the harsh jungle environment made reporting inherently difficult. Second, the two countries accused one another of fabricating "false" versions of the outposts and leading journalists to these phantom outposts to claim victory. See Escobar, "Peru, Ecuador Weigh Peace Terms."

65. Reuters, "Mortar Fire Shatters Truce," *The Times* (London), February 15, 1995.

66. Gabriel Escobar, "Peru, Ecuador Sign Agreement to End Fighting," *Washington Post*, February 18, 1995.

67. Spencer 1998, 144–45.

68. Spencer 1998, 145–46.

69. Associated Press, "Ecuador Says 13 Killed in Peru Clash," *Chicago Tribune*, February 24, 1995. The number was later revised to fourteen; see Klepak 1998, 99.

70. Núñez 2014, 161.

71. William R. Long, "Peru-Ecuador Border Clash Drives Off Peace Team," *Los Angeles Times*, February 23, 1995.

72. Tribune Wires, "Mortar Shells Miss Peruvian President," *Chicago Tribune*, February 26, 1995.

73. "Annex: Press Release Issued on 28 February 1995 by the Ministry of Foreign Affairs of Ecuador," March 2, 1995, United Nations Document Symbol S/1995/173, United Nations Digital Library, https://digitallibrary.un.org/record/175070.

74. Palmer 1997, 123.

75. Viatori 2015, 197.

76. Quoted in Mares and Palmer 2012, 38.

77. Mares and Palmer 2012, 38; Weidner 1996, 55.

78. Jenne 2016, 180; Marcella 1999, 233.

79. Marcella and Downes 1999, 4.

80. Klepak 1998, 100–101.

81. Spencer 1998.

82. James Brooke, "Peruvians at Disadvantage in Border War," *New York Times*, February 8, 1995. See also Mares 1996, 117.

83. Klepak 1998, 95–96.

84. Herz and Nogueira 2002, 45.

85. Brooke, "Peruvians at Disadvantage." See also Mares 1996, 117.

86. Mac Margolis and William R. Long, "Brazil Leader Trying to Mediate Border Dispute," *Los Angeles Times*, February 4, 1995.

87. Mares 1996, 118.

88. Reuters, "Ecuador Rejects Cease-Fire Plan OK'ed by Peru," *The Sun* (Baltimore), February 7, 1995.

89. Quoted in Margolis and Long, "Mediators Halt Peru-Ecuador Talks."

90. Associated Press, "Ecuador Argues Its Case," *South China Morning Post*, February 7, 1995.

91. See the "What's News—Worldwide" column in the *Wall Street Journal*, February 2, 1995, A1.

92. Reuters, "Ecuador Accuses Peru of New Raid," *The Times* (London), February 4, 1995.

93. For example, when Peru began a new assault on Tiwinza on February 22, in direct violation of the Declaration of Itamaraty, President Fujimori claimed that his military was merely responding to Ecuadorian shelling. See Reuters, "Ecuador, Peru Truce Violated," *Globe and Mail* (Toronto), February 23, 1995.

94. Spencer 1998, 147.

95. Mares and Palmer 2012, 39.

96. García Gallegos 1999, 200.

97. Herz and Nogueira 2002, 51.

98. Escobar, "Peru, Ecuador Weigh Peace Terms."

99. Simmons 1999, 32.

100. Marcella and Downes 1999, 3. For more on faits accomplis, refer to Altman (2017, 2020), whose Land Grabs dataset lists the Cenepa Valley War as a fait accompli (conflict 73).

101. Kakabadse, Caillaux, and Dumas 2016, 820.

102. Weidner 1996, 52.

5. FIGHTING WORDS IN THE FIRST ARAB-ISRAELI WAR

1. Gene Currivan, "The Jews Rejoice," *New York Times*, May 15, 1948.

2. The first interstate war to occur after the UN's founding was the First Kashmir War between India and Pakistan, which began in 1947.

3. I briefly discuss the 1877–78 Russo-Turkish War in chapter 1.

4. Schneer 2010.

5. Stein 2009, 11.

6. The Yishuv had already established a sizable government, to the extent that the State Department observed "virtually a state at the threshold of birth." See Jensehaugen, Heian-Engdal, and Waage 2012, 283.

7. Kimche and Kimche 1960, 162. See Shlaim 1995 and Rogan and Shlaim 2007 for more on Arab-Israeli relations.

8. Morris 2008, 197.

9. Stein 2009, 30.

10. Tal 2004, 164.

11. Tal 2004, 160.

12. Karsh 2002, 50.

13. Kimche and Kimche 1960, 161.

14. Quoted in Morris 2008, 198.

15. Bregman 2000, 16; Luttwak and Horowitz 1983, 30.

16. Quoted in Tal 2004, 156.

17. Quoted in Morris 2008, 253–54.

18. Quoted in Lorch 1961, 152.

19. Peter Grose, "Jerusalem's Old Jewish Quarter Is Losing Its Arab Character," *New York Times*, May 29, 1971, https://timesmachine.nytimes.com/timesmachine/1971/05/29/81947827.html?pageNumber=3.

20. Shlaim 2007, 91.

21. Clodfelter 2017, 571; Tal 2004, 229–30.

22. Sachar 1976, 328.

23. Tal 2004, 205.

24. Ilan 1989, 86.

25. Ilan 1989, 116–17.

26. This logic coincides with broader claims made by Kaplow (2016) and Walter (2009).

27. In a July 1949 speech following the war, Foreign Minister Moshe Sharett reflected the sentiments of the Ministry of Foreign Affairs, stating that Israel would not make any "declarations about our desire for peace, since the Arab world interprets them as a sign of weakness and as an indication of our willingness to surrender." Quoted in Caplan 1997, 106.

28. Ilan 1989, 74; Touval 1982, 40.

29. Ilan 1989, 91.

30. Lorch 1961, 250; Sachar 1976, 328.

31. Haganah Information Service, "HIS Information, Daily Precis," June 11, 1948, HA 105/94, quoted in Morris 2008, 267.

32. Sachar 1976, 327.

33. Quoted in Sachar 1976, 327. Carmel's characterization of this respite is further evidence that the Israelis were militarily exhausted but were not in a position to unilaterally stop fighting to recover themselves.

34. Stein 2009, 36–37.

35. Shlaim 1995, 294. The number would rise to eighty-eight thousand by October and ninety-six thousand by December. See Bregman 2000, 16.

36. Bell 1966, 232. On June 11, approximately sixty thousand Jewish and Arab troops existed in Palestine. By the time the truce ended prematurely on July 8, this number had increased to one hundred thousand. See Karsh 2002, 64.

37. Slonim 1979, 498.

38. An assessment submitted by the Central Intelligence Agency on August 5, 1948, underscored the belief that a global arms embargo would "keep the war on a small scale and of a more or less local nature." See "Report by the Central Intelligence Agency," August 5, 1948, *Foreign Relations of the United States, 1948*, vol. 5, part 2, *The Near East, South Asia, and Africa*, document 512, https://history.state.gov/historicaldocuments/frus1948v05p2/d512.

39. See especially Ilan 1996, chap. 6, which emphasizes the impact of Western European weapons in shifting the war in Israel's favor.

40. Morris 2008, 268.

41. Lorch 1961, 254.

42. Morris 2008, 269.

43. Folke Bernadotte, "Text of Suggestions Presented by the United Nations Mediator on Palestine to the Two Parties on 28 June 1948," July 3, 1948, United Nations Document Symbol S/863, United Nations Digital Library, https://digitallibrary.un.org/record/470499.

44. United Nations Security Council, "Resolution 53 (1948)," July 7, 1948, United Nations Document Symbol S/RES/53(1948), United Nations Digital Library, https://digitallibrary.un.org/record/280506.

45. Ilan 1989, 125.

46. Ilan 1989, 139–40.

47. Morris 2008, 270–71. The Jordanians were privately opposed to renewed hostilities but did not want to attract attention by being a sole dissenting vote; see Glubb 1957, 150; Shlaim 1995, 299–300. Throughout the war, the Arab League was hampered by a lack of military and diplomatic coordination. Pollack (2002, 2019) offers an overview of Arab armies' relative ineffectiveness.

48. Morris 2008, 278–85.

49. Morris (2008, 293–94) provides a detailed summary of Operation Dani and how goals shifted over time.

50. Karsh 2002, 64.

51. Persson 1979, 166.

52. Tal 2004, 345–46.

53. Morris 2008, 296.

54. Tal 2004, 346–48.

55. Tal 2004, 358–59.

56. Ilan 1989, 161.

57. Tal 2004, 363.

58. On July 26, Israeli minister of foreign affairs Moshe Sharett stated that Israel would be willing to participate in a roundtable mediation effort if the Arab states would recognize Israel as an equal state. This offer was rejected on September 6. See Persson 1979, 191.

59. Tal 2004, 350.

60. Persson 1979, 201–2.

61. An Egyptian official initiated a peace feeler with Israel on September 21, suggesting a bilateral agreement. Ben-Gurion refused, concealed this development from his cabinet, and proceeded to develop plans for a military attack. See Shlaim 1990, 229–31.

62. Stein 2009, 44.

63. Shlaim 1990, 228.

64. See Gradus 1978 for deeper discussion of the historical and geological importance of Beersheba.

65. Karsh 2002, 68.

66. Waage 2011, 284.

67. Tal 2004, 387.

68. United Nations Security Council, "Resolution 61 (1948)," November 4, 1948, United Nations Document Symbol S/RES/61(1948), United Nations Digital Library, https://digitallibrary.un.org/record/112005.

69. Tal 2004, 396.

70. Sarkees and Wayman 2010, 147.

71. Neff 1995, 93.

72. The Correlates of War marks January 6, 1949, as the official end of the war, due to the ceasefire between Israel and Egypt. I include the subsequent mediation at Rhodes in my discussion of the war's overall resolution.

73. Bell 1966, 241.

74. Shlaim 1995, 300.

75. Quoted in Caplan 1997, 41.

76. Morris 2008, 376.

77. "The Acting Secretary of State to the Special Representative of the United States in Israel (McDonald)," December 30, 1948, *Foreign Relations of the United States, 1948*, vol. 5, part 2, *The Near East, South Asia, and Africa*, document 858, https://history.state.gov/historicaldocuments/frus1948v05p2/d858.

78. Records now show that a British intervention would have been unlikely. See Tal 2004, 456.

79. Ben-Dror (2020) provides an effective summary of the Rhodes conference.

80. McManus 2023; Ramsbotham and Schiff 2018; Zartman 1997.

81. Shlaim 1995, 294.

82. Garfinkle 2015, 61.

83. Mark Landler, "In Middle East Peace Talks, Clinton Faces a Crucial Test," *New York Times*, September 4, 2010, https://www.nytimes.com/2010/09/05/world/middleeast/05clinton.html.

84. Jodi Rudoren and Isabel Kerschner, "Arc of a Failed Deal: How Nine Months of Mideast Talks Ended in Disarray," *New York Times*, April 28, 2014, https://www.nytimes.com/2014/04/29/world/middleeast/arc-of-a-failed-deal-how-nine-months-of-mideast-talks-ended-in-dissarray.html.

85. Ramsbotham and Schiff 2018.

86. See Rudoren and Kerschner, "Arc of a Failed Deal."

6. THE "TALKING WAR" IN KOREA

1. Carson 2016; Huff and Schub 2021; Mastro 2019, chap. 2; Mercer 2013; Slantchev 2010; Stanley 2009.

2. Previous scholars have applied content analysis methods to international negotiation transcripts to study bargaining stages and dynamics. See Druckman 2023, chap. 11, for an example.

3. Stewart 2005, 221.

4. Goncharov, Lewis, and Xue 1993, 146.

5. Fehrenbach 1963, 108.

6. United Nations Security Council. "Resolution 84 (1950)," July 7, 1950, United Nations Document Symbol S/RES/84(1950), United Nations Digital Library, https://digitallibrary.un.org/record/112027.

7. Tucker 2010, 331.

8. In a meeting between President Truman and General MacArthur on October 15, Truman asked about the likelihood of Chinese intervention in the conflict. MacArthur responded that there was "very little" chance of such an event. See Nichols 2000, 39.

9. Whiting 1968, 94.

10. Hannings 2007, 632.

11. Clodfelter 2017, 659–60.

12. Taliaferro 2004, 209.

13. Pillar 1983, 68.

14. Quoted in Kennan 1972, 28–29.

15. "Memorandum by Mr. Lucius D. Battle, Special Assistant to the Secretary of State," December 4, 1950, *Foreign Relations of the United States, 1950*, vol. 7, *Korea*, document 959, https://history.state.gov/historicaldocuments/frus1950v07/d959.

16. Zhu 2001, 27.

17. Zhu 2001, 27.

18. "The United States Representative at the United Nations (Austin) to the Secretary of State," December 9, 1950, *Foreign Relations of the United States, 1950*, vol. 7, *Korea*, document 1017, https://history.state.gov/historicaldocuments/frus1950v07/d1017.

19. For more information on the proposal and the strategic considerations behind China's refusal to accept the ceasefire group's terms, see Chen 2018; Zhihua and Xia 2011.

20. Zartman 2000.

21. Mastro 2019, 47–49.

22. "13 June 1951 Handwritten Letter from Mao Zedong to Gao Gang and Kim Il Sung," *Cold War International History Project Bulletin* 6/7 (1995/96): 61. The

Communist states likely sought another party to bring up talks in order to save face; see Stueck 1995, 217.

23. "Editorial Note," n.d., *Foreign Relations of the United States, 1951*, vol. 7, part 1, *Korea and China*, document 355, https://history.state.gov/historicaldocuments/frus1951v07p1/d355. The term "third party" may feel suspect in this context, given that the Soviets were actively dictating China's involvement in the Korean War. Regardless, the Soviet Union was officially a nonbelligerent at the time, and Malik also made his statement in his capacity as president of the Security Council.

24. Stueck 1995, 216.

25. Stueck 1995, 209.

26. US Department of State 1957, 2637.

27. Mastro 2019, 50.

28. Truman 1955, 438.

29. "The Ambassador in the United Kingdom (Gifford) to the Secretary of State," November 30, 1951, *Foreign Relations of the United States, 1951*, vol. 7, part 1, *Korea and China*, document 757, https://history.state.gov/historicaldocuments/frus1951v07p1/d757. During a conversation between Stalin, Kim Il-sung, and Zhou Enlai in September 1952, Kim Il-sung stated clearly that "in view of the serious situation in which the Korean people have found themselves we are interested in the quickest possible conclusion of an armistice." See "Record of a Conversation between Stalin, Kim Il Sung, Pak Heonyeong, Zhou Enlai, and Peng Dehuai," September 4, 1952, *Archive of the President of the Russian Federation*, f. 45, o. 1, d. 348, ll. 71–82, Wilson Center Digital Archive, https://digitalarchive.wilsoncenter.org/document/114936.

30. Joy would step down from his position as senior UNC delegate in May 1952. Major General William Harrison Jr. assumed the role through the remainder of the war.

31. Tucker 2010, 502–3.

32. Murray 1953, 982.

33. Hermes 1966, 39.

34. Stueck 1995, 230–31.

35. Ridgway 1967, 182–83.

36. Quoted in Toner 1973, 97.

37. Hermes 1966, 507.

38. The line of contact at the time is very similar to the territorial borders between the two Korean states today.

39. Joy stated this plainly during a speech on April 29, 1953: "Instead of showing good faith they dragged their feet at every opportunity and used the thirty days of grace to dig in and stabilize their battle line." See Joy 1978, 5.

40. Carson 2016; 2018, chap. 5. See also Brune 1998.

41. Vatcher 1958, 109–13.

42. "Twentieth Meeting of Staff Officers on Details of Agreement on Agenda Item 3, Held at Pan Mun Jom, 16 February 1952," February 16, 1952, United Nations Command Korean Armistice Negotiations, 1951–1953, Record Group 331, Set T1152, Roll 6, National Archives, College Park, MD.

43. Item 5 was settled in short order at the start of 1952. Both delegations saw the item as being largely insubstantial.

44. The UNC screened POWs in April 1952 and found that about 40,000 out of 132,000 total POWs would refuse to be repatriated; see Hermes 1966, 171. Chang (2020) revises the predominant view that many Communist POWs willingly chose to refuse repatriation.

45. Tierney 2017, 131–32. Truman said, "We will not buy an armistice by turning over human beings for slaughter or slavery." Quoted in Stanley 2009, 158.

46. The fact that the Communist states were not parties to the Geneva Convention weakened their standing to make this charge.

47. Eisenhower's effect on the armistice agreement remains a matter of debate. Calingaert (1988), Eisenhower (1963, 178–81), and Shepley (1956) make the affirmative case; Dingman (1988), Friedman (1975), and Keefer (1986) make the negative case.

48. Boose 2000; Weathersby 1998; Weathersby 2004, 84–85. For more on how leadership changes appear to help break logjams during protracted conflicts, see Croco 2011; Stanley 2009; Weisiger 2016b.

49. In the UNC proposal, any POWs refusing to be repatriated would be transferred to a Neutral Nations Repatriation Committee for ninety days, during which representatives of China and North Korea could try to persuade them to return. See Boose 2000, 27.

50. Some recent scholarship suggests that the UNC may have implicitly allowed this release. See Chae 2017.

51. See Mastro 2019, chap. 2. Reiter (2009, 83) states that "the remainder of the war, from mid- 1951 to mid-1953, can be characterized straightforwardly. . . . On the diplomatic front, a slow dribble of concessions emanated from both sides, eventually culminating in an armistice in July 1953."

52. My work represents a complementary piece to the analysis of the Korean War by Mastro (2019). Her exploration of why the Chinese opted to adopt an open diplomatic posture concludes that "the decision to talk is independent from the decision to settle, and the costly conversations framework seeks to explain the former, not the course of negotiations once they begin" (51).

53. Edwards 2006, 1951.

54. This statistic comes from daily operations reports filed by the UNC, which I describe in greater detail later in this chapter.

55. Zhu 2001, 158.

56. Lindesay Parrott, "Allies Reiterate Final Truce Stand," *New York Times*, June 13, 1952, https://timesmachine.nytimes.com/timesmachine/1952/06/13/84323792.html?page Number=3. Belligerents also did not want to be blamed for ending negotiations. In instructions sent to the UNC delegation on November 28, 1951, the Joint Chiefs of Staff emphasized that "the decision to cease discussion of an armistice must be made by Communists and not the UNC." See "The Joint Chiefs of Staff to the Commander in Chief, Far East (Ridgway)," November 28, 1951, *Foreign Relations of the United States, 1951*, vol. 7, part 1, *Korea and China*, document 748, https://history.state.gov/historicaldocuments/ frus1951v07p1/d748. The UNC's decision to indefinitely suspend talks in October 1952 came after multiple weeks of posturing to publicly signal that the Communists were the obstinate party.

57. Joy 1955, 168–69. See also Hermes 1966, 29.

58. Zhu 2001, 60.

59. Vatcher 1958, 67.

60. Xia 2006, 55.

61. Weathersby 1998, 179.

62. Matray (2012) further argues that much of the bitter tone that negotiations took was spurred by the UNC's opening proposals, which the Communists saw as intentionally humiliating.

63. Foot 1990, 51.

64. "VKP(b) CC Politburo Decision with Approved Message Filippov (Stalin) to Mao Zedong," November 19, 1951, *Archive of Foreign Policy of the Russian Federation*, f. 3, op. 65, d. 828 [9], ll. 42–43, Wilson Center Digital Archive, https://digitalarchive.wilsoncenter. org/document/110833; "Ciphered Telegram No. 25902 from Beijing, Mao Zedong to Cde. Filippov [Stalin]," November 14, 1951, *Archive of the President of the Russian Federation,*

f. 45, op. 1, d. 342, ll. 16–19, Wilson Center Digital Archive, https://digitalarchive.wilson center.org/document/113013.

65. Zhu 2001, 59.

66. Craig and George 1995, 234.

67. Hermes 1966, 110. See also Hastings 1987, 267.

68. Record Group 333 (Records of International Military Agencies), Set T1152 (United Nations Command Korean Armistice Negotiations, 1951–1953) (microfilm).

69. Coverage of UNC reports ends on June 30, 1953, which is twenty-seven days prior to the armistice taking effect.

70. These terms are mutually exclusive to each category; *enemy capture* is an instance of a loss, while any use of the word *capture* not preceded by *enemy* is an instance of a gain.

71. The measures of gains and losses have a correlation of 0.260 at the daily level.

72. Clodfelter 2017, 664.

73. The entirety of negotiation transcripts totals over 1,580,000 words.

74. "Summary of Proceedings, Twenty-Third Session, 17th Meeting at Pan Mun Jom, Sub-delegation on Agenda Item 2, Military Armistice Conference," November 10, 1951, United Nations Command Korean Armistice Negotiations, 1951–1953, Record Group 331, Set T1152, Roll 3, National Archives, College Park, MD.

75. "Transcript of Proceedings, 114th Session, 88th Meeting at Pan Mun Jom, Military Armistice Conference," August 3, 1952, United Nations Command Korean Armistice Negotiations, 1951–1953, Record Group 331, Set T1152, Roll 2, National Archives, College Park, MD.

76. "Eighteenth Meeting of Staff Officers on Details of Agreement of Agenda Item 3, Held at Pan Mun Jom, 14 February 1952," February 14, 1952, United Nations Command Korean Armistice Negotiations, 1951–1953, Record Group 331, Set T1152, Roll 6, National Archives, College Park, MD.

77. "Transcript of Proceedings, Eighty-Fifth Session, 59th Meeting at Pan Mun Jom, Military Armistice Conference," June 17, 1952, United Nations Command Korean Armistice Negotiations, 1951–1953, Record Group 331, Set T1152, Roll 2, National Archives, College Park, MD.

78. See Katagiri and Min 2019 for more information and an application of a comparable technique to study diplomacy during the Berlin Crisis.

79. Full sets of performance metrics for all candidate models are in the online appendix.

80. Refer to Breiman 2001 and Chen, Liaw, and Breiman 2004 for more technical details.

81. Using cross-validation tests, I find that a probability threshold of 0.56 is ideal for determining whether statements are sincere or insincere.

82. All four example statements provided earlier in the chapter were correctly coded as being sincere or insincere by the supervised learning model.

83. Hermes 1966, 160.

84. My balanced random forest model predicts that the speech act featuring this proposal is sincere.

85. A chi-squared test finds this difference to be highly statistically significant ($p \ll 0.01$).

86. There are 1,374 unique speaker-meeting-days in the data.

87. Orr and Fainer 1951.

88. Gaubatz 1991.

89. Plenary sessions serve as the baseline category. Descriptive statistics for all variables are in the online appendix.

90. Full statistical results for all models in this chapter are presented in the online appendix.

91. Almost 12 percent of statements (1,588 statements) were exchanged following Stalin's death.

92. Hermes 1966, 508; Kim 2012. See Downes 2008 and Valentino, Huth, and Croco 2006 for more discussion on the practice of targeting civilians in war.

93. The estimated coefficient for Communist ground losses is significant at the 90 percent level.

94. Zhu 2001, 89.

95. Rummel 1998, chap. 10.

96. Clark 1954, 257.

97. William L. Langer, "Evaluation of Malik's Speech of 23 June 1951," June 25, 1951, Central Intelligence Agency Office of National Estimates, CIA-RDP79S01011A 000400020023–9.

98. Joy 1955, 166.

99. Boose 2000.

CONCLUSION

1. As I noted in chapter 6, we now know that the Communist delegation chose to resume talks using the UNC's previous proposal because of the Soviet Union's insistence. See Boose 2000.

2. United Press, "Red Drive in Korea Blunted by U.N. Units, Van Fleet Says," *New York Times*, October 8, 1952, late city edition.

3. Greg MacGregor, "Panmunjom Talks Viewed Hopefully," *New York Times*, April 19, 1953.

4. Robert Kee and Richard Lindley (hosts), BBC, "TV Interview for BBC1 *Panorama* (2010Z) (Falklands)," Margaret Thatcher Foundation, April 26, 1982, https://www.margaretthatcher.org/document/104783.

5. Dimitar Dilkoff, "Why Russia Is Pushing a Return to Negotiations: The Kremlin Wants to Buy Time to Prepare for a 'Full-Scale Offensive' in Early 2023, Sources Say," Meduza, October 14, 2022, https://meduza.io/en/feature/2022/10/14/why-russia-is-pushing-a-return-to-negotiations.

6. Admati and Perry 1987, 362.

7. Zartman 1989, 2000, 2001, 2022.

8. Saunders 1991; Stein 1989. In the realm of trade disputes, see Busch 2007.

9. Bachrach and Baratz 1962.

10. Romer and Rosenthal (1978) provide an important model of agenda setting. In the realm of international relations, see Bennett and Sharpe 1979; Binder and Golub 2020; Kteily et al. 2013; Murphy 2010; Princen 2007; Tsebelis and Garrett 1996.

11. Quoted in Woolsey 1991, 105.

12. Doyle and Hegele (2021) and Schiff (2008) analyze prenegotiation in armed conflicts.

13. Adler-Nissen 2015.

14. Roberts 2009, 10–11.

15. Ritchie 1932, 122–23.

16. Nicolson (1939) 1963, 67.

17. Sartori 2002, 2005.

18. Joy 1955.

19. Young 1968, 29.

20. Cohen 1991, 144. For more on the attribution of irrationality or infantile qualities to people seen as "Others," see Carson, Min, and Van Nuys (forthcoming).

21. Adair and Brett 2004; Brett et al. 1998; Janosik 1987; Solomon 1995.

22. Lall 1966, 151.

23. Acheson 1961, 105.

24. Huang 2016; Kaplow 2016; Melin and Svensson 2009; Pruitt 2006; Toros 2008; Walter 2006, 2009.

25. Licklider 1995.

26. Howard and Stark 2017/18; Toft 2010.

27. Arreguín-Toft 2001, 2005; Sullivan 2007.

28. DeRouen and Möller 2013; Mattes and Savun 2010; Toft 2009; Walter 1997.

29. Regan, Frank, and Aydin 2009. Greig and Regan (2008) analyze specific factors that influence when and why third parties offer to mediate civil wars.

30. Pechenkina and Thomas 2020.

31. Trager 2017.

32. Siniver and Hart 2021.

33. Bull 1977.

34. Jack Nasher, "Top 10 World Changing Negotiations for 2022," *Forbes*, December 27, 2021, https://www.forbes.com/sites/jacknasher/2021/12/27/top-10-world-changing-negotiations-for-2022/.

35. Reuters, "U.S. Accuses Iran of Trying to Deflect Blame for Nuclear Talks Impasse," July 17, 2021, https://www.reuters.com/world/middle-east/iranian-deputy-foreign-minister-says-vienna-talks-must-await-irans-new-2021-07-17/.

36. Chanlett-Avery et al. 2018.

37. Stacie E. Goddard and Daniel Nexon, "Kim Jong Un Gets to Sit at the Cool Table Now," *Foreign Policy*, June 21, 2018, https://foreignpolicy.com/2018/06/21/kim-jong-un-gets-to-sit-at-the-cool-table-now/.

38. Editorial Board, "Opinion: No More Concessions," *Washington Post*, June 12, 2018, https://www.washingtonpost.com/opinions/global-opinions/the-singapore-summit-was-a-victory-for-kim-jong-un/2018/06/12/3731e970-6e44-11e8-bd50-b80389a4e569_story.html.

39. See Tangredi 1985.

40. Frank Jordans, "Greenpeace Chief Warns of 'Greenwashing' at UN Climate Talks," Associated Press, October 21, 2021, https://apnews.com/article/climate-environment-and-nature-environment-united-nations-greenpeace-308a04052994ecf028ca08c323e109.

41. Organisation for Economic Co-operation and Development, *Climate Finance*, 8.

42. Jocelyn Timperley, "The Broken $100-Billion Promise of Climate Finance— and How to Fix It," *Nature*, October 20, 2021, https://www.nature.com/articles/d41586-021-02846-3.

43. Fankhauser et al. 2021.

44. Death statistics come from the PRIO Battle Deaths Dataset Version 1.0, where data associated with the Correlates of War are limited to the 1900–1997 period.

45. Gaddis 1986, 1987; Pinker 2011. Braumoeller (2019) and Siverson and Ward (2002) offer refutations.

46. For examples of research that addresses broader notions of wartime costs beyond the loss of human lives, see Bellamy and Zajtchuk 1991; Collier 1999; Glick and Taylor 2010; Mansfield and Pevehouse 2000.

47. Luttwak 1999, 36–38.

48. Stedman 1996, 363.

49. Clayton and Dorussen 2022; Frazier and Dixon 2006.

50. Beber 2012; Crescenzi et al. 2011; Favretto 2009; Kydd 2003; Melin 2011; Savun 2008.

51. Regan and Stam 2000.

52. One partial exception is Greig and Regan 2008.

53. Melin 2014.

54. This idea is related to but distinct from the recommendation that third parties must be willing to be committed to enforcing peace for the long term. See Beardsley 2011; Melin 2014; Walter 2002.

55. Corbetta and Dixon 2005; Kim 1991. Scholarship on the impact of third-party military intervention on conflict duration focuses predominantly on civil wars. See Balch-Lindsay, Enterline, and Joyce 2008; Cunningham 2010; Gent 2008; Regan 2002; Sullivan and Karreth 2015.

56. Escribà-Folch 2010.

57. United Nations, "To End Yemen's Tragic Plight, Parties Must Agree on Humanitarian Action, Nationwide Ceasefire, Special Envoy Tells Security Council," press release, April 15, 2021, https://www.un.org/press/en/2021/sc14494.doc.htm.

58. United Nations, "Ceasefire in Tigray More Urgent Than Ever: UN Relief Chief," United Nations News, August 6, 2021, https://news.un.org/en/story/2021/08/1097292.

59. Narang 2015.

60. An additional dilemma regarding humanitarian aid is that militant groups may intentionally create suffering to augment the refugee population, which in turn allows them to exploit humanitarian aid for the purposes of furthering their attacks. See Barber 1997; Terry 2002.

61. Dave Lawler, "Russia Agreed to Open 'Humanitarian Corridors' for Fleeing Civilians: Ukraine Official," Axios, March 3, 2022, https://www.axios.com/2022/03/03/russia-ukraine-peace-talks-belarus.

62. Daniel Boffey and Lorenzo Tondo, "Russia Accused of Shelling Mariupol Humanitarian Corridor," *The Guardian* (US edition), April 26, 2022, https://www.theguardian.com/world/2022/apr/26/russia-accused-of-shelling-mariupol-humanitarian-corridor. See also Carla Babb, Nike Ching, Heather Murdock, Anita Powell, Cindy Saine, and Jeff Seldin, "Ukraine Says Russia Is Shelling Promised Humanitarian Evacuation Corridors," Voice of America, March 4, 2022, https://www.voanews.com/a/ukraine-says-russia-shelling-promised-humanitarian-corridors/6471228.html. Some observers anticipated that Russia would exploit humanitarian corridors in this manner. For instance, see Anna Borschevskaya, "The Sinister Reason Russia Wants Humanitarian Corridors in Ukraine," 19FortyFive, March 4, 2022, https://www.19fortyfive.com/2022/03/the-sinister-reason-russia-wants-humanitarian-corridors-in-ukraine.

63. Reuters, "Nearly 125,000 People Evacuated via Humanitarian Corridors in Ukraine, Says President," March 13, 2022, https://www.reuters.com/world/europe/nearly-125000-people-evacuated-via-humanitarian-corridors-ukraine-says-president-2022-03-13.

References

Acheson, Dean. 1961. *Sketches from Life of Men I Have Known*. New York: Harper.

Adair, Wendi Lyn, and Jeanne M. Brett. 2004. "Culture and Negotiation Processes." In *The Handbook of Negotiation and Culture*, edited by Michele J. Gelfand and Jeanne M. Brett, 158–76. Stanford, CA: Stanford University Press.

Adler-Nissen, Rebecca. 2015. "Conclusion: Relationalism or Why Diplomats Find International Relations Theory Strange." In *Diplomacy and the Making of World Politics*, edited by Ole Jacob Sending, Vincent Pouliot, and Iver B. Neumann, 284–308. Cambridge: Cambridge University Press.

Admati, Anat R., and Motty Perry. 1987. "Strategic Delay in Bargaining." *Review of Economic Studies* 54 (3): 345–64.

Aggestam, Karin. 2006. "Enhancing Ripeness: Transition from Conflict to Negotiation." In *Escalation and Negotiation in International Conflicts*, edited by I. William Zartman and Guy Olivier Faure, 271–92. Cambridge: Cambridge University Press.

Aggestam, Karin. 2012. "Prolonged Peace Negotiations: The Spoiler's Game." In *Unfinished Business: Why International Negotiations Fail*, edited by Guy Olivier Faure and Franz Cede, 318–32. Athens: University of Georgia Press.

Allee, Todd L., and Paul K. Huth. 2006. "Legitimizing Dispute Settlement: International Legal Rulings as Domestic Political Cover." *American Political Science Review* 100 (2): 219–34.

Allen, William Edward David, and Paul Muratoff. 1953. *Caucasian Battlefields: A History of the Wars on the Turco-Cypriot Border, 1828–1921*. Cambridge: Cambridge University Press.

Altman, Dan. 2017. "By Fait Accompli, Not Coercion: How States Wrest Territory from Their Adversaries." *International Studies Quarterly* 61 (4): 881–91.

Altman, Dan. 2020. "The Evolution of Territorial Conquest after 1945 and the Limits of the Territorial Integrity Norm." *International Organization* 74 (3): 490–522.

Anand, Krishnan S., Pnina Feldman, and Maurice E. Schweitzer. 2009. "Getting to NO: The Strategic Use of Instrumental Negotiations." Working paper, David Eccles School of Business (University of Utah) and the Wharton School (University of Pennsylvania).

Anderson, Frank M., and Amos S. Hershey. 1918. *Handbook for the Diplomatic History of Europe, Asia, and Africa, 1870–1914*. Washington, DC: US Government Printing Office.

Arreguín-Toft, Ivan. 2001. "How the Weak Win Wars: A Theory of Asymmetric Conflict." *International Security* 26 (1): 93–128.

Arreguín-Toft, Ivan. 2005. *How the Weak Win Wars: A Theory of Asymmetric Conflict*. New York: Cambridge University Press.

Asmussen, Jan. 2008. *Cyprus at War: Diplomacy and Conflict during the 1974 Crisis*. London: I. B. Tauris.

Avirgan, Tony, and Martha Honey. 1982. *War in Uganda: The Legacy of Idi Amin*. Westport, CT: Lawrence Hill.

Bachrach, Peter, and Morton S. Baratz. 1962. "The Two Faces of Power." *American Political Science Review* 56 (4): 947–52.

Balch-Lindsay, Dylan, Andrew J. Enterline, and Kyle A. Joyce. 2008. "Third-Party Intervention and the Civil War Process." *Journal of Peace Research* 45 (3): 345–63.

Barber, Ben. 1997. "Feeding Refugees, or War? The Dilemma of Humanitarian Aid." *Foreign Affairs* 76 (4): 8–14.

Bartholomees, J. Boone. 2008. "Theory of Victory." *Parameters* 38 (2): 25–36.

Bayer, Reşat. 2006. "Diplomatic Exchange, 1817–2005 (v2006.1)." Correlates of War, https://correlatesofwar.org/data-sets/diplomatic-exchange/.

Beardsley, Kyle. 2008. "Agreement without Peace? International Mediation and the Time Inconsistency Problem." *American Journal of Political Science* 52 (4): 723–40.

Beardsley, Kyle. 2009. "Intervention without Leverage: Explaining the Prevalence of Weak Mediators." *International Interactions* 35 (3): 272–97.

Beardsley, Kyle. 2010. "Pain, Pressure, and Political Cover: Explaining Mediation Incidence." *Journal of Peace Research* 47 (4): 395–406.

Beardsley, Kyle. 2011. *The Mediation Dilemma*. Ithaca, NY: Cornell University Press.

Beber, Bernd. 2012. "International Mediation, Selection Effects, and the Question of Bias." *Conflict Management and Peace Science* 29 (4): 387–424.

Beckley, Michael. 2018. "The Power of Nations: Measuring What Matters." *International Security* 43 (2): 7–44.

Bell, J. Bowyer. 1966. *Besieged: Seven Cities under Siege*. New York: Routledge.

Bellamy, Ronald F., and Russ Zajtchuk. 1991. *Conventional Warfare: Ballistic, Blast, and Burn Injury*. Washington, DC: Office of the Surgeon General, Department of the Army.

Ben-Dror, Elad. 2020. "Ralph Bunche and the 1949 Armistice Agreements Revisited." *Middle Eastern Studies* 56 (2): 274–89.

Bennett, D. Scott, and Allan C. Stam. 1996. "The Duration of Interstate Wars, 1816–1985." *American Political Science Review* 90 (2): 239–57.

Bennett, Douglas C., and Kenneth E. Sharpe. 1979. "Agenda Setting and Bargaining Power: The Mexican State versus Transnational Automobile Corporations." *World Politics* 32 (1): 57–89.

Bercovitch, Jacob. 1991. "International Mediation and Dispute Settlement: Evaluating the Conditions for Successful Mediation." *Negotiation Journal* 7 (1): 17–30.

Bercovitch, Jacob. 1992. "Mediators and Mediation Strategies in International Relations." *Negotiation Journal* 8 (2): 99–112.

Bercovitch, Jacob. 1999. *International Conflict Management, 1945–1995: Official Codebook for the International Conflict Management Dataset*. Christchurch, New Zealand: University of Canterbury.

Bercovitch, Jacob, and Judith Fretter. 2004. *Regional Guide to International Conflict and Management from 1945 to 2003*. Washington, DC: Congressional Quarterly.

Bercovitch, Jacob, and Scott S. Gartner. 2006. "Is There Method in the Madness of Mediation? Some Lessons for Mediators from Quantitative Studies of Mediation." *International Interactions* 32 (4): 329–54.

Bercovitch, Jacob, and Richard Jackson. 2001. "Current Developments in International Conflict Management: Assessing the Relevance of Negotiation and Mediation." *Cambridge Review of International Affairs* 14 (2): 13–38.

Biddle, Stephen. 2004. *Military Power: Explaining Victory and Defeat in Modern Battle*. Princeton, NJ: Princeton University Press.

Binder, Martin, and Jonathan Golub. 2020. "Civil Conflict and Agenda-Setting Speed in the United Nations Security Council." *International Studies Quarterly* 64 (2): 419–30.

Birand, Mehmet Ali. 1985. *30 Hot Days*. London: K. Rustem & Brother.

Birke, Richard. 2000. "Evaluation and Facilitation: Moving Past Either/Or." *Journal of Dispute Resolution* 2000 (2): 309–20.

Birnbaum, Karl E., and Ingo Peters. 1990. "The CSCE: A Reassessment of Its Role in the 1980s." *Review of International Studies* 16 (4): 305–19.

Bjork, Ulf Jonas. 1985. "Excitement, Tinged with Jingoism: British Public Opinion and the Falklands in Four News Magazines." Paper presented at the Annual Meeting of the Association for Education in Journalism and Mass Communication, Memphis, TN, August 3–5, 1985.

Blainey, Geoffrey. 1988. *The Causes of War*. 3rd ed. New York: Free Press.

Bonilla, Adrián. 1999. "The Ecuador-Peru Dispute: The Limits and Prospects for Negotiation and Conflict." In *Security Cooperation in the Western Hemisphere: Resolving the Ecuador-Peru Conflict*, edited by Gabriel Marcella and Richard Downes, 67–89. Miami: North-South Center Press.

Boose, Donald W. 2000. "Fighting While Talking: The Korean War Truce Talks." *OAH Magazine of History* 14 (3): 25–29.

Boroweic, Andrew. 2000. *Cyprus: A Troubled Island*. New York: Praeger.

Bottom, William P. 1998. "Negotiator Risk: Sources of Uncertainty and the Impact of Reference Points on Negotiated Agreements." *Organizational Behavior and Human Decision Processes* 76 (2): 89–112.

Braumoeller, Bear F. 2019. *Only the Dead: The Persistence of War in the Modern Age*. New York: Oxford University Press.

Bregman, Ahron. 2000. *Israel's Wars, 1947–93*. New York: Routledge.

Breiman, Leo. 2001. "Random Forest." *Machine Learning* 45 (1): 5–32.

Brett, Jeanne M., Wendi Adair, Alain Lempereur, Tetsushi Okumura, Peter Shikhirev, Catherine Tinsley, and Anne Lytle. 1998. "Culture and Joint Gains in Negotiation." *Negotiation Journal* 14 (1): 61–86.

Brito, Dagobert L., and Michael D. Intriligator. 1985. "Conflict, War, and Redistribution." *American Political Science Review* 79 (4): 943–57.

Brockett, Linus P., and Porter C. Bliss. 1878. *The Conquest of Turkey: Or, the Decline and Fall of the Ottoman Empire, 1877–1878*. Philadelphia: Hubbard Brothers.

Brune, Lester H. 1998. "Recent Scholarship and Findings about the Korean War." *American Studies International* 36 (3): 4–16.

Bull, Hadley. 1977. *The Anarchical Society: A Study of Order in World Politics*. London: Macmillan.

Busch, Marc L. 2007. "Overlapping Institutions, Forum Shopping, and Dispute Settlement in International Trade." *International Organization* 61 (4): 735–61.

Butterworth, Robert. 1978. "Do Conflict Managers Matter? An Empirical Assessment of Interstate Security Disputes and Resolution Efforts." *International Studies Quarterly* 22 (2): 195–214.

Calahan, H. A. 1944. *What Makes a War End?* New York: Vanguard.

Calingaert, Daniel. 1988. "Nuclear Weapons and the Korean War." *Journal of Strategic Studies* 11 (2): 177–202.

Callaghan, James. 1987. *Time and Chance*. London: Collins.

Cannizzo, Cynthia A. 1980. "The Costs of Combat: Death, Duration, and Defeat." In *Correlates of War II: Testing Some Realpolitik Models*, edited by J. David Singer, 233–57. New York: Free Press.

Caplan, Neil. 1997. *Futile Diplomacy*. Vol. 3, *The United Nations, the Great Powers, and Middle East Peacemaking, 1948–1954*. New York: Routledge.

Carnevale, Peter J. D., and Edward J. Lawler. 1986. "Time Pressure and the Development of Integrative Agreements in Bilateral Negotiations." *Journal of Conflict Resolution* 30 (4): 636–59.

Carroll, Robert J., and Brenton Kenkel. 2019. "Prediction, Proxies, and Power." *American Journal of Political Science* 63 (3): 577–93.

Carson, Austin. 2016. "Facing Off and Saving Face: Covert Intervention and Escalation Management in the Korean War." *International Organization* 70 (1): 103–31.

Carson, Austin. 2018. *Secret Wars: Covert Conflict in International Politics*. Princeton, NJ: Princeton University Press.

Carson, Austin, Eric Min, and Maya Van Nuys. Forthcoming. "Racial Tropes in the Foreign Policy Bureaucracy: A Computational Text Analysis." *International Organization*.

Carter, David B., and Hein E. Goemans. 2011. "The Making of the Territorial Order: New Borders and the Emergence of Interstate Conflict." *International Organization* 65 (2): 275–309.

Castillo, Jasen. 2014. *Endurance and War: The National Sources of Military Cohesion*. Stanford, CA: Stanford University Press.

Chae, Grace. 2017. "Complacency or Complicity? Reconsidering the UN Command's Role in Syngman Rhee's Release of North Korean POWs." *Journal of American-East Asian Relations* 24 (2/3): 128–59.

Chang, David Cheng. 2020. *The Hijacked War: The Story of Chinese POWs in the Korean War*. Stanford, CA: Stanford University Press.

Chanlett-Avery, Emma, Mark E. Manyin, Mary Beth D. Nikitin, Caitlin Elizabeth Campbell, and Wil Mackey. 2018. *North Korea: U.S. Relations, Nuclear Diplomacy, and Internal Situation*. Congressional Research Service Report.

Chen, Chao, Andy Liaw, and Leo Breiman. 2004. *Using Random Forest to Learn Imbalanced Data*. Technical report, University of California, Berkeley. http://statistics.berkeley.edu/sites/default/files/tech-reports/666.pdf.

Chen, Jian. 2018. "Far Short of a 'Glorious Victory': Revisiting China's Changing Strategies to Manage the Korean War." *Chinese Historical Review* 25 (1): 1–22.

Choi, Ajin. 2004. "Democratic Synergy and Victory in War, 1816–1992." *International Studies Quarterly* 48 (3): 663–82.

Clark, Mark W. 1954. *From the Danube to the Yalu*. New York: Harper.

Clausewitz, Carl von. (1832) 1976. *On War*. Translated by Michael Howard and Peter Paret. Princeton, NJ: Princeton University Press.

Clayton, Govinda, and Han Dorussen. 2022. "The Effectiveness of Mediation and Peacekeeping for Ending Conflict." *Journal of Peace Research* 59 (2): 150–65.

Clodfelter, Micheal. 2017. *Warfare and Armed Conflicts: A Statistical Encyclopedia of Casualty and Other Figures, 1494–2007*. Jefferson, NC: McFarland.

Coe, Andrew J. 2018. "Containing Rogues: A Theory of Asymmetric Arming." *Journal of Politics* 80 (4): 1197–210.

Cohen, Raymond. 1991. *Negotiating across Cultures: Communication Obstacles in International Diplomacy*. Washington, DC: United States Institute of Peace Press.

Collelo, Thomas. 1990. *Chad: A Country Study*. Washington, DC: Federal Research Division, Library of Congress.

Collier, Paul. 1999. "On the Economic Consequences of Civil War." *Oxford Economic Papers* 51 (1): 168–83.

Colosi, Thomas. 1984. "A Model for Negotiation and Mediation." In *International Negotiation: Art and Science*, edited by Diane B. Bendahmane and John W.

McDonald, 15–33. Washington, DC: Foreign Service Institute, US Department of State.

Conlon, Donald E., Peter Carnevale, and William H. Ross. 1994. "The Influence of Third Party Power and Suggestions on Negotiation: The Surface Value of Compromise." *Journal of Applied Social Psychology* 24 (12): 1084–113.

Constandinos, Andreas John Louis. 2008. "America, Britain and the Cyprus Crisis of 1974: Calculated Conspiracy or Foreign Policy Failure?" PhD thesis, University of East Anglia.

Cooper, Andrew F. 2008. *Celebrity Diplomacy.* Boulder, CO: Paradigm.

Corbetta, Renato. 2010. "Determinants of Third Parties' Intervention and Alignment Choices in Ongoing Conflicts, 1946–2001." *Foreign Policy Analysis* 6 (1): 61–85.

Corbetta, Renato. 2015. "Between Indifference and Coercion: Third-Party Intervention Techniques in Ongoing Disputes." *Conflict Management and Peace Science* 32 (1): 3–27.

Corbetta, Renato, and William J. Dixon. 2005. "Danger beyond Dyads: Third-Party Participants in Interstate Disputes." *Conflict Management and Peace Science* 22 (1): 39–61.

Craig, Gordon A., and Alexander L. George. 1995. *Force and Statecraft: Diplomatic Problems of Our Time.* New York: Oxford University Press.

Cramton, Peter C. 1992. "Strategic Delay in Bargaining with Two-Sided Uncertainty." *Review of Economic Studies* 59 (1): 205–25.

Crescenzi, Mark J. C., Kelly M. Kadera, Sara McLaughlin Mitchell, and Clayton L. Thyne. 2011. "A Supply Side Theory of Mediation." *International Studies Quarterly* 55 (4): 1069–94.

Croco, Sarah E. 2011. "The Decider's Dilemma: Leader Culpability, War Outcomes, and Domestic Punishment." *American Political Science Review* 105 (3): 457–77.

Cunningham, David E. 2010. "Blocking Resolution: How External States Can Prolong Civil Wars." *Journal of Peace Research* 47 (2): 115–27.

Dahl, Erik J. 2013. *Intelligence and Surprise Attack: Failure and Success from Pearl Harbor to 9/11 and Beyond.* Washington, DC: Georgetown University Press.

Daniel, Donald C., and Katherine L. Herbig. 1982. *Strategic Military Deception.* New York: Pergamon.

Danneman, Nathan, and Kyle Beardsley. 2020. "International Mediation and the Problem of Insincere Bargaining." In *On Mediation: Historical, Legal, Anthropological and International Perspectives*, edited by Karl Härter, Carolin F. Hillemans, and Günther Schlee, 184–207. New York: Berghahn Books.

Dean, Sidney E. 2007. "Treaty of Portsmouth 1905: Theodore Roosevelt's Role as Mediator." *Hampton Roads Military History* 1 (1): 2–3.

Debo, Richard K. 1992. *Survival and Consolidation: The Foreign Policy of Soviet Russia, 1918–1921.* Montreal: McGill-Queen's University Press.

Debs, Alexandre, and Nuno P. Monteiro. 2014. "Known Unknowns: Power Shifts, Uncertainty, and War." *International Organization* 68 (1): 1–31.

Demetriades, Evros I., William J. House, Nabil F. Khoury, and Symeon Matsis. 1992. *Population and Human Resources Development in Cyprus: Research and Policy Issues.* Nicosia, Cyprus: Department of Statistics and Research.

Depledge, Joanna. 2008. "Striving for No: Saudi Arabia in the Climate Change Regime." *Global Environmental Politics* 8 (4): 9–35.

DeRouen, Karl, Jacob Bercovitch, and Paulina Pospieszna. 2011. "Introducing the Civil Wars Mediation (CWM) Dataset." *Journal of Peace Research* 48 (5): 663–72.

DeRouen, Karl, and Frida Möller. 2013. "The Short-Term Effects of Mediation on Low-Intensity Civil Wars." *Negotiation Journal* 29 (4): 413–38.

Desch, Michael C. 2002. "Democracy and Victory: Why Regime Type Hardly Matters." *International Security* 27 (2): 5–47.

Diehl, Paul F. 2004. *The Scourge of War: New Extensions on an Old Problem*. Ann Arbor: University of Michigan Press.

Dilke, Charles W., and Demetrius N. Botassi. 1897. "The Uprising of Greece." *North American Review* 164 (485): 453–61.

Dingman, Roger. 1988. "Atomic Diplomacy during the Korean War." *International Security* 13 (3): 50–91.

Dittman, Andrea G., Nour Kteily, and Emile Bruneau. 2021. "When Getting More Makes Groups Seem Worth Less: Negotiating a 'Better' Deal in Prisoner Swaps Can Ironically Signal Low Self-Regard and Engender Disrespect." *Journal of Experimental Social Psychology* 92 (104056): 1–14.

Documents diplomatiques: Affaires d'Orient; Affairs de Créte, conflit gréco-turc; Situation de l'Empire ottoman; Février–mai 1897. 1897. Paris: Imprimerie nationale, on behalf of the Ministère des Affaires étrangères.

Dodd, Clement. 2010. *The History and Politics of the Cyprus Conflict*. New York: Palgrave Macmillan.

Downes, Alexander B. 2008. *Targeting Civilians in War*. Ithaca, NY: Cornell University Press.

Downs, Chuck. 1999. *Over the Line: North Korea's Negotiating Strategy*. Washington, DC: American Enterprise Institute Press.

Downs, George W., and David M. Rocke. 1990. *Tacit Bargaining, Arms Races, and Arms Control*. Ann Arbor: University of Michigan Press.

Doyle, Lindsey, and Lukas Hegele. 2021. "Talks before the Talks: Effects of Pre-negotiation on Reaching Peace Agreements in Intrastate Armed Conflicts, 2005–15." *Journal of Peace Research* 58 (2): 231–47.

Druckman, Daniel. 2023. *Negotiation, Identity and Justice: Pathways to Agreement*. New York: Routledge.

Duffy, Eamon. 1997. *Saints and Sinners: A History of the Popes*. New Haven, CT: Yale University Press.

Dupuy, Trevor N. 1987. *Understanding War: History and Theory of Combat*. New York: Paragon House.

Duursma, Allad. 2018. "Mediating Solutions to Territorial Civil Wars in Africa: Norms, Interests, and Major Power Leverage." *African Studies Review* 62 (3): 65–88.

Dwight, Theodore. 1851. *The Roman Republic of 1849; with Accounts of the Inquisition, and the Siege of Rome, and Biographical Sketches*. New York: R. Van Dien.

Edmonds, James. 1932. *Military Operations: France and Belgium, 1916*. Vol. 1, *Sir Douglas Haig's Command to the 1st July: Battle of the Somme*. London: Macmillan.

Edwards, Paul M. 2006. *Korean War Almanac*. New York: Facts on File.

Eggenberger, David. 1985. *An Encyclopedia of Battles: Accounts of over 1,560 Battles from 1479 B.C. to the Present*. New York: Dover.

Eisenhower, Dwight D. 1963. *The White House Years: Mandate for Change, 1953–1956*. Garden City, NY: Doubleday.

Ekinci, Mehmet Uğur. 2006. "The Origins of the 1897 Ottoman-Greek War: A Diplomatic History." MA thesis, Bilkent University, Ankara, Turkey.

Engel-Janosi, Friedrich. 1950. "The Return of Pius IX in 1850." *Catholic Historical Review* 36 (2): 129–62.

Epstein, Gil S., and Yosef Mealem. 2013. "Who Gains from Information Asymmetry?" *Theory and Decision* 75 (3): 305–27.

Escribà-Folch, Abrel. 2010. "Economic Sanctions and the Duration of Civil Conflicts." *Journal of Peace Research* 47 (2): 129–41.

Fankhauser, Sam, Stephen M. Smith, Myles Allen, Kaya Axelsson, Thomas Hale, Cameron Hepburn, J. Michael Kendall, Radhika Khosla, Javier Lezaun, Eli Mitchell-Larson, Michael Obersteiner, Lavanya Rajamani, Rosalind Rickaby, Nathalie Seddon, and Thom Wetzer. 2021. "The Meaning of Net Zero and How to Get It Right." *Nature Climate Change* 12 (1): 15–21.

Farber, Henry S., and Joanne Gowa. 1995. "Polities and Peace." *International Security* 20 (2): 123–46.

Favretto, Katja. 2009. "Should Peacemakers Take Sides? Major Power Mediation, Coercion, and Bias." *American Political Science Review* 103 (2): 248–63.

Fazal, Tanisha M. 2007. *State Death: The Politics and Geography of Conquest, Annexation, and Occupation*. Princeton, NJ: Princeton University Press.

Fazal, Tanisha M. 2013. "The Demise of Peace Treaties in Interstate War." *International Organization* 67 (4): 695–724.

Fazal, Tanisha M. 2018. *Wars of Law: Unintended Consequences in the Regulation of Armed Conflict*. Ithaca, NY: Cornell University Press.

Fearon, James D. 1994. "Domestic Political Audience Costs and the Escalation of International Disputes." *American Political Science Review* 88 (3): 577–92.

Fearon, James D. 1995. "Rationalist Explanations for War." *International Organization* 49 (3): 379–414.

Fearon, James D. 2013. "Fighting Rather Than Bargaining." Working paper, Stanford University. https://web.stanford.edu/group/fearon-research/cgi-bin/wordpress/wp-content/uploads/2013/10/frtb6.pdf.

Fehrenbach, Theodore R. 1963. *This Kind of War: The Classic Korean War History*. Washington, DC: Brassey's.

Fey, Mark, and Kristopher W. Ramsay. 2007. "Mutual Optimism and War." *American Journal of Political Science* 51 (4): 738–54.

Filson, Darren, and Suzanne Werner. 2002. "A Bargaining Model of War and Peace: Anticipating the Onset, Duration, and Outcome of War." *American Journal of Political Science* 46 (4): 819–37.

Filson, Darren, and Suzanne Werner. 2004. "Bargaining and Fighting: The Impact of Regime Type on War Onset, Duration, and Outcomes." *American Journal of Political Science* 48 (2): 296–313.

Findley, Michael G. 2012. "Bargaining and the Interdependent Stages of Civil War Resolution." *Journal of Conflict Resolution* 57 (5): 905–32.

Finlan, Alastair. 2002. "British Special Forces and the Falklands Conflict: Twenty Years On." *Defense & Security Analysis* 18 (4): 319–32.

Finnemore, Martha. 2003. *The Purpose of Intervention: Changing Beliefs about the Use of Force*. Ithaca, NY: Cornell University Press.

Fisher, Roger, William Ury, and Bruce Patton. 2011. *Getting to Yes: Negotiating Agreement without Giving In*. New York: Penguin.

Foch, Ferdinand. 1918. *The Principles of War*. New York: H. K. Fly.

Foot, Rosemary. 1990. *A Substitute for Victory: The Politics of Peacemaking at the Korean Armistice Talks*. Ithaca, NY: Cornell University Press.

Fortna, Virginia P. 2004. *Peace Time: Cease-Fire Agreements and the Durability of Peace*. Princeton, NJ: Princeton University Press.

Fortna, Virginia P. 2008. *Does Peacekeeping Work? Shaping Belligerents' Choices after Civil War*. Princeton, NJ: Princeton University Press.

Fournier Coronado, Eduardo. 1995. *Tiwinza con zeta*. Lima: La Oficina de Información del Ejército.

Frazier, Derrick V., and William J. Dixon. 2006. "Third-Party Intermediaries and Negotiated Settlements, 1946–2000." *International Interactions* 32 (4): 385–408.

Freedman, Lawrence. 1982. "The War of the Falkland Islands, 1982." *Foreign Affairs* 61 (1): 196–210.

Freedman, Lawrence. 1998. "Military Power and Political Influence." *International Affairs* 74 (4): 763–80.

Freedman, Lawrence, and Virginia Gamba-Stonehouse. 1990. *Signals of War: The Falklands Conflict of 1982*. London: Faber & Faber.

Freese, John Henry. 1897. *A Short Popular History of Crete*. London: Jarrold & Sons.

Frei, Daniel. 1976. "Conditions Affecting the Effectiveness of International Mediation." *Papers—Peace Science Society (International)* 26 (1): 67–84.

Friedman, Edward. 1975. "Nuclear Blackmail and the End of the Korean War." *Modern China* 1 (1): 75–91.

Gaddis, John L. 1986. "The Long Peace: Elements of Stability in the Postwar International System." *International Security* 10 (4): 99–142.

Gaddis, John L. 1987. *The Long Peace: Inquiries into the History of the Cold War*. New York: Oxford University Press.

García Gallegos, Bertha. 1999. "New Perspectives on Using Diplomacy for the Resolution of the Ecuador-Peru Conflict." In *Security Cooperation in the Western Hemisphere: Resolving the Ecuador-Peru Conflict*, edited by Gabriel Marcella and Richard Downes, 195–209. Miami: North-South Center Press.

Garfinkle, Adam. 2015. *Politics and Society in Modern Israel: Myths and Realities*. 2nd ed. New York: Routledge.

Gartner, Scott S. 1998. "Opening Up the Black Box of War." *Journal of Conflict Resolution* 42 (3): 252–58.

Gartner, Scott S. 2011. "Signs of Trouble: Regional Organization Mediation and Civil War Agreement Durability." *Journal of Politics* 73 (2): 380–90.

Gartner, Scott S., and Jacob Bercovitch. 2006. "Overcoming Obstacles to Peace: The Contribution of Mediation to Short-Lived Conflict Settlements." *International Studies Quarterly* 50 (4): 819–40.

Gartner, Scott S., and Randolph M. Siverson. 1996. "War Expansion and War Outcome." *Journal of Conflict Resolution* 40 (1): 4–15.

Gartzke, Erik A., and Paul Poast. 2018. "Empirically Assessing the Bargaining Theory of War: Potential and Challenges." In *Oxford Research Encyclopedia of Politics*, edited by William R. Thompson. Oxford: Oxford University Press. https://doi.org/10.1093/acrefore/9780190228637.013.274.

Gaubatz, Kurt T. 1991. "Election Cycles and War." *Journal of Conflict Resolution* 35 (2): 212–44.

Geller, Daniel S. 2000. "Status Quo Orientation, Capabilities, and Patterns of War Initiation in Dyadic Rivalries." *Conflict Management and Peace Science* 18 (1): 73–96.

Gelpi, Christopher, Peter D. Feaver, and Jason Reifler. 2009. *Paying the Human Costs of War: American Public Opinion and Casualties in Military Conflicts*. Princeton, NJ: Princeton University Press.

Gent, Stephen E. 2008. "Going In When It Counts: Military Intervention and the Outcome of Civil Conflicts." *International Studies Quarterly* 52 (4): 713–35.

Gent, Stephen E., and Megan Shannon. 2010. "The Effectiveness of International Arbitration and Adjudication: Getting into a Bind." *Journal of Politics* 72 (2): 366–80.

Gibler, Douglas M. 2018. *International Conflicts, 1816–2010: Militarized Interstate Dispute Narratives*. Lanham, MD: Rowman & Littlefield.

Gibler, Douglas M., and Steven V. Miller. 2022. "An Appraisal of Project Mars and the Divided Armies Argument." *International Studies Quarterly* 66 (2): sqc011.

Glantz, David M., and Jonathan M. House. 2015. *When Titans Clashed: How the Red Army Stopped Hitler*. Lawrence: University Press of Kansas.

Glick, Reuven, and Alan M. Taylor. 2010. "Collateral Damage: Trade Disruption and the Economic Impact of War." *Review of Economics and Statistics* 92 (1): 102–27.

Glozman, Edy, Netta Barak-Corren, and Ilan Yaniv. 2015. "False Negotiations: The Art and Science of Not Reaching an Agreement." *Journal of Conflict Resolution* 59 (4): 671–97.

Glubb, John Bagot. 1957. *A Soldier with the Arabs*. London: Hodder & Stoughton.

Goemans, Hein E. 2000a. "Fighting for Survival: The Fate of Leaders and the Duration of War." *Journal of Conflict Resolution* 44 (5): 555–79.

Goemans, Hein E. 2000b. *War and Punishment: The Causes of War Termination and the First World War*. Princeton, NJ: Princeton University Press.

Goertz, Gary, Paul F. Diehl, and Alexandru Balas. 2016. *The Puzzle of Peace: The Evolution of Peace in the International System*. New York: Oxford University Press.

Goldstein, Erik. 1992. *Wars and Peace Treaties: 1816–1991*. New York: Routledge.

Goldstein, Joshua S. 2011. *Winning the War on War: The Decline of Armed Conflict Worldwide*. New York: Plume.

Goncharov, Sergei N., John W. Lewis, and Xue Litai. 1993. *Uncertain Partners: Stalin, Mao, and the Korean War*. Stanford, CA: Stanford University Press.

Gradus, Yehuda. 1978. "Beer-Sheva, Capital of the Negev Desert—Function and Internal Structure." *GeoJournal* 2 (6): 521–32.

Gray, Colin S. 2018. *Theory of Strategy*. New York: Oxford University Press.

Greene, Shane. 2008. "Tiwi's Creek: Indigenous Movements for, against, and across the Contested Peruvian Border." *Latin American and Caribbean Ethnic Studies* 3 (3): 227–52.

Greig, J. Michael. 2001. "Moments of Opportunity: Recognizing Conditions of Ripeness for International Mediation between Enduring Rivals." *Journal of Conflict Resolution* 45 (6): 691–718.

Greig, J. Michael. 2005. "Stepping into the Fray: When Do Mediators Mediate?" *American Journal of Political Science* 49 (2): 249–66.

Greig, J. Michael, and Paul F. Diehl. 2005. "The Peacekeeping-Peacemaking Dilemma." *International Studies Quarterly* 49 (4): 621–45.

Greig, J. Michael, and Patrick M. Regan. 2008. "When Do They Say Yes? An Analysis of the Willingness to Offer and Accept Mediation in Civil Wars." *International Studies Quarterly* 52 (4): 759–81.

Guilbaud, Auriane. 2020. "Diplomacy by Non-state Actors." In *Global Diplomacy: An Introduction to Theory and Practice*, edited by Theirry Balzacq, Frédéric Charillon, and Frédéric Ramel, 183–94. Cham, Switzerland: Palgrave Macmillan.

Gulsby, Seth A. 2010. "Strategic Asymmetric Deception and Its Role in the Current Threat Environment." *Journal of Strategic Security* 3 (1): 65–70.

Halperin, Morton H. 1961. "Nuclear Weapons and Limited War." *Journal of Conflict Resolution* 5 (2): 146–66.

Hamilton, Keith, and Patrick Salmon. 2006. *Documents on British Policy Overseas*. Series 3, vol. 5, *The Southern Flank in Crisis, 1973–1976*. London: Routledge.

Hampson, Fen Olster, Chester A. Crocker, and Pamela R. Aall. 2007. "Negotiation and International Conflict." In *Handbook of Peace and Conflict Studies*, edited by Charles Webel and Johan Galtung, 35–50. London: Routledge.

Hanami, Andrew K. 2003. *Perspectives on Structural Realism*. New York: Palgrave Macmillan.

Handel, Michael I. 1977. "The Yom Kippur War and the Inevitability of Surprise." *International Studies Quarterly* 21 (3): 461–502.

Handel, Michael I. 1982. "Intelligence and Deception." *Journal of Strategic Studies* 5 (1): 122–54.

Hannings, Bud. 2007. *The Korean War: An Exhaustive Chronology*. Jefferson, NC: McFarland.

Hanska, Jan. 2017. "Times of War and War over Time: The Roles Time and Timing Play in Operational Art and Its Development According to the Texts of Renowned Theorists and Practitioners." PhD thesis, National Defence University, Helsinki.

Hastings, Max. 1987. *The Korean War*. New York: Simon & Schuster.

Hatzis, Aristides N. 2018. "A Political History of Modern Greece 1821–2018." In *Encyclopedia of Law and Economics*, edited by Alain Marciano and Giovanni Battista Ramello, 1–12. New York: Springer.

Haythornthwaite, Philip. 2004. *Gallipoli 1915: Frontal Assault to Turkey*. London: Osprey.

Hegre, Høavard. 2008. "Gravitating toward War: Preponderance May Pacify, but Power Kills." *Journal of Conflict Resolution* 52 (4): 566–89.

Hermes, Walter G. 1966. *Truce Tent and Fighting Front*. Washington, DC: Office of the Chief of Military History, US Army.

Herring, George C. 1983. *The Secret Diplomacy of the Vietnam War: The Negotiating Volumes of the Pentagon Papers*. Austin: University of Texas Press.

Herz, Monica, and João Nogueira. 2002. *Ecuador vs. Peru: Peacemaking amid Rivalry*. Boulder, CO: Lynne Rienner.

Holmes, Marcus. 2013. "The Force of Face-to-Face Diplomacy: Mirror Neurons and the Problem of Intentions." *International Organization* 67 (4): 829–61.

Holsti, Kalevi J. 1966. "Resolving International Conflicts: A Taxonomy of Behavior and Some Figures on Procedures." *Journal of Conflict Resolution* 10 (3): 272–96.

Holsti, Kalevi J. 1991. *Peace and War: Armed Conflicts and International Order, 1648–1989*. Cambridge: Cambridge University Press.

Hopmann, P. Terrence. 2012. "Issue Content and Incomplete Negotiations." In *Unfinished Business: Why International Negotiations Fail*, edited by Guy Olivier Faure, 240–68. Athens: University of Georgia Press.

Hougaard, Philip. 1999. "Multi-state Models: A Review." *Lifetime Data Analysis* 5 (3): 239–64.

Howard, Lise Morjé, and Alexandra Stark. 2017/18. "How Civil Wars End: The International System, Norms, and the Role of External Actors." *International Security* 42 (3): 127–71.

Huang, Reyko. 2016. "Rebel Diplomacy in Civil War." *International Security* 40 (4): 89–126.

Huff, Connor, and Robert Schub. 2021. "Segregation, Integration, and Death: Evidence from the Korean War." *International Organization* 75 (3): 858–79.

Iji, Tetsuro, and Siniša Vuković, eds. 2023. *Revisiting the "Ripeness" Debate*. New York: Taylor & Francis.

Iklé, Fred C. 1964. *How Nations Negotiate*. New York: Praeger.

Iklé, Fred C. 1971. *Every War Must End*. New York: Columbia University Press.

Ilan, Amitzur. 1989. *Bernadotte in Palestine, 1948: A Study in Contemporary Knight-Errantry*. New York: Palgrave Macmillan.

Ilan, Amitzur. 1996. *The Origin of the Arab-Israeli Arms Race: Arms, Embargo, Military Power and Decision in the 1948 Palestine War*. London: Macmillan.

Jackson, Michael O., and Massimo Morelli. 2011. "The Reasons for War: An Updated Survey." In *Handbook on the Political Economy of War*, edited by Christopher J. Coyne and Rachel L. Mathers, 34–57. Northampton, MA: Edward Elgar.

Janis, Irving I., and Leon Mann. 1977. *Decision Making: A Psychological Analysis of Conflict, Choice, and Commitment*. New York: Free Press.

Janosik, Robert J. 1987. "Rethinking the Culture-Negotiation Link." *Negotiation Journal* 3 (3): 385–95.

Jaques, Tony. 2007. *Dictionary of Battles and Sieges: A Guide to 8,500 Battles from Antiquity through the Twenty-first Century*. Westport, CT: Greenwood.

Jenne, Nicole. 2016. "The Domestic Origins of No-War Communities: State Capacity and the Management of Territorial Disputes in South America and Southeast Asia." PhD thesis, European University Institute, Florence, Italy.

Jensehaugen, Jørgen, Marte Heian-Engdal, and Hilde Henriksen Waage. 2012. "Securing the State: From Zionist Ideology to Israeli Statehood." *Diplomacy & Statecraft* 23 (2): 280–303.

Jervis, Robert. 1976. *Perception and Misperception in International Politics*. Princeton, NJ: Princeton University Press.

Jo, Dong-Joon, and Erik Gartzke. 2007. "Determinants of Nuclear Weapons Proliferation: A Quantitative Model." *Journal of Conflict Resolution* 51 (1): 167–94.

Joint Chiefs of Staff. 2006. *Military Deception*. Joint Publication 3–13.4, US Department of Defense.

Jones, Benjamin T., and Shawna K. Metzger. 2018. "Evaluating Conflict Dynamics: A Novel Empirical Approach to Stage Conceptions." *Journal of Conflict Resolution* 62 (4): 819–47.

Jost, Tyler, Joshua D. Kertzer, Eric Min, and Robert Schub. 2024. "Advisers and Aggregation in Foreign Policy Decision Making." *International Organization* 78 (1): 1–37.

Joy, C. Turner. 1955. *How Communists Negotiate*. New York: Macmillan.

Joy, C. Turner. 1978. *Negotiating While Fighting: The Diary of Admiral C. Turner Joy at the Korean Armistice Conference*. Stanford, CA: Hoover Institution Press.

Kakabadse, Yolanda, Jorge Caillaux, and Juan Dumas. 2016. "The Peru and Ecuador Peace Park: One Decade after the Peace Settlement." In *Governance, Natural Resources, and Post-conflict Peacebuilding*, edited by Carl Bruch, Carroll Muffett, and Sandra S. Nichols, 817–24. New York: Routledge.

Kang, Polly, Krishnan S. Anand, Pnina Feldman, and Maurice E. Schweitzer. 2020. "Insincere Negotiation: Using the Negotiation Process to Pursue Non-agreement Motives." *Journal of Experimental Social Psychology* 89 (103981): 1–14.

Kaplow, Jeffrey M. 2016. "The Negotiation Calculus: Why Parties to Civil Conflict Refuse to Talk." *International Studies Quarterly* 60 (1): 38–46.

Karsh, Efraim. 2002. *The Arab-Israeli Conflict: The Palestine War, 1948*. Osceola, WI: Osprey.

Katagiri, Azusa, and Eric Min. 2019. "The Credibility of Public and Private Signals: A Document-Based Approach." *American Political Science Review* 113 (1): 156–72.

Kaufman, Chaim. 2007. "An Assessment of the Partition of Cyprus." *International Studies Perspectives* 8 (2): 206–23.

Keefer, Edward C. 1986. "President Dwight D. Eisenhower and the End of the Korean War." *Diplomatic History* 10 (3): 267–89.

Kennan, George F. 1972. *Memoirs, 1950–1963*. Boston: Little, Brown.

Ker-Lindsay, James. 2015. "The Cyprus Problem." In *"Frozen Conflicts" in Europe*, edited by Anton Bebler, 19–34. Opladen, Germany: Barbara Budrich.

Kertzer, Joshua D., Marcus Holmes, Brad L. LeVeck, and Carly Wayne. 2022. "Hawkish Biases and Group Decision Making." *International Organization* 76 (3): 513–48.

Kertzer, Joshua D., Brian C. Rathbun, and Nina Srinivasan Rathbun. 2020. "The Price of Peace: Motivated Reasoning and Costly Signaling in International Relations." *International Organization* 74 (1): 95–118.

Kim, Chae-Han. 1991. "Third-Party Participation in Wars." *Journal of Conflict Resolution* 35 (4): 659–77.

Kim, Taewoo. 2012. "Limited War, Unlimited Targets: U.S. Air Force Bombing of North Korea during the Korean War, 1950–1953." *Critical Asian Studies* 44 (3): 467–92.

Kimche, Jon, and David Kimche. 1960. *Both Sides of the Hill: Britain and the Palestine War*. London: Secker & Warburg.

Kissinger, Henry A. 1969. "The Viet Nam Negotiations." *Foreign Affairs* 11 (2): 38–50.

Kleiboer, Marieke. 1994. "Ripeness of Conflict: A Fruitful Notion?" *Journal of Peace Research* 31 (1): 109–16.

Kleiboer, Marieke, and Paul 't Hart. 1995. "Time to Talk? Multiple Perspectives on Timing of International Mediation." *Cooperation and Conflict* 30 (4): 307–48.

Klepak, Hal. 1998. *Confidence Building Sidestepped: The Peru-Ecuador Conflict of 1995*. Toronto: Centre for International and Security Studies.

Kliot, Nurit, and Yoel Mansfeld. 1997. "The Political Landscape of Partition: The Case of Cyprus." *Political Geography* 16 (6): 495–521.

Knorr, Klaus. 1956. *The War Potential of Nations*. Princeton, NJ: Princeton University Press.

Kowner, Rotem. 2006. *Historical Dictionary of the Russo-Japanese War*. Lanham, MD: Scarecrow.

Krainin, Colin, Caroline Thomas, and Thomas Wiseman. 2020. "Rational Quagmires: Attrition, Learning, and War." *Quarterly Journal of Political Science* 15 (3): 369–400.

Kteily, Nour, Tamar Saguy, James Sidanius, and Donald M. Taylor. 2013. "Negotiating Power: Agenda Ordering and the Willingness to Negotiate in Asymmetric Intergroup Conflicts." *Journal of Personality and Social Psychology* 105 (6): 978–95.

Kuperman, Alan J. 2022. "Muscular Mediation and Ripeness Theory." *Ethnopolitics* 21 (2): 163–77.

Kurizaki, Shuhei. 2007. "Efficient Secrecy: Public versus Private Threats in Crisis Diplomacy." *American Political Science Review* 101 (3): 543–58.

Kurtulgan, Kürşat. 2019. "Cyprus Issue and the Approach of European States in the Historical Development of Turkish-Greek Relations." In *Social, Educational, Political, Economic and Other Developments Occurred in Turkey between the Years of 1938–1980*, edited by Özkan Akman, Mustafa Murat Cay, Fatih Bozbayindir, and Erhan Tunç, 202–12. Konya, Turkey: International Society for Research in Education and Science.

Kydd, Andrew. 2003. "Which Side Are You On? Bias, Credibility, and Mediation." *American Journal of Political Science* 47 (4): 597–611.

Lake, David A. 2010/11. "Two Cheers for Bargaining Theory: Assessing Rationalist Explanations of the Iraq War." *International Security* 35 (3): 7–52.

Lall, Arthur S. 1966. *Modern International Negotiation: Principles and Practice*. New York: Columbia University Press.

Langlois, Catherine C., and Jean-Pierre P. Langlois. 2009. "Does Attrition Behavior Help Explain the Duration of Interstate Wars? A Game Theoretic and Empirical Analysis." *International Studies Quarterly* 53 (4): 1051–73.

Langlois, Jean-Pierre P., and Catherine C. Langlois. 2012. "Does the Principle of Convergence Really Hold? War, Uncertainty and the Failure of Bargaining." *British Journal of Political Science* 42 (3): 511–36.

Lanoszka, Alexander, and Michael A. Hunzeker. 2015. "Rage of Honor: Entente Indignation and the Lost Chance for Peace in the First World War." *Security Studies* 24 (4): 662–95.

Laqueur, Walter. 1980. *The Political Psychology of Appeasement: Finlandization, and Other Unpopular Essays*. New Brunswick, NJ: Transaction Books.

Leatherdale, Clive. 1983. *Britain and Saudi Arabia, 1925–1939: The Imperial Oasis*. London: F. Cass.

Lebow, Richard Ned. 1996. *The Art of Bargaining*. Baltimore: Johns Hopkins University Press.

Lebow, Richard Ned. 2020. *Between Peace and War*. 40th anniversary rev. ed. Cham, Switzerland: Palgrave Macmillan.

Lee, Melissa M. 2020. *Crippling Leviathan: How Foreign Subversion Weakens the State*. Ithaca, NY: Cornell University Press.

Lehmann, Todd, and Yuri Zhukov. 2019. "Until the Bitter End? The Diffusion of Surrender across Battles." *International Organization* 73 (1): 133–69.

Lemke, Douglas, and Suzanne Werner. 1996. "Power Parity, Commitment to Change, and War." *International Studies Quarterly* 40 (2): 235–60.

Levendusky, Matthew S., and Michael C. Horowitz. 2012. "When Backing Down Is the Right Decision: Partisanship, New Information, and Audience Costs." *American Journal of Political Science* 74 (2): 323–38.

Lewicki, Roy J. 1983. "Lying and Deception: A Behavioral Model." In *Negotiating in Organizations*, edited by Max H. Bazerman and Roy J. Lewicki, 68–90. Beverly Hills, CA: Sage.

Licklider, Roy. 1995. "The Consequences of Negotiated Settlements in Civil Wars, 1945–1993." *American Political Science Review* 89 (3): 681–90.

Long, Stephen. 2003. "Time Present and Time Past: Rivalry and the Duration of Interstate Wars, 1846–1985." *International Interactions* 29 (3): 215–36.

Lorch, Netanel. 1961. *The Edge of the Sword: Israel's War of Independence, 1947–1949*. New York: Putman.

Loschelder, David D., Roderick I. Swaab, Roman Trötschel, and Adam D. Galinsky. 2014. "The First-Mover Disadvantage: The Folly of Revealing Compatible Preferences." *Psychological Science* 25 (4): 954–62.

Lukacs, John. 1999. *Five Days in London, May 1940*. New Haven, CT: Yale University Press.

Luttwak, Edward N. 1987. *Strategy: The Logic of War and Peace*. Cambridge, MA: Belknap Press of Harvard University Press.

Luttwak, Edward N. 1999. "Give War a Chance." *Foreign Affairs* 78 (4): 36–44.

Luttwak, Edward N., and Daniel Horowitz. 1983. *The Israeli Army: 1948–1973*. Cambridge, MA: Abt Books.

Lyall, Jason. 2020. *Divided Armies: Inequality and Battlefield Performance in Modern War*. Princeton, NJ: Princeton University Press.

Mallinson, William, and Vassilis Fouskas. 2017. "Kissinger and the Business of Government: The Invasion of Cyprus, 15 July-20 August 1974." *Cyprus Review* 29 (1): 111–34.

Mandel, Robert. 2006. *The Meaning of Military Victory*. Boulder, CO: Lynne Rienner.

Manrique, Nelson. 1999. "Perils of Nationalism: The Peru-Ecuador Conflict." *NACLA Report on the Americas* 32 (4): 6–10.

Mansfield, Edward D., and Jon C. Pevehouse. 2000. "Trade Blocs, Trade Flows, and International Conflict." *International Organization* 54 (4): 775–808.

Marcella, Gabriel. 1995. *War and Peace in the Amazon: Strategic Implications for the United States and Latin America of the 1995 Ecuador-Peru War*. Carisle Barracks, PA: Strategic Studies Institute.

Marcella, Gabriel. 1999. "Epilogue: The Peace of October 1998." In *Security Cooperation in the Western Hemisphere: Resolving the Ecuador-Peru Conflict*, edited by Gabriel Marcella and Richard Downes, 231–35. Miami: North-South Center Press.

Marcella, Gabriel, and Richard Downes. 1999. Introduction to *Security Cooperation in the Western Hemisphere: Resolving the Ecuador-Peru Conflict*, edited by Gabriel Marcella and Richard Downes, 1–19. Miami: North-South Center Press.

Mares, David R. 1996. "Deterrence Bargaining in the Ecuador-Peru Enduring Rivalry: Designing Strategies around Military Weakness." *Security Studies* 6 (2): 91–123.

Mares, David R., and David S. Palmer. 2012. *Power, Institutions, and Leadership in War and Peace: Lessons from Peru and Ecuador, 1995–1998*. Austin: University of Texas Press.

Markides, Kyriacos C. 1977. *The Rise and Fall of the Cyprus Republic*. New Haven, CT: Yale University Press.

Marraro, Howard R. 1943. "Unpublished American Documents on the Roman Republic of 1849." *Catholic Historical Review* 28 (4): 459–90.

Marshall, Monty G., Ted Robert Gurr, and Keith Jaggers. 2016. *Polity IV Project: Political Regime Characteristics and Transitions, 1800–2015*. Vienna, VA: Center for Systemic Peace.

Mastro, Oriana Skylar. 2019. *The Costs of Conversation: Obstacles to Peace Talks in Wartime*. Ithaca, NY: Cornell University Press.

Mastro, Oriana Skylar, and David A. Siegel. 2023. "Talking to the Enemy: Explaining the Emergence of Peace Talks in Interstate War." *Journal of Theoretical Politics* 35 (3): 182–203.

Matray, James I. 2012. "Mixed Message: The Korean Armistice Negotiations at Kaesong." *Pacific Historical Review* 81 (2): 221–44.

Mattes, Michaela, and T. Clifton Morgan. 2004. "When Do They Stop? Modeling the Termination of War." *Conflict Management and Peace Science* 21 (3): 179–93.

Mattes, Michaela, and Burcu Savun. 2010. "Information, Agreement Design, and the Durability of Civil War Settlements." *American Journal of Political Science* 54 (2): 511–24.

Maxwell, Neville. 1970. *India's China War*. London: Jonathan Cape.

Mazower, Mark. 1992. "The Messiah and the Bourgeoisie: Venizelos and Politics in Greece, 1909–1912." *Historical Journal* 35 (4): 885–904.

McDermott, Rose. 2004. "The Feeling of Rationality: The Meaning of Neuroscientific Advances for Political Science." *Perspectives on Politics* 2 (4): 691–706.

McManus, Cathal. 2023. "Political Interventions to 'Ripen' Peace Initiatives: An Analysis of the Northern Ireland and Israeli/Palestinian Conflicts." *Ethnopolitics* 22 (3): 335–52.

McMichael, Scott R. 1990. "Soviet Tactical Performance and Adaptation in Afghanistan." *Journal of Soviet Military Studies* 3 (1): 73–105.

McMillan, Joseph. 1992. *Talking to the Enemy: Negotiations in Wartime*. Technical report, National War College, Washington, DC.

Melin, Molly M. 2011. "The Impact of State Relationships on If, When, and How Conflict Management Occurs." *International Studies Quarterly* 55 (3): 691–715.

Melin, Molly M. 2014. "Commitment Problems: Understanding Variation in the Frequency of International Conflict Management Efforts." *International Negotiation* 19 (1): 221–56.

Melin, Molly M., and Isak Svensson. 2009. "Incentives for Talking: Accepting Mediation in International and Civil Wars." *International Interactions* 35 (3): 249–71.

Mercer, Jonathan. 2013. "Emotion and Strategy in the Korean War." *International Organization* 67 (2): 221–52.

Metzger, Shawna K., and Benjamin T. Jones. 2016. "Surviving Phases: Introducing Multistate Survival Models." *Political Analysis* 24 (4): 457–77.

Michalopoulos, Georgios. 2013. "Political Parties, Irredentism and the Foreign Ministry: Greece and Macedonia; 1878–1910." PhD thesis, University of Oxford.

Miller, James Edward. 2009. *The United States and the Making of Modern Greece: History and Power, 1950–1974*. Chapel Hill: University of North Carolina Press.

Min, Eric. 2020. "Talking While Fighting: Understanding the Role of Wartime Negotiations." *International Organization* 74 (3): 610–32.

Min, Eric. 2021. "Interstate War Battle Dataset (1823–2003)." *Journal of Peace Research* 58 (2): 294–303.

Min, Eric. 2022. "Speaking with One Voice: Coalitions and Wartime Diplomacy." *Journal of Strategic Studies* 45 (2): 303–27.

Montgomery, Evan B. 2013. "Counterfeit Diplomacy and Mobilization in Democracies." *Security Studies* 22 (1): 33–67.

Morey, Daniel S. 2016. "Military Coalitions and the Outcome of Interstate Wars." *Foreign Policy Analysis* 12 (4): 533–51.

Morris, Benny. 2008. *1948: The First Arab-Israeli War*. New Haven, CT: Yale University Press.

Morrow, James D. 1989. "Capabilities, Uncertainty, and Resolve: A Limited Information Model of Crisis Bargaining." *American Journal of Political Science* 33 (4): 941–72.

Morrow, James D. 2007. "When Do States Follow the Law of War?" *American Political Science Review* 101 (3): 559–72.

Mueller, John. 2004. *The Remnants of War*. Ithaca, NY: Cornell University Press.

Murphy, Hannah. 2010. *The Making of International Trade Policy: NGOs, Agenda-Setting and the WTO*. Cheltenham, UK: Edward Elgar.

Murray, James C. 1953. "The Korea Truce Talks: First Phase." *United States Naval Institute Proceedings* 79 (9): 981–89.

Narang, Neil. 2015. "Assisting Uncertainty: How Humanitarian Aid Can Inadvertently Prolong Civil War." *International Studies Quarterly* 59 (1): 184–95.

Neff, Donald. 1995. *Fallen Pillars: U.S. Policy towards Palestine and Israel since 1945*. Washington, DC: Institute for Palestine Studies.

Nichols, Michael R. 2000. "The Chinese Communist Intervention in the Korean War: An Exercise in Analyzing Documents." *OAH Magazine of History* 14 (3): 37–39.

Nicolson, Harold. (1939) 1963. *Diplomacy*. New York: Oxford University Press.

Nish, Ian. 1993. *Japan's Struggle with Internationalism: Japan, China and the League of Nations, 1931–1933*. New York: Routledge.

Noesner, Gary. 2010. *Stalling for Time: My Life as an FBI Hostage Negotiator*. New York: Random House.

Núñez, Macías. 2014. *Brief History of the Ecuadorian Army*. Translated by Raúl López. Quito, Ecuador: Study Center of the Army History.

O'kane, Eamonn. 2006. "When Can Conflicts Be Resolved? A Critique of Ripeness." *Civil Wars* 8 (3–4): 268–84.

Olekalns, Mara, and Philip L. Smith. 2007. "Loose with the Truth: Predicting Deception in Negotiation." *Journal of Business Ethics* 76 (2): 225–38.

Organisation for Economic Co-operation and Development. 2023. *Climate Finance Provided and Mobilised by Developed Countries in 2013-2021: Aggregate Trends and Opportunities for Scaling Up Adaptation and Mobilised Private Finance.* Paris: OECD. https://www.oecd-ilibrary.org/environment/climate-finance-provided-and-mobilised-by-developed-countries-in-2013-2021_e20d2bc7-en.

Organski, A. F. K. 1958. *World Politics*. New York: Knopf.

Orr, K. D., and D. C. Fainer. 1951. "Cold Injuries in Korea during Winter 1950–51." *Medicine (Baltimore)* 31 (2): 177–220.

Palmer, David Scott. 1997. "Peru-Ecuador Border Conflict: Missed Opportunities, Misplaced Nationalism, and Multilateral Peacekeeping." *Journal of Interamerican Studies and World Affairs* 39 (3): 109–48.

Partzsch, Lena. 2014. "The Power of Celebrities in Global Politics." *Celebrity Studies* 6 (2): 178–91.

Pauly, Reid. 2018. "Would U.S. Leaders Push the Button? Wargames and the Sources of Nuclear Restraint." *International Security* 43 (2): 151–92.

Pechenkina, Anna O., and Jakana L. Thomas. 2020. "Battle Stalemates and Rebel Negotiation Attempts in Civil Wars." *Security Studies* 29 (1): 64–91.

Persson, Sune O. 1979. *Mediation and Assassination: Count Bernadotte's Mission to Palestine, 1948*. London: Ithaca.

Pevehouse, Jon C., Timothy Nordstrom, and Kevin Warnke. 2004. "The COW-2 International Organizations Dataset, Version 2.0." *Conflict Management and Peace Science* 21 (2): 101–19.

Phillips, Charles, and Alan Axelrod, eds. 2005. *Encyclopedia of War*. New York: Facts on File.

Phillipson, Coleman. 1916. *Termination of War and Treaties of Peace*. London: T. F. Unwin.

Pillar, Paul R. 1983. *Negotiating Peace: War Termination as a Bargaining Process.* Princeton, NJ: Princeton University Press.

Pinker, Steven. 2011. *The Better Angels of Our Nature: Why Violence Has Declined.* New York: Viking.

Pollack, Kenneth M. 2002. *Arabs at War: Military Effectiveness, 1948–1991*. Lincoln: University of Nebraska Press.

Pollack, Kenneth M. 2019. *Armies of Sand: The Past, Present, and Future of Arab Military Effectiveness*. New York: Oxford University Press.

Polyviou, Polyvios G. 1980. *Cyprus: Conflict and Negotiation, 1960–1980*. London: Duckworth.

Ponting, Clive. 2004. *The Crimean War: The Truth behind the Myth*. London: Chatto & Windus.

Porter-Szücs, Brian. 2014. *Poland in the Modern World: Beyond Martyrdom*. West Sussex, UK: Wiley Blackwell.

Powell, Robert. 2002. "Bargaining Theory and International Conflict." *Annual Review of Political Science* 5 (1): 1–30.

Powell, Robert. 2004. "Bargaining and Learning While Fighting." *American Journal of Political Science* 48 (2): 344–61.

Powell, Robert. 2006. "War as a Commitment Problem." *International Organization* 60 (1): 169–203.

Powell, Robert. 2012. "Persistent Fighting and Shifting Power." *American Journal of Political Science* 56 (3): 620–37.

Powell, Robert. 2017. "Taking Sides in Wars of Attrition." *American Political Science Review* 111 (2): 219–36.

Princen, Sebastiaan. 2007. "Agenda-Setting in the European Union: A Theoretical Exploration and Agenda for Research." *Journal of European Public Policy* 14 (1): 21–38.

Princen, Thomas. 1992. *Intermediaries in International Conflict*. Princeton, NJ: Princeton University Press.

Pruitt, Dean G. 1981. "Kissinger as a Traditional Mediator with Power." In *Dynamics of Third Party Intervention*, edited by Jeffrey Z. Rubin, 136–47. New York: Praeger.

Pruitt, Dean G. 2005. *Whither Ripeness Theory?* Technical report, Institute for Conflict Analysis, George Mason University. https://activity.scar.gmu.edu/sites/default/files/wp_25_pruitt_0.pdf.

Pruitt, Dean G. 2006. "Negotiation with Terrorists." *International Negotiation* 11 (2): 371–94.

Pruitt, Dean G., and Douglas F. Johnson. 1970. "Mediation as an Aid to Face Saving in Negotiation." *Journal of Personality and Social Psychology* 14 (3): 239–46.

Pruitt, Dean G., and Sung Hee Kim. 2004. *Social Conflict: Escalation, Stalemate, and Settlement*. Boston: McGraw Hill.

Pruitt, Dean G., and Piotr V. Olczak. 1995. "Beyond Hope: Approaches to Resolving Seemingly Intractable Conflict." In *Conflict, Cooperation, and Justice: Essays Inspired by the Work of Morton Deutsch*, edited by Barbara B. Bunker and Jeffrey Z. Rubin, 59–92. San Francisco: Jossey-Bass.

Pugh, Jeffrey. 2009. "The Structure of Negotiation: Lessons from El Salvador for Contemporary Conflict Resolution." *Negotiation Journal* 25 (1): 83–105.

Quessard, Maud. 2020. "Entertainment Diplomacy." In *Global Diplomacy: An Introduction to Theory and Practice*, edited by Thierry Balzacq, Frédéric Charillon, and Frédéric Ramel, 279–95. Cham, Switzerland: Palgrave Macmillan.

Ramsay, Kristopher W. 2008. "Settling It on the Field: Battlefield Events and War Termination." *Journal of Conflict Resolution* 52 (6): 850–79.

Ramsay, Kristopher W. 2017. "Information, Uncertainty, and War." *Annual Review of Political Science* 20 (1): 505–27.

Ramsbotham, Oliver, and Amira Schiff. 2018. "When Formal Negotiations Fail: Strategic Negotiation, Ripeness Theory, and the Kerry Initiative." *Negotiation and Conflict Management Research* 11 (4): 321–40.

Regan, Patrick M. 2002. "Third-Party Interventions and the Duration of Intrastate Conflicts." *Journal of Conflict Resolution* 46 (1): 55–73.

Regan, Patrick M., Richard W. Frank, and Aysegul Aydin. 2009. "Diplomatic Interventions and Civil War: A New Dataset." *Journal of Peace Research* 46 (1): 135–46.

Regan, Patrick M., and Allan C. Stam. 2000. "In the Nick of Time: Conflict Management, Mediation Timing, and the Duration of Interstate Disputes." *International Studies Quarterly* 44 (2): 239–60.

Reiter, Dan. 2003. "Exploring the Bargaining Model of War." *Perspectives on Politics* 1 (1): 27–43.

Reiter, Dan. 2009. *How Wars End*. Princeton, NJ: Princeton University Press.

Reiter, Dan, and Allan C. Stam. 2002. *Democracies at War*. Princeton, NJ: Princeton University Press.

Reiter, Dan, Allan C. Stam, and Michael C. Horowitz. 2016a. "A Deeper Look at Interstate War Data: Interstate War Data Version 1.1." *Research and Politics* 3 (4): 1–3.

Reiter, Dan, Allan C. Stam, and Michael C. Horowitz. 2016b. "A Revised Look at Interstate Wars, 1816–2007." *Journal of Conflict Resolution* 60 (5): 956–76.

Repo, Jemima, and Riina Yrjölä. 2011. "The Gender Politics of Celebrity Humanitarianism in Africa." *International Feminist Journal of Politics* 13 (1): 44–62.

Richmond, Oliver. 1998. "Devious Objectives and the Disputants' View of International Mediation: A Theoretical Framework." *Journal of Peace Research* 35 (6): 707–22.

Ridgway, Matthew B. 1967. *The Korean War.* Garden City, NY: Doubleday.

Ritchie, H., ed. 1932. *A Guide to Diplomatic Practice.* 3rd ed. London: Longmans, Green.

Roberts, George. 2014. "The Uganda-Tanzania War, the Fall of Idi Amin, and the Failure of African Diplomacy, 1978–1979." *Journal of Eastern African Studies* 8 (4): 692–709.

Roberts, Ivor. 2009. *Satow's Diplomatic Practice.* Oxford: Oxford University Press.

Robertson, Priscilla Smith. 1952. *Revolutions of 1848: A Social History.* Princeton, NJ: Princeton University Press.

Rogan, Eugene L., and Avi Shlaim. 2007. Introduction to *The War for Palestine: Rewriting the History of 1948,* 2nd ed., edited by Eugene L. Rogan and Avi Shlaim, 1–11. New York: Cambridge University Press.

Romer, Thomas, and Howard Rosenthal. 1978. "Political Resource Allocation, Controlled Agendas, and the Status Quo." *Public Choice* 33 (4): 27–43.

Rose, W. Kinnaird. 1897. *With the Greeks in Thessaly.* London: Methuen.

Rosenbaum, Naomi. 1970. "Success in Foreign Policy: The British in Cyprus, 1878–1960." *Canadian Journal of Political Science* 3 (4): 605–27.

Rubin, Jeffrey Z. 1992. "Conclusion: International Mediation in Context." In *Mediation in International Relations: Multiple Approaches to Conflict Management,* edited by Jacob Bercovitch and Jeffrey Z. Rubin, 249–72. New York: Palgrave Macmillan.

Rubinstein, Ariel. 1982. "Perfect Equilibrium in a Bargaining Model." *Econometrica* 50 (1): 97–109.

Ruhe, Constantin. 2015. "Anticipating Mediated Talks: Predicting the Timing of Mediation with Disaggregated Conflict Dynamics." *Journal of Peace Research* 52 (2): 243–57.

Rummel, Rudolph J. 1998. *Statistics of Democide: Genocide and Mass Murder since 1900.* Piscatway, NJ: Transaction.

Sachar, Howard M. 1976. *A History of Israel: From the Rise of Zionism to Our Time.* New York: Knopf.

Salmon, Patrick, and Keith Hamilton, eds. 2006. *The Southern Flank in Crisis, 1973–1976.* Series 3, vol. 5, *Documents on British Policy Overseas.* London: Routledge.

Sarkees, Meredith R., and Frank Wayman. 2010. *Resort to War: 1816–2007.* Washington, DC: CQ Press.

Sartori, Anne E. 2002. "The Might of the Pen: A Reputational Theory of Communication in International Disputes." *International Organization* 56 (1): 121–49.

Sartori, Anne E. 2005. *Deterrence by Diplomacy.* Princeton, NJ: Princeton University Press.

Saunders, Harold. 1991. "We Need a Larger Theory of Negotiation: The Importance of Pre-negotiation Phases." In *Negotiation Theory and Practice*, edited by J. William Breslin and Jeffrey Z. Rubin, 57–70. Cambridge, MA: Program on Negotiation at Harvard Law School.

Savun, Burcu. 2008. "Information, Bias, and Mediation Success." *International Studies Quarterly* 52 (1): 25–47.

Scheina, Robert L. 2003. *Latin America's Wars*. Vol. 2, *The Age of the Professional Soldier, 1900–2001*. Washington, DC: Brassey's.

Schelling, Thomas. 1960. *The Strategy of Conflict*. Cambridge, MA: Harvard University Press.

Schiff, Amira. 2008. "Pre-negotiation and Its Limits in Ethno-national Conflicts: A Systematic Analysis of Process and Outcomes in the Cyprus Negotiations." *International Negotiation* 13 (3): 387–412.

Schneer, Jonathan. 2010. *The Balfour Declaration: The Origins of the Arab-Israeli Conflict*. New York: Bloomsbury.

Schub, Robert. 2020. "When Prospective Leader Turnover Promotes Peace." *International Studies Quarterly* 64 (3): 510–22.

Schultz, Kenneth A. 1999. "Do Democratic Institutions Constrain or Inform? Contrasting Two Institutional Perspectives on Democracy and War." *International Organization* 53 (2): 233–66.

Schwartz, Adi, and Eytan Gilboa. 2021. "False Readiness: Expanding the Concept of Readiness in Conflict Resolution Theory." *International Studies Review* 23 (4): 1328–48.

Sebenius, James K. 2017. "BATNAs in Negotiation: Common Errors and Three Kinds of 'No.'" *Negotiation Journal* 33 (2): 89–99.

Shannon, Megan. 2009. "Preventing War and Providing the Peace?" *Conflict Management and Peace Science* 26 (2): 144–63.

Shannon, Megan, Daniel Morey, and Frederick J. Boehmke. 2010. "The Influence of International Organizations on Militarized Dispute Initiation and Duration." *International Studies Quarterly* 54 (4): 1123–41.

Shepley, James. 1956. "How Dulles Averted War." *Life* 40 (3): 70–80.

Shirkey, Zachary C. 2009. *Is This a Private Fight or Can Anybody Join? The Spread of Interstate War*. Burlington, VT: Ashgate.

Shirkey, Zachary C., and Alex Weisiger. 2012. "An Annotated Bibliography for the Correlates of Interstate Wars Database." Manuscript, CUNY Hunter College and Columbia University.

Shlaim, Avi. 1990. *The Politics of Partition: King Abdullah, the Zionists, and Palestine, 1921–1951*. New York: Columbia University Press.

Shlaim, Avi. 1995. "The Debate about 1948." *International Journal of Middle East Studies* 27 (3): 287–304.

Shlaim, Avi. 2007. "Israel and the Arab Coalition in 1948." In *The War for Palestine: Rewriting the History of 1948*, 2nd ed., edited by Eugene L. Rogan and Avi Shlaim, 79–103. New York: Cambridge University Press.

Showalter, Dennis E. 2014. *The Encyclopedia of Warfare*. London: Amber Books.

Simmons, Beth A. 1999. *Territorial Disputes and Their Resolution: The Case of Ecuador and Peru*. Washington, DC: United States Institute of Peace.

Simmons, Beth A. 2002. "Capacity, Commitment, and Compliance." *Journal of Conflict Resolution* 46 (6): 829–56.

Singer, J. David. 1987. "Reconstructing the Correlates of War Dataset on Material Capabilities of States, 1816–1995." *International Interactions* 14 (2): 115–32.

Singer, J. David, Stuart Bremer, and John Stuckey. 1972. "Capability Distribution, Uncertainty, and Major Power War, 1820–1965." In *Peace, War, and Numbers*, edited by Bruce M. Russett, 19–48. Beverly Hills, CA: Sage.

Siniver, Asaf, and Dan Hart. 2021. "The Meaning of Diplomacy." *International Negotiation* 26 (2): 159–83.

Siverson, Randolph M., and Michael D. Ward. 2002. "The Long Peace: A Reconsideration." *International Organization* 56 (3): 679–91.

Slantchev, Branislav L. 2003a. "The Power to Hurt: Costly Conflict with Completely Informed States." *American Political Science Review* 97 (1): 123–33.

Slantchev, Branislav L. 2003b. "The Principle of Convergence in Wartime Negotiations." *American Political Science Review* 97 (4): 621–32.

Slantchev, Branislav L. 2004. "How Initiators End Their Wars: The Duration of War and the Terms of Peace." *American Journal of Political Science* 48 (4): 813–29.

Slantchev, Branislav L. 2010. "Feigning Weakness." *International Organization* 64 (3): 357–88.

Slantchev, Branislav L., and Ahmer Tarar. 2011. "Mutual Optimism as a Rationalist Explanation of War." *American Journal of Political Science* 55 (1): 135–48.

Slonim, Shlomo. 1979. "The 1948 American Embargo on Arms to Palestine." *Political Science Quarterly* 94 (3): 495–514.

Smith, Alastair. 1998a. "Fighting Battles, Winning Wars." *Journal of Conflict Resolution* 42 (3): 301–20.

Smith, Alastair. 1998b. "International Crises and Domestic Politics." *American Political Science Review* 92 (3): 623–38.

Smith, Alastair, and Allan Stam. 2003. "Mediation and Peacekeeping in a Random Walk Model of Civil and Interstate War." *International Studies Review* 5 (4): 115–35.

Smith, Alastair, and Allan C. Stam. 2004. "Bargaining and the Nature of War." *Journal of Conflict Resolution* 48 (6): 783–813.

Smith, George Barnett. 1895. *The Life and Enterprises of Ferdinand de Lesseps*. London: W. H. Allen.

Smith, James D. D. 1995. *Stopping Wars: Defining the Obstacles to Cease-fire*. Boulder, CO: Westview.

Snyder, Glenn. 1984. "The Security Dilemma in Alliance Politics." *World Politics* 36 (4): 461–95.

Snyder, Jack, and Erica D. Borghard. 2011. "The Cost of Empty Threats: A Penny, Not a Pound." *American Political Science Review* 105 (3): 437–56.

Solomon, Richard H. 1995. *Chinese Political Negotiating Behavior, 1967–1984*. Santa Monica, CA: RAND Corporation.

Souva, Mark. 2023. "Material Military Power: A Country-Year Measure of Military Power, 1865–2019." *Journal of Peace Research* 60 (6): 1002–9.

Spector, Bertram I. 1998. "Deciding to Negotiate with Villains." *Negotiation Journal* 14 (1): 43–59.

Spencer, David. 1998. "Peru-Ecuador 1995: The Evolution of Military Tactics from the Conflict of 1981." *Small Wars and Insurgencies* 9 (3): 129–51.

St John, Ronald Bruce. 1996. "Conflict in the Cordillera del Cóndor: The Ecuador-Peru Dispute." *IBRU Boundary and Security Bulletin* 4 (1): 78–85.

St John, Ronald Bruce. 1999. "The Ecuador-Peru Boundary Dispute: The Road to Settlement." *Boundary and Territory Briefing* 3 (1): 1–65.

Stam, Allan C. 1996. *Win, Lose, or Draw: Domestic Politics and the Crucible of War*. Ann Arbor: University of Michigan Press.

Stanley, Elizabeth A. 2009. *Paths to Peace: Domestic Coalition Shifts, War Termination and the Korean War*. Stanford, CA: Stanford University Press.

Stasavage, David. 2004. "Open-Door or Closed-Door? Transparency in Domestic and International Bargaining." *International Organization* 58 (4): 667–703.

Stedman, Stephen J. 1996. "Negotiation and Mediation in Internal Conflict." In *The International Dimensions of Internal Conflict*, edited by Michael E. Brown, 341–76. Cambridge, MA: MIT Press.

Stein, Janice Gross. 1982. "Military Deception, Strategic Surprise, and Conventional Deterrence: A Political Analysis of Egypt and Israel, 1971–1973." *Journal of Strategic Studies* 5 (1): 94–121.

Stein, Janice Gross, ed. 1989. *Getting to the Table: The Processes of International Prenegotiation*. Baltimore: Johns Hopkins University Press.

Stein, Leslie. 2009. *The Making of Modern Israel, 1948–1967*. Malden, MA: Polity.

Stewart, Richard A. 2005. *American Military History*. Vol. 2, *The United States Army in a Global Era, 1917–2003*. Washington, DC: Office of the Chief of Military History, US Army.

Sticher, Valerie. 2021. "Negotiating Peace with Your Enemy: The Problem of Costly Concessions." *Journal of Global Security Studies* 6 (4): oga0544.

Stueck, William. 1995. *The Korean War: An International History*. Princeton, NJ: Princeton University Press.

Sullivan, Patricia L. 2007. "War Aims and War Outcomes: Why Powerful States Lose Limited Wars." *Journal of Conflict Resolution* 51 (3): 496–524.

Sullivan, Patricia L. 2012. *Who Wins? Predicting Strategic Success and Failure in Armed Conflict*. New York: Oxford University Press.

Sullivan, Patricia L., and Johannes Karreth. 2015. "The Conditional Impact of Military Intervention on Internal Armed Conflict Outcomes." *Conflict Management and Peace Science* 32 (3): 269–88.

Sun-Tzu. 2010. *The Art of War*. Translated by Lionel Giles. New York: Cosimo Classics.

Tal, David. 2004. *War in Palestine, 1948: Strategy and Diplomacy*. London: Routledge.

Taliaferro, Jeffrey W. 2004. *Balancing Risks: Great Power Intervention in the Periphery*. Ithaca, NY: Cornell University Press.

Tangredi, Sam J. 1985. "Negotiation from Weakness: Achieving National Security Objectives from a Position of Strategic Inferiority." MA thesis, Naval Postgraduate School, Monterey, CA.

Tannenwald, Nina. 2007. *The Nuclear Taboo: The United States and the Non-use of Nuclear Weapons since 1945*. Cambridge: Cambridge University Press.

Tatsios, Theodore G. 1984. *The Megali Idea and the Greek-Turkish War of 1897: The Impact of the Cretan Problem on Greek Irredentism, 1866–1897*. Boulder, CO: East European Monographs.

Terry, Fionna. 2002. *Condemned to Repeat? The Paradox of Humanitarian Action*. Ithaca, NY: Cornell University Press.

Thatcher, Margaret. 1993. *The Downing Street Years*. New York: HarperCollins.

Thucydides. 1972. *History of the Peloponnesian War*. Translated by Rex Warner. Harmondsworth, Middlesex: Penguin.

Tierney, Dominic. 2013. "Fighting While Negotiating in Afghanistan." *Orbis* 57 (1): 171–86.

Tierney, Dominic. 2017. "The Ethics of Unwinnable War." In *Moral Victories: The Ethics of Winning Wars*, edited by Andrew R. Hom, Cian O'Driscoll, and Kurt Mills, 123–39. Oxford: Oxford University Press.

Tincopa, Amaru. 2021. *Air Wars between Ecuador and Peru*. Vol. 3. Wokingham, Berkshire, UK: Helion.

Toft, Monica D. 2009. *Securing the Peace: The Durable Settlement of Civil Wars.* Princeton, NJ: Princeton University Press.

Toft, Monica D. 2010. "Ending Civil Wars: A Case for Rebel Victory?" *International Security* 34 (4): 7–36.

Tomz, Michael R. 2007. "Domestic Audience Costs in International Relations: An Experimental Approach." *International Organization* 61 (4): 821–40.

Toner, James H. 1973. "Power and Politics in the Korean War: A Study in Negotiatory Naiveté." MA thesis, College of William & Mary.

Toros, Harmonie. 2008. "'We Don't Negotiate with Terrorists!': Legitimacy and Complexity in Terrorist Conflicts." *Security Dialogue* 39 (4): 407–26.

Touval, Saadia. 1982. *The Peace Brokers: Mediators in the Arab-Israeli Conflict, 1948–1979.* Princeton, NJ: Princeton University Press.

Trager, Robert F. 2017. *Diplomacy: Communication and the Origins of International Order.* Cambridge: Cambridge University Press.

Trevelyan, George M. 1912. *Garibaldi's Defence of the Roman Republic.* London: Longmans, Green.

Triandafillov, Vladimir. 1994. *The Nature of the Operations of Modern Armies.* Translated by William A. Burhans. Portland, OR: Frank Cass.

Truman, Harry S. 1955. *Memoirs.* Vol. 2, *Years of Trial and Hope, 1946–1952.* New York: Doubleday.

Tsebelis, George, and Geoffrey Garrett. 1996. "Agenda Setting Power, Power Induces, and Decision Making in the European Union." *International Review of Law and Economics* 16 (3): 345–61.

Tucker, Spencer C. 2010. *The Encyclopedia of the Korean War: A Political, Social, and Military History.* Vol. 1, *A–L.* Santa Barbara, CA: ABC-CLIO.

Tversky, Amos, and Daniel Kahneman. 1973. "Availability: A Heuristic for Judging Frequency and Probability." *Cognitive Psychology* 5 (2): 207–32.

United Nations. 1945. *Charter of the United Nations and Statute of the International Court of Justice.* New York: United Nations, Office of Public Information.

United Nations. 1960. "Treaty of Guarantee, Signed at Nicosia, on 16 August 1960." *Treaty Series* 382 (5475): 4–6.

United Nations. 1974. "United Nations: Documents concerning Cyprus." *International Legal Materials* 13 (5): 1275–91.

US Army. 2017. *Field Manual No. 3–0: Operations.* Washington, DC: Headquarters, US Department of the Army.

US Congress. 1935. "National Labor Relations Act." 29 U.S.C. 99151–169.

US Department of State. 1957. *American Foreign Policy, 1950–1955: Basic Documents.* Vol. 2. Washington, DC: US Government Printing Office.

US Department of the Army. 1994. *Field Manual 34–1: Intelligence and Electronic Warfare Operations.* Washington, DC: Headquarters, US Department of the Army.

Valentino, Benjamin A., Paul K. Huth, and Sarah E. Croco. 2006. "Covenants without the Sword: International Law and the Protection of Civilians in Times of War." *World Politics* 58 (3): 339–77.

Valentino, Benjamin A., Paul K. Huth, and Sarah E. Croco. 2010. "Bear Any Burden? How Democracies Minimize the Costs of War." *Journal of Politics* 72 (2): 528–44.

Van Evera, Stephen. 1999. *Causes of War: Power and the Roots of Conflict.* Ithaca, NY: Cornell University Press.

Vatcher, William H. 1958. *Panmunjom: The Story of the Korean Military Armistice Negotiations.* New York: Praeger.

Vatikiotis, Panayiotis Jerasimof. 2014. *Popular Autocracy in Greece, 1936–1941: A Political Biography of General Ioannis Metaxas.* New York: Routledge.

Viatori, Maximilian. 2015. "Rift, Rupture and the Temporal Politics of Race in Ecuador: Whiteness and the Narration of Neoliberal Futures during and after the Cenepa War." *History and Anthropology* 26 (2): 187–205.

Vuković, Siniša. 2022. "Expanding Ripeness beyond Push and Pull: The Relevance of Mutually Enticing Opportunities (MEOs)." *Ethnopolitics* 21 (2): 190–201.

Waage, Hilde Henriksen. 2011. "The Winner Takes All: The 1949 Island of Rhodes Armistice Negotiations Revisited." *Middle East Journal* 65 (2): 279–304.

Wagner, R. Harrison. 2000. "Bargaining and War." *American Journal of Political Science* 44 (3): 469–84.

Walch, Colin. 2016. "Rethinking Ripeness Theory: Explaining Progress and Failure in Civil War Negotiations in the Philippines and Colombia." *International Negotiation* 21 (1): 75–103.

Walgrave, Stefaan, and Yves Dejaeghere. 2017. "Surviving Information Overload: How Elite Politicians Select Information." *Governance* 30 (2): 229–44.

Wallensteen, Peter, and Isak Svensson. 2014. "Talking Peace: International Mediation in Armed Conflicts." *Journal of Peace Research* 51 (2): 315–27.

Wallihan, James. 1998. "Negotiating to Avoid Agreement." *Negotiation Journal* 14 (3): 257–68.

Walter, Barbara F. 1997. "The Critical Barrier to Civil War Settlement." *International Organization* 51 (3): 335–64.

Walter, Barbara F. 2002. *Committing to Peace: The Successful Settlement of Civil Wars.* Princeton, NJ: Princeton University Press.

Walter, Barbara F. 2006. "Building Reputation: Why Governments Fight Some Separatists but Not Others." *American Journal of Political Science* 50 (2): 313–30.

Walter, Barbara F. 2009. *Reputation and Civil War: Why Separatist Conflicts Are So Violent.* Cambridge: Cambridge University Press.

Waltz, Kenneth N. 1979. *Theory of International Politics.* Long Grove, IL: Waveland.

Wang, Kevin, and James Lee Ray. 1994. "Beginners and Winners: The Fate of Initiators of Interstate Wars Involving Great Powers since 1495." *International Studies Quarterly* 38 (1): 139–54.

Ward, A. W., G. W. Prothero, and Stanley Leathes, eds. 1909. *The Cambridge Modern History.* Vol. 11, *The Growth of Nationalities.* Cambridge: Cambridge University Press.

Warner, Geoffrey. 2009. "Review Article: The United States and the Cyprus Crisis of 1974." *International Affairs* 85 (1): 129–43.

Weathersby, Kathryn. 1998. "Stalin, Mao, and the End of the Korean War." In *Brothers in Arms: The Rise and Fall of the Sino-Soviet Alliance,* edited by Odd Arne Westad, 90–116. Stanford, CA: Stanford University Press.

Weathersby, Kathryn. 2004. "The Soviet Role in the Korean War: The State of Historical Knowledge." In *The Korean War in World History,* edited by William Stueck, 61–92. Lexington: University Press of Kentucky.

Weeks, Jessica L. 2008. "Autocratic Audience Costs: Regime Type and Signaling Resolve." *International Organization* 62 (1): 35–64.

Weidner, Glenn R. 1996. "Operation Safe Border: The Ecuador-Peru Crisis." *Joint Force Quarterly* 11 (Spring): 52–58.

Weisiger, Alex. 2013. *Logics of War: Explanations for Limited and Unlimited Conflicts.* Ithaca, NY: Cornell University Press.

Weisiger, Alex. 2016a. "Exiting the Coalition: When Do States Abandon Coalition Partners during War?" *International Studies Quarterly* 60 (4): 753–65.

Weisiger, Alex. 2016b. "Learning from the Battlefield: Information, Domestic Politics, and Interstate War Duration." *International Organization* 70 (2): 347–75.

Weitsman, Patricia A. 2014. *Waging War: Alliances, Coalitions, and Institutions of Interstate Violence*. Stanford, CA: Stanford University Press.

Werner, Suzanne, and Amy Yuen. 2005. "Making and Keeping Peace." *International Organization* 59 (2): 261–92.

Wheeler, Mark. 2011. "Celebrity Diplomacy: United Nations' Goodwill Ambassadors and Messengers of Peace." *Celebrity Studies* 2 (1): 6–18.

Whigham, Thomas L., and Barbara Potthast. 1999. "The Paraguayan Rosetta Stone: New Insights into the Demographics of the Paraguayan War, 1864–1870." *Latin American Research Review* 34 (1): 174–86.

White, John A. 1964. *The Diplomacy of the Russo-Japanese War*. Princeton, NJ: Princeton University Press.

White, Sally Blount, and Margaret A. Neale. 1991. "Reservation Prices, Resistance Points, and BATNAs: Determining the Parameters of Acceptable Negotiated Outcomes." *Negotiation Journal* 7 (4): 379–88.

Whiting, Allen S. 1968. *China Crosses the Yalu*. Stanford, CA: Stanford University Press.

Whitman, J. E. A. 1941. *How Wars Are Fought: The Principles of Strategy and Tactics*. New York: Oxford University Press.

Winham, Gilbert R. 1977. "Negotiation as a Management Process." *World Politics* 30 (1): 87–114.

Wittman, Donald. 1979. "How a War Ends: A Rational Model Approach." *Journal of Conflict Resolution* 23 (4): 743–63.

Wohlforth, William C. 2009. "Unipolarity, Status Competition, and Great Power War." *World Politics* 61 (1): 28–57.

Wolford, Scott. 2017. "The Problem of Shared Victory: War-Winning Coalitions and Postwar Peace." *Journal of Politics* 79 (2): 702–16.

Wolford, Scott, Dan Reiter, and Clifford J. Carrubba. 2011. "Information, Commitment, and War." *Journal of Conflict Resolution* 55 (4): 556–79.

Woolsey, Robert E. D. 1991. "The Fifth Column: La Méthode de Charles-Maurice de Talleyrand or Maximized Acceptance with Optimized Agendas." *Interfaces* 21 (6): 103–5.

Wright, Quincy. 1924. "Changes in the Conception of War." *American Journal of International Law* 18 (4): 755–67.

Xia, Yafeng. 2006. *Negotiating with the Enemy: U.S.-China Talks during the Cold War, 1949–1972*. Bloomington: Indiana University Press.

Young, Kenneth T. 1968. *Negotiating with the Chinese Communists: The United States Experience, 1953–1967*. New York: McGraw-Hill.

Zacher, Mark W. 2001. "The Territorial Integrity Norm: International Boundaries and the Use of Force." *International Organization* 55 (2): 215–50.

Zartman, I. William. 1989. *Ripe for Resolution: Conflict and Intervention in Africa*. New York: Oxford University Press.

Zartman, I. William. 1997. "Explaining Oslo." *International Negotiation* 2 (2): 195–215.

Zartman, I. William. 2000. "Ripeness: The Hurting Stalemate and Beyond." In *International Conflict Resolution after the Cold War*, edited by Paul Stern and Daniel Druckman, 240–65. Washington, DC: National Academy Press.

Zartman, I. William. 2001. "The Timing of Peace Initiatives: Hurting Stalemates and Ripe Moments." *Global Review of Ethnopolitics* 1 (1): 8–18.

Zartman, I. William. 2008. "Ripeness Revisited: The Push and Pull of Conflict Management." In *Negotiation and Conflict Management: Essays on Theory and Practice*, edited by I. William Zartman, 303–17. Athens, GA: Routledge.

Zartman, I. William. 2022. "Understanding Ripeness: Making and Using Hurting Stalemates." In *Contemporary Peacemaking: Peace Processes, Peacebuilding and Conflict*, edited by Roger Mac Ginty and Anthony Wanis-St. John, 23–42. Cham, Switzerland: Springer Nature.

Zartman, I. William, and Alvaro de Soto. 2010. *Timing Mediation Initiatives.* Washington, DC: United States Institute of Peace.

Zhihua, Shen, and Yafeng Xia. 2011. "Mao Zedong's Erroneous Decision during the Korean War: China's Rejection of the UN Cease-Fire Resolution in Early 1951." *Asian Perspective* 35 (2): 187–209.

Zhu, Pingchao. 2001. *Americans and Chinese at the Korean War Cease-Fire Negotiations, 1950–1953.* Lewiston, NY: Edwin Mellen.

Index

Page numbers followed by *f* or *t* refer to figures or tables.

www.ingramcontent.com/pod-product-compliance
Lightning Source LLC
Chambersburg PA
CBHW051729260326
41914CB00040B/2024/J